ISBN-13: 978-0997326444

First Edition

COMPUTERS AND TECHNOLOGY BASICS *PILOT* DICTIONARY

Written by: Jack C. Stanley and Erik D. Gross,
Co-Founders of The Tech Academy

PILOT DICTIONARY

The word "pilot" means "done as an experiment or test before introducing something more widely." In 2017, we published our first dictionary. It was a massive success but since that time, technology has evolved and changed. Not only that, our knowledge base and experience has grown. As an example, whereas originally we only offered one coding bootcamp (intensive training program in software development), we now offer *eleven*.

With this expansion came a host of new technical definitions that needed to be written. This is something we took upon ourselves due to the sheer lack of beginner-level technical definitions available in society.

We have not only added hundreds of new definitions to this dictionary, we have reviewed, updated and edited all of the definitions included in the original. In addition to these upgrades, we have improved and added over a hundred images. Simply put: this version of the dictionary is much better than any previous edition.

This is a pilot dictionary because we want to hear from you before we release our finalized edition. Therefore, if you come across any errors, missing terms or have suggestions, please email them to us at: dictionary@learncodinganywhere.com. This will ensure our final dictionary is perfect.

The terms in this dictionary are sequenced alphabetically, with symbols defined first.

We hope you find this to be a valuable text. We have attempted to include every technical term used within our definitions in this dictionary so as to provide you with a "one-stop-shop" experience. Happy studies!

-The Tech Academy, July 2021

PREFACE

Written by Jack C. Stanley, Co-Founder of The Tech Academy

Why did we write a computer dictionary? There are already so many in existence. Plus, you can simply search online for any definition you need at any time, right?

In the beginning of 2014, Erik Gross and I co-founded The Tech Academy (a school that trains students in a wide variety of technical subjects). When we started the school, I quickly found that the existing definitions of technical terms were often over the head of the average person.

Go ahead and try it: choose a computer term and Google it. More likely than not, the definition will contain other technical words you do not know. Even a relatively simple term like "Internet" uses other technical terms that the average person does not understand within its definition.

At the beginning of my journey into technology, I was immediately hit with a mountain of terminology that was difficult to comprehend. So often I found that to understand "X," I must first understand "Y," which requires an understanding of "Z," and so on. The problem we had to solve was creating a curriculum that could teach *anyone* (not just nerds) how to code. If, in the beginning, I was having a difficult time comprehending the terminology, chances were others would have that same issue.

The vocabulary required to work in I.T. is *the* reason more people are not training as computer programmers and why we have a shortage of technical personnel. It is probably the reason nerds and geeks were bullied so much in the past – people tease those things they do not understand.

After struggling with the technical terms and concepts contained within existing dictionaries for a while, I had a revelation: *Virtually all existing technology dictionaries assume prior knowledge on the part of the student.*

This is a concept that can easily be glossed over but it deserves attention: the difficulty in learning technology stems from the assumption that readers know the meaning of technical terms contained within definitions, when actually most do not!

And so, instead of utilizing existing resources, we set out to define all relevant computer and technology-related words needed for our curriculum in-house. It took thousands of hours of my time and many others contributed. Eventually, we had defined all basic computer terms required for an understanding of the subject.

Then one day on a whim, I decided to count up how many definitions we had written and it was over a thousand! I became curious and grabbed a small, basic technology dictionary we had in the office and found out it had a little less than 500 entries in it. It was then that I realized that we could – with some editing and further work – create a dictionary of our own!

I then compiled all the definitions we had written, did some thorough research and wrote a list of an additional couple hundred terms that should be included in the dictionary. As part of this process, we went through every Tech Academy course and gathered any technical term we defined within them. This is our finished product.

So, what sets this dictionary apart from others? *A beginner can use this dictionary to define highly technical terms.*

We are surrounded by technology. Our phones, cars and most machinery we use now contain computers. Frankly, not understanding computers can be dangerous. Conversely, understanding computers and technology puts you more in control of the subject as a whole because the more we understand something, the more effective we can be regarding it.

Whereas there are tools and machine designs that have existed and remained relatively unchanged for thousands of years, technology is a rapidly changing arena. Knives, for example, have been used for over a million years but computers from the 1960s are completely obsolete. The passing of just a decade can make certain computer technology superannuated. This factor alone makes understanding this subject difficult. But here's the deal: the better you know the basics and understand the fundamental words associated with computers, the better you are able to keep up with the changing times. Regardless of any new gadgets and advances, much of the basic information regarding computers and how they operate has remained the same for decades, and will remain the same for a long time to come.

So, to bring up the initial question I asked. Why create a Technology Dictionary? Because a dictionary did not exist that defined technology terms in plain English and in a way that the average person could understand. There was no dictionary that did *not* assume prior knowledge on the part of the student.

This is not just another dictionary. It is completely unique. This is the dictionary your grandfather could use to define the tech words he does not know. It is also of tremendous value to children and teenagers. Frankly, everyone can benefit from this dictionary.

The Tech Academy's logo contains a bridge in it. The reason for this is that our purpose is to bridge the gap between general society and technology experts. I feel this dictionary is a large step forward for us in achieving this purpose.

Computers and technology *can* be understood by anyone. My sole reason in creating this dictionary was to help people. And I sincerely hope this dictionary helps you.

In closing, I have created a list of key terms that I highly recommend you look up in this dictionary. These are words I believe that every person on Earth should understand. They are arranged in a logical sequence – when studied in order, they will provide you with an understanding of the basics of technology. Think of it as a mini-course. Enjoy!

Basic technology terms to look up and study in sequence:

1.	technology	33.	boot
2.	machine	34.	install
3.	computer	35.	format
4.	device	36.	initialize
5.	instruction	37.	configure
6.	data	38.	database
7.	process	39.	network
8.	hardware	40.	router
9.	digital	41.	server
10.	memory	42.	client
11.	graphics	43.	hack
12.	CPU	44.	firewall
13.	chip	45.	website
14.	RAM	46.	Internet
15.	core	47.	email
16.	drive	48.	modem
17.	driver	49.	mobile
18.	hard drive	50.	wifi
19.	USB	51.	fiber optics
20.	USB drive	52.	Ethernet
21.	base	53.	web browser
22.	binary	54.	cache
23.	input	55.	host
24.	output	56.	cloud computing
25.	mainframe	57.	bandwidth
26.	algorithm	58.	HTML
27.	program	59.	HTTP
28.	bug	60.	domain
29.	computer programmer	61.	colon (:)
30.	programming language	62.	slash (/)
31.	code	63.	address
32.	OS	64.	IP address

65.	URL	98.	BMP
66.	GUI	99.	JPEG/JPG
67.	desktop	100.	Blu-ray
68.	dot (.)	101.	streaming
69.	download	102.	MP3
70.	update	103.	cell phone
71.	computer security	104.	printer
72.	virus	105.	spooling
73.	run	106.	search engine
74.	power supply	107.	SEO
75.	read	108.	social networking
76.	cookie	109.	blog
77.	bit	110.	wiki
78.	byte	111.	hashtag
79.	I/O device	112.	add-on
80.	mouse	113.	interface
81.	cursor	114.	interactive
82.	character	115.	virtual
83.	keyboard	116.	cyber
84.	return key	117.	link
85.	ALT key	118.	G (cell phone)
86.	CTRL key	119.	G (wifi)
87.	tab key	120.	Internet of Things
88.	font	121.	home page
89.	icon	122.	hertz
90.	folder	123.	HDMI
91.	import	124.	GPS
92.	screen	125.	GIF
93.	PC	126.	motherboard
94.	online	127.	buffer
95.	LED	128.	aspect ratio
96.	VGA	129.	artificial intelligence
97.	resolution, levels of		

This list may seem long, but as you look it over you may notice you've come across most of (if not all of) these definitions in the past. Good luck with your studies!

Introduction

Written by Erik D. Gross, Co-Founder of The Tech Academy

As a kid, I read a lot. My parents were avid readers, and I inherited that love of the written word.

I remember once, in my teens, taking an afternoon and counting all the books in the house. It's been many years, so I may be off about the exact total, but I recall that it was 1,600, or maybe 2,000. This is what happens when you get old.

Either way, it was a lot of books – and at that point I had read nearly every one of them.

Over the years, I have learned that this isn't a particularly unusual story. What is unusual though, is an aspect of reading in my house that I don't believe was part of many kids' upbringing: Mom made me clear up (look up; define) any words I did not understand when I was reading.

It didn't matter whether I was reading a science textbook or *Dragonriders of Pern* by Anne McCaffrey – I always had a dictionary right next to me, and I was expected to look up any words I didn't know.

It wasn't until many years later that I came to understand my mother's true wisdom. While I was in the Navy, I spent a couple of years working on a submarine – in the middle of the desert in Idaho. That's an interesting story; if we ever meet up, you can buy me a cup of coffee and I'll tell you how that came to be.

In the training program I was in, we were learning to operate nuclear reactors. I had done pretty well in my training, so I was assigned as an instructor.

That was great, and I was pretty happy about it – until they told me that my first job was going to be "Classroom Instructor." With basically no prep, I was given a lesson plan and dropped in front of a bunch of students who were punk kids just like me.

I learned a number of things over the several months I did that job. I learned that I love teaching. I learned that there aren't many things more satisfying than helping a person to have one of those really awesome "ah-ha!" moments that come with a sudden understanding. And I learned that definitions matter.

What I mean is this: every subject has its own particular vocabulary – those terms specific to that subject. They cover many things – the tools of the trade, the specialized actions, the slang, etc. If a person is studying that subject, they had better make sure they understand those terms well and that includes understanding the terms *as they are used in that context.*

I kept seeing students bog down on complex engineering concepts. At first, I thought the problem was simply how complex the concept was. But as I dug in, I actually found that in pretty much every case, the student had confusions or misunderstandings on just one or two key terms in the subject – and once those were cleared up, the student was able to work out the rest of their understanding by themselves.

What I developed out of this was a couple of basic ideas about education. One: Dictionaries and glossaries are awesome, and if you don't have one you better make one. Two: If you can explain complex technical concepts in a clear, simple way that others can understand, you become very valuable and you can really help people.

By the time I started The Tech Academy with Jack a few years ago, these ideas had been proven true to me over and over again. Because of that, a technology dictionary for our students was inevitable. And when we did create technical definitions that were simple, clear and easy to understand, our students loved them. In fact, that body of definitions emerged as one of the main factors in the success of our school.

As word of what we were doing got around, though, I found myself having some pretty interesting conversations with people from all walks of life about technology and education.

What I came to realize is that *everyone* needed what we were creating. We all deal with technology in one form or another, and we usually do so with little or no education in the key terms of the subject. Instead, we're expected to somehow just "figure it out as we go along."

That just doesn't work for me. So, we did something about it.

The dictionary you're reading now is really a labor of love – love of technology, love of learning, and love of people. I really hope it helps you. If it does, let me know. And if it can be improved, please let me know as well. I'm interested in being effective, and I just wanted to create an effective tool.

I hope this helps.

SYMBOLS

<> (angle brackets): 1. Punctuation marks that are used to mark certain text as different from the surrounding text. Angle brackets can be used to let the computer know that certain text needs to be handled differently than other text – the text inside the two symbols is different.

EXAMPLE: There can be <italic>no more than</italic> 4 passengers in each vehicle. Here, the words inside the angle brackets are instructions to the computer, not words to be displayed on a screen. These particular instructions direct the computer to make the letters between the two instructions appear in italics, like this: There can be *no more than* 4 passengers in each vehicle.

2. The "not-equal" symbol. "<>" is used to show that a comparison should be made. Specifically, this "less-than or greater-than" symbol is an instruction to check whether the data on the left side of the symbol is either less or greater in amount or quantity than the data on the right side. The answer to this comparison is either "true" or "false."

EXAMPLE: 3 <> 4. This means "check whether 3 is less than or greater than 4." Since three is, in fact, less than four, the answer is " true." Another example: 5 <> 4. This means "check whether 5 is less than or greater than 4." The answer is "true." A final example: 4 <> 4. This means "check whether 4 is less than or greater than 4." Since 4 is neither less than or greater than 4, the answer is "false." This is useful in computers since we may want to have it perform one or another action, based on the answer to a comparison.

== (double equal sign): This symbol is used to show that a comparison should be made. Specifically, this "==" symbol is an instruction to check whether the data on the left side of the symbol is equal to the data on the right side. The answer to this comparison is an answer of "true" or "false." This is useful in computers since we may want to have it perform one action or another action, based on the answer to a comparison. Computers are often used to check how one piece of data compares to another piece of data. Some examples of this are: Checking whether a person is old enough to order a specific item from a company; checking whether there are enough items of a specific product left in a warehouse for a company to fill a specific order; or checking whether a computer has been idle for a certain period of time. You can probably think of other examples. When the "==" symbol is used to check for equality, usually it is used like this: [first item to be compared] == [second item to be compared]

EXAMPLE: (10 + 5) == 15. In this example, we are asking the computer to check whether the result of adding 5 and 10 is equal to 15. When the "==" symbol is used in this manner, we are asking the computer to give a response after checking for equality. Usually, this result is given in a "true" or "false" manner. Here, the response would be "true," since (10 + 5) is equal to 15. Another example: (10 + 6) == 15. Here, the computer would respond with "false" since (10 + 6) is not equal to 15.

= (equal sign): In computers, this symbol is used mainly to set the value of a thing that the computer is keeping track of. Usually the "=" symbol is used to set the VALUE of a variable (data that has a name and a value [type/amount], and can be changed). When the "=" symbol is used to set the value of a variable, it is usually used like this: [NAME of the variable] = [VALUE that is being assigned to that variable]

EXAMPLE: fabricColor = "blue" Here, there is a piece of data that the computer is keeping track of that has been given the name" fabricColor." By using the "=" symbol, we can set the value of the piece of data called "fabricColor." In this case, we are setting that value to the series of letters "blue."

> (greater-than sign): This symbol is used to show that a comparison should be made. Specifically, this "greater-than" symbol is an instruction to check whether the data on the left side of the symbol is more in amount or quantity than the data on the right side. The answer to this comparison is an answer of "true" or "false."

EXAMPLE: 5 > 4. This means "check whether 5 is greater than 4." Since five is in fact greater than four, the answer is "true." Another example: 3 > 6. This means "check whether 3 is greater than 6." The answer is "false." This is useful in computers since we may want to have it perform one action or another action, based on the answer to a comparison.

>= (greater-than sign followed by an equal sign): This symbol is used to show that a comparison should be made. Specifically, this "greater-than or equal" symbol is an instruction to check whether the data on the left side of the symbol is more than or equal in amount or quantity than the data on the right side. The answer to this comparison is an answer of "true" or "false."

EXAMPLE: 5 >= 4. This means "check whether 5 is greater than or equal to 4." Since five is in fact greater than four, the answer is "true." Another example: 3 >= 6.
This means "check whether 3 is greater than or equal to 6." The answer is "false." A final example: 6 >= 6. This means "check whether 6 is greater than or equal to 6." The answer is "true." This is useful in computers since we may want to have it perform one action or another action based on the answer to a comparison.

< (less-than sign): This symbol is used to show that a comparison should be made. Specifically, this "less-than" symbol is an instruction to check whether the data on the left side of the symbol is less in amount or quantity than the data on the right side. The answer to this comparison is an answer of "true" or "false."

EXAMPLE: 3 < 4. This means "check whether 3 is less than 4." Since three is, in fact, less than four, the answer is "true." Another example: 15 < 6. This means "check whether 15 is less than 6." The answer is "false." This is useful in computers since we may want to have it perform one or another action based on the answer to a comparison.

<= **(less-than sign followed by an equal sign):** This symbol is used to show that a comparison should be made. Specifically, this "less-than or equal" symbol is an instruction to check whether the data on the left side of the symbol is less than or equal in amount or quantity with the data on the right side. The answer to this comparison is an answer of "true" or "false."

EXAMPLE: 3 <= 4. This means "check whether 3 is less than or equal to 4." Since three is, in fact, less than four, the answer is "true." Another example: 15 <= 6. This means "check whether 15 is less than or equal to 6." The answer is "false." Another example: 6 <= 6. This means "check whether 6 is less than or equal to 6." The answer is "true." This is useful in computers, since we may want to have it perform one or another action, based on the answer to a comparison.

/: See "slash."

//: See "slash."

=== **(triple equal sign):** This symbol is used to show that a comparison should be made. Specifically, this "===" symbol is an instruction to check whether the data on the left side of the symbol is equal to the data on the right side, *and* that it is the same type of data as that on the right. The answer to this comparison is an answer of "true" or "false." This is useful in computers since we may want to have it perform one action or another action, based on the answer to a comparison.

EXAMPLE: You want to check whether two birth dates are equal. You have two pieces of data in the computer that represent these two birth dates:
"DateOfBirth1" is data of type "Date," and the value of the data is "1/1/1970";
"DateOfBirth2" is data of type "Date," and the value of the data is "1/1/1970."
You would use the "===" symbol like this: DateOfBirth1 === DateOfBirth2. This tells the computer to check whether the two pieces of data are equal in both VALUE and TYPE. Since they are, the computer responds with " true."

A

abstract class: A generic (template) class or type of object that is used as a basis for creating other objects that conform with its specifications. Classes have properties (attributes) and methods (behaviors), which can be based on other, previously-defined classes. Developers can utilize inheritance (the act of taking on the characteristics [structure and behavior] of another class) to derive the specific implementation of abstract classes. Classes that are derived from abstract classes are called inherited classes or derived classes. When inheritance is performed multiple times, the result is a hierarchy (an arrangement of items in terms of rank, so that some are "higher," "below," or "at the same level as" one another) of classes. When this occurs, an abstract class is at the root of the hierarchy.

EXAMPLE: You might create an abstract class named "fruit." Other classes may be derived from the fruit class (e.g., apple class, orange class, grape class, etc.).

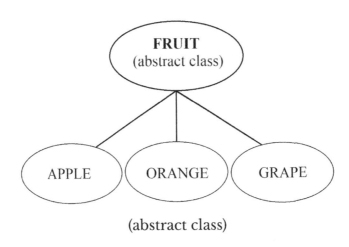

(abstract class)

abstract data: "Abstract" indicates ideas, thoughts and theories as opposed to physical or concrete existence. Abstract data refers to data where we are only concerned with it in terms of its items and operations – not the implementation. In other words, we only care about what it's supposed to do – not about how it does it.

EXAMPLE: A common example would be what happens when you step on the brakes of a car. The driver knows the expected behavior – a gradual slowing of the car, and eventual stoppage if the braking continues. What the driver often does not know, and does not need to know in order to use the braking system, is HOW the system accomplishes this behavior. Different cars could have different methods for accomplishing this type of behavior; to the driver, the use of the system is the same. This is a demonstration of "abstracting out" the implementation, so that only the items and operation need to be known to the users of a thing – not the mechanics of how it is done. See "abstraction" for more information.

abstraction: "Abstract" indicates ideas, thoughts and theories, as opposed to physical or concrete existence. Abstraction is a general idea about a type of situation, thing, or person rather than a specific example from real life. Regarding computers, abstraction is the hiding away of the implementation details, and only providing the description of the behavior to be performed. Abstraction is a less complicated way to say what task a computer is doing, without displaying the long list of details that are happening behind the scenes that are part of how the computer is doing the task.

EXAMPLE: An automatic coffee dispenser machine will simply have a button that says "Make Coffee." It does not display information on how exactly it is done, and you do not necessarily need to know what functions the machine performs – you just know the expected behavior. This is abstraction.

abstraction (design): See "design abstraction."

A/B test: This is a test that provides two options for the target audience. Two different versions of the product are tested to see which is preferred. This eliminates any design bias.

EXAMPLE: In an A/B test, two designs could be displayed to a group of customers to see which one is preferred.

ACC: Short for "accumulator." This is a computer component used in a part of the computer called the Central Processing Unit. The ACC temporarily stores the results of math performed inside the CPU. It is called this because the results of mathematical operations "accumulate" (stack up) there. The arithmetic itself is performed in the ALU (Arithmetic Logic Unit) in the CPU. After the ALU executes a math problem, the resulting number is stored in the ACC. The ACC is simply a storage location for data, not an element of the CPU that performs functions.

EXAMPLE: You type in 2 + 5. The ALU takes 2, adds 5 to it, and determines the answer is 7. The result, 7, is then stored (accumulated) in the ACC.

acceptance test environment: See "environment."

access modifier: See "private."

access: To get information from a computer. If you access something in a computer, you are ordering the computer to pass something over to you.

EXAMPLE: If you click on a file on a computer in order to modify it, you are accessing it.

access time: The amount of time needed by a memory device to transfer information to the CPU. It is measured from the instant the CPU requests information until the instant that the CPU receives the information.

EXAMPLE: If you click a file in order to open it, the CPU tells the memory to deliver the file. It then reports back to you with an opened file. If that took 30 seconds, the access time was 30 s (seconds).

accumulator: See "ACC."

Active Directory: Software from Microsoft that provides central authentication (the process of verifying that an individual is who they say they are) and authorization (the process of determining what data [files, programs, databases, etc.] a user is allowed to access, and allowing such access only after they've been authenticated [proven to be who they say they are] and authorized) services for computers. It is used by a system administrator (someone that manages a system of computers and their associated equipment and computer software) to store information about users, assign security policy and deploy software. It can be used in organizations of all sizes, from administering one user to hundreds of thousands of users.

EXAMPLE: Active Directory could be used in a large company to store all user names and passwords on a network.

ADC: See "digitize."

adder: The part in a computer that adds numbers together. A computer will use many adders. They are made up of very small electronic parts. The adder takes numerical information passed into it and is able to determine amounts. There are two types of adders: half adder and full adder. They both are used in adding numbers, but they operate in slightly different ways. The full adder has more parts than the half adder and is used to perform larger math functions. It's also called an "adding machine."

EXAMPLE: If you type 13 + 3 into a computer, the adder will determine that it equals 16.

adding machine: See "adder."

add-on: An additional item that is included or added to something so that it can do more work for you, or it can do some very specific work for you.

EXAMPLE: You buy a special case for your phone that has a bigger battery in it. That case and bigger battery could be called an add-on for your phone. Another example of an add-on would be if you had a computer game and you bought an add-on. This would allow you to play more levels, etc. Add-ons are also used in combination with web browsers to increase the performance of internet searches, etc.

address: In the real world, an address signifies a specific property in your town, city, neighborhood, apartment building, etc. It is called a "unique identifier" in that no two physical properties will ever have the same address, so the address can be used to identify a specific property. In the computer industry, "address" refers to the location of a specific piece of information, device, or other item that can be accessed by computers. The word address has the following specific meaning:

1. This often applies to a network of computers and other devices – a system where those computers and devices are all connected to each other in some way. Each computer or device on that network will have a unique "address" that is known by the other computers and devices in the network. When a computer in the office wants to connect to another computer or device, it has a special computer program that sends out a signal which contains the address of the desired device. When the desired device receives that signal, it responds with a return signal to the original device using the address of that device and now the two devices can share information back and forth.

EXAMPLE: An example would be a shared printer in an office. When you want to print something from that printer, your computer looks up the address of the printer, and then sends a signal to it. When the printer responds, your computer starts sending it the electronic file you wish to print. As the printing process proceeds, your computer and the printer send information back and forth – each using the address of the other device to ensure the information arrives at the intended device.

2. Anything that can be accessed over the Internet is called a "resource." This can be a website, of course, but it could also be a security camera, a printer, a machine that manufactures auto parts, etc. – if the item has a computer inside it, and that computer is connected to the Internet, it is a "resource." Every resource on the Internet has a unique address, so that every other resource on the Internet can identify that device. The most common system used for addresses on the Internet uses a series of numbers separated by three dots. An example would be: `127.0.0.1`.

EXAMPLE: Your own personal computer has a unique address that it uses when interacting with the various resources on the Internet; it might be something like 123.45.67.890. When you use your browser to request a web page from a web server, the web server usually makes a record of which computer asked for the web page, what web page was requested, and whether or not the web page was successfully sent to the requesting computer. The record will contain, among this other information, the address of your computer – 123.45.67.890 in our example.

3. The locations in a computer where information is stored for use by the Central Processing Unit. A CPU makes use of physical data storage devices in order to do its job of processing data. A data storage device could be thought of as a collection of boxes. Each box can contain one piece of data. Each box has an individual identifier so that the CPU can keep track of it. These "boxes" are called memory locations. The

individual identifier for a memory location is called an address. The CPU can "read" or "write" to these memory locations.

EXAMPLE: If the CPU was processing an addition operation where two numbers were being added together, it would likely need three addresses to work with – the address where it could find the first number, the address where it could find the second number, and the address where it would store the result of the addition (the "total").

address bus: A bus inside the computer that connects the CPU to the memory in the computer. It is used to specify the memory location to be used for an individual operation by the CPU.

EXAMPLE: If the CPU were processing an addition operation where two numbers were being added together, it would likely need three addresses to work with – the address where it could find the first number, the address where it could find the second number, and the address where it would store the result of the addition (the "total"). These addresses, one at a time, would be placed on the address bus for use by the CPU as it performs the steps of an addition operation.

ADO.NET: Stands for "ActiveX Data Object." A software library that is part of the .NET framework and is used to interact with data from multiple sources. It allows developers to create applications where a user can connect to a data source to retrieve and update data.

EXAMPLE: If you were to browse an e-commerce site (a site for selling items or services online) that uses ADO.NET, the item you click on will probably retrieve and display information from the website's database. This retrieval process is due to ADO.NET.

A drive: See "hard drive."

aggregator: See "RSS."

Agile: a project management methodology that is popular in the computer industry. It is best understood in terms of how it differs from more traditional methods for project management. Traditional project management is characterized by a linear (step-by-step; sequential) approach that usually has some or all of these broad steps:
1. Initiation (starting the project)
2. Planning
3. Execution
4. Monitoring
5. Completion

Agile project management methodology, first introduced in the late 1980s, is characterized by a non-linear approach. Instead of being completed in the "Planning" step, requirements and solutions evolve through collaboration between self-organizing, cross-functional teams. Execution of project work is done continuously throughout the life of the project. Agile methods involve adaptive planning, evolutionary development, early delivery, and continuous improvement. Agile encourages rapid and flexible response to change. This method is increasingly popular, and is often used to manage the process of creating software. It focuses on teamwork and finishing one feature of the software at a time fully before moving onto the next.

EXAMPLE: In software development, Agile is the most popular form of project management in the world.

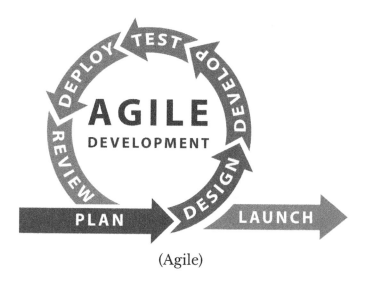
(Agile)

AI: See "artificial intelligence."

AJAX: Stands for "Asynchronous JavaScript and XML." AJAX is a set of tools that can be used in creating asynchronous (no set pattern and not occuring at the same time; in asynchronous data transfer, one operation is completed before the next is begun, as opposed to all data being transmitted simultaneously) functions for websites. AJAX is best understood by relating it to the way a normal web page is accessed by a user. With a web browser (the program you use to view web pages), a user issues a "request" to see a specific web page. That request is sent to the web server. That server gathers those requested files and sends them to the user's computer as a "response" to the "request," and the browser then converts them to a visual form and displays them for the user. If the creator of that web page wants to make it so some content on the web page can change based on a user action, they have a number of different options. One method is to just send a new request for the web page, along with some instruction to provide the new content that is desired. This can take a long time, though, as every file needed to display that web page has to be sent back to the user's computer by the web server. This is where AJAX can come in. Instead of requesting that the entire page be recreated, the creator of the website can make it so that just the new content is requested from the web server. The way this works is that user action triggers an asynchronous request to the web server for JUST a specific section of the web page. It is asynchronous in that it is not tied to the full "request" – "response" – "page display" process used for a full web page. The technologies used to accomplish this feature are JavaScript and XML (short for "extensible markup language"; XML is a customizable markup language, used primarily in the displaying documents on the internet [i.e., websites]) – hence the name "AJAX," or <u>A</u>synchronous <u>J</u>avaScript <u>A</u>nd <u>X</u>ML.

EXAMPLE: If you are viewing a web page, AJAX can make it so that when you click on a video, the video is sent over from the server – as opposed to both the video and the rest of the web page.

algebra: A type of math that uses letters and other symbols to represent numbers and amounts.

EXAMPLE: $1 + n = 4$. This is an algebra problem. In this case, "n" is used to represent "what amount, when added to 1, results in a total of 4?" You can see that "n" in this case would be "3."

ALGOL: A computer programming language developed in the late 1950s that was mainly used to solve math problems and scientific equations. The name ALGOL was taken from the word "algorithm" (a set of steps to solve a problem or perform an action); ALGOL is short for "Algorithmic Language."

EXAMPLE: Many of the first computer programs that aided scientists in creating military craft and equipment were written in ALGOL.

algorithm: A mathematics word that literally means "a plan for solving a problem." An algorithm consists of a sequence of steps to solve a problem or perform an action. Computers use algorithms. It is a set of instructions that is used to get something done.

EXAMPLE: An algorithm for selecting the right kind of shirt might have the following steps:
1. Pick a shirt from your closet.
2. Put the shirt on.
3. Look at yourself in the mirror.
4. Decide whether you like the way you look in that shirt. If you like how you look, leave the shirt on and go to step 6. If you do not like how you look, take the shirt off and put it back in the closet where you got it from.
5. Repeat steps 1 - 4
6. End this procedure.
Algorithms are very important in computers because most computer programs include algorithms, so you will learn more about this subject on this course.

alias: "See "shortcut.""

alphanumeric: Containing both numbers and letters. Alphanumeric code consists of characters that represent both the letter of the alphabet and the digits 0 to 9. Alphanumeric code also contains characters that represent various symbols, including punctuation marks and the signs for mathematical operations. The term was created in the 1950s by combining the words "alphabet" and "numerical."

EXAMPLE: The numbers, letters and symbols on your keyboard are alphanumeric.

alpha test: "Alpha" is the first letter of the Greek alphabet and is often used to describe things that come first in an ordered system. Alpha testing is a form of testing done while creating a software program. It is often the first form of testing done, hence the name "alpha." It is done by having people use the actual computer program, or a simulation of it. Often this is done on premises – meaning, at the location where the software is being developed. The people doing the testing can be the intended users of the software, a team of professional testers, or others.

EXAMPLE: In creating a website for newlyweds, a person could bring in a group of newlyweds and have them go through the site to identify any problems or mistakes, give feedback on usability, etc. That would be alpha testing.

ALT key: Short for "Alternate key." Like the CTRL key, this key is usually used in combination with other keys, and it provides a way for one key to have two different functions. Often, a key will have its primary output written on it (say, the number 1), as well as a secondary output (say, an exclamation point). Normally the key will produce the primary output when not accompanied by another key. However, in the earlier example, when the 1 key is pressed while the SHIFT key is being held down, it will perform the secondary function: !.

EXAMPLE: Sometimes the ALT key can be used to access a menu of some sort on a computer program.

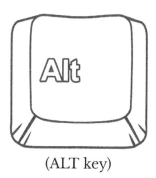
(ALT key)

alternate key: A key is a piece of data that is used to uniquely identify a specific row in a table in a database and no two rows in a table can have the same key. A primary key is an attribute (column) or a combination of attributes that is used to uniquely identify all the tuples (records; rows) in a table. There are certain rules regarding a primary key:

A. It must contain a unique value for each row of data,

B. It cannot contain null values.

An alternate key is a key associated with one or more attributes (columns) that uniquely identifies every tuple (row) but which is not the primary key.

EXAMPLE: The primary key may be a series of numbers, and the alternate key could be a combination of the first and last name of every customer. In that second example, using those two columns as the key would mean that you could not have two rows in that table where the first and last name were the same in each of the rows. When you tried to add the second row with an identical combination of first and last name, the database would not allow the row to be added.

ID	f_name	l_name	Gender
001	Jeremy	Burke	M
002	Arthur	Smith	M
003	Hannah	Young	F
004	Lindsey	Patterson	F

Primary key   Alternate key

(alternate key)

alternative hypothesis: See "hypothesis testing."

ALU: Stands for "Arithmetic Logic Unit." The part of the CPU that performs mathematical functions and logic operations. "ACC" stands for "accumulator." The accumulator is also in the CPU. The ACC temporarily stores the results of math performed. It is called this because the results of mathematical operations "accumulate" (stack up) there. The arithmetic itself is performed in the ALU in the CPU. It does addition and subtraction and moves things around inside the memory of the computer. It can be made to operate when you type exact instructions into a computer. After the ALU executes a math problem, the resulting number is stored in the ACC.

EXAMPLE: You type in 2 + 5. The ALU takes 2, adds 5 to it, and determines the answer is 7. The result, 7, is then stored (accumulated) in the ACC.

AMD: Stands for "Advanced Micro Devices." This is a computer company that was founded in 1969 that makes computer parts, including CPUs and microprocessors. AMD is an international company based in California and is one of the largest computer parts manufacturers on the planet. They are one of the largest competitors of Intel, the biggest computer parts manufacturer in the world.

EXAMPLE: If you wanted to increase the speed of your computer, there are electronic parts that you can purchase from AMD that would make that possible.

(AMD)

amplifier: *Amplify* means to increase or enlarge the size of something. An amplifier is a device that increases an electronic signal.

EXAMPLE: The most common type of amplifier is a device that makes sound louder.

Anaconda: A free and open-source distribution software used for scientific computing in data science, machine learning, large data processing and predictive analytics. It comes with more than 1,500 libraries for R and Python. It also comes with RStudio and Jupyter Notebooks built in.

EXAMPLE: The package manager used by Anaconda is called *Conda*. One of the uses of Conda is that when you're downloading any Python libraries, it'll look for conflicts with the ones already preinstalled.

(Anaconda)

analog: See "digital."

anchor tag: HTML code used to create a link to another page. It instructs the browser to display content from another document (typically a web page).

EXAMPLE: As a note, by default, most browsers display such links as follows:

-An unvisited link is underlined and blue

-A visited link is underlined and purple

-An active link is underlined and red

The anchor element needs an attribute called an "href attribute." "Href" is short for "hypertext reference." This attribute contains the location of the resource or document that the author intends to link to. Here is what it looks like:

```
<a href="https://learncodinganywhere.com/">Check out The Tech Academy!</a>
```

This would display as check out The Tech Academy and would take the user to the page at https://learncodinganywhere.com/.

ANN: See "neural network."

anonymous functions: See "lambda."

android: A robot with a human-like appearance. For example, androids usually have "skin" made of material that looks and feels similar to human flesh. Androids typically include AI. The word was coined from two Greek words: *andr-* meaning "man; male" and the suffix *-oid* "having the form or likeness of."

EXAMPLE: Data, from Star Trek, was an android:

(android)

Android: An operating system created by Google; it is used on mobile devices like smartphones and tablets.

EXAMPLE: Samsung phones run on Android.

(Android)

anti-phishing software: Software is a tool to help you detect something coming from a non-legitimate source so you do not mistakenly get your information stolen – it protects you from phishing attacks.

EXAMPLE: If you receive a phishing email from an entity pretending to be your bank, anti-phishing software may notify you with a statement like: "This is likely not a legitimate email from your bank." This gives you an opportunity to contact your bank and verify the validity of the email.

antivirus software: "Anti-" means against. Antivirus software is software that protects the computer from viruses (harmful programs).

EXAMPLE: If someone tried to send a virus to your computer, antivirus software could warn you and stop the virus from infecting your computer.

API: Stands for "Application Programming Interface." A special part of a computer program that allows other programs to give information to that program and also to get information from them. It is basically a way that a computer program can tell other programs: "If you want to give or get information, here is the exact way you'll need to ask me." The reason programs would have an API is so there is a description of the standard way other programs can access that program. That way, any programmer who has a description of the API can make software that can connect to the API. If there is no API for a program, other programs can't access that program easily.

EXAMPLE: If there were a software program that kept track of the inventory for a bicycle manufacturer, that program might have an API that would allow the company's dealers to connect to the program and find out how many of a certain type of bicycle were available at the manufacturer. In this case, the dealers could have a software program of their own, which would connect to the API of the software at the manufacturer and request that inventory information.

app: See "program."

Apache: A popular web server software. The actual name of the software is "Apache HTTP Server." HTTP stands for HyperText Transfer Protocol, and is the protocol for sending web page files between the computers that make up the Internet. Apache is a free software program.

EXAMPLE: You can lower the costs to start up a business by putting your business' website on a computer that uses Apache, since you won't need to pay for the Apache software.

Apache Hadoop: Software that allows for large sets of data to be distributed for processing across multiple computers. It is designed to scale up from single servers to thousands of machines.

EXAMPLE: A large social networking company might want to store and process user information in order to connect like-minded individuals. With such a large amount of information, Hadoop could help to process that information.

(Apache Hadoop)

Apple 2: A personal computer released by Apple in 1977. It was the first computer from Apple that was sold to the public. The Apple II was highly successful and many units were sold. It was often used in school computer labs for educational purposes, and it helped to popularize the personal computer around the world. Also written as Apple II.

EXAMPLE: You could type documents in an Apple 2.

(Apple 2)

application: See "program."

application program interface: See "API."

architecture: The design and construction of buildings. In technology, architecture refers to the design of a computer. It is the organizing of all the parts of the computer. Different computers have different architecture depending on what they are meant to handle. Architecture is also used to describe the overall design of a computer program. This means how the various parts of the program are organized relative to each other, and also how that program is designed in terms of how it will interact with other programs in a computer as needed.

EXAMPLE: Some computers' architecture is set up so that the computer does the same thing over and over all day. Other computers' architecture is set up so that people can use them for personal reasons.

archive: A collection of historical records. In computers, it means a collection of data that provides a record of what's happened over time. Usually the data in an archive is all related in some way.

EXAMPLE: You may have a bunch of emails related to a project. Many computers can present those emails to you organized by the date you received each email. You now have an archive of those emails – that is, a collection of the emails that present a historical record.

arithmetic operator: See "operator."

artificial neural network: See "neural network."

Apache Subversion: See "Subversion."

Apple: A computer and technology company that was founded by Steve Jobs and Steve Wozniak in 1976. It is one of the top companies on the planet and is based in Cupertino, California. As a note, per Steve Jobs at a conference in 1998, the "i" at the beginning of some Apple products represents several things, including: internet, individual, instruct, inform and inspire.

EXAMPLE: Apple offers many popular products, including: the iPhone, iPad and Apple Watch.

(Apple)

application: See "program."

argument: See "parameter."

arithmetic logic unit: See "ALU."

arithmetic operator: See "operator."

array: A collection of data, arranged so that each piece of data in the collection can be individually identified. In coding, an array is a group of related things that are stored together in a sequence. It is a way things can be organized in a computer in a logical way. Arrays can be quite simple, or quite complex. A simple array would be something like the numbers 7, 3 and 15. It would be written out like this:

[7, 3, 15]

These three pieces of data are called elements – they are the elements of the array. A system is needed for identifying each element of an array. This is done by labeling each position in the array. The simplest method for this is to start numbering them at zero, starting at the left position and counting up from there. It is important to understand that the index only tells the position of the element in the array, and not the value of the element at that position. In the above example, the element with a value of "7" would be at position 0, the element with a value of "3" would be at position 1, and the element with a value of "15" would be at position 2. Another word for the position of an element is the "index" of the element – for the above example of an array, the element at index 0 has a value of "7," the element at index 1 has a value of "3," etc. Each element, therefore, has two properties: its index and its value.

EXAMPLE: Let's say you have three pictures of your cat, and you could save them in an array: CatPic1, CatPic 2, and CatPic 3. Here, the element at index 1 has a value of "CatPic2."

arrow key: One of the keys used to move the cursor around in a text document. There are four arrow keys – left, right, up, and down. They are often used in other ways, depending on the computer program being used.

EXAMPLE: A computer game that lets the user direct the path of a vehicle might use the arrow keys to "steer" the vehicle on the screen.

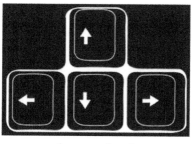

(arrow key)

artificial intelligence: Abbreviated "AI." A machine or a program that is built to "think" like humans think. It refers to a machine or a program that has been programmed to learn and to change its behavior based on its experiences. One of the purposes of AI is for computers to perform actions typically handled by people. A robot that handled all housekeeping and cooking and that could learn from its mistakes as well as come up with creative new food ideas, could be considered an AI. AI can refer to robots that look like humans, but at its root, AI is software that is programmed to "observe and learn." An example of AI is voice recognition software (computer programs that attempt to process words that human's say). When you use "voice to text" on your phone (having text messages written out for you based on the words you say), this is AI.

EXAMPLE: Many science fiction TV shows and movies contain AI. Some even make the case for "AI rights" and argue that they should be treated as human. The folly in this is that everything that AI could do was predetermined by a human and, no matter how advanced they get, they're still just a machine and, thereby, only a distant "extension" of humans. One could program a computer to feel "pain" when a component is broken, but this "pain" would only be a series of 1s and 0s contained within the software of the AI unit. Only those who believe they are a computer (a machine made of plastic and metal into which commands are inputted and processed) would believe a computer to be human. This point is being stressed so that the reader understands that no matter how realistic AIs become, they are soulless machines. Humans and machines are not the same – they are very different. In the future, some people may attempt to marry an AI or assert that they're forming an undeniable human connection with these advanced robots. But at the end of the day, the true connection is between them and the designers and programmers behind the AI. The true source of whatever affection one feels for the machine is its human creators, and/or the aesthetics (visually appealing elements) they designed and created.

ASCC: See "Mark I."

ASCII: Stands for "American Standard Code for Information Interchange." An ASCII chart provides a standard way to represent text characters using numbered codes. These include upper and lowercase English letters, numbers, and punctuation symbols. In this system, the commonly-recognized English letters, numbers and punctuation marks each have a unique number that identifies them. This helps computer manufacturers by providing a standard way to refer to every character used in the English language. ASCII uses binary numbers with 7 digits to represent each character. Often, these binary numbers are converted to decimal to make them more easily read and understood by people.

EXAMPLE: In ASCII, the capital letter "T" is represented by 1010100 in binary or 84 in decimal.

ASCII Code: Character to Binary

a	01100001	x	01111000	U	01010101
b	01100010	y	01111001	V	01010110
c	01100011	z	01111010	W	01010111
d	01100100	A	01000001	X	01011000
e	01100101	B	01000010	Y	01011001
f	01100110	C	01000011	Z	01011010
g	01100111	D	01000100	1	00000001
h	01101000	E	01000101	2	00000010
i	01101001	F	01000110	3	00000011
j	01101010	G	01000111	4	00000100
k	01101011	H	01001000	5	00000101
l	01101100	I	01001001	6	00000110
m	01101101	J	01001010	7	00000111
n	01101110	K	01001011	8	00001000
o	01101111	L	01001100	9	00001001
p	01110000	M	01001101	0	00000000
q	01110001	N	01001110		
r	01110010	O	01001111		
s	01110011	P	01010000		
t	01110100	Q	01010001		
u	01110101	R	01010010		
v	01110110	S	01010011		
w	01110111	T	01010100		

(ASCII)

aspect ratio: Refers to how something is positioned or the direction it faces. For example, "The front aspect of the building faced south." *Ratio* is the comparative amount between values. Such as, "There were three females to every one male in the class," or, "A 90/10 ratio of ice cream to chocolate syrup." *Aspect ratio* refers to the comparative size of width to height on a screen. This is best understood visually.

EXAMPLE: Here are various image sizes being displayed on different screen sizes:

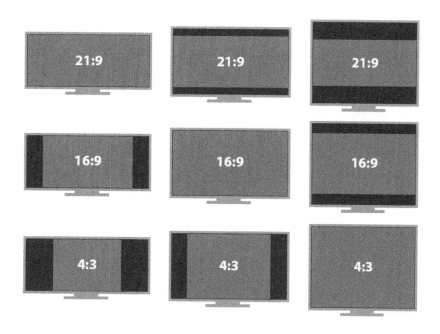

In this image, all of the televisions on the left have a 21:9 aspect ratio display size. The televisions in the middle have a 16:9 display size. The display size for the televisions on the right have a 4:3 aspect ratio. Take the 21:9 examples in this above image. What this indicates is that the image is 21 "units" wide (width) and 9 "units" tall (height). This would mean that an image with a 21:9 aspect ratio would reach the edge of a display device with a 21:9 aspect ratio (as can be seen in the top left image). Yet an image with a 21:9 aspect ratio on a 16:9 display device (top middle) or 4:3 (top right) would have black bars around the edges. 4:3 is considered "full screen" while 16:9 is "widescreen." The image below was cropped to fit different aspect ratio sizes (1:1 = 500 x 500 pixels, 4:3 = 1280 x 960 pixels and 16:9 = 1280 x 720 pixels):

(aspect ratio)

ASP.NET: Stands for "Active Server Pages dot (.) NET." Early on in the development of the Web, web pages were static – they just had text and images, and the text and images did not change unless the creator of the web page edited the files that make up the web page. Website creators needed a way to make some of the content on a web page dynamic – meaning that the exact content could change based on one or more factors such as the specific identity of the person requesting to see the web page; the time or date; the specific inventory available for sale at any point in time, etc. One such method was Active Server Pages. This was a way to combine the standard language of web pages (HTML) with specific computer code that would create web page content on the fly, as needed. It was quite popular in the late 1990s and early 2000s. ASP.NET is a framework for making complex websites. ASP.NET is simply a set of tools offered by Microsoft used when making websites. ASP.NET allows one to develop complicated websites that contain large amounts of data and sections. It is considered an advanced tool for those interested in making websites and web pages. The term "ASP.NET" uses the letters "ASP," but ASP.NET has very little to do with ASP. The creators of ASP.NET used the "ASP" acronym basically as a marketing element when they released ASP.NET.

EXAMPLE: As an example of its use, the website MySpace was created using ASP.NET.

ASP.NET Core: A framework (code written by others [and documentation on how to use it] that can be used by developers to enhance their programs) created by Microsoft. It boasts considerable performance over the original ASP.NET Framework and, with

Microsoft's open-source (a software's code made available to the public) approach, developers can contribute to the GitHub (a web application where people can store and share code) repository, adding newer features for the entire community to share. ASP.NET Core is essentially the first major release since the original ASP.NET 1.0 Framework and, while it features several enhancements, many of the popular core features remain very similar to the original ASP.NET Framework.

EXAMPLE: A large business enterprise might choose ASP.NET Core to create and maintain their business applications.

assembly language: Computers "speak" and "think" in numbers and this is called "machine language" (1s and 0s). Due to the fact that people speak in words, it is sometimes difficult for us to read and write in machine language (even though it is what the computer would prefer). To handle this, people invented assembly language, a simple language that replaces the numbers used in machine language with easily-remembered English words and phrases that people can understand. An assembler is a program built into the computer that automatically translates the assembly language (easily understood by people) into machine language (the numbers a computer can use to perform its functions). Assembly language is also called assembly code.

EXAMPLE: Instead of writing "01100110" to tell the computer to begin its work, assembly language would let you write a word like "LOAD" to do it. The assembler would then convert the instruction "LOAD" into "01100110" and pass that onto the CPU.

assignment: This is the action of giving a value to a variable (data that has a name and a value [type/amount], and can be changed). In most programming languages, you assign a value to a variable using an equal sign (=). You are stating that that variable now has a certain characteristic.

EXAMPLE: You could write a computer instruction that looked like this:
```
WeeklySalary = $1000.00
AnnualSalary = WeeklySalary x 52
```
There are two assignments here. In the first line, we are assigning the value "$1000" to the variable named "WeeklySalary." In the second line, we are multiplying the value of the variable "WeeklySalary" ($1000) times the number 52, and assigning that number ($52,000) to the variable named "AnnualSalary."

associative array: See "mapping."

asynchronous: "Synchronous" means that two things exist or happen at the same time. In technology, synchronous means that something is happening in a set way, and in regular intervals (set periods of time). It is a smooth, predictable flow. "A" (as a prefix) means "not" or "without." For example, "atypical" means "not typical." So when you add "a" in front of "synchronous," you get "asynchronous," which means two things *can* exist or happen at different times, or that something can occur without being subject to a regular set of intervals. When a synchronous process is occurring, each of the separate steps of the process are done consecutively, and each step has to be fully completed before the next step is begun. This is the type of program flow we have been describing thus far in your training. It is best illustrated by looking at one of the five basic elements of a computer program: the "sub-program." A sub-program is a set of instructions that exists outside the normal flow of execution (the order in which instructions are performed). The subprogram contains a set of instructions that is likely to be used at various points in the execution of the main program, and rather than repeat those exact instructions every time they are needed, the main program instead calls for that sub-program to be executed. In synchronous program execution, the main program would call for the sub-program to be performed, and it would wait for that to finish happening before it continued on with the main program execution. An asynchronous action, on the other hand, does not have to complete before the next steps of the process can continue. This would mean that if a sub-program is designated as asynchronous, the main program would not have to wait for it to be completed before moving on with the main program. Instead, it would continually monitor the sub-program to see if it was done working, and when it was done, it would use whatever the product of its work was.

EXAMPLE: A computer program is processing a list of students. The program is supposed to search through a collection of documents, find the documents that have the name of the student in the document title, and count up how many documents each student has. This is a synchronous process. An asynchronous element of this could be: If no matching documents are found for a particular student, the program could send an email to that student alerting them of that fact. Since that action is asynchronous, the program can continue on checking the next student without having to wait for the entire email process to occur. Later, when the email action is done, the program can be informed of that fact.

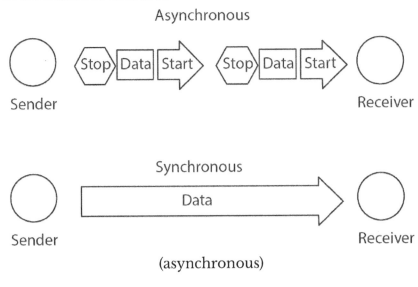

attachment: Something added onto something else, and sent along with it. If you have a piece of paper and you paperclip a card to the back of it, the card is the attachment. In computers, an attachment is information connected to the primary thing being created or sent to another.

EXAMPLE: If you sent someone an email and attached a picture to the email, the picture would be an attachment.

attribute: 1. A characteristic of a thing. In computers, this is a piece of information that determines the character of a piece of computer code or of an electronic file. Computer code and files can have various attributes. The attribute tells something about how the code or file can be used.

EXAMPLE: An electronic file could have an attribute of "Read Only." This means that the file's contents can be viewed, but not changed.

2. See "database attribute."

augmented reality: To augment means to make something better, bigger, expanded or increased. Augmented reality can be thought of as looking at the real world in front of your face through a computer. This computer could be your phone. You look at the world through the camera of your phone and you see the world on the screen of your phone. Augmented reality would then add things to the view of the world that you see on the screen of your phone. These things do not actually exist; they are only added to the image you see on your phone – in other words, they augment the image.

EXAMPLE: If you were visiting another country, and were looking at a menu written in a foreign language, an augmented reality application on your smartphone could help. You could point the camera at the menu, and the augmented reality program could read the foreign language, interpret it, and change the image you see on your phone to show the translated words instead of what was actually printed on the menu.

Automatic Sequence Controlled Calculator: See "Mark I."

automation: The utilization of automatic machines, typically to increase efficiency. Automatic refers to a machine or computer that does things without human interaction.

EXAMPLE: ATMs (automatic teller machines) are an example of automation. They automate the process of taking a debit card, verifying the user's identity, handing over the requested paper currency and returning the debit card.

axis: Coordinates are a set of two numbers that can locate any point on a grid or chart. For example, by using the coordinates longitude and latitude, you can find a location on a map:

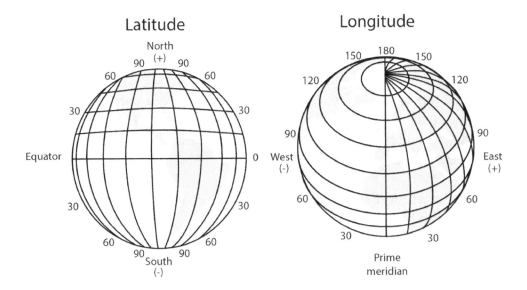

An axis is a line that measures coordinates – in the above example, longitude is an axis, and latitude is an axis. The line that runs left or right (horizontal) is called the X-axis. The line that runs up or down (vertical) is called the Y-axis.

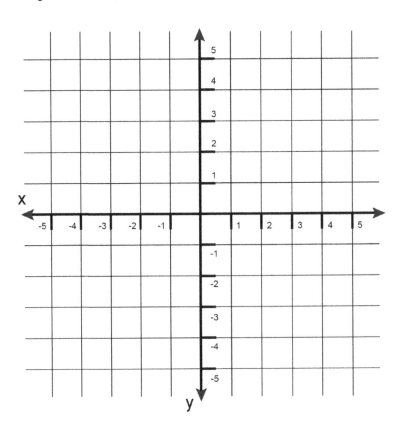

These axes can be used to point to exact locations on a grid.

EXAMPLE: Let's say we want to place these symbols at these coordinates:

Symbol	X axis	Y axis
%	3	4
$	-3	-2
&	-2	2
@	4	-4

The output on the grid would look like this:

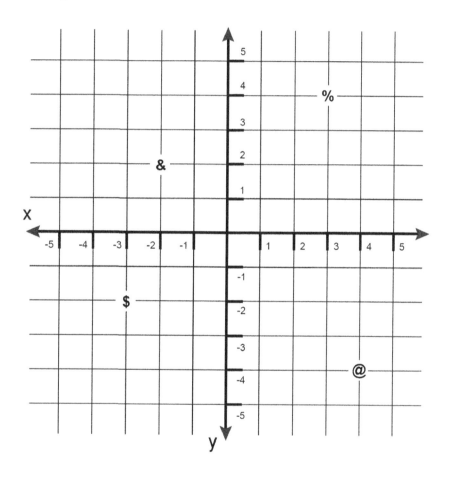

Here is a picture showing the X and Y axis intercepting:

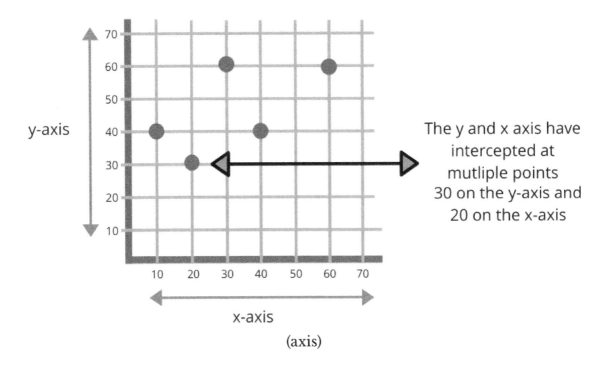

The y and x axis have intercepted at mutliple points 30 on the y-axis and 20 on the x-axis

(axis)

Azure: See "Windows Azure."

B

B: A programming language developed at Bell Labs around 1969 by Ken Thompson and Dennis Ritchie. B was a refinement of an earlier programming language (a system of specialized words and symbols used to communicate with a computer and to create programs) BCPL (Basic Combined Programming Language) and the first version of it was very similar to BCPL, except that it only included the components of BCPL that Thompson felt were necessary (meaning, it left out aspects of BCPL that weren't necessary). As time went on, B was improved and some of what you see in modern programming languages originated in B. They also began changing the syntax used in BCPL. For example, The assignment operator (i.e., symbol used to create variables) in BCPL was ":=" but in B, they changed this to "=." Here is an example of some code written in B:

```
function computeG(a, b, c) {
  let d = use (a, b) {
    ... // some code that calculates d from a and b
    return d;
  };
  let [e, f] = use (d) {
    ...
  };
  let g = use (c, e, f) {
    ...
  };
  return g;
}
```

Note: It is not necessary that you understand every line of code included here, this is just shown as an example so you can see the similarity between this language and modern-day languages.

BA: See "business analysis."

Babbage, Charles (1791-1871): An English philosopher, mathematician and inventor. He is best known as one of the first people to come up with the idea of a programmable computer.

EXAMPLE: Babbage wrote out the theory and design of a mechanical computer called a "Difference Engine." Two other popular devices he invented during his life were the speedometer and the locomotive cow catcher (a metal frame at the front of a train for pushing aside cattle or other obstacles on the tracks).

(Babbage, Charles)

backbone: See "network backbone."

back end: Refers to the parts of a website or software program that perform vital
computing functions, but are not typically seen by the user of the site or program. This
includes things like a database (an organized collection of stored information by the
site or program). This is as opposed to the "front end" of a web site or program, which
is the user interface where the user interacts with the program (usually through a visual
interface). Back end developers are those skilled in the technology required to create
and organize the back end. For example, in a software program that allows a warehouse
manager to monitor and manage the contents of the warehouse, the back end would be
the collection of data about the warehouse contents. The front end would be the
screens she uses to view and change that data. As a further clarification, the term "front
end" has to do with how websites are presented and interacted with. The front end of a
website is the part of the site that a user directly interacts with and sees, as opposed to
the back end, which consists of things behind the scenes that users do not typically deal
with directly. The front end is handled by the web browser. It encompasses things like
preparing the requested website files for display, formatting the text and image that
appear on the screen, handling user interaction with the web page (clicking on text and
images, etc.), and sending information back to the web server (things like requests for
further web pages or user information that was entered in on a web page).
EXAMPLE: When you look at a website and you see the text and pictures, that is all the
"front end." The back end would be all the functions that happen on the web server for
that site.

backing store: An extra backup to the computer's main memory storage. Backing stores
can typically hold more information than the computer itself, but can take longer to
load the data.

EXAMPLE: A compact disc could be used as a backing store.

backlog: You may have heard the word "backlog" used to refer to work that is overdue or should have been done already. For example, if you did not answer your emails for a month, you would have a backlog of emails. In project management, a backlog is slightly different. It is often used in managing computer software development projects. It simply means: work needing to be done. Any work that is supposed to happen is considered a backlog. Often it refers to upcoming work that has not yet been assigned a worker or a target completion date. The word "backlog" is often used in reference to the project management methodologies Agile and Scrum.

EXAMPLE: If you were making a software program that would allow you to manage the members, vehicles and schedules for a car club, you would break down what you had to do or build in order to implement those functions into many individual tasks. That list is your backlog. As you completed items, they would be removed from the backlog.

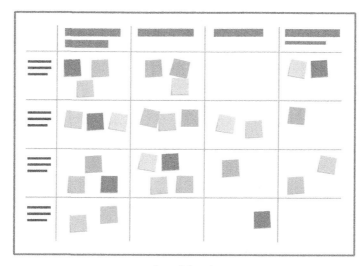

(backlog)

backlog grooming: See "story time."

backlog item: See "PBI."

backlog refinement: See "story time."

backslash: See "slash."

backspace key: Often abbreviated just BACK. A key used to move the cursor back one space. It can delete text just written.

EXAMPLE: Computer programmers have often made use of it for other functions in various different types of computer programs – for example, in a program that lets you access the internet, the BACK key might be used to navigate to the last web page you were visiting.

(backspace)

backup: A copy of information created as an alternate in case the original information is lost or becomes unusable. It is used to store information for safekeeping. Many different systems, devices and services exist to facilitate backing up electronic information. Losing vital electronic records can have a damaging effect.

EXAMPLE: You can copy important files that are on your computer and save the copies of those files on a thumb drive (a small electronic storage device that you plug into a computer that allows you to give and take information). This could be considered "backing up" information.

bak (suffix): A file extension that is typically used to indicate a backup copy of a database file.

EXAMPLE: It is common for an SQL Server to save database backups with the .bak extension.

bandwidth: The capacity for traffic flow on the path that information travels both to and from a computer. The more bandwidth there is, the more information can be sent at once. Bandwidth determines how fast information can be transferred from computer to computer. If some computer operation takes a lot of bandwidth up, it means that it is working with a lot of information and it takes up a lot of the "path."

EXAMPLE: Bandwidth is similar to a pipe in that the wider the pipe (bandwidth), the more water (data) can flow through.

base: A number system is how many unique symbols are used in that number system. A number system is a system that uses symbols to represent quantities. The number system you are most used to using is a base ten number system, which uses only ten unique symbols: 0, 1, 2, 3, 4, 5, 6, 7, 8, and 9. We are so used to only using these symbols that we may not think about the fact that other number systems exist. There are many different number systems, each using a specific number of unique symbols to express different quantities. Another term for these symbols is "digits." Not all symbols used in number systems are numbers like 0, 2, 3 etc. – some number systems use letters, like A, B and C, as the symbols. Base ten is the number system that all math and counting that you have learned is based on. This number system is called "decimal," from Latin decimalis meaning "tenth."

EXAMPLE: a "base four" number system would count, add, subtract, etc. using only four digits: 0, 1, 2 and 3. Digits like 7 and 9 would not exist in a base four number system. This does not mean you couldn't represent quantities like 7 and 9 in a base four number system; it just means you'd have to do so using only the digits 0, 1, 2, and 3.

Bash: Short for "Bourne again shell." A command-line user interface for Unix. A command language is a programming language made up mostly of commands that are mainly used for communicating with the operating system of a computer. Bash is a shell and a command language. Users can type commands that cause actions in the bash.

EXAMPLE: Bash can be used to find a specific file within the computer.

BASIC: Stands for "Beginner's All-purpose Symbolic Instruction Code." BASIC is a computer programming language that was developed in the mid-1960s to provide a way for students to write simple computer programs. BASIC has evolved into a more advanced and powerful language that can be used to create programs for modern computers.

EXAMPLE: Many computer games from the 1970s and 1980s were created using BASIC.

batch file: A computer file containing a list of instructions to be carried out in order. These are most often used in the Windows operating system.

EXAMPLE: Batch files are usually saved as plain text files – such as batch.txt.

batch processing: A batch is a group of things. Processing is when a computer carries out a series of commands and performs instructions. Batch processing refers to the act of processing multiple pieces of data at once. In batch processing, a person gives the computer a batch of information and waits for the computer to process it all at once. The computer does not process the batch until all the information is gathered by someone in one location. Some benefits to batch processing include that the processing takes place when you are not using your computer, and that it is done automatically. It therefore does not require you to intervene throughout.

EXAMPLE: You could compute and send detailed sales reports overnight from a branch office to the headquarters using batch processing.

Baud rate: Baud was named after J. M. E. Baudot (1845-1903). Baud rate is a way to indicate how fast information is being transferred over a communication channel. Since we are talking about computers, which use binary digits (ones and zeroes) to represent data, Baud rate is given in "bits per second," or "bps." A bit is a single binary digit, meaning, a one or a zero. The term "baud" was originally used when telegraphs were used to transmit data over long distances electronically. At that time, "baud" was a unit of telegraph signaling speed in Morse code of "dots per second."

EXAMPLE: A device that had a 14,400 bps baud rate would mean that a maximum of 14,400 bits could be transferred per second by that device.

BCPL: *BCPL* is short for "Basic Combined Programming Language." A programming language that is no longer in general use but it served as an inspiration for many modern-day programming languages. It is rumored that the first ever instance of "Hello, World" was written in BCPL, by a computer programmer named Brian Kernighan in 1970.

EXAMPLE: BCPL was developed by Martin Richards in 1967 at Cambridge University. You can see some BCPL code here:

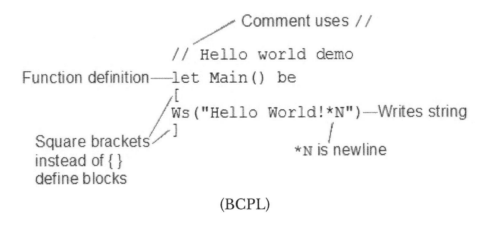

(BCPL)

B drive: See "hard drive."

behavior: See "class."

Bell Labs: An American scientific and research company headquartered in Murray Hill, New Jersey. Bell Labs has been awarded nine Nobel Prizes (a set of prestigious annual awards given out to several categories). They are owned by the I.T. company Nokia.

EXAMPLE: They are credited with several major inventions, including:
- The laser. A laser is an extremely focused beam of light. The difference between a laser and normal light is this: Normal light sources, like light bulbs, emit (send out) light that has several different frequencies. In a laser, the light that is emitted is all the same frequency.

- The transistor. A transistor is a device that can alter the flow of electricity in a machine. It can let electricity flow through it, it can stop the flow of electricity, or it can increase the flow of electricity. In other words, it is basically a switch (device that regulates the flow of electricity).
- Multiple popular programming languages.

NOKIA Bell Labs

(Bells Labs)

Bernoulli distribution: Jacob Bernouli was a Swiss mathematician. Bernoulli distribution is a discrete probability distribution that is only concerned with having two outcomes. This distribution is concerned with the "Bernoulli random variable" which has two values: either 1 or 0. These are considered output values and labeled as:
- n = 1 (success)
- n = 0 (failure)

The probability of which outcome is more likely to occur would be if either 1's or 0's sum is higher.

EXAMPLE: If a store manager wanted to know how many customers bought something and how many customers did not, they could use Bernoulli distribution. Let's say there were a total of 100 customers that came into the store – 70 of them made a purchase and 30 did not.
- Purchasing customers 70% = 1
- Non-purchasing customers 30% = 0

In this case, a customer would more likely purchase something in the store than not.

beta test: *Beta* is the second letter of the Greek alphabet. Beta testing is a form of testing done while creating a software program. It is often the second form of testing done on the software, hence the name "beta." It is done by releasing the software to a limited number of actual end users (the person for whom a program or website is being developed, and who will use it "in the end") for the purpose of identifying defects that earlier testing did not identify. After passing beta testing, the software would usually be released to all end users (the person or persons for whom a computer program is being developed).

EXAMPLE: In creating a website for newlyweds, a person could first have another software programmer go through the site to identify any problems or mistakes. After fixing any issues found, the person could then share their site with twenty-five newly married couples and gather further feedback. This second wave of testing would be beta testing.

BI: See "business intelligence."

big data: The storage, maintenance and use of a very large amount of electronic data, often from multiple sources – so much data that a special database and/or special software must be used to store, maintain and use the data. It can also refer to the business or technology impact of having access to, or responsibility for, such collections of data.

EXAMPLE: If you had a huge company with 10,000 offices and billions of dollars a year in revenue, work that you did involving the data produced and stored by your company would be considered "big data."

bimodal distribution: *Bi* means *two. Modal* means "having to do with mode." A probability distribution that has two different modes. Each of these modes has its own distinctive peak.

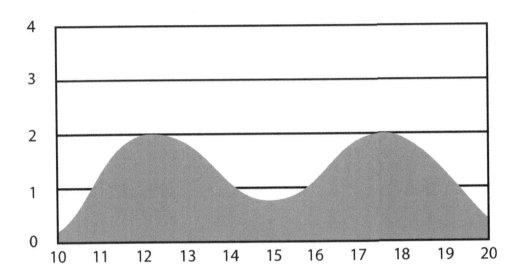

Like two mountains side by side, the mean and median of this kind of data would sit in the "valley."

EXAMPLE: Let's say we have a marketing company that has taken on a new client that provides skincare. This skincare company has stated that their targeted demographic (audience) is between the ages of 14-25. However, based on a recent survey, their data is telling them that their products are not only bought by their targeted demographic, but also by ages 35-48. This opens the door to the possibility of creating a new line of skincare for that second peak. This would be bimodal distribution.

binary: The base two number system (a way of counting that utilizes only two numbers) used by computers. The only two digits computers use to operate are: 0 and 1. The word *binary* comes from the Latin word *binarius*, meaning "two together" or a "pair." All quantities in binary are represented by numbers that use a 1 and/or a 0. In fact, *any* number can be written in binary.

EXAMPLE: Here is how to count to ten in binary: 0 (zero), 1 (one), 10 (two), 11 (three), 100 (four), 101 (five), 110 (six), 111 (seven), 1000 (eight), 1001 (nine) and 1010 (ten). Written another way, here is binary converted to decimal (the base ten number system we are all used to):

Base 2	Base 10 (decimal)
0	0
1	1
10	2
11	3
100	4
101	5
110	6
111	7
1000	8
1001	9
1010	10

To further clarify this, here are places in binary:

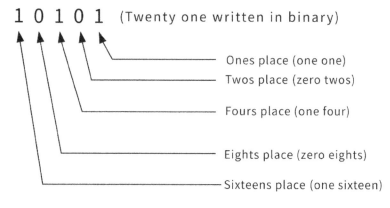

(binary)

binomial distribution: A discrete probability of success or failure outcome from a repeated experiment, survey, poll, etc.

EXAMPLE: A binomial distribution could calculate the probability of an email being spam or not spam.

bionics: The attempt to make machines emulate functions performed by living things. Most commonly, bionics utilizes machine parts to replace body parts on human beings. The term is a combination of the words "biology" and "electronics."

EXAMPLE: In some Star Wars films, Luke Skywalker has a bionic hand.

BIOS: Stands for "Basic Input/Output System." One of the programs that handle the booting process. This is a special computer program that is built into a computer. It is the first computer program that is executed when a computer is turned on, and it is executed every time the computer is turned on. It provides access to the fundamental input and output systems on the computer. If a computer did not have an operating system installed yet, such as Windows, when you turned it on you would see a screen that presented the BIOS. You would be able to perform certain very basic functions of the computer from here. The BIOS is mainly used by whatever operating system gets installed on the computer, so users rarely have to interact with it. There are times that is needed, though, and it looks like this:

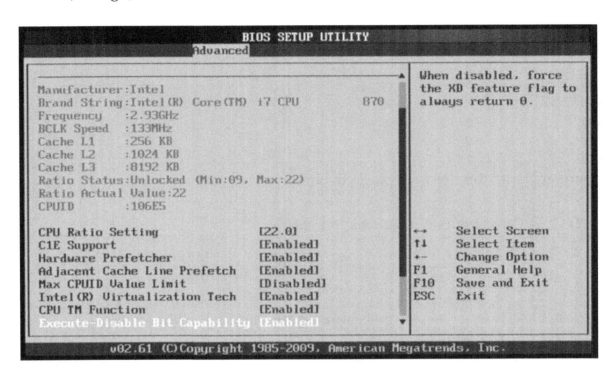

EXAMPLE: A computer, when it is first manufactured, is just a potential tool. The CPU on it has several instructions that can be performed, but there's nothing to tell the computer to do any of those instructions – so the computer has the potential to do work. It needs a program, or a set of instructions, in order to do anything. That's why the BIOS is the first program installed on the computer.

bit: Short for "binary digit." Binary digits are the way computers represent information. Again, binary is a number system that uses two digits (0 and 1) to represent quantities. A binary digit is just that – a 0 or a 1. Inside the computer, a bit is represented in a number of different ways. In terms of storing information in the computer, a bit is represented by the state of a location in the computer's memory storage device. These locations are physical objects that have only two possible states: 1 or 0. In terms of transferring information from one location to another, the computer sends bits as electronic signals on a physical piece of metal wiring. Here, a 1 bit is represented by the presence of electricity on the wire, and a 0 bit is represented by the absence of electricity on the wire. You can also use the term "bit" to describe the size of electronic files. A picture, a document, a movie, etc. are saved on a computer as electronic files. These files are all composed of a certain number of bits. The larger the file, the more bits the file is made up of. When a group of 8 bits are put together for certain purposes, this group is given a special name: a byte.

EXAMPLE: A small file might have 25,000 bits. A large file might have 50 million bits. Note: Computers are often characterized by the size of the instructions and information that they can process at once. This measurement is given in bits. This would mean that an 8-bit computer could only handle an instruction that was made up of 8 binary digits (a byte), whereas a 64-bit computer could handle an instruction that was made up of 64 binary digits. This means that the 64-bit computer could process information much faster than the 8-bit computer, since each instruction could contain much more data.

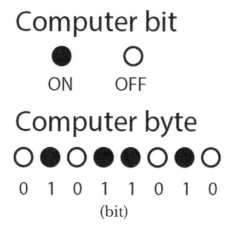

Bitbucket: A web-based version control repository hosting service owned by the company Atlassian. It is specifically used for source code and development projects that use either Git or Mercurial revision control systems. Mercurial is a distributed revision-control tool for software developers. Distributed revision control (also called distributed version control) is a form of version control where the complete codebase, including its full history, is mirrored on every developer's computer. Bitbucket offers both free accounts and paid plans for businesses.

EXAMPLE: Paypal has used Bitbucket.

bitmap: See "BMP."

bit pattern: A particular layout of bits (binary digits). Binary digits are the numbers 0 and 1, and they are the only digits a computer uses. A bit pattern is the arrangement of binary digits that have been arranged in a sequence. Bit patterns are used to represent numbers, characters, etc. It is a pattern of bits that stand for something.

EXAMPLE: In certain instances in a computer, the combination of binary digits "100 0001" is a bit pattern used to represent the letter "A."

BitTorrent: A protocol for sharing large electronic files over the Internet. This gives computer users a way to share information across computers that sometimes works faster than the traditional methods of downloading. It is a "peer-to-peer" protocol for transferring data, meaning all computers involved in the file transfer can act as both providers and consumers of data. (In computers, a peer is another computer you can hook up to directly to give and share information with. This differs from earlier systems in which your computer is required to go through a specialized third-party computer called a server in order to access information from another computer.) Traditional downloading usually means one central computer has the electronic file that you want, so you send a request to that machine to send your computer the file. For example, if you download a video, you are having your computer pull the electronic files for the movie from another machine somewhere so that you can watch the video on your computer. If 100 computers are downloading a specific video from the same machine at once, the video would download slower than if only 5 computers were downloading it at once. Peer-to-peer file transfer protocols (like BitTorrent) provide a way to download the file you want from several computers at once; each computer would only be providing you with a smaller portion of the overall file. In BitTorrent, you are also offering your computer (in a safe way) to be a machine that others can download from. So the more people that are downloading using BitTorrent, the faster it will download because more people are sharing information and fewer people are using the same physical "roads" for data transfer. This is done by installing one of several software programs called a "BitTorrent client." This is a file transfer program that uses the BitTorrent protocol to transfer files. Note: BitTorrent systems are often used for illegal activities, such as downloading copyrighted works like music and videos.

EXAMPLE: If you used a BitTorrent client to download a particular video about waterfalls, your computer would communicate with other computers that have that video and will download small pieces of the video from several sources at once. The more people that have this video, the faster your computer will download. And later, when others want to download the video, your BitTorrent client could receive requests for that video, and it could send out small pieces of that video as part of the process for another BitTorrent user.

bivariate: See "statistical modeling."

biz (suffix): A suffix added to websites that are business websites (biz is just short for business). Usually, websites created for companies are under the .com top level domain (a section of the internet indicated by a suffix, such as: .com, .org, .gov, etc.), but companies can use .biz in two scenarios:
1. If .com is already taken for that particular name (let's say you wanted to call your website hotdogs.com, but someone else is already using that name; you could call it hotdog.biz instead), or
2. If you prefer to call your business' website ".biz."

EXAMPLE: neustar.biz is a website for a marketing company.

black box: In science and engineering, a system where there is a transformation between the input and output without visually seeing and understanding what occurs between. It is called this because it is figuratively a black box that is in between the process of inputting something and getting some output. This concept is used often in a variety of ways in computers. What it is based on, though, is the concept that the system takes in data, does something based on that data, and delivers an output – and the user does not get to see what is being done inside the system. They only get to see what goes in and what comes out.

EXAMPLE: When playing a video game on a console, the system that allows the user to control the actions on the screen is a "black box." The player moves the joystick, presses buttons, etc. and inside the joystick and the console many actions take place that the user does not see. All that is observed by the user is the input (moving the joystick) and the output (the display on the screen changes in accord with the movement of the joystick).

block: A smaller piece that makes up a whole. Usually it refers to pieces of code that make up a program. The pieces of data that form a block are connected (adjacent in a line). Blocking something is to put together segments of data.

EXAMPLE: "ABCD" is a block of characters.

blog: Short for "web log" or "weblog." A log is a written record with descriptions of things that happen, which is then added to over time. A blog is a collection of written communications that is published on the World Wide Web. It is a website where a person or group writes about a certain subject over a period of time.

EXAMPLE: Each time the person writing the blog writes something on the blog, what they wrote is called an "entry" or "post" in the blog. This can be a blog about politics, a blog about animals, a blog about how that person is doing, or whatever is on their mind. Blogs are stored on the web.

blogosphere: The term blog is short for "web log," or "weblog." A log is a description of things that happened, added to over time. A blog is a collection of written communications that is published on the World Wide Web. Blogosphere is a term that describes all blogs and their interconnections. The term implies that blogs exist together as a connected community or as a social network in which everyday authors can publish their opinions.

EXAMPLE: Bill says, "Hey Jane, where did you hear about that new band?" Joe replies, "Somewhere in the blogosphere."

Blu-ray: A standardized way of storing data on plastic discs so the data can be used by computers. Also used to refer to the discs themselves. These are a type of Digital Video Disc (DVD). The data storage method was designed to display high definition videos and store a large amount of data.

EXAMPLE: You could go to a store and buy a copy of the movie "Superman" in the Blu-ray format. You would have to have a DVD player that could read the Blu-ray data format and convert that data into the images and sound for your television.

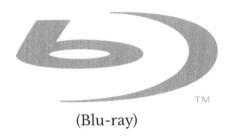
(Blu-ray)

BMP: Stands for "bitmap." Bits are "binary digits" – the 1s and 0s that are used to store information for computers to process. Mapping something means to lay it all out in detail. A bitmap is a type of file used when saving images on a computer. It is a type of picture saved on a computer. If your computer has been set up so it can process data stored in the BMP format, the computer can process those files and display the images they represent.

EXAMPLE: If you were on the Internet (the largest and most-used computer network [connection that allows data transfer between machines] in the world, which is mainly utilized to access the World Wide Web) and saw a picture of a tiger that you liked, you could click on it and save it as a bitmap file type. The resulting image file would be "tiger.bmp," where "tiger" is the name of the file and "bmp" is the format of the data in the file.

board: See "printed circuit board."

bookmark: A marker set on an electronic document so you can easily return to that document or to a specific location in the document. Creating a "bookmark" is when you save the location of a website on the Web so that you can easily return to that website again. When you "bookmark" something, you save it in a list of bookmarks so that when you are on the Web, you may simply select the bookmark in that list and be taken to that website. It comes from the idea of saving your spot in a book using a bookmark. Bookmarks are used by, and stored in, browsers.

EXAMPLE: If you have a website that you visit often that has articles about upcoming movies, you could bookmark that website so that you are taken to it with one click of a button, instead of having to type out the website name every time.

Bookmark Bar

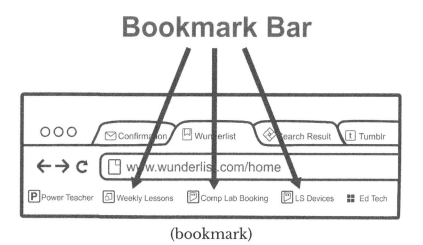

(bookmark)

Boole, George (1815-1864): An English mathematician, educator and philosopher.

EXAMPLE: George Boole was the father of Boolean logic.

(Boole, George)

Boolean logic: A form of logical analysis in which the only possible results of a decision are "true" and "false." In Boolean logic, there are not any vague or 'almost' answers to a calculation or decision. Boolean logic is especially important for the construction and operation of digital computers because it is relatively easy to create a machine where the result of an operation is either "true" or "false." This is done by comparing two or more items – items that can only be "true" or "false." Some examples of the types of comparisons that are performed are "AND" and "OR." They are used like this:
`[true/false condition #1] AND [true/false condition #2]`
That is an example of a Boolean comparison, using the Boolean operator "AND." In Boolean logic, the "AND" operator (a symbol used to carry out a computation – logical operators like "and," "or," and "not" are used to evaluate whether an expression is true or false) is used to see whether ALL the true/false conditions are "true" or not. If ALL of them are "true," then the answer to the overall comparison is "true." If any of the true/false conditions are not "true," then the answer to the overall comparison is "false."

EXAMPLE:

```
[6 > 3] AND [22 <= 23]
```

In this Boolean comparison, each of the true/false conditions are "true" – six is greater than three, and twenty-two is less than or equal to twenty-three. Therefore, the answer to the overall Boolean comparison (AND) is "true." In computers, this becomes valuable because we can build very precise instructions for the computer that allow it to make the same decisions we would make if we did not have the computer as a tool but the computer can make those decisions very quickly, and can perform many such decisions in a very short period of time – much faster than a human could.

boot: To start up a computer. Booting up a computer means that you have turned it on and now it is preparing to operate. It is actually short for "bootstrapping," which means "starting a self-sustaining process that is supposed to proceed without external input." The term "bootstrap" originated in America in the early 1800s through use of the phrase "pull oneself up over a fence by one's bootstraps." A strap is a tab, loop, or handle of cloth or leather. Boots often have straps near the top of the boot that the wearer can use to help pull the boots on without another person's help. The phrase "pull oneself up by one's bootstraps" came to mean "perform a difficult task without external help." The computer industry adopted this term to describe the process of getting a computer running because, once it has started up, it can operate on its own – but it can't start up without a person's external action. The only thing a person has to do is turn on the computer – from there, the boot process begins automatically. During the boot process, a computer is doing several things that are needed before the computer can be used for its routine tasks. These are things like connecting to external equipment (such as a monitor, keyboard, or mouse), installing all required instructions into the computer's temporary data storage for use as the computer is operated, and turning on any specific computer programs that the user has indicated to be turned on when the computer starts.

EXAMPLE: A user usually presses the power button to boot a computer.

Bootstrap: An extremely popular HTML, CSS, and JavaScript framework (code written by others [and documentation on how to use it] that can be used by developers to enhance their programs). It is used for developing responsive websites. Bootstrap websites are particularly good at cross-platform display (e.g., mobile). Bootstrap allows developers to build their projects quickly without spending a lot of time to write and design custom HTML and CSS, while still ensuring cross-browser and multiple viewport compatibility. The Bootstrap framework was originally built by Twitter developers and is now one of the most popular open-source, front-end frameworks in use. Bootstrap offers preconfigured HTML5, CSS, themes, user interfaces, and content layout styles, menu dropdown features, and JavaScript tools.

EXAMPLE: Walmart uses Bootstrap.

(Bootstrap)

bot: A program that runs scripts (lists of commands the computer performs automatically without your involvement) over the internet. These tasks are usually simple and repetitive. Bots perform these tasks at a much greater speed than a person could. Web scraping is the utilization of bots to gather data and content from a website. During web scraping, bots extract HTML code and data. Web scrapers are able to replicate entire websites. Technically speaking, any software that analyzes content and extracts data is a scraper. Bots are automated entities that perform rapid, repetitive actions. Also called "internet bot," "web robot" or "robot."

EXAMPLE: Bots are most commonly used in web spidering (the use of a computer program to systematically browse the web pages that make up the World Wide Web) in which an automated program gathers, analyzes and files information from web servers (a specialized computer used to store and transmit data, such as "serving up" websites through the World Wide Web) at many times the speed of a human.

bounce rate: The percentage of visitors that leave a website after viewing only one webpage. It typically refers to individuals that do not stay on a website long and leave quickly after only looking at the first page they arrive at.

EXAMPLE: A 46% bounce rate would mean that 46 out of 100 visitors to a web page leave without looking at more than that single page.

box: See "quartile."

box plot: See "quartile."

bps: See "byte."

branch: One of two or more possible series of actions that may be performed in a computer program – also known as a "leg." A fundamental aspect of a computer program is the idea of a "path of execution." This means the sequence in which the instructions of a program will be executed. In general, this means, "start at the first instruction, do it, then move on to the next instruction." Because we use computers for work that involves making decisions, we need a way to control that path of execution depending on certain conditions. We make this happen by providing multiple possible actions the computer can perform, depending on the data the computer is evaluating. That is, the computer can be told to perform one of two or more available actions depending on the state of certain information. As an example, the computer might be told to check the test scores of a student, and depending on whether or not the student's test scores were above a minimum level, send them a message inviting them to an advanced class. This type of operation would require two important types of instructions for the computer: an instruction to evaluate information for the purpose of determining what to do, and the actual instructions to be performed once that evaluation has occurred. This is basically the concept of "if this, then that," as applied to computer programming. The first part, the evaluation instruction, is called a "conditional statement" – because which steps the computer will do next are conditional, and are based upon the evaluation of the information given to the conditional statement. An example might be: "if age is greater than 19," or "if the number of items in the order is equal to or less than 10." The second part, the actual instructions to be executed based on the evaluation of the conditional statement, is called "branches." These are each separate paths of execution. There are always at least two branches. Based on the result of the conditional statement, only one of the sets of instructions is performed. An example might be "mark this student as an adult learner," or "apply a 10% discount to the order." Each of these possible sets of instructions is called a "branch" (or "leg").

EXAMPLE: If you are using a computer program to order food from a restaurant, and the restaurant has a different procedure for ordering, depending on whether you want the food to be delivered instead of being set aside for you to pick up, there will be a point in the computer program where the user will be prompted as to whether their order is for pickup or delivery; the computer will have two possible branches it can perform. The conditional statement in the computer program will take in the choice the user made, evaluate that information, and execute one or the other of these branches based on the user's choice.

breadcrumb: In the real world, *breadcrumbs* can be used to leave a trail so one can find their way back. You may have heard of this in stories. In website design and development, breadcrumbs are elements that help user's recall where they are on a website.

EXAMPLE: You can see breadcrumbs within the rectangular box below:

Baking & Pastry Tools

Target / Kitchen & Dining / Bakeware / Baking & Pastry Tools (136)

| Cookie Cutters | Baking Mats | Flexible Spatulas | Cake Decorating Sets |

(breadcrumb)

breakpoint: A marker at a specific instruction in a computer program that tells the computer to pause at that point when executing the computer program. It is a tool for computer programmers that is used when creating a computer program. The breakpoint allows the programmer to analyze their computer program by stopping it at a specific point. They can then investigate the current state of various aspects of the computer program. This is particularly important when a computer program is not producing the results the programmer expects. The origin of the term is based on the idea of breaking the continuous execution of a program at a specific point – hence, a "breakpoint."

EXAMPLE: If a computer program was supposed to be calculating the tax amount on a product sale and was coming up with incorrect tax amounts, a programmer could insert a breakpoint at the exact instruction in the program where the tax calculation was being performed. She could then see the exact data the program was using to perform the calculation and use that data to correct the program.

broadband: A type of access to the Internet. It is used to describe a high-speed connection, meaning computers accessing the Internet can send and receive digital information at a high rate of speed. The primary use of the Internet is to access the World Wide Web (a collection of linked electronic documents known more generally as the "web"). When broadband came into heavy use in the 1990s, it provided a much faster form of access to the Web than the prior Internet access technology, which relied on the use of conventional telephone lines.

EXAMPLE: Broadband Internet requires a computer user to switch from equipment that uses their telephone line to equipment that uses their cable television line. A provider of telephone Internet service might have been a company such as AT&T; a provider of broadband cable Internet service might be a company such as Comcast Cable.

broadcast: The act of sending out audio and/or video content over any one of several systems. Usually this involves the distribution of a signal from one source, which is received by many target devices – hence the term: the content is cast out over a broad area. The first popular use of broadcasting was in the early part of the 20th century, as radio stations started sending out audio programs across a wide geographical area. In any broadcasting system, the transmitting devices convert the information they want to send into an electronic signal; the receiving devices are capable of converting the electronic signal they receive into the needed format; typically this lets the device reproduce the original content from the sending device. This term is now applied in many areas, all based on the physical system used to transmit, receive and present the content. These include radio, television, and Internet (the largest and most-used computer network [connection that allows data transfer between machines] in the world, which is mainly utilized to access the World Wide Web).

EXAMPLE: A professional football game takes place in San Francisco, California. At the stadium, equipment is available that allows audio and/or video of the game to be broadcast over radio, television, and Internet. A fan of the game could use any one of these mediums to listen to or watch the game, depending on what receiving equipment they owned.

browser: See "web browser."

browser engine: An "engine" is the central part of a computer program. A "browser engine" is the core software component of every major web browser. The primary job of browser engines is to transform HTML documents and other resources of a web page into an interactive visual representation on a user's device.

EXAMPLE: The name of Google Chrome's browser engine is called Blink.

brute force: A brute is a violent person or animal. Brute force literally refers to actions taken to accomplish something through use of strength as opposed to mechanical aids or intelligent thought. In coding, brute force refers to two things:
1. Solving a problem in an inefficient way. I.e., having a computer try every possible computation through a sort of trial and error until the end result is achieved. An example of this is a brute force sorting algorithm. Instead of sorting data in the most efficient fashion, a brute force sorting algorithm would find the smallest element in the array and exchange it with the element in the first position, then find the second smallest element in the array and exchange it with the element in the second position, etc.
2. Brute force can also refer to a security attack where the attacker submits several passwords in an attempt to eventually guess it correctly. All possible passwords are checked until the correct one is found.

EXAMPLE: In 2016, a successful brute force attack was made against the massive e-commerce site, Alibaba.

bubble sort: A type of sorting algorithm. In a bubble sort, the list of items is gone through, one item at a time, starting at the beginning. As each item is reached, it is compared to the item previous to it in the list. It is swapped if the desired outcome requires it – for example, if the algorithm is meant to sort a list of numbers in ascending order, the current item would be swapped with the previous item if it is lower than the previous item. This entire process is repeated for the whole list until all the items are in the desired order.

EXAMPLE: You could use a bubble sort to sort a list of students alphabetically by last name.

bucket: You are familiar with the normal definition of bucket: something used to hold a liquid or other material. In computers, a bucket is a system for grouping information together. A bucket is something that similar information is stored in. Where you have various different categories of information to collect and store, each category might have a different bucket to go in.

EXAMPLE: If you were putting together a collection of household receipts on your computer, you might have buckets like "Mortgage," "Groceries," "Clothing," "Cell phones," etc. You could take pictures of each receipt and store the pictures in the appropriate bucket on your computer.

buffer: An area where information is stored for later use. Buffers are usually needed where information is being put into a computer faster than the computer can process it. A special part of the computer's memory is used to store the incoming information until such time as it can be processed by the computer. That part is called a buffer. You may also have a case where not enough information has arrived for the computer to perform the requested action. In this case, the incoming data is stored in a buffer for later use. Buffering means to preload data into the buffer.

EXAMPLE: When a video is loading up on your computer, you may occasionally get a message saying "buffering."

(buffer)

bug: An error in a computer program that impairs or prevents its operation. A bug could slow something down in your computer or stop your computer altogether. Some say this term came from incidents during the early days of computers where actual bugs (insects) got inside the computer and caused malfunctions.

EXAMPLE: Something that causes your computer to freeze whenever you click on a specific image is a bug.

burn: To copy digital information onto a storage device. In the recent past, this referred to the use of plastic discs called "Compact Discs" (CDs); these discs can be "written" on in a process where the surface of the disc is changed so that data is stored for later retrieval. This action has the slang term "burning." As other forms of data storage have come onto the scene, the term "burn" is still used to mean the action of committing data to that storage medium.

EXAMPLE: If you save music on a Compact Disc, you are burning the CD.

burndown chart: A chart that shows how many hours of work are left on the project day by day during a sprint. The days are displayed left to right at the bottom of the graph and the hours are displayed bottom to top on the left side of the graph. You can look at the burndown chart to see if the project is on target, running ahead or falling behind.

EXAMPLE: You can see a burndown chart here:

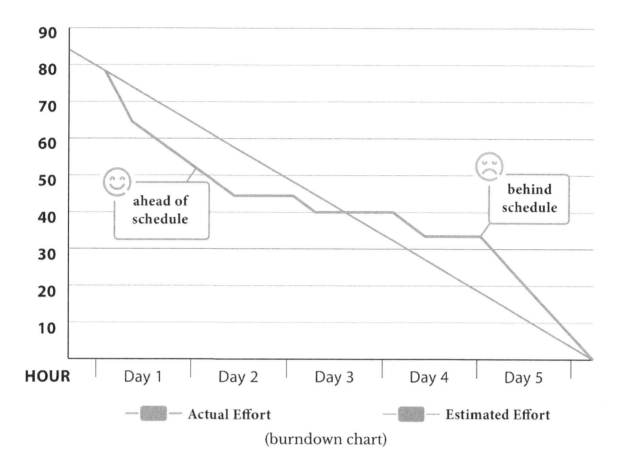

(burndown chart)

bus: You are familiar with buses that drive people around on exact routes. In a computer, a *bus* is a group of wires that reside inside the computer. Electronic signals flow along the wires to reach a specific destination in the computer. Buses are used to connect parts of the computer to each other. They carry information, electricity, etc., through a computer. A full understanding of this involves going back to the fundamentals of how computers work that we covered earlier. We've talked about the fact that the information computers operate with is composed of ones and zeros, and that those ones and zeros are represented by the presence or absence of electricity. The wires in a computer bus are one of the main ways this information is routed to various places inside the computer. The wires in the bus can have electricity applied to them, or not – and that determines whether the signal on that wire means "on" or "off," respectively. Remember, as well, that a computer only does one thing at a time. So the way the bus is used is this: Let's say there are 8 wires in a bus. A piece of data needs to be sent along that bus from one point to another in the computer. The computer will do these things in order:

1. Read the values that need to get sent (the specific combination of ones and zeroes). Let's use the value 11001010 as an example.
2. Apply electricity to those wires that are supposed to send a "one" signal, and do nothing to those wires that are supposed to send a "zero" signal. Using our example value of 11001010, this means that:
   a. Wire 1 would have electricity
   b. Wire 2 would have electricity

    c. Wire 3 would not have electricity

    d. Wire 4 would not have electricity

    e. Wire 5 would have electricity

    f. Wire 6 would not have electricity

    g. Wire 7 would have electricity

    h. Wire 8 would not have electricity

3. Tell the part of the computer that is supposed to receive the data that the data is ready and that it should check the bus for the data.

4. Check for the presence of electricity on each of those eight wires.

5. Use that data on the wires to do work.

6. Remove all electricity from the wires in the bus so it is ready to hold another set of data.

EXAMPLE: Most computers have a device, either internal or external, to store information on. This device is called a "hard drive." To send or receive information to and from this hard drive, the computer uses a bus.

(bus)

bus network: A network is where two or more things (such as computers) are connected to each other. There are several different types of networks, mainly based on the form of the connections and the relationship of each computer to the other computers on the network. A bus network is a form of network where you have several computers connected to a single main wire. Data is transferred between the computers along this one line. An advantage here is that if one of the computers fails, the bus network still works because each computer is connected to the main line. A disadvantage here is that it will take longer to transfer data if they are farther apart, since there is only one line to be used for data transfer; also, you have to wait for data to stop flowing on the line before you can start another data flow.

EXAMPLE: You may decide to have your computers operate on a bus network if you can't afford a great deal of connecting wire for your network.

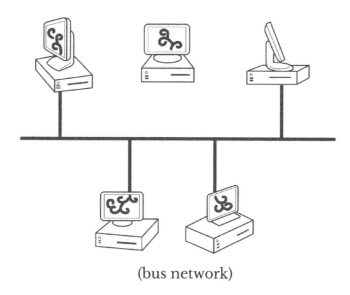

(bus network)

Bush, Vannevar (1890-1974): An American engineer, inventor and scientist. He began developing a computer that could solve complex mathematical problems.

EXAMPLE: For many, Vannevar Bush is considered the first person to use an electronic computer (as opposed to a machine that uses mechanical devices like levers and gears) to perform calculations and store information.

(Bush, Vannevar)

business analysis: Abbreviated "BA." A research discipline of identifying business needs and determining solutions to business problems. Solutions often include the development or modification of software used in implementing business processes, but may also consist of process improvement, organizational change or strategic planning and policy development. The person who carries out this task is called a business analyst, or BA. This is a common position in modern companies.

EXAMPLE: Business analysts may interpret complex reporting requirements that the government might place on a business, and advise various sections of the company on what to do in order to satisfy those requirements.

business case: A description of the reasons for starting a project or tasks. The "why" for a particular project is its business case. Business cases should include the specific business need behind the project and the benefits that it brings. They can be written or conveyed verbally. In addition to the reasons why and the benefits, business cases can include:
- The various options associated with the project,
- The cost of the project,
- The expected risks connected to the project.

Another element of business cases can be a "gap analysis." A gap analysis is a comparison between current performance and the potential or desired performance.

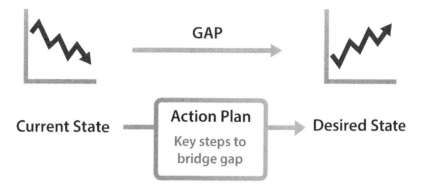

EXAMPLE: A thorough business case for a project includes: the reasons behind it, the associated risks, benefits, various options or approaches, an executive summary and a gap analysis.

business intelligence: Called "BI" for short. BI is the capture and presentation of data in various meaningful forms for useful business purposes. BI can handle enormous amounts of raw data and organize it into forms that give the people in a business valuable insight to improve their business practices. A clarification is needed here on the concept of "raw data." The data is only considered "raw" in relation to the actions or analysis about to be performed on it. For example, in the area of Business Intelligence, the data captured for analysis might have been previously analysed and processed in some fashion – but not for the purposes of performing business analysis with the data. Therefore, the data is considered raw data as far as the BI efforts are concerned, until those BI actions are taken.

EXAMPLE: If you had five branches in your company, business intelligence could be used to gather all historical sales information into one location, organize it, and create various graphs, diagrams, etc. that demonstrate the change of that data over time. Executives could then use this to determine whether or not to close one of those branches, or instead to change some aspect of how that branch is manned or operated so as to improve its performance.

business logic: At a high-level, "business logic" is another word for "code." Technically, business logic is the code that manages communication between a user interface and a database. It is the part of the program that describes how data can be created, stored, changed, and deleted. It can be composed in tiers, as diagrammed below:

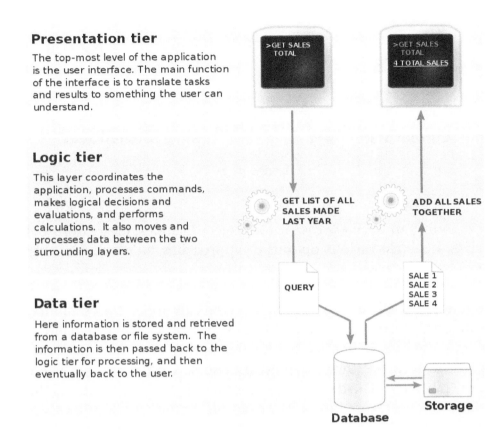

Presentation tier

The top-most level of the application is the user interface. The main function of the interface is to translate tasks and results to something the user can understand.

Logic tier

This layer coordinates the application, processes commands, makes logical decisions and evaluations, and performs calculations. It also moves and processes data between the two surrounding layers.

Data tier

Here information is stored and retrieved from a database or file system. The information is then passed back to the logic tier for processing, and then eventually back to the user.

EXAMPLE: If you log into your amazon.com account, it is the business logic tier that first requests your account information from the database, then displays the appropriate information to your screen.

button: An image on a computer screen that can be used to interact with the computer; it is often used to tell a computer what you want to do. It can often look like a small circle or a rectangular bar. They usually represent a choice to be made. The computer user would choose the button that represents the choice they would like, typically by moving the mouse pointer over the button and clicking the mouse button.

EXAMPLE: If you were using a computer program to handle paychecks for a company, you might have a button in the program that you would click on when the checks were ready to be printed.

byte: Eight binary digits (see "bit"). Size and speed are measured in bits using prefixes telling what magnitude (size) of number they are in. These are taken from Greek words. They are:
- Kilo, meaning "thousand";
- Mega, meaning "million";
- Giga, meaning "billion"; and
- Tera, meaning "trillion."
"Kb" stands for "kilobit." In computers, a kilobit means one of two things:
1. A kilobit is one thousand bits, or

2. More accurately, a kilobit is considered to be 1,024 bits. That's because computers commonly operate off of powers of two. "Power" refers to multiplying a number against itself – for example: 2 to the first power is 2; 2 to the second power is 4 (2 x 2); 2 to the third power is 8 (2x2x2), etc. 2 to the tenth power is 1,024. Since 1,024 is the closest "2 to the power of ____" can get to one thousand, the computer industry uses the term "kilo" to describe that number (1,024). "Kbps" stands for "kilobits per second." This indicates that a network can transfer data at a rate of ____ thousand bits a second – e.g., 20 Kbps indicates a transfer speed of 20,480 bits in a second. If an internet connection had an upload speed of "500 Kbps," it would take 10 seconds to upload a 5,000 Kb file from your computer to another computer on the internet. A notepad document like this might be around 16 Kb in size (16,448 bits – i.e., it would place over 16,000 transistors in various states of on and off within your computer):

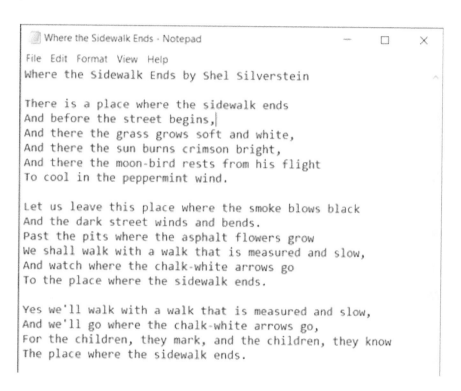

KB stands for "kilobyte." Notice the capital B. A lowercase b indicates "bit," whereas uppercase indicates "byte." Like Kb, a KB is one of two amounts:
1. One thousand bytes (or 8,000 bits). E.g. 3.4 kilobytes is 3,400 bytes, or
2. More accurately, a kilobyte (KB) is 1,024 bytes (8,192 bits).
In the past, kilobytes were used to measure computer memory (how many bytes a computer can store). You saw computers promoting 16KB. That would mean the computer could hold 16,384 bytes of memory (or 131,072 bits). For example, a 1981 IBM computer could store up to 256 KB of memory (very small by today's standards). KBps indicates the transfer of digital information from one location to another at a speed of 1,024 bytes (8,192 bits) per second. Remember, the "K" actually stands for 1024, not 1000. The other four common measurements of bit sizes and transfer speeds are:

1. Megabits – abbreviated as "Mb." Mega means "million," so a Mb is 1,048,576 bits (it is not exactly one million because, as we covered, computers operate off the power of two – in this case 2 to the 20th power).
2. Megabytes – abbreviated as "MB." A MB is 1,048,576 bytes (8,388,608 bits).
3. Gigabits – abbreviated as "Gb." Giga means "billion," so a Gb is 1,073,741,824 bits.
4. Gigabytes – abbreviated as "GB." A GB is 1,073,741,824 bytes (8,589,934,592 bits).

Just like "Kbps" and "KBps," "Mbps," "MBps," "Gbps" and "GBps" refer to how many bits/bytes are being transferred per second. A Mb is a thousand times more bits than a Kb. A Gb is a million times more bits than a Kb and a thousand times more than a Mb. To help give you an idea on sizes, a high-quality image would be around 2MB in size (2,097,152 bytes, or 16,777,216 bits). If your computer had a download speed of 1 MBps (quite slow by today's standards), it would take two seconds to download (move from the internet to your computer) the picture. This picture would utilize 16,777,216 bits of available memory in your hard drive. A high-definition movie that's about an hour and a half long would be around 4 GB in size (4,294,967,296 bytes, 34,359,738,368 bits or 32 Gb). Let's say the download speed of your internet was 1 Gbps (a good speed by today's standards). That means it would take 32 seconds to download. Notice that we said 1 Gbps, not GBps.

EXAMPLE: There are larger file sizes than KB, MB and GB. As you've probably noticed, for each order of magnitude, there is a new name. The next size above GB is terabyte (TB). Again, "tera" is a trillion. A TB is 1,099,511,627,776 bytes (8,796,093,022,208 bits). There are more.

bytecode: The code which makes up a program that has been compiled from source code designed to be processed by the software interpreter. An interpreter performs the same function as a compiler with this one difference: *one instruction at a time, rather than converting the entire set of instructions in the program prior to execution.*

EXAMPLE: If you were to view the byte code of a file, you would notice that while there are numbers and some English words, it does not appear to be human readable.

C

C: One of the most widely-used programming languages. C was developed between 1969 and 1973. Many other languages have borrowed concepts and technology from C. The most up to date version (called C11) was approved in December 2011. C is used in the creation of many things, from operating systems, to apps, games, and business productivity programs. It is a very wide-ranging language with many capabilities.

EXAMPLE: When you buy a new printer, you often need to put a special program on your computer that allows the computer to interact with that printer. That special program might be written in C.

cache: A collection of items stored somewhere for use at a later time. For example, a weapons cache is a place where weapons are kept until they are needed. In computers, a cache is a set of computer memory where information can be stored for later use. One of the most common uses for a cache in computers relates to situations where there is a significant time delay in acquiring certain information. In order to provide a faster user experience, the computer will store the information in a cache after the first time that information is obtained, in order to avoid having to read the information from a slower device, or avoid having to dig around in the computer to find the information again. Pronounced "cash."

EXAMPLE: Things that you view from a cache may only take 2 or 3 seconds to display on your screen, while something new could take 30 seconds to be acquired, prepared for display, and then displayed. On PCs, you can erase a "cached" webpage, and reload the page, by pressing CTRL and F5 together. Here is what cache memory looks like:

(cache)

CAD: See "computer-aided design."

calculator: A device used to perform mathematical calculations. They are usually electronic devices, although certain mechanical calculators have been created over time. Electronic calculators usually contain a display to view numbers, symbols, etc., and physical keys used for inputting data into the calculator.

EXAMPLE: School students often have calculators for use in their classes and most phones have calculators built in.

(calculator)

calibration: The act of correlating (establishing a mutual relationship or connection between) the readings of an instrument against a standard in order to check the instrument's accuracy.

EXAMPLE: The chart below (called the PLUGE pattern – PLUGE stands for *Picture Line-Up Generation Equipment*) can be used to calibrate the black level (the brightness of the darkest areas in the picture) of a computer monitor:

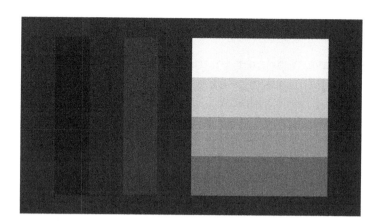

call: To demand or direct something. In normal English this could be used like, "This calls for celebration!" In computers, a call is a direction by a main computer program to execute the tasks of a subprogram. A subprogram is a small program that is often used repeatedly to perform specific tasks. More specifically, a "call" happens when a main program temporarily transfers control of the computer to a subprogram. Once the subprogram is done executing, control of the computer is returned to the main program. A program could make many "calls" to multiple subprograms as the program performs its sequence of tasks.

EXAMPLE: If you were playing a video game, the video game program could call a "high score" subprogram after every game ended in order to make the words "High Score" pop up on the screen.

callback: See "subprogram" and usage note under "function."

call to action: See "CTA."

candidate key: See "primary key."

canonical: A "canon" is a set of rules, principles or laws. There are a few different definitions or usages of this term in the computer industry. "Canonical" means "relating to officially recognized general rules or laws of science." In the computer industry, canonical can mean "having to do with the generally accepted standard items or features of a thing."

EXAMPLE: If there is a generally accepted way to write out a technical description of a section of your computer program and you follow that method in doing so, your technical description could be considered "canonical."

Another way this term is used in computers is when naming the items or objects used in programming or operating computers. There are usually several ways to identify a particular item. Often, the name you use for an item may not be complete – that is, it is possible to confuse it for another, similar item. The canonical name for an item is a name that is unique to that item.

EXAMPLE: You may have a printer in the office that is called "AccountingPrinter2." Inside your office, it would usually be okay to refer to the printer by that name and to program the computers in the office to connect to the printer using only that name. However, you may have another branch of the company, located in another city that happens to have a printer with that exact same name. If the two computer systems in your branches get linked up using the name "AccountingPrinter2" when you set up your computer, it is no longer satisfactory – you'll need a more precise name for each of the two printers. That name could include some unique data related to location – for example: "Branches/NewYork/AccountingPrinter2," and "Branches/Boston/AccountingPrinter2" could be unique names for those two printers. Those are the canonical names for the printers. You will also often find this term used in terms of popular works of entertainment, such as the Star Wars or Star Trek franchises. It is used to indicate whether or not a particular plot line, character, etc., is "canon" – that is, does it come from the official works created and authorized by the creator and/or owner of the entertainment work?

EXAMPLE: In Star Wars, there are novels published in the 1990s that tell about events surrounding Luke Skywalker. The events in those novels are not considered to be part of the official Star Wars canon, as they were not described in the Star Wars movies.

card: Short for "expansion card." A card is a physical component that you can put inside your computer or other electronic equipment to have it perform better or perform additional functions. When you buy a computer, there are cards within it that each perform its own functions.

EXAMPLE: There are cards you can buy that allow you to hook up cable TV to your computer so that you can watch TV on your computer – no television needed.

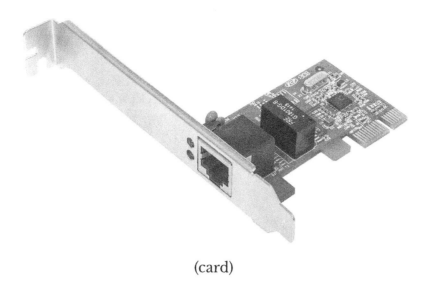

(card)

card (website): See "website card."

carriage return: A character (a symbol used in communication; such as a letter or number) that performs an action, rather than producing a visible letter or number in the document. The action it performs is to cause the text in the document to stop printing on one line, and instead start printing on the next line down, all the way to the left. This is called a control character – it is a character that controls how a document is displayed or printed rather than being part of the words in the document. The carriage return concept, as it is used in computers, comes from mechanical typewriters. A typewriter has a printing mechanism that actually imprints the letters on the paper. It also has a part called a carriage that moves the printing mechanism from left to right. When the typist wants to end off typing on the current line and move down one row and start a new line of writing, they press the "return" key. This makes the carriage move down one row and back all the way to the left. In other words, the carriage "returns" to its default position. On computer keyboards, you use the key marked "return" or "enter" to create this control character.

EXAMPLE: If you are writing an essay on a computer and you are done with one paragraph and wish to start another, you would press the "return" or "enter" key. This would end the paragraph you were writing and start over one line down and over to the left.

carry-in wire: A wire inside the computer that brings (carries) electricity into a part of the computer.

EXAMPLE: A wire connected to a section of your computer that allows the travel of electricity into that section would be a carry-in wire.

carry-out wire: A wire inside the computer that brings (carries) electricity out of a part of the computer.

EXAMPLE: A wire connected to a section of your computer that allows the travel of electricity out of that section would be a carry-out wire.

cartridge: A plastic container that contains hardware and software. Cartridges are inserted into a computer so the software on them can be run. They were more common in the 1990s and earlier, but were replaced by CDs.

EXAMPLE: The classic video game console, Nintendo Entertainment System, used game cartridges.

(cartridge)

Cascading Style Sheets: See "CSS."

case: See "computer case."

case-sensitive: Referring to a programming language where capital and lowercase letters affect the syntax. Some languages allow you to write code with no attention given to capitalization or lowercase letters, while others won't operate unless you write the code exactly.

EXAMPLE: Python is a case-sensitive programming language. In Python, the following code would print Hello, World! on the screen (note: the only "code" in the following line would be print() – the text within the quotation marks is not code):
```
print("Hello, World!")
```
But if you wrote your code as follows, there would be a syntax error and the text wouldn't be displayed. This is because, in Python, the print command does not begin with a capital P:
```
Print("Hello, World!")
```

cassette tape: A device used to store information on magnetic film (tape). Originally released in the 1960s, cassette tapes are commonly used to store audio recordings and digital information for use by computers. While they are no longer in common use for personal computers, they are often used for large computers as a location for long-term storage of valuable information.

EXAMPLE: The 'Disaster Recovery' section of a large company might routinely store operational data on large magnetic tapes, so that if the main computer systems in the company are destroyed, that data is available for recovery.

(cassette tape)

casting: The action of converting a value from one data type (a specific category of information handled by a computer – such as numbers or comparisons) to another. Often in programming, you do not control the initial data type of a value. For example, querying the United Postal Service API for a shipping rate gives back the value "12.85" as a string data type. This data type is useful if you want to display that rate to a customer, but useless if you want to perform any math operations to it first (such as adding it to the total price).

EXAMPLE: In a database, a column in a table could be set up to only accept strings, yet the data type produced by your program is an integer. The integer would need to be cast as a string.

catch: A block of code that is executed if an exception (error) is encountered during a try block (a block of code that tests/risks failure).

EXAMPLE: A catch block might be written in order to "catch" a user input before an unforeseen error occurs.

categorical data: Categorical literally means "clearly explicit; direct." Categorical data refers to a particular subject that has a name or label.
EXAMPLE: The color of a car (blue, red, green, etc.) or yes/no values are examples of categorical data.

CD: 1. Short for "compact disk." A flat, plastic disk that you can store information on for later use by computers. Information on CDs can be accessed by computers and other specialized machines.

EXAMPLE: Music is commonly stored on CDs.

2. Stands for "continuous delivery." It is an element of DevOps CD that encourages development teams to produce software in short cycles. CD automates the delivery of applications to environments. Since teams sometimes work with multiple environments (such as testing and development), CD ensures that there is an automated way to push code changes to the applicable environment. See also "CI."

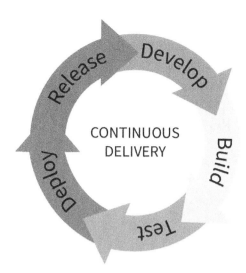

EXAMPLE: CI and CD include continuous testing to ensure that the end product that is delivered to users has no errors. CI/CD are commonly used together to refer to the following:
- DevOps is being utilized.
- Software is being developed by a team.
- Each stage of the process is separated into different environments.
- Only small changes are made.
- Every change is checked in.
- Every step is fully tested before moving forward.

CDN: Stands for "Content delivery network." A specialized service that helps deliver digital files to those who request them over the internet.

EXAMPLE: If you had a website where the pages mainly contained text, but also included the occasional video, and you expected to receive a lot of requests to view the videos, it would be a good idea to put the videos on a CDN, so that users of your website wouldn't have to wait for long when they tried to play the video.

C drive: See "hard drive."

CD-ROM: Stands for "Compact Disk – Read-Only Memory." A compact disk is a flat plastic disk that you can store information on for later use by computers. A CD-ROM is a CD that has some information stored on it at the time it is manufactured, and from that point forward, the information can be read by a computer, but not changed. See also "ROM."

EXAMPLE: Many computer games come on a CD-ROM.

CD-ROM drive: Stands for "Compact Disk – Read-Only Memory drive." A compact disk is a flat plastic disk that you can store information on for later use by computers. A

CD-ROM is a CD that has some information stored on it at the time it is manufactured, and from that point forward, the information can be read by a computer, but not changed. The CD-ROM drive is a device in a computer that can access the data on CDs and deliver that information to the computer. Typically, it has a thin, flat tray that can move outward from the computer, allowing a CD-ROM to be inserted or removed from the computer. See also "ROM."

EXAMPLE: Here is a CD-ROM drive:

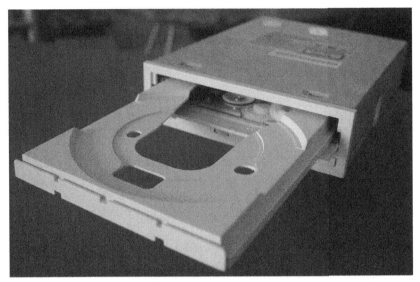

(CD-ROM drive)

cell phone: A type of mobile device; a mobile phone. A cell is the smallest functioning part of your body. This term is part of how the phrase "cell phone" came about. It is related to how the phones interact with the towers that allow them to send and receive information. Here are what cell phone towers look like – you've probably seen them around:

Each tower has a range around it in which it can send and receive data to various computer devices, as long as the device has the correct receiver and transmitter in it. Once you go beyond that range, the device and the tower can't detect each other anymore. In most places now, when you pass out of the range of one tower, you pass into the range of a new tower.

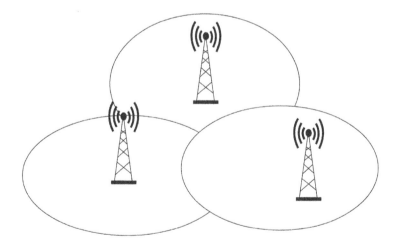

This area around a tower in which the signal is effective is called a "cell," from its resemblance to a physical cell in a body. Towers are physically placed close enough to each other that these "cells" overlap – so that information can be passed from one "cell" to another. That way information can go from your cell phone, across this network of "cells," to the cell phone of the person you're talking to. You can be on a phone call while you are in a car and the call can continue for quite some time, as the connection to your phone is transferred from one cell tower to another, based on your changing location. A cellular network (or mobile network) refers to the total coverage of cell towers. Nowadays, most carriers (cell phone service companies) have cellular networks that span entire countries. In the present day, all cell phones are smartphones. A smartphone is a handheld mobile computer that can connect to the internet. This makes it so the smartphone can function as a cell phone, but also as an internet-connected computer.

EXAMPLE: In addition to phone calls, you can use a cell phone to access websites, perform work tasks, play games, etc.

cell tower: See "cell phone."

central processing unit: See "CPU."

central tendency: In normal English, *tendency* is a likelihood to behave in a certain way or go a particular direction. *Central tendency* is a single value that attempts to describe a set of data by identifying the central position in the data set. Central tendency asks the question, "Where does the center of the data tend to be most?" Central tendency can be measured by mean, median or mode.

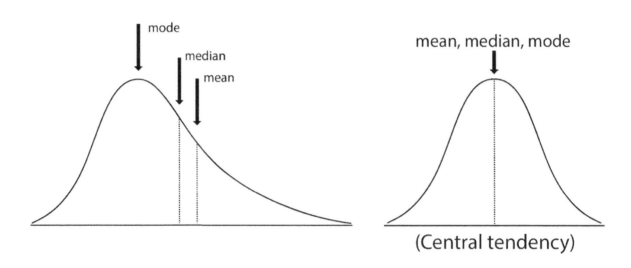

EXAMPLE: The central tendency of female height is 5ft 4in.

certificate authority: A company that gives out digital certificates. Digital certificates are specially-formatted data that gets saved on a web server. They are evidence of a certain degree of trust you can have that the website you're using is safe to use, as far as not letting any valuable private data you might submit to the website fall into the wrong hands. Essentially, the website is given a digital "passport" proving that they are who they say they are and that it is okay for website users to send their information. Certificate authorities are official organizations that state that a company appears to be safe to deal with over the Internet.

EXAMPLE: Most websites that have received a certificate from a certificate authority will display a logo that looks something like a padlock or a green checkmark. It is very important to understand that having an icon like these is not proof that a website has a valid certificate – the actual certificate is a file saved on the web server for the website. Anyone can put these icons on the pages of their website. The actual proof that the website has a valid certificate is found in one of two ways:

1. The address of the website in the web browser has an "s" after the "http" – the "s" stands for "secure," and is only there if the website has a valid certificate on its web server.

2. Some browsers have a padlock icon somewhere in the browser that is NOT where the web pages are displayed. This can be found at the very bottom of the browser, at the top near the website address, or in other places – but not in the web page being displayed. Remember, the web page creator can put whatever symbols they want on a web page, including that padlock icon – but they can't make the browser itself display the icon in the non-web page areas of the browser. The presence of this icon indicates the browser has verified the web server has a valid certificate.

chaining: The action of executing or taking in one section of a program at a time. This is most commonly done if the program is too large to fit into the computer's memory all at once.

EXAMPLE: If someone bought a large software program that was too large, the computer may utilize chaining to run the program.

channel: Something that other things can pass through. It is a passageway for something to travel; a path.

EXAMPLE: A wire is a channel for electricity.

char: A data type (a specific category of information handled by a computer – such as numbers or comparisons) that represents a single text item – that is, a single letter, number or other symbol. The word "char" is short for "character." The behavior of this data type includes things you would do with text – convert the text to uppercase etc. A char variable would be "declared" and "assigned" like this:

```
char [variable name] = '[alphanumeric character]'
```

EXAMPLE: You could have a computer keep track of the middle initial of a student using a char variable named "middleName." You could set it to 'M' like this:

```
char middleName = 'M'
```

Note that the actual data stored in memory for the variable are the letters in between the single quote marks – the quote marks are not part of the data itself; they are just used to show where the char begins and ends.

character: An individual letter, number, symbol, etc.

EXAMPLE: "A" is a character. "7" is also a character. "A,#$Sf1247SA^D" is 14 characters.

character code: See "character encoding."

character encoding: A system where numbers, letters, etc. are represented by codes. The codes used are in a form that computers can easily understand. The system used for each type of code depends on how that code is going to be used. Also called an "encoding system" or "character code."

EXAMPLE: The letter "A" could be represented by the code "65."

Usually, the actual codes for a letter, number, etc. are in binary. Every letter or symbol has a unique number so that the computer knows what letter or symbol you mean, and this is called character encoding.

EXAMPLE: The letter "B" might have 1000010 as its character encoding.

character set: Fixed collections of characters (a symbol used in communication; such as a letter or number).

EXAMPLE: The English written language is a character set containing almost 100 symbols. This includes 26 upper-case letters of the English alphabet, 26 lower-case characters of the English alphabet, the numeric digits 0 through 9, and a collection of punctuation marks.

chassis: A container that consists of a frame or other internal supporting structures on which the parts that make up the device are mounted. You can think of it as the skeleton of the machine – it's the frame on which the actual working parts are attached. The internal framework of a structure is its chassis. Other parts of the structure are attached to the chassis. Pronounced "CHA-see."

EXAMPLE: The chassis of a car is the internal frame, including the axle and wheels that the remainder of the car rests on. Here is a computer chassis:

(chassis)

check bit: A binary digit (a 1 or a 0) that is used to check for possible errors in the transmission or storage of a piece of data. Because all data is stored in 0s or 1s on a computer, the computer can simply check if there is an even or odd number of 1s in that piece of data. If there should be an even number, but there is an odd number, the computer then knows there has been an error somewhere in the storage or sending of the data and vice versa. The check bit would be a 0 if the number of 1s was even, or it would be 1 if the number of 1s was odd. The computer would compare the check bit to what it received and then determine if there was an error or not. It is a built-in quality control function inside computers.

EXAMPLE: Computer A sends data to computer B. Computer A tells computer B that the check bit was 1 for that particular chunk of data. Computer B looks at what it received and sees that it received an even number of 1s. It now knows that there was an error somewhere, since the check bit should be a 0 if there are an even number of 1s in the data.

check in: To add code changes to a set of computer code, into the code that is being managed by a version control system. Conversely, "checking out" code means marking a certain part of the code that is being managed by a version control system as being subject to modification. That section of code can then be managed by the version control system in such a manner that the system acts to prevent conflicts that could be caused if another person wanted to work on that exact same section of code simultaneously to you working on it. Checking in is sometimes referred to as "committing" code.

EXAMPLE: If you were working with a team of two other developers on a computer program that tracked the students in a school, and you wanted to work on the part of the code that calculated grade point averages, you might "check out" that section of code. The version control system would then mark that section of code in some way, and could notify the other two developers that the section of code has been checked out should they attempt to change it.

check out: See "check in."

checkpoint: A named set of data in the computer's memory that can be restored in the future if needed.

EXAMPLE: If during an update a computer had an error, one could restore an earlier checkpoint. This would bring the computer back into the earlier state when things were operational.

checksum: A number that is used to verify the integrity of a set of transmitted data. You use this checksum to ensure that the correct data has been transmitted. A special computer program is used to calculate a unique number, based on the exact contents of an electronic file. When that file is sent from one computer to another, the checksum is also sent. If the computer receiving the file performs the same calculation and compares the number it calculated to the checksum it received, it can determine if any part of the data it received is different from what was sent. Checksums are a type of quality control method used by computers to ensure files are transmitted properly.

EXAMPLE: Let's say your file has a checksum of 1234567890. You then transmit the file to your friend's computer. Your friend then creates a checksum for the file she received, using the same method you used to create your checksum. If the checksum she gets is 1234567890, it means her file is identical to yours. If the checksum she gets is 0798645321, the file is not identical – likely there were errors in transmitting the file.

chemical element: Any of the more than 100 known substances (92 of which occur naturally) that cannot be separated into simpler substances, and that singly or in combination constitute all matter.

EXAMPLE: Carbon, oxygen, lead, silver, and gold are all chemical elements.

child class: See "parent class."

chip: Short for "microchip." As a reminder, "micro" means "very small." Chips are very small parts of a computer that are usually made of an element called silicon. A single chip can contain millions of parts that store and pass on information. There are many types of chips, but they all share the same basic operation of handling different functions in a computer using electricity. Examples of different types of chips in a computer are the CPU and certain digital storage devices.

EXAMPLE: When you save something on a computer, it can be saved on a chip.

(chip)

Chi-Square Test: *Chi* is the twenty-second letter of the Greek alphabet (**X**, χ). It is pronounced "kigh" (think "high" with a *k*, instead of an *h*). The *Chi-Square Test* determines whether or not a data set is dependent upon one or more independent variables. It also gives us a value to determine how dependent the data set is upon this/these variable(s). The symbol for chi-square test is: χ^2 test

EXAMPLE: Let's say that we are looking at the advance (ahead-of-time) ticket sales to Comic-Con versus the total attendance. With the Chi-Square test we can determine to what extent the advance ticket sales affects the total ticket sales.

CI: Stands for "Continuous Integration." An approach to software development and a set of practices that encourages developers to implement small changes and check in code to version control repositories frequently. Each time developers merge their code changes into a central repository, CI includes ensuring automated builds and tests are run on the code in the repository. This is as opposed to not checking in code often or not testing code after every push. See also "CD."

EXAMPLE: CI is a component of DevOps.

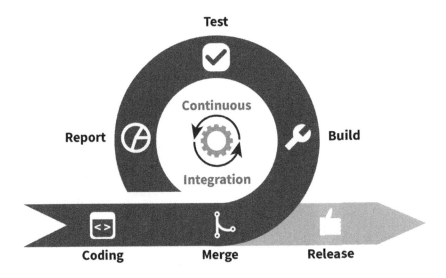

(continuous integration)

circuit: You've probably heard of negative and positive electricity. "Negative" and "positive" are the two main types of electricity, and as the saying goes, "Opposites attract." Positive energy is drawn toward negative, and vice versa. On the other hand, negative electricity pushes away other negative electricity and positive electricity repels positive electricity. Here is an illustration showing this (negative electricity is indicated by a minus sign, -, while a plus sign, +, is used for positive):

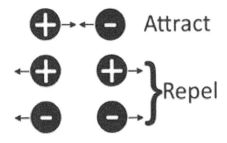

You can see the negative and positive written on batteries:

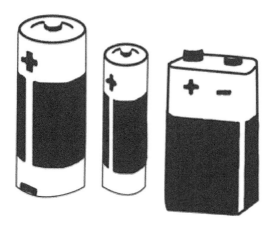

A "circuit" is a path that electricity flows along from beginning to end – it is a complete path of electricity. Along that path, there might be certain machine parts that do work or control the flow of the electricity. The electricity that travels through this circuit will come from a source (such as a battery or an electrical outlet in a wall), travel through wires and devices, and return back to that source. Batteries utilize the negative and positive energy to draw electricity through circuits, as can be seen in this illustration:

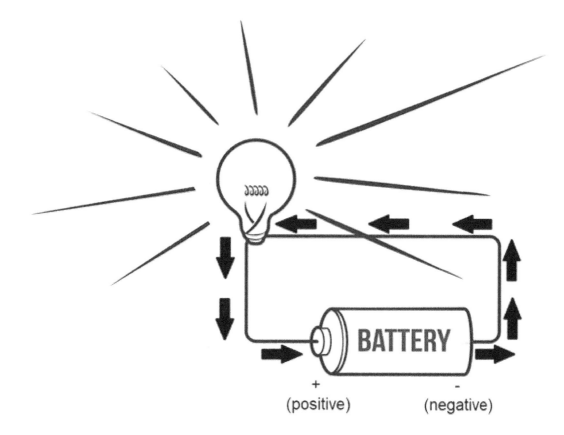

EXAMPLE: All of this directly relates to computers because they're connected to an electricity source (a plug in a wall; an internal battery) – and that electricity runs through circuits in the computer and performs functions along the way.

circuit board: See "printed circuit board."

Cisco: Short for "Cisco Systems." A major company that specializes in building and selling computer networking equipment. It has about 70,000 employees internationally and is based in San Jose, California.

EXAMPLE: You could purchase all hardware required to build a computer network from Cisco.

(Cisco)

class: In OOP, a class is an object, created from the mind of the computer programmer, that represents a type of thing the programmer wants to represent in the computer program. Examples of objects include things like "integer," "string," "Student," "Teacher," "Email Processor," etc. Objects have three aspects: Their structure, their behavior and their state. Most computer programming languages have certain built-in objects that the programmer gets to use automatically. These are the common data types like "integer," "string," etc. As an example of the concepts of "structure," "behavior" and "state," we can look at the object known as an integer. Structure here is relatively simple: an integer is a quantity – a number. It usually can be positive (10.5, for example), negative (-1560.7, for example), or zero (0). Due to the need to manage the use of the available memory locations in the computer, it will have maximum positive and negative limits – say, from 65,536 to -65,535. Behavior here is also pretty straightforward – an integer object has behavior related to mathematical operations. That is, the object can be used to perform operations like addition, subtraction, multiplication, division, etc. State refers to the value or condition of the data represented by the object at any given point in time. Here, with an integer, the "state" is the actual number for a given object of the type "integer" at any point in time. For example, if a program were making use of an integer called "Age," its state might be "24," and be used to represent the age of a person. The programmer does not need to define the structure and behavior of these built-in objects. They are often called "primitive types," in that they are data types that are the simple, well-known, common data types any programming language will need to do usual common operations. The programmer can simply write a computer program that creates objects of those types, gives them a certain state, and performs the built-in behaviors with them. Often, though, the programmer will need to define their own objects. In the examples given above, these are objects like "Student," "Email Processor," etc. Here, the object needed is unique to the problem the programmer is trying to solve through the creation of a computer program. These custom objects, also called custom types, are one of the main tools a programmer has to create useful computer programs. Here, the programmer can represent useful objects, often modeled on real-world objects, that the program can create, modify and delete in order to make a useful computer program. One of the more important custom data types a programmer can create is a type of object called a "class." Classes are not actually objects themselves. Instead, they provide a template that actual objects can be created from. The programmer defines the structure of a potential object, as well as the behaviors available to that potential object. Then, when the program needs to make use of an object of the type defined in a certain class, the program creates an actual object of that type, gives it state, and then performs the behaviors defined for it in the class definition. This action of creating an actual example of the object defined by a class is called "instantiation," and the created object is called an "instance" of the class. Objects so created can also be referred to as a "class object" or "class instance." You can think of the class definition as an answer to the question of, "If I were a [type of object], what would I look like and what could I do?" Here, "what would I look like" refers to the structure of the potential object, and "what could I do" refers to the behavior of the potential object.

EXAMPLE: Let's say the question was, "If I were a vehicle, what would I look like and what could I do?" The structure of a vehicle would include such things as: An energy source that can provide the motive force to move the vehicle. Examples might be "a gasoline engine" or "an electric motor." A physical form that implements the primary purpose of the vehicle. Examples might be "sedan," "convertible," "pickup truck," etc. One or more doors to provide entrance and egress for the people operating or being transported by the vehicle. A mechanism for increasing the speed of the vehicle. Examples might be "an accelerator pedal" or "a speed lever." A mechanism for decreasing the speed of the vehicle. Examples might be "a brake pedal" or "a brake lever." A mechanism for steering the vehicle. Examples might be "a steering wheel" or "a steering lever." A speed at which the vehicle is traveling. Examples might be "55 miles per hour," "10 feet per second," or "0." Another term for these structure elements is "Properties." The behaviors of a vehicle would include such things as: accelerate the vehicle, slow the vehicle, stop the vehicle, steer the vehicle to the right, and steer the vehicle to the left. This would be an example of the definition of a "Vehicle" class. Again, this wouldn't be referring to any vehicle in particular, but instead to the concept of a vehicle – what things must any vehicle have, and what things can you do with or to a vehicle, if you had one. When the computer program had need for a vehicle, it would be directed to use this class definition to create, or "instantiate" one. Specifically, it would create an object of type "Vehicle." At that point, the program would set aside parts of the computer memory to keep track of the properties of that particular object of the Vehicle class. The computer program would then be directed to set the state of this new object of the Vehicle class. It would have to have specific values for the properties of this Vehicle – what type of engine it had, what physical form it was built to, what kind of steering mechanism it had, etc. Probably it would get these values from the user of the computer program. Here are two examples of instantiated objects of the type Vehicle:

Vehicle 1:

```
Energy source: gasoline engine
Physical form: Pickup truck
Number of doors: 2
Mechanism for increasing speed: Accelerator pedal
Mechanism for decreasing speed: Brake pedal
Mechanism for steering the vehicle: Steering wheel
Speed: 0
Vehicle 2:
Energy source: electric motor
Physical form: Sedan
Number of doors: 4
Mechanism for increasing speed: Accelerator pedal
Mechanism for decreasing speed: Brake pedal
Mechanism for steering the vehicle: Steering wheel
Speed: 0
```

At this point, the computer program can make use of the defined behaviors for objects of the Vehicle class. That is, the computer might execute an instruction to "Increase speed of Vehicle1 by 10 miles per hour once a minute until its speed property is 40 miles per hour," or "Steer Vehicle2 to the right." Certain computer programming languages implement another concept related to this concept of "classes": They allow for the definition of classes that inherit the structure and behavior of another class, while also allowing for the addition of new properties and new behaviors. This concept is called "inheritance" – that is, the second class "inherits" the structure and behavior of the first class. In this system, the first class is called the "parent" class and the inheriting class is called the "child" class. Using our "Vehicle" class as an example, the programmer might create child classes like "Airplane" and "Helicopter." Each of these child classes would automatically get the structure and behavior of the parent class ("Vehicle"), but the programmer could add certain structure and behavior elements particular to that type of object. For example, the "Airplane" class might add properties like: A number of wings to provide lift, and a number of engines. This "Airplane" class might add behaviors like: Take off, and land. This way of programming adds certain benefits for the computer programmer. One primary benefit is that they do not have to write the same code more than once. Besides the fact that it saves time, this is valuable because the programmer can make a change in the parent class and all its children then can make use of that change. For example, the programmer might add the properties to the Vehicle class "A number of passengers" and the behaviors "Load a passenger" and "Remove a passenger." Now, the children of the Vehicle class ("Airplane" and "Helicopter") can use those properties and behaviors with no further work from the computer programmer.

classifier: An item used in machine learning models (mathematical representations of real-world processes) to pinpoint a certain type of data and to sort that data into categories. It is how the computer learns to recognize what data is what.

EXAMPLE: If you fed the computer two different pictures (one of a cat and one of a dog), you would classify picture one as "dog" and picture two as "cat," then continue giving the computer different pictures of dogs and cats until it recognizes the pattern of each classifier ("dog" or "cat").

CLI: 1. See "command-line interface." 2. See "Common Language Infrastructure."

click: See "mouse."

client: A computer that is requesting service from another computer. The client is the computer that requests and receives information from a server (a powerful computer that sends out information to other computers).

EXAMPLE: If you have one computer in an office that stores all the appointment data for the office employees, and many people need access to that information, the individual computers that connect to that "appointment data" computer are clients of the "appointment data" computer, which is the server. Your web browser (program that you use to look at things on the Internet) is also a client.

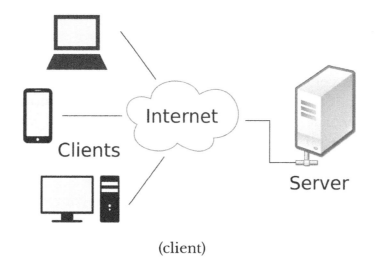

(client)

client side: See "server side."

clip: A short video that is typically made up of a scene or scenes from a longer video.

EXAMPLE: A movie preview is composed of clips.

clock: The device on the computer that controls the timing of the CPU (Central Processing Unit – the "brain" of the computer; a physical piece within the computer that processes [handles; performs actions with and on] data). It is a device that, once turned on, continuously operates to produce an exact electronic output signal. This signal increases and decreases in electrical strength at an exact, unchanging rate. The signal is delivered directly to the CPU, and it is one of the most important aspects of how a computer works. It is this signal that actually controls the CPU, and therefore the entire computer. Since a computer can only really do one thing at a time, and the operations it can perform are built into the CPU, what remains is some instruction to the CPU to "perform the next instruction, please." It is the signal from the clock that performs this function. When the output signal from the clock is "high," it is putting out electricity. When it is "low," it is not. The moment the clock goes "high," the CPU detects that this has occurred, and then knows it should start its next action.

EXAMPLE: The faster your computer's clock can operate, the better your computer can perform. This is called "clock rate."

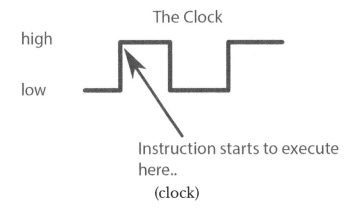

(clock)

clock rate: The rate of operation for the device on the computer that controls the timing of the CPU (Central Processing Unit – the "brain" of the computer; a physical piece within the computer that processes [handles; performs actions with and on] data). It is measured in "Hertz," with one full "high-to-low" cycle per second being 1 Hertz. Hertz is abbreviated Hz.

EXAMPLE: The faster a computer's clock rate, the better your computer can perform.

closed loop: A system that does not accept inputs from or create outputs to another system. Once the system is up and running, it does not receive any input from any user or other system, and it does not send any information to any other systems.

EXAMPLE: The pump on a fish aquarium is a closed loop. Once the pump is turned on, it just continues to operate until power is removed. It does not receive any input from any other system, and it does not give any input to other systems.

close tag: See "tag."

closing tag: See "tag."

cloud, the: See "cloud computing."

cloud computing: To understand cloud computing, you need to understand the usual way that people store information on computers. For many years, people and businesses would use computers that were located at their home or place of business to store data on or to run special computer programs on. At some point in the early part of the 21st century, new businesses started appearing that offered customers the use of large computers owned by these new businesses and located in their facilities These computers could be used by the customers to store information and programs on. The customers could connect to these computers from wherever they lived or worked, using the Internet, and access the information or use the programs. Since the actual physical computers were no longer located in the home or office of the customer, they started being described as being "in the cloud," as in "well, they're somewhere up there in the clouds; I do not know exactly where..." The cloud is other people running computers on your behalf so that you can reach over the Internet.

EXAMPLE: You could take several pictures with your camera and then use a program to get the pictures off your camera and store them in the "cloud." Later on you could access those pictures using other devices.

cluster: 1. A set of connected computers that work together as one. In many ways, clusters can be viewed as a single system. One special computer program manages the use of the collection of computers in performing complex computer operations, typically by having each computer in the cluster perform some small part of the overall operation, and then managing the process of combining the work of each computer into an overall result.

EXAMPLE: A company that provides users with information about travel destinations all around the world might have an incredibly large collection of data to be processed in order to rapidly find and display needed information. They could set up a cluster of computers, each of which had the entire set of data on it, and then have each computer search only a small section of the data. The computer that found the desired data first could provide it to the user, and then all computers in the cluster would cease searching.

2. In normal English, a *cluster* is "a group of similar people or things placed or occurring closely together." In statistics, when data is seen to form in a group, it is called a cluster. There can be many clusters in one set of data. Clusters can be data that have similar traits and values. Clustering is dividing the population into a number of groups that are considered more or less the same, and assigning them to clusters. This is useful when you want to compare groups of data.

EXAMPLE: If we were to take a poll on favorite movie genres, we might see a variety of clusters.

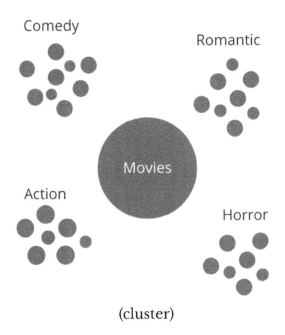

(cluster)

CMD key: Short for "command key." This key exists on some keyboards and is most commonly used in combination with other keys (shortcuts). For example, pressing CMD and the letter B at the same time, can make text **bold**. The command key is found on Apple (major technology company) laptops.

EXAMPLE: Originally the Apple logo was going to be listed on the key but Apple's Co-Founder (Steve Jobs) decided that having it displayed would be an overuse of the company's logo. An American designer named Susan Kare came up with using a looped square:

⌘

Most CMD keys have that symbol displayed.

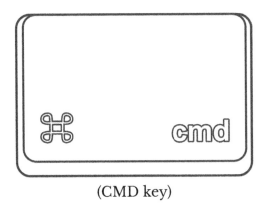

(CMD key)

CMOS: Stands for "Complementary Metal-Oxide Semiconductor." Metal-oxide is a combination of metal and oxygen. A semiconductor is a substance (most commonly a material called silicon) that switches between either conducting electricity or blocking it; they are used in computers and there are many different types. A CMOS is a semiconductor that uses very little power.

EXAMPLE: The manufacturer of a small hand-held electronic device might choose to use CMOS semiconductors in the device in an effort to give it longer battery life.

CMS: Stands for "Content Management System." A specialized kind of computer program that is used to create and manage the text, pictures, videos, etc. (content) of a website. A CMS allows a person who does not have the specialized training needed to create web pages and websites to do so anyway. It does this by providing the user with a graphical representation of the various text, pictures, etc. that could be in a web page, and letting the user move those parts around on the screen into the final appearance they want for their web pages. The CMS then creates the actual files for the website.

EXAMPLE: WordPress is a popular CMS. A company that sells framed art might use WordPress to create their website. They would take pictures of the art they wanted to sell, load those pictures into WordPress, write any needed descriptions for the artwork, and use WordPress to lay out the pictures and text of the website. When they were done designing the website, WordPress would convert those layouts into actual website files.

CMY: Stands for "Cyan, Magenta and Yellow." This is also called CMYK. The "K" stands for "Key." A key refers to a key plate, which is a plate (a thin sheet used to press ink when printing) that prints the detail of an image. Since the ink color of the key plate is usually black, the "Key" (K) in CMYK means "black." And so, the CMY color model and color wheel are also called CMYB (B for black). CMY are the main colors used for printing on paper. You may have used printers that use cyan, magenta, yellow and black ink.

EXAMPLE: Here is the CMY color model:

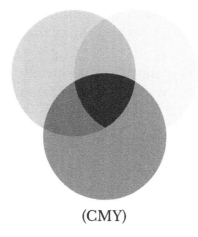

(CMY)

COBOL: See "FORTRAN."

code: 1. The instructions typed into a computer to create a program (a set of written instructions, entered into a computer by people, that make it execute [perform] specific tasks). Code is written in specialized computer languages.

EXAMPLE: In the popular programming language Python, the following code could cause a computer to display the sentence "Perhaps one did not want to be loved so much as to be understood." on the computer screen:

```
print ("Perhaps one did not want to be loved so much as to be understood.")
```

2. To type instructions (using a particular computer language) to create a program that will make the computer perform specific actions.

EXAMPLE: Computer programmers code for a living.

code injection: When someone intentionally causes a bug by processing invalid data. Code injections can be used by an attacker to introduce (or "inject") code into a computer program to change the course of execution. The results of a code injection attack can be disastrous. Code injection techniques are popular in system hacking to gain information or to gain unauthorized access to a system. It can be used malevolently (in an evil way) for many purposes.

EXAMPLE: A hacker might attempt to inject malware (dangerous software) into a server (a specialized computer used for storing and transmitting information).

code introspection: "Introspect" means "to look inward; examine one's inner feelings and thoughts." Code introspection refers to examining elements of code – such as functions, classes and keywords – so that you know what these things are, what they're for, what they do, etc.

EXAMPLE: A software developer may need to use a new library of code for a project. In order to use this new library effectively, it would be wise to use code introspection to get a better understanding of its features and functionality.

code point: The numerical value assigned to a specific character (a symbol used in communication; such as a letter or number) or format used in a character encoding system.

EXAMPLE: ASCII (American Standard Code for Information Interchange) has 128 code points. In the chart below, you can see some of the code points in the ASCII character set (033-095 – note: the left column is the decimal code point, the middle column is the hexadecimal code point, and the right column is the character):

033	21	!		081	51	Q
034	22	"		082	52	R
035	23	#		083	53	S
036	24	$		084	54	T
037	25	%		085	55	U
038	26	&		086	56	V
039	27	'		087	57	W
040	28	(		088	58	X
041	29	)		089	59	Y
042	2A	*		090	5A	Z
043	2B	+		091	5B	[
044	2C	,		092	5C	\
045	2D	–		093	5D	]
046	2E	.		094	5E	^
047	2F	/		095	5F	_

(code point)

coder: See "computer programmer."

coding: See "computer programming."

coding language: See "programming language."

colon (:): A symbol used when separating the HTTP from the rest of the address of a website. The colon is placed after http to create a separation point to help the computer find the address you want to go to. The colon is used in a browser's (the program you use to view web pages) address bar to separate two things. To the left of the colon, you'll find the protocol (a standard way to format [arrange; structure] and pass data between computers) that the browser uses in requesting, receiving, and displaying information found using the Internet (the largest and most-used computer network [connection that allows data transfer between machines] in the world, which is mainly utilized to access the World Wide Web). To the right of the colon, you'll find the particular information being displayed.

EXAMPLE: You've probably noticed that most websites have http: at the beginning of them. If you've ever noticed your browser showing something else to the left of the colon, you should know that it was telling you what protocol the browser used to find, retrieve and display the information you were seeing. Colons are used in lots of other ways in the computer industry. A colon nearly always is used to separate two things that have some sort of a relationship to each other.

color filter: See "image filter."

color model: A system that uses three main colors to create a large range of other colors. There are various color models – each having their own purpose. Each color model displays a different range of colors. The range of colors included in and produced by a color model is called a color space. Here are three color models visualized:

Color models can be represented by color wheels.

EXAMPLE: There are three types of color wheels:
1. RYB: This stands for Red, Yellow and Blue and looks like this:

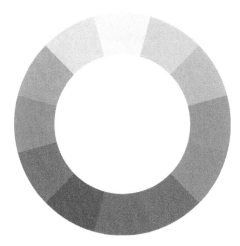

2. RGB: This stands for Red, Green and Blue. These are the primary colors for light, and are used in digital publication since computer screens emit light. The RGB color wheel looks like this:

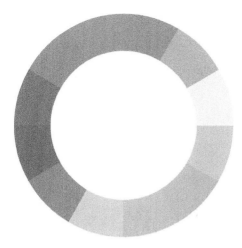

3. CMY: Stands for Cyan, Magenta and Yellow. This is also called CMYK. The "K" stands for "Key." A key refers to a key plate, which is a plate (a thin sheet used to press ink when printing) that prints the detail of an image. Since the ink color of the key plate is usually black, the "Key" (K) in CMYK means "black." And so, the CMY color model and color wheel are also called CMYB (B for black). CMY are the main colors used for printing on paper. You may have used printers that use cyan, magenta, yellow and black ink. Here is the CMY color wheel:

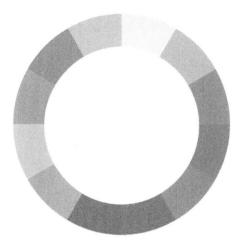

color palette: A *palette* is literally a thin board where artists place and mix their paint colors. Here is the famous painter, Bob Ross, holding a palette:

The term *color palette* is interchangeable with *color scheme*. A *scheme* is a specific arrangement or ordered system. A *color scheme* is how you choose to arrange or combine colors. Here's an example of a color scheme for a house:

A color palette is the colors you choose to use in your design. All designers (home, website, car, building, app, etc.) use color palettes.

EXAMPLE: A color palette might consist of a stack of colors, with the top color being the dominant, and the lower colors being the accents.

color psychology: The idea that colors can affect the mood, attitude and feelings of the user. It is the use of colors to attempt to influence a user's impression of a product.

EXAMPLE: A light blue is generally used to indicate a feeling of calm.

color scheme: See "color palette."

color value: This is a way to define colors. Color value refers to an exact color and how light or dark it is – each color having its own value. This is done to standardize how computers created by many different manufacturers present the various visible colors. Often this is done by telling the computer how much of the three main colors (Red, Green and Blue) to use. In this way, many different colors can be created. This works because you can use some combination of red, green and blue to create nearly all visible colors.

EXAMPLE: The code "rgb(255, 0, 0)" is a way to write the color value for the color red (r = red, g = green, b = blue; 255, 0 and 0 are numbers indicating the degree of the color).

color wheel: See "color model."

column: A vertical (up and down) arrangement of numbers or information. The opposite of a column is a row (side to side). A column can have a "header" that is basically a title explaining what type of information is stored in a given column.

EXAMPLE: If you were creating a written document to track the academic progress of the students in a school, you might have columns such as "Full Name," "Overall Grade Point Average," "Age," etc.

(column)

com (suffix): .com is short for commercial (refers to a company that exists for profit) and is a suffix added to the name of a website to show that the website belongs to the .com domain.

EXAMPLE: Chipotle (a restaurant) is a company that makes money by providing a service, so their website is chipotle.com.

command: Something the computer is told to do. Commands are usually typed in by a person and cause the computer to respond in some fashion. These commands can be stored in files on the computer for use at a later time.

EXAMPLE: You could tell the computer to print a document on a printer. This would be a "print" command.

command key: See "CMD key."

command line: See "command-line interface."

command-line interface: Abbreviated "CLI." An interface is a device or program that enables a user to communicate with a computer, or that enables one program to communicate with another program. A CLI is a method of operating a computer that uses a visual prompt and accepts typed instructions. A command line has an input symbol, called a prompt that tells the user the computer is ready to receive an instruction. The prompt usually looks something like this:
>
Or this:
>>
Or this:
:
Or this:
$
The user types instructions for the computer immediately after the prompt. A special computer program then converts the text instructions into commands the computer can understand. The command line allows you to perform many actions, including: moving files, deleting things, copying files, etc. In the early days of computers, a CLI was the primary method for running a computer. Nowadays, most computers are run by interacting with graphical representations of the things on the computer. Most computers, however, can still be operated from a CLI if the user wants to do so. Also just called "command line."

EXAMPLE: You might type the following instructions at a command line prompt:
>copy activestudents\nancydrew.doc graduates
This would mean to copy the file "nancydrew.doc" that is in the "activestudents" folder over to the "graduates" folder.

command-line option: A command that modifies the operation of a command; the effect is determined by the command's program. In many CLIs, these options are written by typing a hyphen, followed by the desired option (or switch). Also called "option," "flag" or "switch."

EXAMPLE: the command "ls" tells the computer to list the files in the current directory (another word for "folder"; a location where a file or files are stored within a computer). Adding the switch "-lS" will modify the command so that the list of files is sorted from largest file size to smallest.

command prompt: A visual indication that a computer is ready to accept input from the user. It is used in a Command Line Interface (CLI), a method of operating a computer that uses a visual prompt and accepts typed instructions. A command line has an input symbol, called a prompt, that tells the user the computer is ready to receive an instruction. The prompt usually looks something like this:

>

Or this:

>>

Or this:

:

Or this:

$

The user types instructions for the computer immediately after the prompt. A special computer program then converts the text instructions into commands the computer can understand. Note that you would not type the ">" character – that character represents the command line prompt.

EXAMPLE: You might type the following instructions at a command line prompt:
```
>copy activestudents\nancydrew.doc graduates
```
This would mean to copy the file "nancydrew.doc" that is in the "activestudents" folder over to the "graduates" folder. Note that you would not type the ">" character – that character represents the command line prompt.

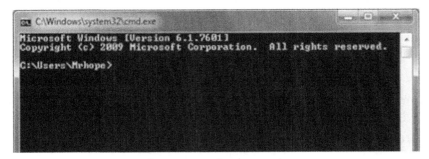

(command prompt)

comment: Descriptive messages written by a computer programmer inside their computer program. Comments are not instructions to the computer; comments are notes that describe the computer program or provide other useful information for computer programmers. Comments can make programs easier to understand when viewing the code. In some computer languages, comments are preceded by double slashes: "//."

EXAMPLE: Print "John" //John is the name of the main character
Here, the computer will print "John" on the screen, but it will not print the text "//John is the name of the main character," as that is a comment.

commit: To submit desired changes to an existing file. This is used often in computers where the user has an existing file or set of files, and has been working on one or more changes they want to make to those files. In this case, the user might create a copy of the files, and make the changes they want on those copies. When the changes are ready, the user can perform a computer action where they ask to make the changes to the original files. This is called "committing" or "making a commit." This operation is unique in that the requested changes are evaluated before they are made permanent. This is done to make sure it is "safe" to make the changes.

There are certain things that can be used to define when it is "safe" to make the requested changes. They usually revolve around making sure the original set of data or files does not get corrupted – that is, the data in the files maintains the desired format and content. One example of a situation where it would not be "safe" to make the requested changes is where a second user happened to be making changes to the same original file as the first user, and they both try to commit their changes to the original file at the same time. The computer then won't know what changes to actually use. When this occurs, the usual solution is for one of the users to review both proposed changes and select one or the other to actually be made permanent – in other words, they select which change to commit. See also "check in."

EXAMPLE: If you and a colleague are collaborating in creating a large written document, you may each have a copy of the original document where you are making changes to different areas in the document. At various points, you may each decide you're done with that part of the document, and you'll try to commit your changes to the original document. If no issues are found by the computer, the changes will be committed.

Commodore 64: A very old computer (released in 1982) that was extremely popular. It was one of the first computers that made it possible for average families to own and use a computer in their homes.

EXAMPLE: KoalaPainter was one of the applications on the Commodore 64, allowing users to create drawings on their computer.

(Commodore 64)

Common Language Infrastructure: Abbreviated "CLI." A product developed by Microsoft and allows applications written in one of the common .NET framework languages (e.g. C#) to be run on any operating system. CLI is made up of the Common Intermediate Language (CIL) and the Common Language Runtime (CLR). This combination allows applications to be run on any OS using a general runtime program rather than a language-specific runtime program. CLI uses a compiler to convert source code into CIL that can then be delivered to the CLR, where it is then compiled to a platform-specific machine language (commands given in a way the computer "understands" and that reflects the construction of its components – 1s and 0s).

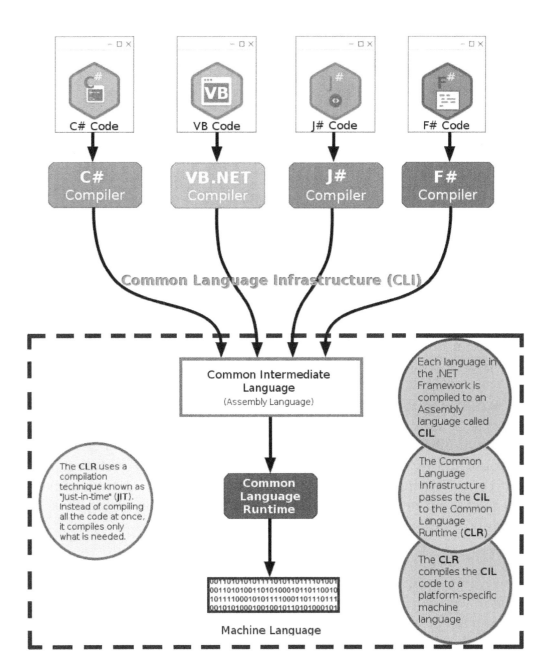

C# Code   VB Code   J# Code   F# Code

C# Compiler   **VB.NET** Compiler   **J#** Compiler   **F#** Compiler

Common Language Infrastructure (CLI)

Common Intermediate Language
(Assembly Language)

Each language in the .NET Framework is compiled to an Assembly language called **CIL**

The **CLR** uses a compilation technique known as "Just-in-time" (JIT). Instead of compiling all the code at once, it compiles only what is needed.

Common Language Runtime

The Common Language Infrastructure passes the **CIL** to the Common Language Runtime (**CLR**)

001101010101011110101101111101001
001101010011010100010110110010
1011110001010111110001101110111
00101010001001001011010101000101

Machine Language

The **CLR** compiles the **CIL** code to a platform-specific machine language

EXAMPLE: xbox.com (written in the C# language) was created with the help of the CLI.

compiler: A special computer program that is used to convert source code (the original code of a program as written by the program's creator[s]) to a form that the computer can actually use. A compiler is a special program that converts the source code, written in a programming language (a system of specialized words and symbols used to communicate with a computer and to create programs), into the machine language (commands given in a way the computer "understands" and that reflects the construction of its components – 1s and 0s) that the CPU (Central Processing Unit – the "brain" of the computer; a physical piece within the computer that processes [handles; performs actions with and on] data) can understand and operate off of. The product of a compiler is a set of machine language instructions understandable to the CPU , and that the CPU can execute. This would make the computer do what the source code described. This collection of compiled code is called an "executable," because the CPU can actually execute the instructions contained in it.

EXAMPLE: You type this instruction into a computer program:

```
if (age > 18)
{
        print("You are an adult");
}
```

A compiler would take what you wrote, change it into a form the CPU can understand (1s and 0s), and then relay that command to the CPU so it will be executed. One important aspect of how a compiler works is that it takes all of the instructions in the program and turns them all into machine language – all before actually executing the program. There are other methods of converting high-level languages (code that is human-readable) to machine language that do not involve converting the entire program before it is executed; instead, each instruction is converted and executed one at a time. This is not how a compiler works.

complement: Something that completes something else. It is used in how computers do math. This relates to positive and negative numbers. Positive numbers are greater than zero; negative numbers are less than zero (e.g. 8 is a positive number; -4 is a negative number). You could represent the positive number 8 with a "+" before it, like this: +8. This is not common, though, since people are usually talking about positive numbers and rarely talk about negative numbers. In doing subtraction, it can look like you're taking away one number from another, like this:

6 - 4 = 2
6 + (-4) = 2

This means you are using negative numbers to do subtraction. This kind of math is challenging in computers because representing negative numbers in computers is difficult. Computers can work with numbers a lot more easily than they can work with symbols like "-." In order to get around this challenge, computer designers came up with a way to represent negative numbers without using a symbol before them. In other words, these negative numbers look like positive numbers – but you can use them to do things you normally need negative numbers for, like subtraction. That is how complements are used. The "complement" of one number is the exact number you'd have to ADD to another number in order to do subtraction.

EXAMPLE: If you wanted to do the math 260 – 200, but you only wanted to use positive numbers to do it, you could do this math: 260 + 800 = 1060, and then remove the "1" from your answer. You would be left with 60, which is the answer to 260 - 200. In this example, the number 800 is a complement, since it ends up being the exact number you would need to add to 260 so that your answer would be 60 (after removing that "1"). Every binary number has a complement (binary is a number system that uses only the digits 1 and 0, instead of the ten digits you are used to). That means every binary number has another binary number that can be used by the computer to do subtraction, without having a problem because the computer can't understand a "-" symbol. So in computers, the complement is the positive number you use to "subtract" from another positive number.

component: One of the pieces of something that, along with the pieces, adds up to the whole thing. For example, there are different components to a car, like the engine, wheels, seats, etc. There are also different components to a computer.

EXAMPLE: Your hard drive is a component of your computer that stores information.

compress: In normal English, *compress* means to make something smaller. In computers, compression is the changing of data in such a way that it can be stored in a computer using less space than if it were stored in its original form. Compression programs are special computer programs that convert electronic files to a smaller format so that they take up less room, making it easier and/or faster to send those files to other locations. This can also free up available storage space in a computer, as the files do not use as much space.

EXAMPLE: You have a large document that uses the phrase "This page intentionally left blank" many times. A compression program might assign that exact phrase a code like "#blnk123#." Then, it would replace the text "This page intentionally left blank" with the code "#blnk123#." This will make the document smaller, since there are significantly fewer characters in the code than there are in the text. Later, when the user wants to view that document, that same compression program can reverse the process, restoring the actual text in the file wherever it finds the code "#blnk123#."

CompSci: See "computer science."

computation: The action of calculating an answer to a problem, usually by using math. This can be done with a computer, a calculator or your own mind. When you are performing addition, subtraction, multiplication or division, you are involved in computation. Computers are able to evaluate, calculate, and figure out the amounts of things because people designed them to do so.

EXAMPLE: If you type "8 x 2" into a computer, it performs a rapid computation and gives you the result "16."

compute: To determine the answer to something. Computing can refer to figuring out a problem using numbers. To compute is to evaluate something and look it over with the purpose of coming to a conclusion. A computer is a machine that computes. In computers, compute means that you are using a computer to help you solve a problem or get something done.

EXAMPLE: You want to know what 2 + 2 is. You type it into a calculator and it gives you the answer of 4. The calculator computed the math problem.

computer: An electronic machine that stores and deals with information. It is made up of many different parts through which electricity passes. Computers are a tool that people use to help them do things. Computers follow instructions entered into them by people. They can store instructions to be done at later points in time so that people do not have to re-enter the same instructions over and over again. Computers automatically perform a series of functions when they are on and also respond to commands that people enter into them. The way computers respond to commands is all set up beforehand by individuals. Machines, such as cars and phones, can have computers inside them that perform specific functions related to that machine. Computers typically exist to help people by performing repetitive activities, storing information and making certain activities faster or more efficient.

EXAMPLE: An electronic calculator is a very basic type of computer.

(computer)

computer-aided design: Abbreviated "CAD." A type of computer program that can be used to help in designing physical objects. Blueprints, engineering plans, floor plans, etc. can be created utilizing CAD programs. CAD programs can allow two-dimensional or three-dimensional sketches/diagrams. An interior designer can use a CAD to design a room. The output of CAD programs can often be used to control the actions of special manufacturing equipment, so that the equipment will create the actual object that has been designed using the CAD program.

EXAMPLE: A manufacturer of bicycles might use a CAD program to design bicycle wheels, and feed the CAD output files to special manufacturing equipment to make the actual wheels.

computer case: The plastic or metal structure that forms the outside of a computer.

EXAMPLE: Most cases are solid metal or plastic, and you can't see through them. However, certain cases are made of transparent plastic (as a design element), and you can see the computer parts through the case.

(computer case)

computer ergonomics: "Ergonomics" is a science concerned with designing and arranging things people use with the intention of assuring an efficient and safe interaction between people and things. It is a field of study that attempts to reduce strain, fatigue, and injuries by improving work space arrangement with a goal of comfortable, relaxed posture.

EXAMPLE: There are ergonomic chairs made specifically for reducing bodily injury or fatigue while using a computer.

computer ethics: "Ethics" refers to the actions that affect one's quality of survival. Abusing illegal substances would be an example of poor ethics because of the adverse effects it has on one's life – including the potentiality of an early death. Good ethics would be eating vegetables or exercising as these enhance one's quality of life. Like any tool, computers can be used for good or bad. Computer ethics refers to intelligent and responsible use of computers. It includes not using them to harm others.

EXAMPLE: One tenet of computer ethics is that a computer should not be used to steal information from someone else.

computer generation: See "generation."

computer graphics: Pictures created on a computer. These can be 2D or 3D images and videos. They can be used for many kinds of displays, including computer screens, televisions and movie screens.

EXAMPLE: In the movies based on the popular "Transformers" cartoon, the robots that transform from vehicles to large robots are created using computer graphics.

computer language: 1. See "programming language." 2. See "machine language."

computer processor: See "CPU."

computer programmer: A person who can create computer programs (written instructions, entered into the computer, that make it perform certain tasks). A programmer can type exact commands and instructions in a computer to create many of the things we use computers for on a day-to-day basis. Computer programmers are also referred to as "coders," "software developers," "developers," or "software engineers." All these terms refer to professionals that create software (programs).

EXAMPLE: Lots of computer programmers work at Google and help design many of Google's products.

computer programming: The act of creating computer programs (prepared sets of computer instructions designed to accomplish certain tasks). It consists of typing exact commands and instructions into a computer to create many of the things we use on a day-to-day basis. To do computer programming, you must learn various computer languages (systems of specialized words and symbols used to communicate with a computer and to create programs) and use these languages to create things on a computer that others can use. Computer programming is also called "coding," "software development," "software engineering" or "development."

EXAMPLE: The program on your computer entitled "Calculator," which you can use to do math, is the result of computer programming.

computer science: Abbreviated "CS" or "CompSci." A subject having to do with the mathematical and scientific study of the principles and possible uses of computers. It is a wide-ranging field including mathematics, engineering, and even the study of how people think in comparison to how computers operate. CS covers all the subjects related to the operations and functions of computers. People interested in learning about computers typically take a Computer Science course to find out how they work.

EXAMPLE: Some people who want to work in the computer industry go to college to major in Computer Science.

computer security: Actions and practices concerned with keeping private information safe. The following points are standard precautions when using a computer:
- Use secure passwords,
- Use different passwords for different websites (do not reuse passwords),
- Do not email any private data – do not send credit card numbers, social security numbers, etc.,
- Do not send money to people you do not know and only use secure payment systems on trustworthy sites for actual services and products,
- Be careful about trusting people online – impersonation of others is too easy to pull off and happens often,
- Install regular computer updates,
- Log out of or shut off computers after use.

See "cyber security" for more information.

EXAMPLE: Not downloading an attachment included with a strange email would be considered a good computer security practice.

concatenate: To connect things together, like links in a chain. To take one piece of data and stick it on the end of another piece of data.

EXAMPLE: Concatenating the text "device" and the text "s" makes the text "devices."

condition: Something which other things depend on. In math, a condition is something that is required for something else to be true. Conditions are points that are necessary to be present for other points to be present. If you say something is "conditional," that means it relies on the state of another thing.

EXAMPLE: "Electricity is allowed to flow through this part of the computer if you type 1" could be a condition. Or say you have a word problem like this: "Come up with two digits that when added together, equal six but the digits 2 and 4 are never to be used to get the answer." Here, the part that tells you that "you can't use the numbers 2 or 4 in your answer" is a condition.

conducting channel: To conduct means to allow electricity to flow through. A channel is a path that something moves along. A conducting channel is something that passes electricity through it.

EXAMPLE: There are many conducting channels inside a computer. A common example would be a wire. Certain objects can be manufactured where the object is made up primarily of materials that do not allow electricity to flow, but certain parts of that object are designed so that they allow electricity to flow. These parts of the object would be called conducting channels.

conductor: Material that allows electricity to flow through it. Metal is a conductor, while rubber is not a conductor.

EXAMPLE: Many tall buildings have a large metal pole at the top, and metal wires connecting the pole to the ground at the base of the building. These poles are called lightning rods, and their purpose is to conduct the electricity from a lightning strike from the top of the pole, through the wires, and down into the earth below, so that the electricity does not flow through the building itself, possibly causing damage or hurting people.

configure: To set up a machine to be used in a particular way. When there is a function that the computer does and you make that function behave in a certain way, you are configuring that function. Computers configure things so that they communicate smoothly with other things and work properly. As a note: When a computer displays "configuring..." that means the computer is arranging and ordering its system or a program so that it is prepared for a particular task. Simply put: it is setting everything up.

Preparing to configure Windows.
Do not turn off your computer.

EXAMPLE: If you bought a new computer game, your computer would have to configure some of its functions relating to how it displays things, so that the image quality would align with what your monitor is able to do. Some monitors would have a lower quality picture than others, for example, and the computer might individually configure the best possible picture for that monitor.

console: 1. An input/output device for a computer. It allows the user to view certain data about the computer, and to enter data and instructions into the computer. A console typically consists of a screen (for output) and a keyboard (for input).

EXAMPLE: When setting up very large computers, a common arrangement is to have the computer itself in a large room where the temperature and humidity can be controlled, and where physical access to the computer can be controlled. In order for users to see information and enter information, consoles are placed in locations outside the computer room. The consoles are connected to the computer, and computer operators use the consoles to give the computer instructions and see the results of the computer's operations.

2. Short for "video game console." A specialized computer used for playing video

games. Consoles function like a PC and contain the same essential components, including: a CPU, GPU and RAM. Consoles commonly utilize television screens as "monitors."

EXAMPLE: PlayStation5 and Nintendo Entertainment System are consoles.

constant: The name given to a location in a computer's memory that a program (a set of written instructions, entered into a computer by people, that make it execute [perform] specific tasks) has set aside for use in storing data, a situation where the value of the data stored in that memory location will NOT change over time.

EXAMPLE: You could program a video game character to always have the same height (6' 0" tall) by creating a constant. It would not make sense to use a constant for the game character's "health" rating, as the character would likely see its health decrease and increase as the video game is played.

constraint: Things that hold other things within certain limits or boundaries. In computer science, constraints are used to not allow certain actions by the person using the computer, so the computer can work effectively. With regards to databases, constraints are the enforced rules regarding the columns of a table. The purpose of constraints is to limit the type of data that can be inserted into a table so that the data is accurate and reliable.

EXAMPLE: If you are using a computer to facilitate the sale of bicycles, and if the computer had access to the records of the unique serial numbers of the bicycles in the warehouse, a constraint could be created that prevents an inventory worker from adding a bicycle to the database that has the same serial number as one already stored in the database. You can specify the constraints you want applied to a table. As an example: the NOT NULL constraint can be used to ensure that a column cannot have a NULL value – data must be present in that field for any row you try to add to the table.

constructor: A special part of a common computer programming tool called a class (a representation in a program of a type of thing [such as "animal"], which can be broken down further into individual objects [such as "dogs," "cats," "fish," etc.]). Classes are used in a type of computer programming called "object oriented programming." In the world, you are surrounded by objects – your dog, the TV, etc. Objects have state and behavior. The state of an object would be the size, color, etc. The behavior of an object would be what the object does – the actions it takes. In object oriented programming, objects are parts of computer programs. They share a similarity to real life objects: they have a state and behavior. You create these objects by creating "classes," using a programming language (a system of specialized words and symbols used to communicate with a computer and to create programs). You could create (or "declare") a class called a "Customer" class. It is important to know that when you first create this class, you are describing the POTENTIAL characteristics and behavior of that TYPE of thing – you still need to create an actual one of those things. This process is called "creating an INSTANCE" of the class, where "instance" means "an actual one" of the things described when you declared the class. A class can have a constructor. The constructor is a special part of the class that describes the default state of any new instance of the class that gets created. In other words, it gives default values for the properties of the class.

EXAMPLE: Let's say you had a class called "Customer." The computer code to create the "customer" class might look something like this:

```
class Customer
{
string FullName;
Boolean Active;
}
```

(Here, the term "Boolean" means "data that can only be 'true' or 'false.'")
Now let's say that whenever you created a new instance of the "customer" class, you wanted it to be an active customer – in other words, you wanted the property "Active" to be set to "true." You would make a constructor for the "customer" class. It would be a small subprogram, inside the class, that would be used every time an instance of the "customer" class was created. The constructor might look something like this:

```
Customer(string name)
{
Fullname = name;
Active = true;
}
```

The entire class would look like this:

```
class Customer
{
string FullName;
Boolean Active;
Customer(string name)
{
Fullname = name;
Active = true;
}
}
```

The constructor would be used by asking for an instance of the "customer" class to be created, and passing along the desired name of the customer. The call to create the instance of the class would look like this:

```
Customer cust = new Customer("Brenda Smith");
```

This creates a new instance of the "customer" class, using the constructor inside the class. The constructor uses the "Brenda Smith" it was given to set the value of the property "FullName," and uses the instruction in the constructor to set the property "Active" to "true." The new instance of the "customer" (cust) will therefore have the properties:

```
FullName = "Brenda Smith"
```

Active = true

container: 1. A standard unit of software that packages up code and all its dependencies so the application runs quickly and reliably from one computing environment to another. It is a lightweight, standalone, executable package of software that includes everything needed to run an application: code, runtime, system tools, system libraries and settings.

EXAMPLE: One of the most popular containers in use today is the Docker software.

2. See "Docker." 3. See "website container."

content: The substance that makes up a book, article, website, etc. Content includes words, pictures, videos, and all other relevant material – as opposed to form or design. In the context of a web page, "content" is the information being presented – the text, images, videos, sounds, etc. This is different from the layout or physical appearance of that information.
EXAMPLE: The content of a website that centered around a particular popular band might include information about upcoming concerts, videos from past performances, photographs of the band members, catalogs of merchandise available for purchase, etc.

content curation: To curate means to select and organize something. The word curate is used here in reference to the content of websites or web pages. In this context, "content" is the data being presented on a web page – the text, images, videos, sounds, etc. Content curation is determining what content to include on a web page or website. It includes sorting through the massive amount of content on the Web and presenting it in a useful and organized way.

EXAMPLE: There might be a web page dedicated to efforts to perform manned missions to other planets. The company that owns that website could give someone the job of regularly searching the Web for any information related to these types of missions. That person could then present that select data on the website. That select data is curated content.

content delivery network: See "CDN."

content management system: See "CMS."

continuous data: Quantitative data that would literally take forever to count or measure – there is no possible end or final count because it is constantly changing. Continuous data is numerical and the amounts change.

EXAMPLE: A person's weight is an example of continuous data. Not only can this fluctuate day to day (for example, people typically weigh slightly less in the morning than at night), but we can also continue to measure weight in more and more exact ways (pounds, ounces, fractions of a pound, fractions of ounces, etc.).

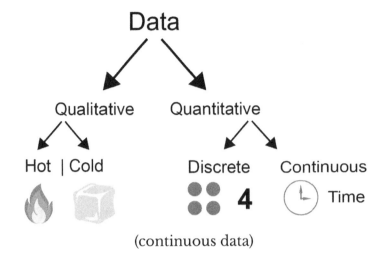

(continuous data)

continuous development: See "CD."

continuous integration: See "CI."

control bus: A bus that carries the commands issued by the CPU to control the devices in the computer system, and also carries certain status signals from those devices to tell the CPU the result of the commands.

EXAMPLE: If you click on a video you want to watch, the bus will have data on it specifying the exact actions the display screen is to perform so that the video is displayed. It will also have instructions on it to tell the speakers what to do.

control character: See "LF."

control key: See "CTRL key."

controller: In an MVC (see "MVC") application, the part of the program that interprets what is being requested by the user, makes sure any business logic is done, then returns the proper view back to the user. You can liken it to the Air Traffic controller at an airport, directing incoming and outgoing planes to the proper destination.

EXAMPLE: In your Bike Shop application, you may have a file called OrderController.cs, where any methods related to ordering would go. So if someone hit the "Place Order" button on the OrderPage.cshtml, that request would go to a specific method in a controller, which would do things like process a credit card and update a database table with a new order.

control unit: See "CPU."

convention: See "naming convention."

conversion: The act of turning a potential customer into a paid customer. Many websites are designed to facilitate the sale of various products and/or services. The more effective a website is at getting the people who visit the site to purchase a product or service, the better. This action is called conversion – you are converting a visitor to a paid customer.

EXAMPLE: If you have 100 people visit your website in a day and 5 end up buying your product or service, that would be five conversions. Also, it would be a 5% conversion rate for that day.

cookie: A session is a span of time in which a web browser (the program people use to view web pages) maintains a connection to a particular web server (a specialized computer used to store and transmit data, such as "serving up" websites through the World Wide Web). A cookie is a set of data that a website causes to be stored on your computer for use during a session in which you visit that website. These cookies are managed by your browser (e.g., Chrome, Safari, etc.). Cookies can be a tool to help make a particular website display the way you want it faster, or to personalize your experience on that site. In general, there are two types of cookies: temporary and persistent. A temporary cookie expires when a web browser session ends – usually, this happens when the browser program is closed down. This is a session cookie. The cookie's data is not stored on your computer permanently. The data in a persistent cookie is stored on your computer for a specified time period. These cookies always have expiration dates; the cookie is erased from your computer after the expiration date. It is considered good practice for a website to inform you if it uses cookies. The word "cookie" originated from a computer programmer named Lou Montulli. He derived it from the term "magic cookie," which means "a packet of data a program receives and sends back unchanged."

EXAMPLE: If you regularly visited a shopping website, the cookie for that website might store the most common type of product you liked to purchase, so that those types of products would be displayed first when you next visited the website.

coordinates: See "axis."

core: 1. An old term for the main memory of a computer. The word core in this case is a special word that describes a small physical device used to store information in a computer. The full name for this type of computer memory device was "magnetic-core memory." Core memory had an arrangement where wires were run around a round magnetic ring several times and through the hole in the middle of the ring. The round magnet was called the "core." It was shaped like a doughnut.

Older computers used these cores as memory to store information in since you could set the magnet up in one of two distinct states; and that state wouldn't change unless you used electricity to make it change. This meant it could store the ones and zeroes that make up digital information. Even though computers do not use this type of memory any longer, the memory of a computer is sometimes still called "core."

EXAMPLE: Erasing memory could be called wiping the core or dumping the core.

2. A slang term for a key part of a Central Processing Unit. The CPU is basically the "brain" of the computer. It controls all the different tasks a computer can do. The processor does one action at a time – things like taking in data from a keyboard, or storing data in the computer's memory, etc. It can do billions of these types of actions every second, but it only ever does one thing at a time. The basic job of all processors is to execute a sequence of stored instructions built into them. While a CPU handles many types of tasks related to communicating with and controlling the devices connected to it (screen displays, keyboard, etc.), the primary purpose of a CPU is to process data – take data in, perform operations on that data, and use the results of those operations to control the rest of the computer. The part of the CPU that does this data processing is called the processor. The term "core" is a slang term for this processor.

EXAMPLE: A dual-core processor includes two cores, while a quad-core contains four.

(core)

corruption: See "data corruption."

count: The number representing the result of a process of counting; the total number.

EXAMPLE: The count of students in a class is the total number of students in that class.

C++: A programming language (a system of specialized words and symbols used to communicate with a computer and to create programs) that was created in the beginning of the 1980s. It is based on one of the most popular computer programming languages: C. It can be used in conjunction with some other programming languages. C++ has many uses and can be used to create several types of things. Many computers contain something on them that was created using C++ as it is one of the most common programming languages. Pronounced "C plus plus."

EXAMPLE: Many computer games have been made using C++.

CPU: Stands for "Central Processing Unit." The CPU is basically the "brain" of the computer. It is the part of a computer that controls all the actions the computer does. A CPU is a small device that contains billions of tiny electronic components (parts). Most CPUs have a set of built-in "instructions." They define the various actions the CPU can take – things like taking in data from a keyboard, storing data in the computer, sending data to a display, etc. The basic job of all processors is to execute various combinations of those simple instructions built into them. It only ever performs one of these instructions at a time, but modern computers can perform billions of instructions per second. All actions you can make a computer do will be composed of various combinations of these actions that are built into a CPU. CPUs are also called "microprocessors," "processors," "control units," or "computer processors."

EXAMPLE: If you have a list of students in a computer file and you give the computer an instruction to put the list in alphabetical order, it is the CPU that performs the analysis and re-ordering of the list.

(CPU)

crash: The action of a computer program (a set of written instructions, entered into a computer by people, that make it execute [perform] specific tasks) malfunctions and stops operating normally. It typically causes the currently-used program to shut down; sometimes the entire computer stops operating and needs to be restarted.

EXAMPLE: If you were playing a game on a computer and it froze and then shut off, that would be the game crashing.

crawler: See "web spider."

CRC: Stands for "Cyclic Redundancy Check." "Cyclic" refers to a cycle (something that repeats, start to finish, over and over, like a circle). A CRC is a set of steps taken by a computer to determine if data has been corrupted during transmission and storage on the receiving device. When you store information in a computer, it is normally followed by a Cyclic Redundancy Check to make sure the information did not develop any errors during the storage process. This process works by comparing the information received by the computer with the original information from where it was sent.

EXAMPLE: If you transferred a file from one computer to another, a CRC would occur. If there was any alteration or mistake, an error message would pop up.

crippled mode: This is when part of a computer or a program is not working properly, but the system continues to operate in a reduced capacity. Not all computers or programs have a crippled mode.

EXAMPLE: If the computer cannot display colors correctly due to an error, it could run in crippled mode, displaying everything in black and white.

critical value: In normal English, *critical* means "having a decisive or vital importance in the success, failure, or existence of something." When testing a hypothesis in statistics, a critical value is a point on the test that is compared to the test statistic to determine whether to reject the null hypothesis (the expected result). A critical value can be used this way: if the absolute value of your test statistic is greater than the critical value, you can declare statistical significance and reject the null hypothesis.

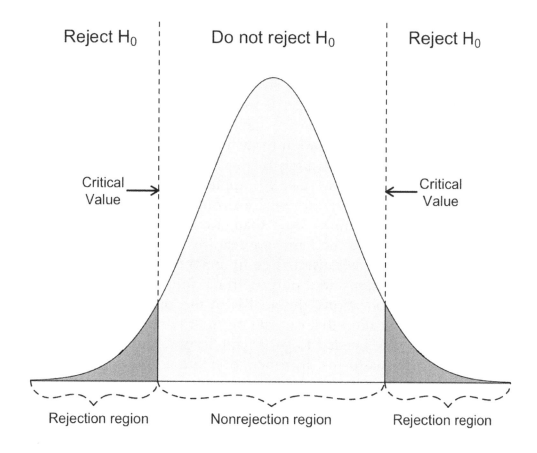

EXAMPLE: A critical value plays an important role in election polling.

CRM: Stands for "customer relationship management." Software used to track customers and manage relationships with them.

EXAMPLE: Items like customer contact information and appointments can be monitored with CRMs.

cross-platform: Refers to a computer program that is developed so it can operate on multiple platforms. Here, the term "platform" refers to the environment in which a computer program runs, specifically the environment on a particular mobile device – a "mobile platform." An example of this type of platform is the iPhone, a smartphone manufactured by the technology company Apple. Another example of a platform is Android smartphones. These are manufactured by many different companies, but they all use many things in common, regardless of who manufactured them. There are a few key parts of the mobile platform:

-The *physical hardware* of the device. This includes things like the camera, the motion sensors, the physical controls for such things as power and sound volume, the speaker, and the Central Processing Unit. The physical hardware of an iPhone is not the same as that of an Android smartphone.

-The *operating system* installed on the device. An operating system is a special-purpose computer program that supports the computer's basic functions, such as scheduling tasks, running other computer programs, and controlling peripherals (external devices such as speakers and displays). iPhones have an operating system called iOS. iOS uses its own methods for performing those tasks; these methods are different from those used by Android, the operating system used on Android smartphones. The Android operating system is owned by Google, a technology company. When creating a computer program for a mobile device (an "application"), you have two broad approaches: You can write the application in such a way that it only works on a specific platform, or you can write it in such a way that it can easily run on multiple platforms. The first approach is called a "native" application; the second is called a "cross-platform" application. There are usually strong advantages to creating a native application – they generally perform faster than cross-platform applications, and they generally have greater access to the hardware features of the device (camera, motion sensors, buttons, etc.) This is because the computer programming language used to create those native applications was purpose-built for that exact platform. When creating cross-platform applications, the goal is to use one computer programming language to create an application that can run on multiple platforms. This can greatly reduce the time and money needed to get an application into the market that can be used by multiple device platforms. In order to create a cross-platform application, though, you usually have to rely on special computer programs that can translate your instructions in the programming language you used into instructions that are specific to the platform your application is actually running on. This has many challenges, including the fact that device manufacturers often make changes to their hardware or operating systems that can make it so a cross-platform application no longer has the full functionality as it once did.

EXAMPLE: If you were creating a computer game and you wanted it to be available for both iPhones and Android phones, and you wanted to minimize your expenses and time, you could create the game as a cross-platform application.

crowdsourcing: The action of getting other people (outside of your company and other than yourself) to help you with a project. There are different ways to crowdsource, including publicly displaying your project at a location where people may be able to find out about it and decide to help you if they wish to. There are web sites that help facilitate this process.

EXAMPLE: If you wanted to create a new consumer product, like a drone, you might crowdsource the funding for the funds you needed to start the project. You could write up a description of the drone, explain what makes your design and your business worth supporting, and ask people to help contribute funds to get the business started. In exchange for their financial help, you might give them discounts on the first drones produced.

crt (suffix): A file extension that indicates the file contains a digital certificate for validating the authenticity of a website in a web browser.

EXAMPLE: On a secure website, the file containing the website's security certificate may be named "cert.crt."

CS: See "computer science."

C#: A programming language that was invented in 1999 by Microsoft. C# has many uses and can be used to create several types of things. The purpose of C# is to precisely lay out steps of instructions that a computer can perform to accomplish a task. Anything that a computer can physically do can be programmed using C#. C# is one of the most commonly used programming languages. It is well-suited to make large software programs that enable businesses to automate business processes. Some uses of C# are:
-Sending or receiving information to and from a database,
-Displaying a very clear picture in movies and video games,
-Controlling other machines that you connect to your computer, and
-Playing music and sound effects on a computer.

EXAMPLE: Some parts of the Windows operating system were created using C#.

CSS: Stands for "Cascading Style Sheets." Cascading Style Sheets are used to control the appearance of the text, images, video, etc., on web pages. Cascading is a term that comes from the idea of water flowing down a series of drops in height. Think of it as a series of small waterfalls. Information can cascade, meaning it can be stored at one central, most important location and then can be applied to other locations that are considered to be lower than, or derived from, that more important central location. This is a benefit to the people making a website because if they want to change any of the things that they set up in the style sheet, they only have to change it in that one place. Those changes will then be applied to all pages in the website at once. A style sheet is a tool used to design the format of a web page. Style sheets are a central place to store data about how that page will appear and how it will behave. It can be used to store information about how to display colors, pictures, text, etc. It is a sheet that handles the style of the website. With Cascading Style Sheets (CSS), the people who make a website can create one master style sheet, and then make the functionality described in that style sheet apply automatically to all the web pages in that website. As of today, CSS3 is the newest version of CSS.

EXAMPLE: You write a website using CSS. In the main style sheet for the website, you specify the color of all text to be used on all pages of the site to dark blue. Later, you decide you want to have all text be red. You would change that one setting in the style sheet for text color, and now all text on all web pages for the website would be red.

CSS precedence: See "precedence."

CSS rule set: See "rule set."

CSV: Stands for "Comma Separated Values." CSV is a popular file extension and format where text or numbers are separated with commas.

EXAMPLE: You could take the spreadsheet below and change it to a CSV format:

Make	Model	Year	Color
Nissan	Altima	2021	Red
Ford	Focus	2022	Silver
Kia	Optima	2025	Blue

The CSV file would look like this:
Make, Model, Year, Color
Nissan, Altima, 2015, Red
Ford, Focus, 2010, Silver
Kia, Optima, 2007, Blue
You can save Microsoft Excel spreadsheets with the .csv extension.

CTA: Stands for "Call To Action." An item on a website that asks the visitor to perform an action. It might be a piece of text, a button or image, etc. These actions might include "read more about this," "sign up," "buy now," "subscribe," etc.

EXAMPLE: On a web page for a school, there could be a Call to Action button that states "Enroll today!" You could click on this button and be taken to an application form.

CTRL key: Short for "control key." This key does not do anything by itself. Instead, it is used in keyboard shortcuts (keys pressed in combination with other keys). Instructions to do something like this are written as follows: CTRL-[Other key to be pressed].

EXAMPLE: "CTRL-P" means to hold down the Control key and press the "P" key, then release both keys. This key combination, by the way, is a common shortcut to activate the "print a document" function in various computer programs.

curate: See "content curation."

current: A flow of electricity. It is a measure of the flow of electrons through a material. Electrical current can have different levels. A current is electricity moving from one point to another. This flow of electricity is actually a flow of energy, and that energy can be used to do work – turn on a light bulb; turn a motor, etc. Not all materials will let electricity flow through them. A material that will allow electricity to flow through itself is called a conductor. Some conductors allow electricity to flow more easily than others. Most metals (like copper, gold, silver, etc.) are good conductors. Rubber is a very poor conductor, so it is often used to protect people and things so that electricity can't connect to those people and things. If you receive an electrical shock, it is the current (the rapidly-moving electrons) that causes the actual damage to your body.

EXAMPLE: A blender has a cord. The cord has two wires inside it. When you plug in the blender, a current is sent through one wire, to the blender, and back to the outlet through the second wire. The blender will now work when you push the buttons that control it.

current directory: See "working directory."

current working directory: See "working directory."

cursor: An indicator on the display screen of the computer that indicates where you can type in text. Early computer systems needed to have a way to tell users that the computer was ready to accept input. The common way to do that was to have a small square or thin vertical line located at the point where text could be accepted, and to make the square or line blink when the computer was ready to receive input. This is still used as the most common way to show a computer user where they will be entering data.

EXAMPLE: That flashing up and down vertical line (or bar) that shows you where you are typing on a computer screen is a cursor. It looks something like this: |
Note: Often, people mistake "pointers" for cursors. Pointers are the various symbols used to show where the mouse is on the display screen.

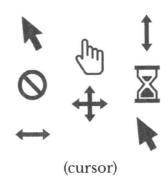

(cursor)

custom type: See "class."

CWD: See "working directory."

cyber: Relating to computers and technology. The word comes from "cybernetics," which means "the science of communications in people and machines." Cybernetics has to do with automated control systems – ways to cause actions to occur automatically. Cybernetics is derived from the Greek word *kubernan*, meaning "to steer."

EXAMPLE: Cybercrime refers to illegal activities committed with a computer or over the internet.

cybernetics: The scientific study of communication and control in animals, people and machines. Cybernetics is a field that explores systems in many areas and industries. It embraces many topics including learning, communication and efficiency. The word cybernetics was coined by the French physicist Andre-Marie Ampere in an 1834 essay where he describes the science of civil government. The modern use of the word began with the American mathematician and philosopher Norbert Wiener in his 1948 book "Cybernetics." He used the term to refer to the general analysis of control systems and communication systems in living organisms and machines. More recently, cybernetics has been used mainly to refer to controlling any system using technology; communication and control of systems utilizing technology. The word is a recent one, and you may find it used in inconsistent ways.

EXAMPLE: An educational researcher who was examining the factors related to various changes in educational practice and their resulting effects on student academic performance, teacher job satisfaction, and employment outcomes for the graduates could be engaged in the science of cybernetics.

cybersecurity: Actions and practices concerned with keeping computers, networks, websites and software safe from digital attack. It is a field in its own right, with its own professionals. Also called "computer security" (see "computer security").

EXAMPLE: A cybersecurity professional could implement protective measures to keep hackers from breaking into your website.

D

D/A: Stands for "Digital-to-Analog." Digital refers to data made up of exact, distinct parts. Analog refers to data flowing out in a continuous stream. An example of a machine that uses an analog method would be a record player. As the record turns beneath the needle, a continuous stream of data is sent from the needle into the record player, and then on to the speakers. An example of a machine that uses a digital method would be a portable media player, such as an iPod. The songs on the player are stored as digital files. This means that the files themselves are just a series of the digits 1 and 0. The pattern those digits are in represents the original audio recording, and that pattern can be processed by a computer and converted to sound coming out of a speaker or headphones. D/A is conversion of data from a digital format to an analog format. D/A converters are used for a variety of things.

EXAMPLE: When an iPod (or similar portable media player) plays music, it is performing a Digital-To-Analog conversion. This is because the files on the player are digital, and they need to be converted to an electrical signal that makes the speakers vibrate, thereby producing sound. That electrical signal is an analog signal, in that it is a continuous signal. The D/A converter reads in the digital data one digit at a time, very rapidly, and creates a continuous electrical signal that represents the sounds described by the digital information.

DAC: See "digitize."

daily stand-up: A daily meeting involving certain employees who are working on a project. It is meant to last 5-15 minutes. Often the attendees actually stand up. This is meant to encourage participants to make the meeting short. Each person tells the group the answers to these three questions:
1. What did I accomplish yesterday?
2. What will I do today?
3. What obstacles are impeding my progress?

EXAMPLE: Daily stand ups help ensure that obstacles to getting your work done are identified and handled rapidly.

(daily stand-up)

DAL: See "data access layer."

data: Information – things like words, symbols, pictures, etc. An input device is something that is used to input (input means to put something into something else) information into a computer – a common input device would be a keyboard. Data is most often put into a computer using input devices.

EXAMPLE: Data is the main thing that a computer handles.

data access layer: A part of a computer program which provides simplified access to data stored in persistent storage (like a database); the point where the interactions between an application and a database exist. Just as it sounds, the Data Access Layer is what coordinates accessing data. The DAL is literally the code written in your program that accesses the database for you.

EXAMPLE: In the image below, you can see the various layers of software:
1. Presentation (what the user sees and interacts with),
2. Business logic (the main code of the program itself), and
3. Data access (DAL – that code in your program that coordinates with the database).

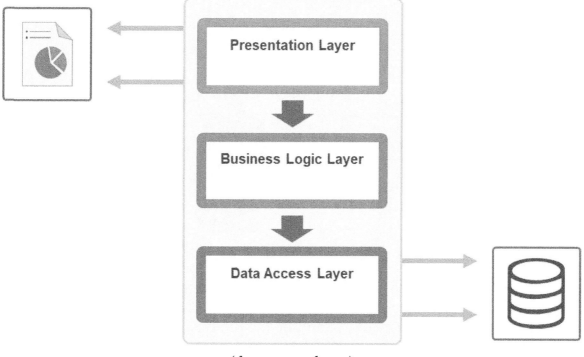

(data access layer)

data analyst: A position name referring to one who performs data analysis (the evaluation of data to discover useful information and assist in decision-making). Data analysis includes:

- Data cleaning – the process of preparing data for analysis by changing or removing information that is wrong, inaccurate, duplicated, incomplete, irrelevant, or not formatted correctly.
- Interpreting (reading and evaluating) the data.
- Creating visual representations – such as graphs that show the data as a diagram and creating reports.

EXAMPLE: Data analysts use information to answer questions and communicate results in order to help make intelligent business decisions. They sift through data – seeking trends, finding common denominators, making predictions and spotting correlations.

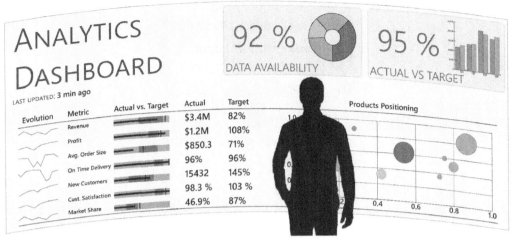

(data analyst)

data architecture: The manner in which information is stored, collected and accessed. There are many different possible data architectures. Data architecture is a set of regulations and standards that control and define the type of data that is collected and how it is utilized within an organization.

EXAMPLE: A smaller company would most likely have simpler data architecture than a large, complex business.

database: An organized collection of related data, typically for use on a computer. Other computers might connect to a database that is stored on another computer in order to access the data in the database. This is the symbol for a database:

The symbol represents a series of disks stacked upon one another in a hard drive (main storage within a computer). Usually, the data in a database is organized into tables (data structures made up of rows and columns). Each column would represent a type of data that could be stored in the table; each row would represent one entry into the table. For example, if you had a table that was meant to hold data about students, the columns might be:

- Last Name
- First Name
- Date of Birth
- Grade Point Average
- Teacher

A row in that table might have the values:

Smith, John, 5/24/1969, 3.52, Mrs. Huber

A table often has many rows of data in it.

EXAMPLE: A large collection of data containing all the names of a school's students, along with data about their grades and attendance, organized in a logical way, would be a database.

FIRST NAME	LAST NAME	ADDRESS	CITY	AGE
Mickey	Mouse	123 Fantasy Way	Anaheim	73
Bat	Man	321 Cavern Ave	Gotham	54
Wonder	Woman	987 Truth Way	Paradise	39
Donald	Duck	555 Quack Street	Mallard	65
Bugs	Bunny	567 Carrot Street	Rascal	58
Wiley	Coyote	999 Acme Way	Canyon	61
Cat	Woman	234 Purrfect Street	Hairball	32
Tweety	Bird	543	Itotitaw	28

(database)

database attribute: In databases, a column (up and down section in a table) is called an attribute. It is a set of data values made up of a particular data type (a specific category of information handled by a computer – such as numbers or comparisons). Sometimes the word "field" is used interchangeably with attribute or column, but technically a field is one single cell in a database/table.

EXAMPLE: An attribute may consist of text or numbers.

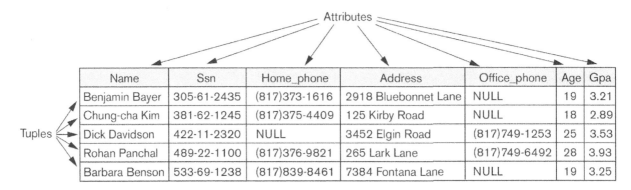

(database attribute)

database engine: The main software behind a DBMS or database server. DBMSs and database servers are sometimes referred to as database engines.

EXAMPLE: Microsoft SQL Server can be referred to as a database engine.

database field: A single piece of information stored in a database. It means the same thing as a cell within a table.

EXAMPLE: The name "Jeff" might be stored in a field that asks for a name.

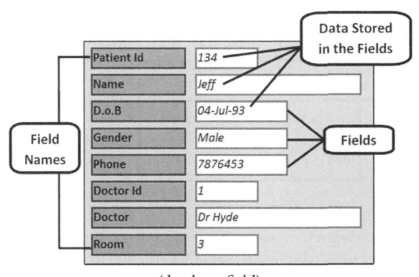

(database field)

database index: A part of the data model that makes data retrieval faster. It is a way of sorting records. In its most basic form, it is one or more columns in the table that can be used to make looking up data in the table happen more easily. A common use of an index is to determine the physical order in which the rows in a table are stored on the computer. This way it is easier to find a particular row in a table.

EXAMPLE: Here is an example index:

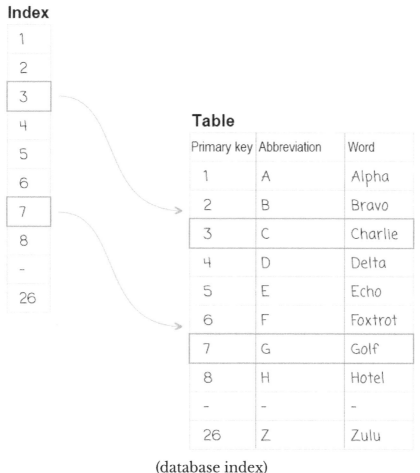

(database index)

database instance: A database instance refers to a complete database environment, including the: RDBMS, table structure, stored procedures, and other functionality. There can be multiple instances of the same database.

EXAMPLE: Here is an example of having three instances of a database:
1. The production database instance (this is the database that contains live data – the database being utilized in the real-world by users).
2. The test database instance, also referred to as the pre-production database. This can be used to test out upgrades and new functionality prior to live (production) release.
3. The development database instance. This is where developers can create new functionality, prior to testing.

database management system: See "RDBMS."

database migration: "Migrate" literally means to move from one place to another. A database migration is the moving of a database from one database to another.
EXAMPLE: One type of migration involves transferring database information from a business computer to the cloud.

(database migration)

database object: A data structure that is used to store or reference data. The most common objects that you'll interact with are tables. Here are some examples of database objects:

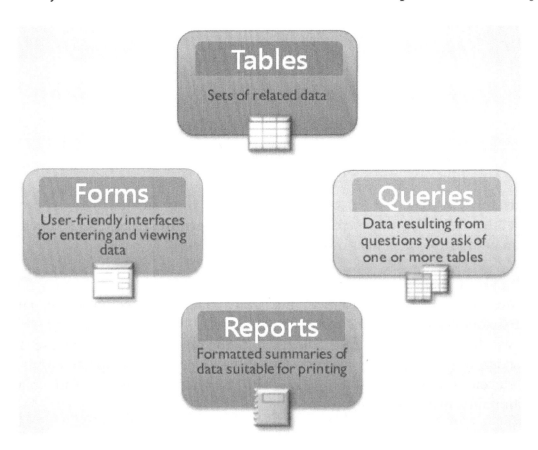

EXAMPLE: A database table named "Customer Information" is a database object.

data bus: The data bus carries the actual electronic data used by the CPU and the various devices in the computer.

EXAMPLE: When you click on a video to play it, the data bus would contain the electronic information about the video images to display. It would also contain the data about the audio sounds to play. Here is a diagram:

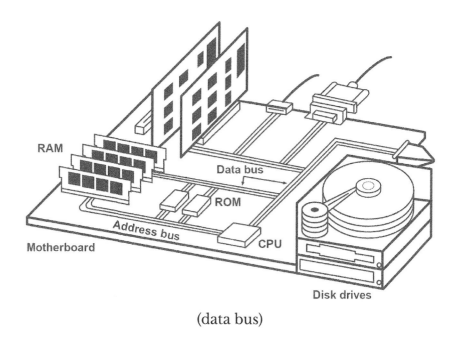

(data bus)

data corruption: Errors in computer data that occur during writing, reading, storage, transmission, or processing, which introduce unintended changes to the original data and cause errors. When electronic data is stored, there is a predetermined form as to how the data will be stored. If that form gets distorted, the data will not be usable by the computer in the future.

EXAMPLE: Let's say you were creating a file that would store the records of a group of students. You decided that the data would be stored in this order:

```
Student Name ** Teacher ** Grade Point Average
```
A set of uncorrupted data might look like this:
```
Jane Brown ** Mr. Henderson ** 3.58
Marte Jonsson ** Mrs. Andrews ** 3.97
David Jones ** Mr. Tolliver ** 2.66
```
If a particular computer program knew the format of this data, the program could read the data in and use it in performing the program's tasks. Here is an example of corrupted data:
```
Jane Brown ** Mr. Henderson ** 3.58
Marte Jonsson ** 3.97 ** David Jones
Mr. Tolliver ** 2.66 **
```
A computer program would not be able to read this information and use it since the individual pieces of data are not in the order it is programmed to expect.

data-driven programming: A programming paradigm in which the program statements describe the data to be identified and the instructions to be completed based on that data, rather than defining a sequence of steps to be taken. The data controls the flow of a program as opposed to some other thing controlling program flow. A data-driven application would be an application that accepts different data sets and then makes a predetermined decision for each specific data set and gives an outcome as a result.

EXAMPLE: An example of a data-driven application could be one which is meant to display a calendar showing upcoming events in a city where event data is stored in a database and is updated at random times. Each time the user requests the calendar to be displayed, the application must read the event data from the database, and then format the calendar so as to best present whatever event data was retrieved.

data dump: See "dump."

data engineer: Data engineering is the utilization of programming languages to ensure data is clean, reliable and usable. Data engineers build the systems that allow data scientists and data analysts to perform their work. They ensure that data is properly received, transformed, stored and accessible. Data engineers are trained in software development and databases. They write the code behind the platforms (a specific combination of hardware and an operating system) and systems used.

EXAMPLE: Google Data Engineers create and maintain software that allows data to be collected and processed.

data engineering: See "data engineer."

data format: See "format."

data integrity: The validity of data; the accuracy and consistency of the stored data. This can also be used as a verb, where it means "to maintain and assure the accuracy and consistency of data over its entire life-cycle." Often, this term is used when describing the creation and operation of databases. A database is an organized collection of related data, typically for use on a computer. Data integrity is imposed within a database as it is being designed and is consistently maintained through checking to see if the data being added and updated are up to standards. These standards are defined by the database management system (software used to edit databases) and by the software developer. Say you have a form you are filling out on your computer in order to sign up for a library card. The data you enter into the form will eventually be stored in a database, where it can be retrieved at a later date by computers. There could be a spot on this form where you have to enter your age. If the database is expecting you to enter a number, and you do in fact enter a number, like "29," the data integrity of the database will be maintained. If you instead spell out your age, like "twenty-nine," it could produce problems if that were actually to be stored in the database.

EXAMPLE: If the computer were to try to identify all people in the database who were older than 21, it would most likely not be able to properly interpret the words "twenty-nine" as a number, and therefore would not identify you as being over 21. That would be an example of not maintaining data integrity. If, on the other hand, the computer checked the data quality before storing it in the database and prompted you to enter a number instead of letters, then it would be an example of maintaining data integrity.

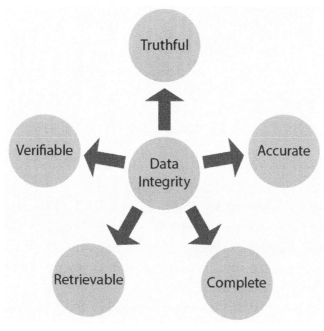

(data integrity)

data lake: A centralized data repository that holds structured data, unstructured data and semi-structured data. This could be almost any kind of data in different file formats – text, video, spreadsheets, consumer transactions, etc. In its simplest form, a data lake could be considered a container in the cloud where you can store almost any kind of data in any type of format. Bigger companies with thousands and thousands or millions of pieces of data, organized (or not) in several different kinds of data structures, could use data lakes.

EXAMPLE: Data lake software offers analytics tools like NoSQL, SQL and Python so analysts can sift through millions of data elements. To make the data in the data lake useful for analysis, it is usually necessary to process it in some way so that it has a structure that can be easily searched through to gather the data for analysis. This process is called transforming the data.

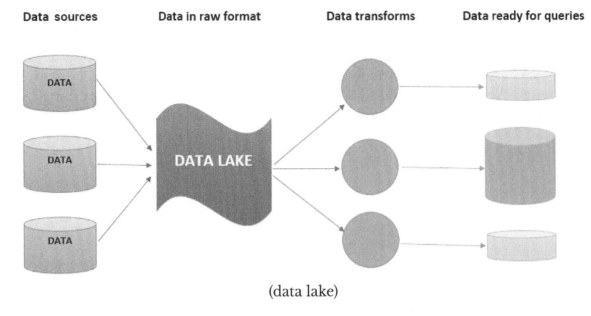

Data sources	Data in raw format	Data transforms	Data ready for queries

(data lake)

data lifecycle: "Life cycle" describes a series of changes in the life of a living organism from birth all the way to death. A data lifecycle refers to the data's stages of change from initial creation to its destruction. There are typically 5 stages in a data lifecycle:
1. Data creation: This can come in many different forms from data input, data extraction from SQL databases, Word documents, etc.
2. Data storage: This is where data is processed and stored according to the required specifications and security requirements.
3. Usage: At this stage the data is being actively used to make decisions and or predictions.
4. Archived: The data is no longer needed but is stored for possible later use and is set aside to make space for newer incoming data.
5. Data deletion: This is the final stage when the data is no longer needed at all and gets erased. This would be done on archived data and not at any other point in the data lifecycle.

EXAMPLE: In order to provide clear insight from Big Data, businesses will use the data lifecycle as a framework.

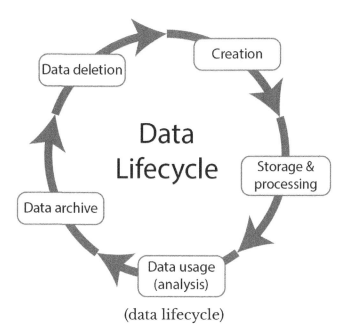

(data lifecycle)

data manipulation: The action of changing data to make it more organized and easier to read. SQL is a data manipulation language and most commonly used to work on databases.

> EXAMPLE: Let's say you have a list of students and you need to find a student with a first name that starts with a "K," but the list is out of order. You can manipulate the list to sort the students by first name and in alphabetical order.

data manipulation language: Abbreviated "DML." A sublanguage of SQL (Structured Query Language – the most common language used to create, manage, interact with, delete and edit databases). It is used for adding (inserting), deleting, and updating (modifying) data in a database.

> EXAMPLE: The INSERT command (used in SQL) is DML and is used to enter (insert) rows into a table.

data mapping: See "data wrangling."

data mining: The process of going through large amounts of information to locate new and useful data. Similar to mining for gold, except in this case one is mining for data – usually online.

> EXAMPLE: A company could thoroughly inspect its sales and manufacturing records that provide data for the past several years in an effort to discover unknown patterns. This would be data mining.

data modeling: A part of the software development process. This is the designing and planning of what kind of information will be needed and how that data will be organized and structured. Data modelling is typically done prior to the development of computer software so that it is laid out beforehand.

EXAMPLE: In developing a way to store all client information, data modeling could be used in determining exactly how a company would structure and organize the information (for example: name, phone, address and email for each client, etc.).

data munging: The process of making data more accessible for analysis. *Mung* means to manipulate (control; handle) data. The origin of the term is uncertain, but some say it is an acronym for "mash until no good." *Data wrangling* is another term for *data munging*. See also "data wrangling."

EXAMPLE: If a business is interested in analyzing data, they will need to first convert it from raw data into a form that is prepared for analytical evaluation. This is the job of data munging.

data pipeline: A series of actions for handling data. The output of one action becomes the input for the second action. Just like putting data into a Data Warehouse, there needs to be a flow in which the data is processed before it gets stored. This could even be an automated process using specific software. One of the many tasks of a data scientist is to set up this pipeline and decide where and how the data gets from point A to point B. Part of the Data Pipeline process is called ETL. ETL stands for Extract, Transform and Load. The first step would be to take your data from its many sources of consumer information, then extract them for placement into the Data Warehouse or Data Lake. The data must be transformed in order to be loaded into a Data Warehouse or Data lake due to the fact that, upon setup, they are directed to only allow a limited amount of data formats. There's no shortage of software out there that can help you set this up. By transforming the data, you are making it compatible with your predefined formats. After the data is loaded into the Data Warehouse or Lake, it can then be prepared for further processing and Data Analytics.

EXAMPLE: When a social media post is extracted for analyzing, it has entered a data pipeline.

data preprocessing: The action of taking raw data and putting it into a consistent format for data warehouse inclusion. Data scientists spend about 80% of their time cleaning and processing data for it to be in a proper condition for analyzing. If you were to take data in its complete raw format and try to analyze it, you could spend days trying to get results by sifting through improperly imported data or missing values. Not only that – not all data warehouses are built the same. A data warehouse is built with specific needs in mind and, therefore, the data needs to be transformed so that the warehouse can ingest it (absorb the data) properly. There are three main factors that contribute to the quality of data that needs to be processed:

1. Accuracy: Some data might have erroneous values that deviate from what is expected. This can be caused by:
   a. Human error during the data entry process,
   b. Incorrect formats for input fields, or
   c. Data that has been duplicated and merged together.
2. Completeness: Some data might lack attribute values. This can be caused by:
   a. Unavailability of data,
   b. Deletion of inconsistent data, or
   c. Incorrect deletion of data that was deemed irrelevant.
3. Consistency: The aggregation of some data may be inconsistent.

EXAMPLE: Let's say that a business has a large amount of data about the types of shoes people prefer. This data needs to be preprocessed before being included in a data warehouse.

data query language: Abbreviated "DQL" – query language for short. A computer language that is used to make queries (requests for data) to databases. The SQL (Structured Query Language – the most common language used to create, manage, interact with, delete and edit databases) commands that are used to retrieve data from databases are DQL. DQL is a sublanguage of SQL.

EXAMPLE: The SELECT statement (used in SQL) is DQL and is used to select data from a database. In the following example, we are specifying which table to get data from:

SELECT * FROM table_name;
This is DQL *and* SQL.

data science: An industry that embraces a wide range of scientific methods, systems and processes to extract knowledge and insights from data. The term was first used by an American computer scientist named William S. Cleveland in his article "Data Science: An Action Plan for Expanding the Technical Areas of the Field of Statistics." The purpose of data science is basically to make decisions based on data. Data science includes such topics as:
- Data visualization – Representing information in pictorial form (like graphs or pie charts).
- Statistical analysis – Identifying trends in different data sources.
- Data analysis – Evaluating data to discover useful information and assist in decision making.
- Artificial intelligence – As covered earlier, programming a machine to perform human-like actions, such as facial recognition or voice recognition.
- Machine learning – A subcategory of AI that deals with a computer's ability to "learn" – meaning, the ability to perform certain actions based on past experience without explicit instructions.

EXAMPLE: Data scientists can apply exact techniques and utilize various tools to attempt to predict future occurrences based on past data.

data set: Collections of data. Literally "sets of data."

EXAMPLE: In a school, the grades of a particular class of students could be a data set. Or, in databases, a data set could correspond with one or more tables.

data store: See "store."

data striping: In computer data storage, the technique of segmenting logically sequenced data, such as a file, so that consecutive sections are stored on different physical storage devices. Striping is useful when a processing device requests data more quickly than a single storage device can provide it.

EXAMPLE: If a large file is saved in two different drives (storage mediums) on a computer that would be data striping.

data structure: The organization of related pieces of information. There are many different ways to organize data. A particular data structure is often created because that structure makes it easier to perform the common operations that are expected with the type of data being organized. A data structure refers to how the data is organized in terms of implementation (use of the data; relation of the various parts of the data). It is a particular way to organize data in a computer so that it can be used efficiently.

EXAMPLE: Consider two different areas of business: The shipping industry and the manufacturing industry. The types of data the shipping industry may need to collect and organize will center around vehicles and their capacity, shipping rates, fuel costs, travel times between various geographical points, etc. The types of data the manufacturing industry may need to collect and organize will center around raw materials, product manufacturing methods and times, inventory locations and amounts, shipping information, etc. The structure of the data used by computers in these two industries may have similarities, but it is certain that the data structures wouldn't be identical.

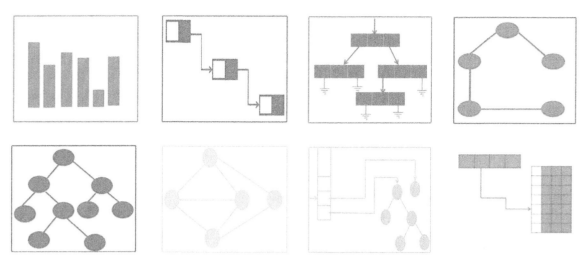

(data structure)

data type: There are many different kinds of information. Common types of information used in computers could be letters and numbers. When information is used in a computer, that information will have a "data type." A data type is two things: "what kind of information is this?," and "what kind of things can we do with this data?" Different data types can be used in different ways. When data is stored in a computer, its type is also stored – that way the computer knows how to work with that particular piece of data. The various different things you can do with data are called operations. Not all data types have the same operations available to them.

EXAMPLE: "Decimal numbers" (0-10) is a data type. Typical operations you could do with decimal number data are addition, subtraction, multiplication, etc. "Text" is another data type. Typical operations you could do with text data are "convert the text to uppercase" or "concatenate." (Concatenate means to link together, as in a chain. For example, you could take the individual text elements "purple" and "?!," and then concatenate them into "purple?!," etc.). When creating computer programs, every piece of data being kept track of by the computer is a certain type of data. For example, the datum 342.98 is data of type "decimal." The datum "casserole" is data of type "text." It would not make sense to apply mathematical operations to text data – for example, trying to tell a computer to add the number 34 to the text "banana" wouldn't work – because the two types of data are different, and mathematics do not apply to text data.

data visualization: The creation and study of the visual representation of data. Data visualization is often done so the data can be more easily understood. This is commonly done through taking data and showing it as graphs, tables, charts, etc.

EXAMPLE: Pie charts are a type of data visualization.

data warehouse: A data storage system that gathers and stores data from different databases and external sources. It contains mostly structured data, but also unstructured data and combines both into a comprehensive database. A company could use data warehouse software to look at all the historic data to analyze data about its products, customers and trends. Common sources of data for a data warehouse are:

- CRMs – stands for "customer relationship management." CRM is software used to track customers and manage relationships with them. Things like customer contact information and appointments can be monitored with CRMs.
- ERPs – stands for "enterprise resource planning." ERP is software and technology used to manage various business processes. Various office functions and HR (human resources – the department in a company that handles personnel) can be automated using ERP.
- Billing – the section of a company and the associated documentation that deals with charging for services.

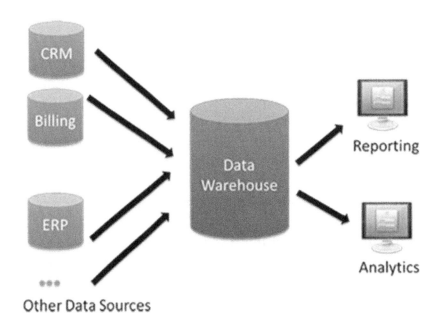

EXAMPLE: Let's say a car manufacturing company pulls data from its many data-gathering sources and uploads it into the data warehouse. Sources for this data could include: Employee time clock (tracking system for work hours), Sales Software, Customer rewards systems, an inventory database etc.

data wrangling: In normal English, *wrangle* means "to round up, take charge or herd (typically referring to livestock)." Data wrangling is the process of taking data in its raw and messy form, and cleaning, transforming and structuring the data in a unified format. This is done by data mapping. *Data mapping* is the process of establishing relationships between separate elements of data and connecting them. Much like a map, the roads and highways all connect so that you can get from one place to another. Data mapping connects data from its source to its targeted destination. The process can be set up automatically by a data scientist by creating mapping rules with some sort of software to take the data elements and match them to their targeted data fields. See also "data munging."

EXAMPLE: Here is data mapping diagrammed:

Source Data

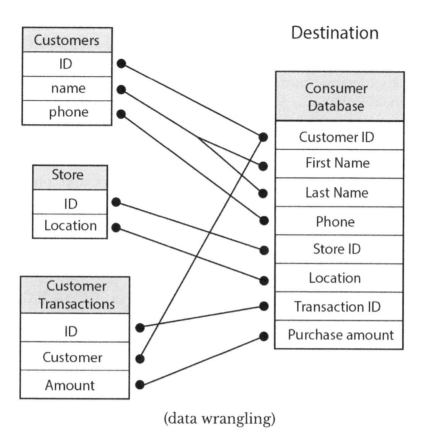

(data wrangling)

dB: *dB* is short for *decibel.* A unit used to measure the power level of an electronic signal. dB is most commonly used to measure how loud a sound is.

EXAMPLE: A helicopter produces 100 decibels, whereas a whisper sits around 30 decibels.

DBMS: See "RDBMS."

dbo: Short for "database owner." A dbo is the user account associated with a database that is granted permissions to perform all activities in the database. Dbo is also the default schema for a newly created database. The dbo schema is owned (fully controlled) by the dbo user account. When executing a user-defined procedure, it is recommended to define the procedure name with the schema name. Doing so gives a small performance boost because the database engine does not have to search multiple schemas. It also prevents executing the wrong procedure if a database has procedures with the same name in more than one schema.

EXAMPLE: If your account is part of the Dbo schema, you have access to all the objects within that schema.

D drive: See "hard drive."

decibel: See "dB."

decimal: A number system based on the amount "ten." "Decimal" comes from Latin *decimalis* meaning "tenth." The decimal number system uses only the ten digits (unique symbols) 0, 1, 2, 3, 4, 5, 6, 7, 8 and 9 to represent quantities.
EXAMPLE: Using the decimal number system, you count like this: 1, 2, 3, 4, 5, 6, 7, 8, 9, 10, 11, etc. This is the number system you've been using since a very young age.

decode: Have you ever opened a file and the document was displayed incorrectly? In order to properly display characters when opening a file, a program (like a text editor) must know which encoding system was used. In most browsers and programs, you can choose which encoding system to use. You can also typically specify the encoding type when saving a file. One of the encoding options for Notepad documents is UTF-8. This can be seen in the picture below:

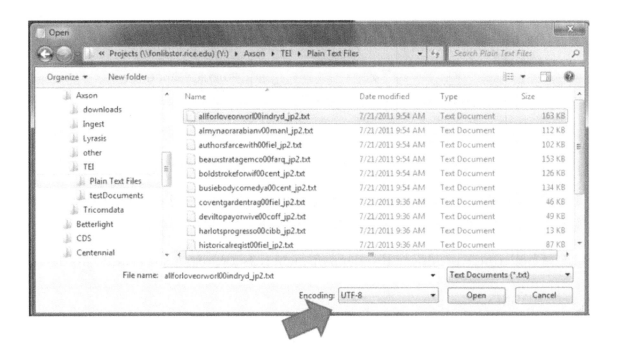

EXAMPLE: If you were to open a Microsoft Word document, it must be opened with the Microsoft Word software in order to be decoded correctly.

decorative typeface: Like the name states, *decorative typeface* (also called *display typeface* or *ornamental typeface*) is used for decorative purposes, such as posters. Typically, it is not recommended to use a decorative typeface for body text. Decorative typeface can be either casual or formal. Here are some examples of decorative typeface:

AMATIC

BUNGEE SHADE

Cabin Sketch

Chewy

EXAMPLE: If you were to create a baby shower invitation, you might consider using a decorative typeface.

decrement: See "increment."

dedicated: Set apart or reserved for a specific use or purpose. When this term is used in the computer industry, it means a computer is assigned to one particular user or function.

EXAMPLE: A dedicated Disaster Recovery computer would be a computer that is only used to provide access to vital operational data in the event the usual computers used to run a business were to fail for some reason.

deep learning: A subfield of machine learning that teaches machines to do what humans can do naturally. Deep learning is composed of networks that have the purpose of learning (unsupervised) from unstructured (see "structured data") and unlabeled data. Deep learning is also called a *stacked neural network, deep neural learning* or *deep neural network.*

EXAMPLE: A car that can "self-drive" (such as recognize streets, stop lights, pedestrians, etc.) would be a product of deep learning.

deep neural learning: See "deep learning."

deep neural network: See "deep learning."

default: A value that a computer assumes, or a course of action that a computer will take when the computer user specifies no overriding value or action. This usually refers to the settings you may find in a computer program or electronic device when it is initially started up. These settings are usually configured to provide the most common setup for the program or device; a user who wishes to change one or more of these settings can usually do so. They may also be able to restore the program or device to its original "default" settings after making changes.

EXAMPLE: If you print something from a computer, the default printer is the printer the computer automatically prints to.

definition: See "resolution, levels of."

defrag: See "defragmentation."

defragmentation: To reformat the data on a digital storage device so that the individual electronic files on the device are not broken up and stored in multiple locations in the device. This usually applies to the central storage device on computers, called the hard drive. When a hard drive is defragmented, all the files on the hard drive are examined, and are then rearranged such that all files are undivided, if at all possible. This often leads to more efficient computer operation. See also "fragmentation."

EXAMPLE: If your computer is running slowly, defragmenting the hard drive often makes the computer run faster.

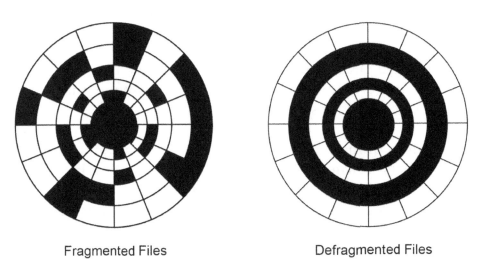

Fragmented Files   Defragmented Files

(defragmentation)

degrees of freedom: Refers to the number of independent values (a value that does not depend on a separate value) that can be assigned to a statistical distribution (a statistical distribution of a data set shows us all the possible values or intervals of data, as well as how often each piece of data occurs and is observed). In statistics, the number of degrees of freedom is the number of values in the final calculation of a statistic that is able to vary (change). The number of allowed movements that do not violate existing constants are referred to as the number of degrees of freedom.

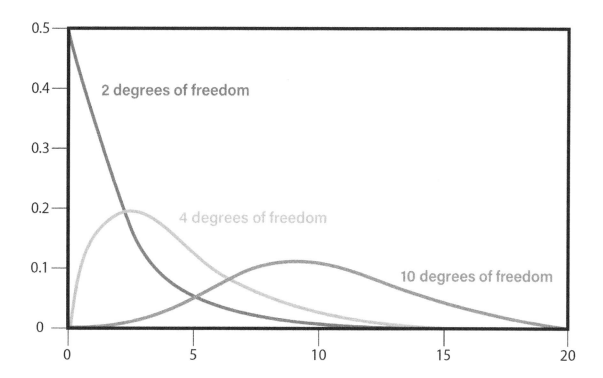

EXAMPLE: If you flipped a coin a set number of times, then tried to find the average result, the degree of freedom would be 1. This is because we have subtracted 1 from the total number of coin-flip possibilities.

deliverable: A measurable thing that is brought about as the result of work. A deliverable is a "done" – something completed. They're quantifiable goods or services that are produced.

EXAMPLE: A completed website presented to a client is a deliverable.

density: A measure of the compactness of data – that is, how much data there is in a given area on a physical device. This is used mainly in two areas of the computer industry: data storage devices and display devices. When used in relation to storage devices, density refers to how many bits are stored in a given area of a physical storage device. Bits are "binary digits" – the 0s and 1s that are used to represent data for use in computers. Storage density is usually given in "Bits per Inch," meaning "the number of bits in one square inch of the device's storage medium." Devices with a higher density are generally preferred over those with a lower density, as they can hold the same amount of data in a smaller device, which often means that the computer data can go between the device and the computer at a faster rate. When used in relation to displays, density refers to how many pixels are present in a given area of a display device. Pixels are the smallest element of an image that can be displayed on a screen. Each pixel can be a different color; put together, the individual pixels make up the overall image to be displayed. Display density is usually given in "Pixels per Inch" (PPI), meaning "the number of individual pixels in one square inch of the display screen." Displays with a higher density are generally preferred over those with a lower density, as they can present images more clearly.

EXAMPLE: Typically, with each new phone that comes out, the density of the screen is increased. This means that photos, games, etc. are clearer and have more vivid colors than on previous models with a lower PPI rating.

deploy: To spread something out or arrange it in a strategic fashion. In technology, deploy means to ensure software (or hardware) is fully set up and running properly. This includes installation, testing, making necessary changes and more.

EXAMPLE: If you have a big company with many computer users, and you have a new computer program that all users will need, you would deploy that program to all computers.

descriptive statistics: Shorter pieces of data that help explain a larger body of information. The most common descriptive statistics are: mean, median and mode.

EXAMPLE: Grade point average (GPA) is a descriptive statistic.

design: To decide upon the look and function of a product. A *designer* is a person that creates the plans for how something will operate or appear. A designer may or may not be the person who implements such plans. For example, a furniture designer would decide what furniture to use and where to place it, but might not be the one who actually purchases, transports and physically places the furniture. In development, a designer is the one who provides the "blueprints" for a website or application. Again, they may or may not do the development themselves. It is common for developers to work on completing projects according to plans created by a designer.

EXAMPLE: Before ebay.com developed their website, they first decided on a design.

design abstraction: The design that differs from the physical realities of a thing. You can see degrees of abstraction of a panda here:

Low abstraction   Medium abstraction   High abstraction

Design abstraction can also refer to designs that hide implementation with smooth and user-friendly interfaces. For example, a UI that had the person manually type in the state they live in would have a lower level of abstraction than one that allowed them to choose their state from a scrollable dropdown menu. Back to the earlier definition of design abstraction (artistic interpretations that are different from their real-world sources or motivations). Here is an example of design abstraction:

Design
Abrastraction

Lorem ipsum dolor sit amet, consectetur adipiscing elit, sed do eiusmod tempor incididunt ut labore et dolore magna aliqua. Ut enim ad minim vanim Lorem ipsum dolor sit amet, consectetuer adipiscing elit, sed diam nonummy nibh euismod tincidunt ut laoreet dolore magna Lorem ipsum dolor sit amet, consectetuer adipiscing elit, sed diam nonummy nibh euismod tincidunt ut laoreet dolore magna aliquam erat

While this may seem to violate consistency and typical layout approaches, this abstract design could work. Here are some other examples of design abstraction:

And:

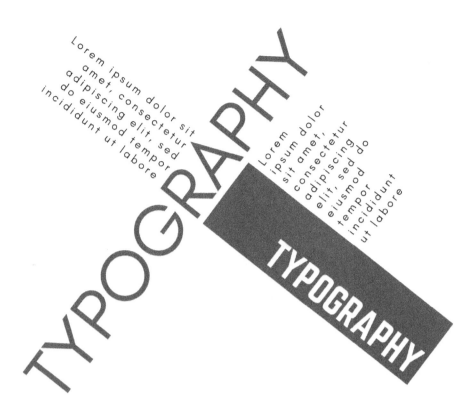

The point is, at the end of the day, design is art. Art is creativity and communication. What we are going for in design are products that convey a feeling, a message. There are many approaches to this and they don't always have to follow pre-established templates or approaches.

designer: See "design."

desktop: 1. Another term for a "desktop computer." This is a computer that is typically created for use in one location, such as a desk in an office (hence the name). This is different from a laptop computer which is typically created for use wherever the user wishes. Desktops typically consist of a display screen, a tower (the computer itself), a keyboard and a mouse.

EXAMPLE: Many companies provide desktops to their employees.

2. A graphical image of a desktop on a computer display, provided so the user can have a simulation of a real-world desktop where they can store the various electronic files they store on the computer.

EXAMPLE: On most computer desktops, there is a program called "Recycle Bin" where items can be moved for deletion from the computer.

desktop computer: See "desktop."

desktop sharing: See "screen sharing."

developer: See "computer programmer."

development: See "computer programming."

development environment: See "environment."

device: Machine with a purpose. It is a tool that you use for a particular purpose. Anything that you use for a job or specific purpose could be considered a device. In computers, a device is something that is external to a computer that can be connected to the computer and can work with the computer. Devices are also the physical parts of the computer that you can see, touch and interact with – such as the computer screen, the keyboard, or the mouse.

EXAMPLE: When you hook up a camera to your computer, the camera is considered a device.

DHTML: To understand DHTML, you must know what "dynamic" means. Dynamic refers to actions that take place the moment they are needed, rather than in advance. A restaurant that prepares your food to your specifications, when you order, would be dynamic. The opposite of dynamic is "static," meaning "unchanging." A restaurant that has the food pre-cooked and waiting before you order would be static – the food does not change in regards to time or circumstance. In computers, dynamic means the computer processes your request right when you ask it to; it does not have a predetermined result ahead of time. Dynamic relates to the Internet by describing websites that have content that changes while the website is being viewed, depending on things like what part of the web page you move to with the mouse. This is important because a web page made only with HTML is "static" – that is, the content of the page does not change unless the actual file stored on the web server changes. This means that you could view that page using a browser over and over, and it would always have the same appearance. As the World Wide Web increased in popularity, a technology was needed that could modify the HTML that was used in the browser without having to replace the HTML file on the web server, so that web pages could change based on the instructions of the web page designer. Such web pages are called "dynamic" pages. DHTML stands for Dynamic HyperText Markup Language. It is essentially HTML (which we have covered) combined with additional technologies. This set of technologies can be used to make web pages that are displayed differently based on various factors (meaning the web pages are dynamic). You type certain things into a computer, using the DHTML technologies, and you can make a web page that behaves differently based on various user actions taken on the web pages. Conventional HTML is not able to do this. Instead, web pages written in HTML will always show up the same in a web browser, regardless of any user actions. While the concept of creating web pages that have dynamic content and functionality are still very much in use today, the term DHTML has fallen out of use.

EXAMPLE: With DHTML you could develop a web page with a calendar where the appointments scheduled for a specific day would be displayed in larger size letters when the user rolled the mouse pointer over that specific day.

dial-up: A method of connecting a computer to a network through a telephone line. This usually refers to an early system for accessing the Internet (the largest and most-used computer network [connection that allows data transfer between machines] in the world, which is mainly utilized to access the World Wide Web). A phone line is connected to a computer and the computer dials up (makes a "phone call") through a wire to connect to a network. Instead of carrying a voice signal like a telephone call, the telephone wires carry electronic signals that can be received and processed by computers.

EXAMPLE: Dial-up Internet was popular in the 1990s; a computer usually made funny sounds while connecting via dial-up. These sounds were provided to let the computer user know when their computer had successfully made a connection to the network being accessed.

digit: A symbol that represents a quantity. The symbol "3" is a digit and represents the quantity three. By combining the digits (symbols) "2" and "4" into 24, the quantity twenty-four can be represented.

EXAMPLE: The quantity of eight cubes can be written as the digit 8, like this image shows:

(Quantity)   (Digit)

(digit)

digital: Describing things that are made up of exact, distinct parts. These parts are always in one precise state. "State" refers to the condition of a thing – such as, "green," "empty," "50 years old," etc. Things that are digital can only be in one of the available states for that thing, and not "in between" any of the states. A light bulb with a regular light switch is digital because it only has two states: totally on or totally off. A light bulb with a dimmer switch that could be set somewhere between "totally on" and "totally off" is not digital. The photograph below is digital:

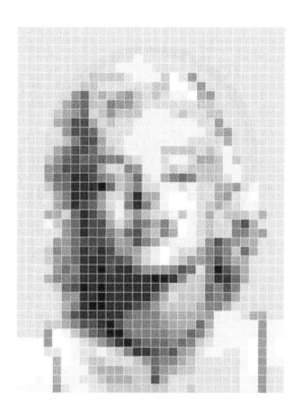

Each square in the photo is its own distinct part with its own distinct state – black, white, gray, dark gray, etc. This does not mean that every blurry photo is digital. Most digital photos are composed of so many "squares" that, to the eye, they look just like the real world shown in the photo. One of the ways to understand digital is to compare it to a different term: "analog." "Analog" refers to devices or objects that represent amounts in a continuous stream. It means that the item gradually increases or decreases or stays the same in a steady flow over time. "Analog" comes from the Greek word analogy, meaning "analogous" (similar; related to). Due to the fact that "digital" means "distinct" and "analog" means "gradual," the two terms are commonly considered opposites. In fact, one of the definitions of "analog" is "not digital." This car speedometer is an analog device:

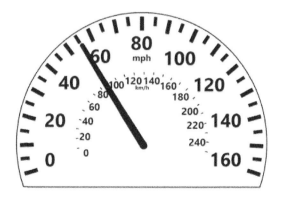

The needle changes position in relation to the physical movement of the wheels. On the other hand, this is a digital speedometer:

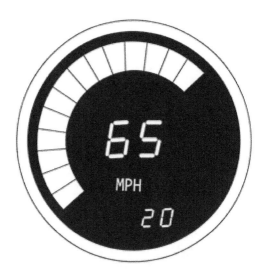

Many speedometers nowadays are digital because modern cars have computers built into them. You commonly see a combination of both speedometer types, analog and digital:

These two types of speedometers provide a great way to really show the difference between analog and digital. These devices operate with electricity. Small currents (flows) of electricity go through them. There are several words used to describe these small electrical currents, including: impulses, signals and pulses. In both types of speedometer, a device will measure the speed of the car, create an electrical signal based on that speed, and send that signal to the speedometer. That signal is used to control the speed that is displayed. The two types differ in how they can represent that speed to the driver. Let's say you're going exactly 54 miles per hour (MPH). Both types of speedometers (the digital number displayed and the needle on the dial) are showing 54 MPH. See also "digitize."

EXAMPLE: As a further example of machines that can be either analog or digital, there are analog watches:

And digital watches:

And just as a loose final example, let's compare analog and digital to physical objects. A slide or a hill could be considered "analog" because the slopes are gradual. Whereas a staircase, with its distinct steps that are each separate from each other, could be considered "digital." This can be seen in the picture below – the waves are analog and the steps are digital:

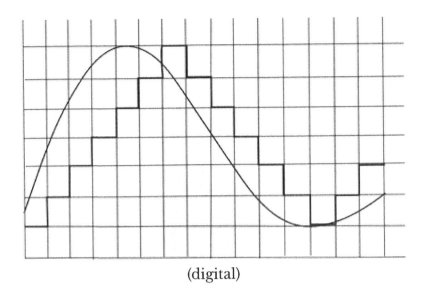

(digital)

digital certificate: See "certificate authority."

digitize: To digitize something is to make it digital. Digital means "of or related to a circuit or device that represents magnitudes in digits." Computers are digital devices; information in computers is represented using digits. The best place to start with the concept of "digitizing" something is the idea of converting a real-world object to a form that can be represented in a computer. For example, let's say you have an actual watercolor painting, and you want to convert it into a form that can be displayed on a computer system. There are scanning devices that can help with this process. These scanners can look at the colors in real world objects and come up with the electronic data for how to display those colors. They do this by viewing the object with a camera and then creating an electronic "grid" made up of many individual points that will represent the image it sees in the camera. In our example, it could treat the watercolor painting as if it were made up of thousands of tiny individual points, and it could come up with a grid that represented the color of each of those points. All that information could be put into a file on a computer, and then the computer version of the painting could be displayed on the computer display. This electronic file of the image is digital – it is made up of ones and zeroes, which are binary digits. It is VERY important to understand that there is no guarantee that the digital version of the painting will be identical to the actual painting. This is because there is always a degree of accuracy in real-world objects that a computer can't reproduce. To illustrate this, let's use that watercolor painting again. Remember, the scanner viewed the painting and then created a grid of tiny individual points to represent the painting. It then determined the color of each point and converted that color to an electronic form. So what happens if one of those individual points on the actual painting is not all one color? Perhaps the point is right at the edge of an object in the painting, and it contains two colors. How does the scanner handle this? It has to decide on a color, and ONLY ONE color, for that point. It does not have the concept of "mostly one color but some of another color." It has to convert what is perceived in the real world into one color that the computer can understand and display. If the scanner can break an image down into enough tiny points, the digital version of the painting may look very similar to the real painting. If not, the digital version may look substantially different – colors not as accurate; sharpness of the image is degraded, etc. The final thing to cover in terms of creating digital representations of real-world things is how to work with real-world things that can change over time. In our first example, we had a watercolor painting. It is not going to change at all – it is static. But how would we work with something that changes over time – like sound?

EXAMPLE: To work this out, let's take the example of using a computer to record a music concert. In very basic terms, we will have a live musical performance, and we want to end up with a computer file containing electronic data that represents the sounds of that performance as closely as possible. The systems that are actually used for this can be really complex, but for our purposes let's say we have only a few parts to our system: The actual musical instruments and singers that are creating the sound, a microphone that listens to that sound and produces an electrical signal based on what it hears, a special piece of equipment called an "analog to digital converter" (ADC) that can take in the electrical signal from the microphone and convert it to electronic data that a computer can use – binary data, and the actual computer where the electronic data is stored for later use. So let's see how this works: As the artists play their instruments and sing, the microphone is creating a constantly-changing electronic signal that represents the sounds they are creating. "Analog" means "of or relating to a mechanism that represents data by measurement of a continuous physical variable, as voltage or pressure." The microphone is an analog device, and the signal coming from the microphone is an analog signal – it is a wave, with volume and frequency. Its volume and frequency follow the actual sound perfectly, changing in real time as the sound changes. We need to somehow get that signal into a form the computer can work with. That's where the analog to digital converter comes in. The way the analog to digital converter works is this: on a repeating basis, it checks ("reads") the level of that electrical signal coming out of the microphone, and converts the voltage level it reads into a binary number. For example, it might check the signal from the microphone at one point and see it is at a level of 2 volts. It will convert that amount to binary and store it in a file. Just a moment later, it checks again, and sees that the signal from the microphone is at 2.1 volts – it has gone up a small amount. It converts that amount to binary and stores it in a file. This process is called "sampling" – the converter samples the incoming signal periodically. Later, when we want to play back this audio, the computer will take the electronic file representing that audio and output it to a device called a "digital to analog converter" (DAC). It does the opposite of an analog to digital converter – it uses the digital information to create an analog wave signal, with voltage and frequency, that can be used by a speaker to recreate the audio sounds. The problem here is that, just like we saw with the watercolor painting, we will never be able to make the digital information we store about this audio signal be exactly identical to the sound that was created in the real world. Let's look at this closely, since this is VERY important: Let's say the singer suddenly starts signing much more loudly. You're there, listening, and you can hear the singer's voice rise in volume quickly. It is not instant – you can hear the change. The signal coming out of the microphone and going into the analog to digital converter will suddenly jump up in voltage – again, it is not instant. If you were looking at the signal, you'd be able to see that the increase takes a little time. Let's say it jumps from 2 volts to 10 volts in just half a second. It is not instantaneous, but it happens pretty fast. At the quarter-of-a-second mark, it might be at 5 volts or so. Now (and here's the problem) let's say the analog to digital converter can only sample the microphone's signal once a second. It checks it at one second, sees it is at 2 volts, and converts that to binary form. Then, a second later, it checks it, sees it is at 10 volts, and converts that to binary. It has no way of detecting the values that the signal goes through as it increases from 2 volts to 10. And there is the issue – the electronic version of this musical performance did not capture the actual rise in volume. If you used this file to replay the music, you'd hear a sudden increase in volume, and not the actual rise that happened in the real world. The only solution would be to sample the incoming audio signal at a faster rate – and for sure that could be done, but remember that each time the signal is sampled, a piece of digital information is created. So the higher the sampling rate, the larger the digital file is that gets created. This can be taken to extremes, and produce a huge digital recording of the sound that is virtually indistinguishable from the real thing – but it will never be able to exactly duplicate it. This is the difference between analog (real-world, changing) and digital (composed of exact values; having no concept of amounts between those values).

dingbat: In the mid 19th century, the word *dingbat* was used to refer to various vaguely specified objects. The term originated from the idiom "have bats in the belfry (the part of a building where bells are housed – like in a church steeple)" – this idiom means to be crazy or odd. In typography (the art of arranging characters and words), a dingbat is a character or spacer (something that indicates or maintains distance between things). They're often used in typesetting (the preparation of the arrangement of printed characters for display) to create frames around text or as a spacer between lines. Dingbats are composed of images or symbols, such as ordering lists with bullet points:

EXAMPLE: The following are examples of a dingbat:

- Bullet point
  - Default sub point of *bullet* in google docs

- Square
  - Default sub point of *square* in google docs

- Star
  - Default sub point of *star* in google docs

- Arrow
  - Default sub point of *arrow* in google docs

Another example of a dingbat is a symbol that separates bodies of text, like this:

Lorem Ipsum

Chapter One: Ipsum

Lorem ipsum dolor sit amet, consectetur adipiscing elit, sed do eiusmod tempor incididunt ut labore et dolore magna aliqua. Ut enim ad minim veniam, quis nostrud exercitation ullamco laboris nisi ut aliquip ex ea commodo consequat.

– *"Duis aute irure dolor in reprehenderit in voluptate velit esse cillum dolore eu fugiat nulla pariatur. Excepteur sint occaecat cupidatat non proident, sunt in culpa qui officia deserunt mollit anim id est laborum."*

(dingbat)

diode: See "LED."

directory: 1. See "folder." 2. See "working directory."

disc: See "disk."

discrete data: *Discrete* literally means "distinct" and "individually separate." Discrete data is quantitative data that can be counted within a finite amount of time.

EXAMPLE: The change in your pocket/purse/wallet is an example of discrete data.

discrete distribution: In statistical distribution, when the probabilities of outcomes are considered discrete (countable) data, it is called a *discrete distribution*.

EXAMPLE: The probability distribution of a 6-sided die being 1, 2, 3, 4, 5, and 6 is an example of discrete distribution.

disk: Also spelled *disc*. A disk is a flat, thin, round object that can be used to store electronic information for use in a computer. Disks operate by rapidly rotating while information is put onto them or retrieved from them.

EXAMPLE: A CD (compact disk) is a type of disk, commonly used to store music for replay.

disk drive: See "drive."

disk-on-key: Another word for "USB drive."

dispersion: See "refraction."

display: See "screen."

display typeface: See "decorative typeface."

distribution: The distribution of a variable is a description of the relative number of times each possible outcome will occur within a number of attempts.

EXAMPLE: Take the game "rock paper scissors."
```
R = Rock
P = Paper
S = Scissors
```
If we wrote a computer program that automatically chose these at random and played against itself, technically the distribution of each would be:

Variable	Attempts	Possible outcome
R	100	.333333333
P	100	.333333333
S	100	.333333333

distribution software: A software program that has been developed for the manufacturing and distribution industry. It is designed to help order processing, accounting, supply chain, sales, customer support and customer relationship management. It is an all-in-one solution software that can be accessed by anyone in an area that deals with any associated tasks, and it ensures everyone is in sync.

EXAMPLE: NetSuite is a popular distribution software that many companies use to assist in the management of their business.

div tag: A tag that defines a division or a section in an HTML document. The div element is often used as a container for other HTML elements to style them or make specific changes to the content within that particular div tag.

EXAMPLE: Review this code:

```
<!DOCTYPE html>
<html>
  <head>
    <title>Your title here</title>
  </head>
  <body>
    <h1>Your heading here</h1>

    <div style="color: blue">
      <h2>Your div heading here</h2>
      <p>Your div paragraph here</p>
    </div>
  </body>
</html>
```

All of the elements contained within the <div> element will be written in blue.

Django: A free and open-source Python web framework (code written by others [and documentation on how to use it] that can be used by developers to enhance their programs) that can be used to create complex websites. It is covered on The Tech Academy's Python Course.

EXAMPLE: Youtube utilized Django in the creation of their website.

dll: See "dynamic link library."

DML: See "data manipulation language."

DNS: Stands for *Domain Name System*. It is a naming system for computers that are connected to the Internet. Typically, the name for a computer is represented in the DNS by a series of four numbers, separated by periods – for example, 127.0.0.1 is a DNS name. DNS is something that works in the background when you are on the Internet. DNS changes domain names from human language (e.g. doughnuts.com) to computer language (e.g. 131.235.98.45). It does this because your computer does not understand "doughnuts.com." Your computer and the Internet communicate with numbers. DNS is sometimes compared to a phone book. You tell your computer where you want to go on the Internet, DNS translates that to your computer and the Internet, and voila!, you are taken there. DNS helps people navigate the Internet.

EXAMPLE: You type in cheeseburgers.com, and DNS changes it to 452.376.12.32 so that your computer can find the web server for cheeseburger.com on the Internet.

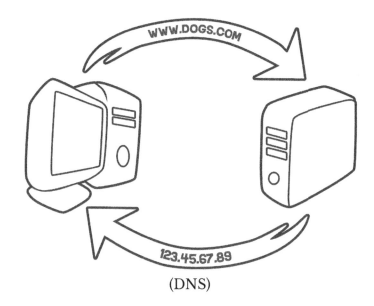

(DNS)

Docker: A *container* is an object that can be used to hold or transport something. In computing, a container is used to hold and deliver software. More specifically, the software and all its necessary libraries and files are packaged together to create a container. The container allows the application to run quickly and reliably from one computing environment to another. A popular software used to create and deliver these containers is called *Docker*. Docker was originally created as a free open source program in 2013 by Solomon Hykes. To date, over a thousand individuals have contributed code to Docker, including huge technology companies like Google, IBM, and Microsoft.

EXAMPLE: Docker creates containers by encapsulating the program with all of the necessary libraries and configuration files into a self-contained package. Software developers can then access these containers and have a fully running computer program on any operating system. This is possible because all of the necessary items for the program to run are already stored in the container with it.

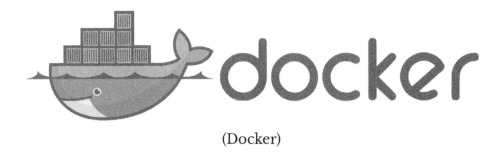

(Docker)

document.getElementById method: A "method" is an action that an object can perform. It is a named sequence of events. The document.getElementById method returns (executes and provides relevant output) an element. An "attribute" is a specification that assigns a property (name; characteristic) to something. Basically, an attribute is metadata (data that describes other data). The element returned by document.getElementById has an Id attribute with a specific value assigned to it. The Id is a variable (data that has a name and a value [type/amount], and can be changed).

EXAMPLE:

```
<h1 id="Header_1">This is my heading</h1>
```

We have assigned the h1 element the Id "Header_1." To run and display (return) this element, we write:

```
document.getElementById("Header_1").innerHTML
```

"innerHTML" gets or sets the HTML markup (the action of adding instructions to a document to control the style, format and appearance of the content [text, pictures, videos, etc.] of the document) contained within the element. Document.getElementById is used mainly to control or get information from an element within your code. If it can't find the element with the specified Id, it will return "null."

Document Object Model: See "DOM."

docx (file format): "Docx" is short for "document XML." This means that developers can create their own document structure, and then use XML (short for "extensible markup language"; XML is a customizable markup language, used primarily in the displaying documents on the internet [i.e., websites]) to specify markup (the action of adding instructions to a document to control the style, format and appearance of the content [text, pictures, videos, etc.] of the document) instructions for the data in those documents. Tags are the markup language (a system of specialized words and symbols used to add instructions to a document in order to control the style, format and appearance of the content [text, pictures, videos, etc.] of the document – markup languages are primarily used to make websites) words that usually have two parts, a start tag and an end tag. They have these symbols before and after them: < and >. XML is similar to HTML except that the code itself can be customized (i.e. the developer can create their own tags). The .docx file format is what Microsoft Word documents are typically saved as (previously, Word used .doc).

EXAMPLE: If you attempted to open a .docx file in a program that does not support Word document formats, you would either get an error message or a scrambled document.

DOM: The interface for HTML documents exists and it is called the Document Object Model, or the DOM. It is pronounced "dom," not "dee-oh-em." The middle word is "object" and in its simplest form, an object is just "something the computer is keeping track of." Usually it is a variable, or a data structure, or similar item. It is essentially a value stored in computer memory, so it has a location and an identifier that can be used to identify and use it. So the DOM is a <u>model</u> of the various <u>objects</u> in the HTML <u>document</u> – a document object model. The DOM presents the HTML document as a tree structure, where each node in the tree is an object representing a part of the HTML document. Take a look at this HTML code:

```html
<html>
    <head>
        <title>
            My title
        </title>
    </head>
    <body>
        <h1>A heading</h1>
        <a href="https://www.learncodinganywhere.com">Link text</a>
    </body>
</html>
```

Here is an example of a Document Object Model for this HTML code:

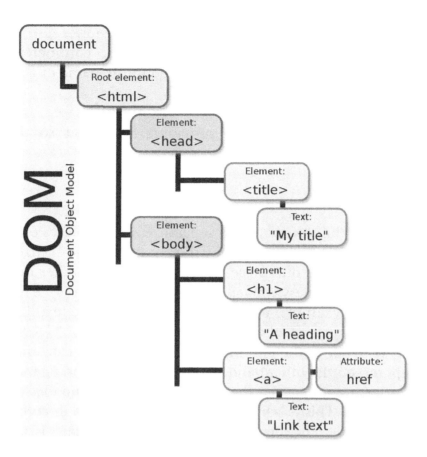

A DOM for an HTML page is generated by specialized computer programs. These programs scan through an HTML file, locating the various elements in the page described by that file, and then they create the tree structure that represents the unique arrangement of elements on that page. That tree structure, the DOM, is itself then held in computer memory. Once the DOM is generated for a particular HTML document, other programs can access the Object Model and the various parts of the document that are represented in it. They can get data about the various elements on the page, and can even modify the page.

EXAMPLE: Suppose you wanted to find all paragraph elements in an HTML document. You might use code like this:

```
var foo = document.getElementsByTagName("p");
```

The variable called "foo" would now contain a collection of all the paragraph tags in the document. Many different programming languages can be used to work with the DOM. One of the most common is JavaScript; in fact, the code example above is actually JavaScript.

domain: The various high-level categories of websites that are available on the World Wide Web. Typically, these are categories like "websites for commercial companies," "websites for educational institutions," etc. These categories are given two- or three-character names. For example, .com is short for commercial (refers to a company that exists for profit) and is a suffix added to the name of a website to show that the website belongs to the .com domain.

EXAMPLE: Chipotle makes money by providing food and so their website is chipotle.com.

domain name system: See "DNS."

dot (.): A dot (period) is used in computers to separate multiple pieces of data, where the entire set of data is meant to be processed by the computer. The "." character is used by the computer to show where one piece of data ends and another begins. The basic concept here is important: Unless you tell the computer when a piece of data starts and ends, it won't know. For example, what if you and I saw some text like this: "The zoo had three types of animals on display: lionstigersandbears." Obviously someone ran all the words together at the end of the sentence but we can still determine the meaning. A computer, on the other hand, has no idea what lions, tigers and bears are – it actually needs a separator between the words or it will have no idea that it is actually dealing with four words. This is why we need data separators in computers – to tell where data starts and ends. The separator is not part of the data; it is a way of marking out what the data actually is.

EXAMPLE: When you type google.com, you are telling the computer that the name of the place you want to go is "Google," and that Google is a "com" (stands for commercial -- something that exists for profit) entity. Google and com are different things. One is a name, the other is a type of thing, and the "." separates the two.

.bak: See "bak (suffix)."

.biz: See "biz (suffix)."

.com: See "com (suffix)."

.crt: See "crt (suffix)."

.docx: See "docx (file format)."

.gov: See "gov (suffix)."

dot matrix: A grid of dots which are filled selectively to create an image on paper or a screen.

EXAMPLE: Dot matrix printers print characters composed of tiny dots.

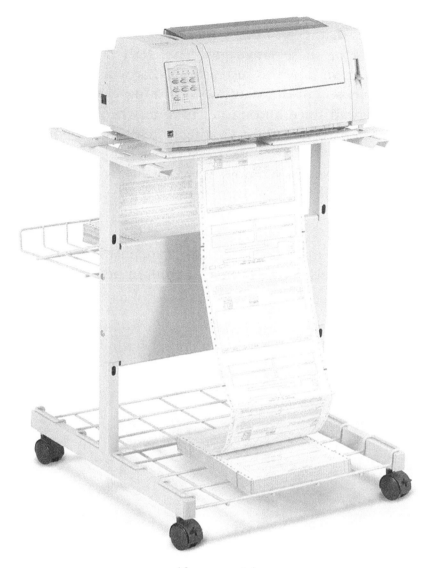

(dot matrix)

.net: See "net (suffix)."

.NET: A large collection of software development tools from Microsoft.

    EXAMPLE: .NET Core and the .NET Framework are elements of .NET.

.NET Core: The successor of the .NET Framework. It is a framework from Microsoft that is free and open-source. .NET Core is cross-platform and can run on Windows, macOS and Linux. It is compatible with all Microsoft programming languages (including C#). Like the .NET Framework, .NET Core can be referred to as just .NET.

    EXAMPLE: You can build web applications using .NET Core.

.NET Framework: Also called .NET. A collection of tools and pre-made software that help developers to make computer programs. It was created by Microsoft. It has several programming languages that it can work with. As a developer, you can write a program that uses one or more of these languages. The .NET Framework can take these programs and convert them down to instructions that will work on pretty much any computer that runs a version of the Windows operating system. This means you only have to write the program once and do not have to write variations of it for all the various combinations of hardware and operating systems that are out there.

EXAMPLE: The operating system Windows was made using the .NET Framework.

.org: See "org (suffix)."

dot plot: *Plot* literally means to mark (a route, path, road, position, etc.) on a chart (usually some sort of map). Plot can also mean to mark a point or points on a graph.

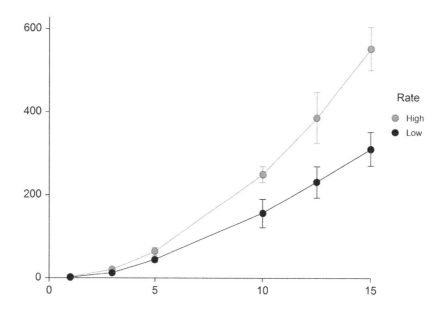

In statistics, we can visualize the frequency of data using a dot plot. A dot plot is a statistic visualization where each dot represents one piece of information.

EXAMPLE: The following image shows how many of each type of coffee drink has been ordered within an unspecified amount of time. This dot plot also tells us that one dot represents a value of 3 coffee drinks.

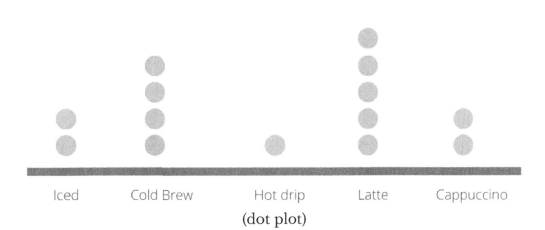

Types of coffee ordered   ● = 3 drinks

Iced   Cold Brew   Hot drip   Latte   Cappuccino

(dot plot)

double click: See "mouse."

double equal sign: == is used to show that a comparison should be made. Specifically, the "==" symbol is an instruction to check whether the data on the left side of the symbol is equal to the data on the right side. The answer to this comparison is an answer of "true" or "false." When the "==" symbol is used to check for equality, usually it is used like this: [first item to be compared] == [second item to be compared]

EXAMPLE: (10 + 5) == 15 true

down: When a machine is down, it is not operational. This can either be due to the power being off or some sort of error or issue with the machine. See also "downtime."

EXAMPLE: If a computer network is down, it means the network is not passing communication at that time between the interconnected computers on the network.

download: To get an electronic file from a website and then put a copy of that file onto your computer. If you download a video, you are having your computer pull the video file over the Internet from another computer and store that file on your computer so you can watch it later. The opposite of download is upload, which is when you take a set of data on your computer and send it to a website.

EXAMPLE: If you wanted to save a music video on your computer, you could download the video onto your computer and then watch it whenever you wanted.

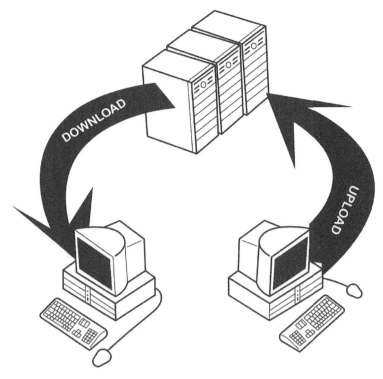

(download)

downtime: The period of time a computer, website, network of computers, etc. is down (not operational). When a machine is down, it is not operating as expected. This can either be due to the power being off or some sort of error or issue with the machine. It is very common for people to use computer programs that are not even on their computer – they are instead, on a remote computer, and the user connects their computer to that remote computer in order to use the computer program. In this case, it would be very important that the remote computer not go down often, as it would be very inconvenient to users. The performance of a resource (a computer or computer network, for example) that is used in this way is often given as "downtime percentage" – that is, a resource that is operational 99% of the time would have a 1% downtime.

EXAMPLE: If a server crashes, the time in between the point it crashes and the point it becomes operational again is the downtime. If a computer had a 1% downtime, this would mean it was down about 3 days a year, on average.

DQL: See "data query language."

drag and drop: See "mouse."

drain: A place where stuff can leave an area. In computers, a drain is the section of a computer part where electricity flows out.

EXAMPLE: Electricity flows into a computer part and exits through the drain.

drive: A device that the computer can use to store data for later use. The creation of storage drives was a major breakthrough in the computing industry, as it allowed users to set up data in an organized fashion, store it on a device that the computer could access, and then have the computer use the data when needed. Before this, users would have to manually enter data for the computer to use. If the computer was turned off, the data was gone, and it would have to be entered again when the computer was turned on again. Drives are often referred to as "disk drives" because the first designs made use of one or more metal disks that could be used to store computer data. The surface of these disks are magnetic and can be modified so that it stores data for use in computers. When the computer needs to access data on the disk drive, the disk spins quickly. As the disk spins, the data on the magnetic surface is read by the computer.

EXAMPLE: A CD-ROM drive is where CD-ROMs are inserted into a computer and processed. You can see one on a laptop here:

(drive)

driver: A special computer program that helps that particular model of computer work with certain devices. The driver acts as a "translator" between the computer and the device so that they can understand each other and work together. It is software that coordinates the functions of the hardware.

EXAMPLE: In order to use a printer with your computer, it is usually necessary to install a driver so that your computer understands how to control that exact printer model. These drivers are usually created by the printer manufacturer. The manufacturer needs to get the technical information about how that particular computer communicates with devices that get connected to it, and then make a computer program that aligns how their printer is controlled with how that particular computer works.

DSL: Stands for *Digital Subscriber Line*. A *subscriber* is someone that requests to receive information from a particular source. In terms of connected computers, DSL is a way to transfer data over telephone lines at a high speed and is mainly used to allow computers to access the internet. What this means is that the subscriber connects to the Internet through the telephone line leading to their home or building. Back when people utilized dial-up internet (internet access through their phone line), the phone companies saw the need for both a faster connection to the internet, as well as a way to allow users to access the internet at the same time they were using their telephones for voice calls. The technology they created was DSL. This technology became popular in the late 1990s as the use of the Internet gained in popularity.

EXAMPLE: A homeowner who had access to the internet through dial-up connection could pay their phone provider (e.g., AT&T) for DSL. AT&T would come to the house and install special DSL equipment, and then the homeowner could access the internet at faster speeds and make phone calls at the same time.

(DSL)

dual-core: See "core."

dump: Short for "data dump." A large amount of information transferred from one location to another.

EXAMPLE: If you dumped information from one computer to another, you would be moving all the information from the first computer onto the second computer.

DVI: Stands for "Digital Video Interface." A type of connector that is used to connect a video source to a display device. This came out in the 1990s and allows higher quality video displays than VGA. There are several different types of connectors that relate to passing video and audio signals. This is because manufacturers of audio and video equipment have continued to improve the performance of their equipment over the years, and this means that often, earlier connectors can't take advantage of the newer, better features of that equipment – so new connectors had to be designed. Here is a DVI cable:

EXAMPLE: Higher-end laptops have DVI ports which can be used to connect your laptop to a high definition monitor. On the left is a DVI port and on the right is a VGA port:

(DVI)

dynamic: Refers to actions that take place the moment they are needed, rather than in advance. A restaurant that prepares your food to your specifications, when you order, would be dynamic. The opposite of dynamic is "static," meaning "unchanging." A restaurant that has the food pre-cooked and waiting before you order would be static – the food does not change in regards to time or circumstance. In computers, dynamic means the computer processes your request right when you ask it to; it does not have a predetermined result ahead of time. Dynamic relates to the Internet by describing websites that have content that changes while the website is being viewed, depending on things like what part of the web page you move to with the mouse. This is important because a web page made only with HTML is "static" – that is, the content of the page does not change unless the actual file stored on the web server changes. This means that you could view that page using a browser over and over, and it would always have the same appearance. As the World Wide Web increased in popularity, a technology was needed that could modify the HTML that was used in the browser without having to replace the HTML file on the web server, so that web pages could change based on the instructions of the web page designer. Such web pages are called "dynamic" pages.

EXAMPLE: A website that displays dark colors in the evening, and light colors during the day, is a dynamic website.

dynamic link library: A Windows file format that indicates the file contains a library of functions and other information that can be accessed by programs. Abbreviated "DLL."

EXAMPLE: The .NET Framework file is entitled mscoree.dll.

dynamic memory: Dynamic refers to actions that take place the moment they are needed, rather than in advance. A restaurant that prepares your food to your specifications when you order, would be dynamic. The opposite of dynamic is "static," meaning "unchanging." A restaurant that has the food pre-cooked and waiting before you order would be static – the food does not change in regards to time or circumstance. In computers, dynamic means the computer processes your request right when you ask it to – it does not have a predetermined result ahead of time. Memory is physical components in a computer where information can be stored for later use. Dynamic memory is memory where the stored information is not maintained when the computer is shut off. The information is cleared each time the computer has no power.

EXAMPLE: When typing a document on a computer, if your computer abruptly turns off you can sometimes lose your data. This is due to the fact that unsaved documents are dynamic memory.

E

ECMA: The ECMA is an organization that oversees various technical standards. Prior to 1994, ECMA stood for European Computer Manufacturers Association. In 1994, this name was changed to European association for standardizing information and communication systems, but EMCA was kept as the acronym for the organization. JavaScript is an implementation of the ECMAScript Language (a programming language) Specification standard. Acronyms like ES6, ES2015 and ES2016 refer to various versions of this standard.

EXAMPLE: ES6 introduced the "let" and "const" statements in JavaScript.

E drive: See "hard drive."

EF: See "Entity Framework."

8K: See "resolution, levels of."

electric signal: An electric current that can be modified by electronic devices. That modification of the current is a signal, and it can be used to convey information from one place to another. Also referred to as just "signal."

EXAMPLE: Music is conveyed from your music player to your speaker via an electrical signal.

electronic: Having to do with electronics (the science of controlling electricity). The origin of the word has to do with the fact that electricity involves the movement of electrons from one point to another. Electrons are one of the smallest parts of the physical universe. They are part of the atoms that make up physical matter. When electrons move from one point to another, certain physical actions take place. This is electricity – the movement of electrons. We can use electricity to make machines perform tasks.

EXAMPLE: Most of the devices you use to consume audio, video, etc. are electronic devices.

element: 1. Tags and the code written between them. Here is a diagram that shows this:

EXAMPLE: To define an element on the HTML document, you use an opening and closing tag. For example: to create a paragraph, write:

```
<p> This is a paragraph. </p>
```

Which would simply display:

This is a paragraph.

If we fail to include either the opening or the closing tag for our element, we will create errors within the document. There are exceptions to this rule; there are a few elements that do not require closing tags. However, for the sake of simplicity, assuming all tags require a closing tag is a good rule to follow.

2. See "chemical element."

email: Stands for "electronic mail." Email is used for sending "mail" to someone using your computer. It is written communication sent person-to-person using computers. As you know, you type out what you want to say and then send it to another person. The other person receives the email and then can read it and reply if they choose.

EXAMPLE: Roughly 306.4 billion emails are sent and received each day, and the figure is expected to increase to over 361.6 billion daily emails in 2024.

email client: A client is a software program that can request information from a server, receive the requested information, and do something with it. A web browser (the program people use to view web pages) is a kind of a client. Another kind of client is an email program. It helps a user contact special servers over the Internet where email messages are stored, and retrieves them for the user. The first versions of these email clients were programs you would put on your computer. You'd set the program up to use whatever email address you were using, and when you wanted to get your messages, the client would request them from a server and store them on your computer. Later versions of these email clients were actually put on websites, so you could view your email messages without saving them to your computer.

EXAMPLE: Microsoft Outlook is a popular email client.

embed: To fix something inside another thing. Content from another source that is included as part of a page is referred to as "embedded content." This typically refers to content that exists on another website.

EXAMPLE: A common example is an embedded video. This would be like taking a video from YouTube and displaying it on your website.

embedding: Most elements of a web page will be stored on the web server for that website. When you use something from another web server on your website, it is called "embedding." This information can be a video, picture, etc. Instead of being stored on your site, it remains stored on the other site. Usually, people can see it on both websites.

EXAMPLE: It is common for companies to put a video on YouTube, and also embed it on their website. The video would then be visible in two places (the company site and the YouTube site), but only takes up storage space on the YouTube web servers.

Ember: Short for "Ember.js." An open-source, JavaScript web framework that allows developers to create dynamic web applications.

EXAMPLE: Many major companies have utilized Ember within their organizations, including: Microsoft, LinkedIn and Netflix.

(Ember)

enable wire: "Enabled" means that something is turned on and active. An enable wire would be a wire that causes something to turn on. Enable wires are used by the CPU to control the operation of the memory locations in the computer. Each memory location has its own enable wire. The enable wire is used by the CPU when it wants to retrieve information from a specific memory location. The CPU turns the enable wire for that memory location "on" (by applying electricity to it), and then the CPU tells the memory location to send the information it has stored in it. There is also a "set" wire for each memory location. It is used when the CPU wants to store information in a specific memory location. The CPU turns the set wire for that memory location "on" and then it sends the information to be stored to that memory location.

EXAMPLE: The CPU has designated memory location 10002 with the name "age." This would have happened because the program initialized a variable (data that has a name and a value [type/amount], and can be changed) called "age." Now the program wants to store the value "40" in that memory location. The CPU turns the set wire on for the memory location, and then sends the value "40" to it. That information is then stored in the memory location. Later, the program needs to get the value of the variable "age."

The CPU knows that this variable's value is stored in memory location 10002, so it turns the enable wire on for location 10002, and tells it to send its information. The value "40" is sent to the CPU.

encapsulation: To wrap something or cover it completely. Often when creating computer programs, you will have certain tasks that you need to do over and over again. In this case, it is helpful to create computer instructions that perform that task, and then turn those instructions into a small program that itself can be used by other computer programs. A common term for this is "sub program." For example, there may be a subprogram that can receive some numbers, add them together and give the answer. You can imagine that this subprogram might get used quite often. There are two aspects of a task in a computer program: WHAT it does, and HOW it does it. In computer programming, encapsulation means setting up a computer program so that the details of HOW are hidden away and only WHAT it does is visible.

EXAMPLE: Let's say that two different people were assigned the task to write a subprogram called 'MultiplyTwoNumbers' which is intended to receive two numbers and give back the result of multiplying those two numbers. The subprogram can be written in more than one way, because you can do the math in more than one way: You can multiply the two numbers, or you can do the whole operation using addition. An example: If you want to multiply 3 times 4, you can do it with addition by adding up the number 3, four times: 3 + 3 + 3 + 3 = 12. Or you can do it with multiplication: 3 x 4 = 12. Either approach gives you the correct answer. This applies to encapsulation, and to computer programming, like this: If two people each solved the task differently, but the way they did it resulted in the correct answer, either one of the subprograms could be used when a person wanted to do multiplication. They wouldn't need to see HOW the subprogram arrived at the right answer – they would only need to know WHAT to give the subprogram in order for it to do its job, and WHAT they would receive as an answer. In both cases, the WHAT to give the subprogram is "the two numbers you want to multiply', and the WHAT you get back is "the product of the two numbers" (in math, "product" means "what you get when you multiply numbers"). So here, we encapsulate the implementation of the subprogram, and only give the user what they need to see to use the subprogram.

encode: To turn something into a code (a system where you can use a symbol to represent another thing). If you encode a message, you convert it into code. Doing this usually makes it difficult to figure out the original message.

EXAMPLE: Britain intercepted encoded German messages during World War II that might have contained information vital to the war effort. Due to the brilliant work of an early computer pioneer named Alan Turing, the British military was able to figure out how the encoding was done and reverse it so the English could view the original German messages.

encoding system: See "character encoding."

encrypt: To change information into a form that can't be understood by regular means, but can be converted back to its original form through certain means. If you have the password "catsarefun," and then encrypt it, it might look like "4s(7_G⌃k" to anyone else viewing it. If you needed to send that password to another person but wanted to keep it safe, you would encrypt it and tell the other person the method you used to encrypt it. Computers work the same way; there are several standard ways of encrypting data, and if the computer that is receiving encrypted information knows the way it was encrypted, it can restore it to its original form.

EXAMPLE: Encryption is used to keep personal information secure. Your bank will encrypt your personal information when its computers send that data to each other so that if anyone intercepts the information they won't be able to understand what they are seeing.

End key: See "Home key."

end-to-end testing: A technique used to test if the process of an application, from start to finish, is behaving as expected. The purpose is to identify system dependencies and verify that data integrity is maintained between various system components.

EXAMPLE: End-to-end testing for a text message app could look something like this:
1. Log into the application.
2. Access message boxes (Inbox, Sent, Drafts, Trash, and Folders).
3. Open and close each message box.
4. Compose a message.
5. Check if the message was sent.
6. Log out of the application.
This can be applied to any day-to-day use items other than just software, like a car manufacturer could ensure safety with end-to-end testing.

end user: See "user."

engine (software): See "software engine."

engineering: The application of mathematics combined with scientific, economic, social, and practical knowledge in order to invent, design, build, maintain, research, and improve structures, machines, tools, systems, components, materials, processes, and organizations. The discipline of engineering is extremely broad and encompasses a range of more specialized fields of engineering, each with a more specific emphasis on particular areas of applied science, technology, and types of application. From building bridges to combining chemicals in a lab, engineering embraces many fields. There are many types of engineering, such as civil engineering (design and maintenance of physical structures) and mechanical engineering (design, construction, and use of machines). Computer and software engineering have to do with the building and operation of computers and the designing of programs that run on those computers.

EXAMPLE: Intel (a major computer company) employs computer engineers.

enter key: See "return key."

enterprise resource planning: See "ERP."

enterprise software: "Enterprise" means "a company or a business." Enterprise software is used to satisfy the needs of an organization, as opposed to individual users. Software designed for use by companies, schools, governments, charities, etc., is enterprise software.

EXAMPLE: Salesforce is a popular enterprise software that assists in the area of customer relationship management.

Entity Framework: An O/RM from Microsoft. It is abbreviated "EF." It gives developers an automated mechanism for accessing and storing the data in the database from within the program code. EF is capable of connecting C# code and the database, allowing the user to code and directly interact with the database through using C#. It allows the programmer to code a lot more effectively. *Entity Framework Core* is an open source and cross-platform version of Entity Framework.

EXAMPLE: You could create a whole database, with many tables, and the Entity Framework could automatically create all the C# classes and methods needed to create, read, update and delete data in the database. Alternatively, you could start with your code, creating your C# classes, and EF could create the entire database and all of its tables for you.

(Entity Framework)

entry-level developer: See "junior developer."

enum: In normal English, enumerate means "to establish the number of something." For example, "The U.S. census for 1950 enumerated 150,697,361 residents in the country."

Enums or enum is short for enumerated. In coding, enum is a data type that consists of a set of named values. These named values are called elements, members, enumeral, or enumerators of the type. Enumerator names are usually identifiers that behave as constants (names given to locations in a computer's memory that a program has set aside for use in storing data, in the situation where the value of the data stored in that memory location will NOT change over time).

EXAMPLE: Consider playing card suits (Clubs, Diamonds, Spades and Hearts). Each suit could be an enumerator, belonging to an enumerated type named Suit. You could then assign a new variable (such as "Queen," 8, "Ace," etc.) and declare that the suit is that data type. Once the data type of suit has been declared, you can assign one of the four values (Clubs, Diamonds, Spades or Hearts) to it.

environment: 1. The overall structure within which a user, computer, etc. operates. This is often used to mean "the combination of physical hardware and operating system that my computer uses."

EXAMPLE: Your computer might have an environment that is specifically set up for creating and modifying detailed artistic drawings. This could mean that the computer's display, operating computer programs and the speed the computer operates at would be set up in order to best facilitate those tasks.

2. A computer system where computer programs are executed and deployed. An example of an environment is developing and executing a program on a single machine (such as your laptop). Environments range in size from the single machine just mentioned, to networks of multiple, separate servers (large computers used to store and transmit data). An environment is the overall structure within which a user, computer, or program operates. A staging environment (stage) is a nearly exact copy of a production environment (the actual code composing a product) for software testing. Staging environments are made to test code and to ensure quality before deploying software. Everything in a staging environment is as close of a replica to the production environment as possible to ensure the software works correctly.

EXAMPLE: In some companies, the following environments are used:
1) Development environment – This is where all the coding occurs.
2) Test environment or Quality Assurance (QA) environment – This is where the code is tested by other developers.
3) Acceptance test environment or staging environment – This is where the client tests the software.
4) Production environment or operations environment – This is the live software that users can access.

As you may have guessed, the above environments are actually a sequence that the software moves through. Once a stage is complete, the code is passed along to the next stage. If rejected, it moves back for corrections – if accepted, it moves forward.

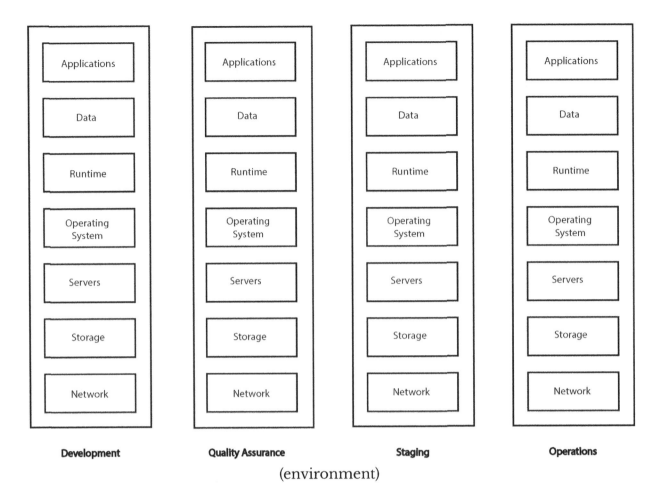

| Development | Quality Assurance | Staging | Operations |

(environment)

environment variable: A variable set outside of a computer program, whose functionality is used by the computer's operating system. They are made up of name/value pairs. Environment variables serve various purposes, including:

- Indicating where to store temporary files,
- Helping programs to know which directory (another word for "folder"; a location where a file or files are stored within a computer) to install files in,
- Where to locate user profile settings, and more.

EXAMPLE: PATH is an environment variable that can be used on the command line to specify a set of directories where executable programs are located. An executable is a file or program that can be run by the computer. The PATH environment variable basically allows you to run any executables that are located inside the paths specified in the variable using the command prompt, without having to give the absolute path to the executable.

epic: In Agile, this refers to a larger body of work (big tasks) that can be broken down into user stories (smaller tasks).

EXAMPLE: Developing one video game level could be an epic.

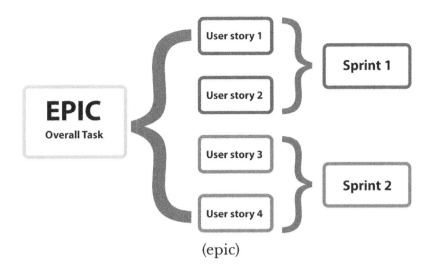

(epic)

epsilon: The fifth letter in the Greek alphabet. The uppercase epsilon looks like the regular E that is used in our alphabet and the lower case takes two forms: ε and ϵ. In statistical modeling, the lowercase epsilon is referred to as the "error term" or the "random error component." The value of error is used to describe how the predicted value of y, may actually vary from a predicted line.

EXAMPLE: Let's say the stock value of a shoe company is observed at $4.99 a share on Saturday. Based on a linear regression analysis, the predicted amount for that day was $5.23 – the variance is .24 cents. In this case, the random error component would be .24.

equation: In math, an equation is when you say two or more things are the same using numbers. The root of the word is "equal." An equation is a statement that states one thing is equal to another thing. Computers are able to perform equations. A computer can take numbers, run them through a series of steps, and determine an exact outcome.

EXAMPLE: 2 + 4 = 6 is an equation. We are saying here that 2 + 4 is the same as 6. An equation can also be a math problem where you do not know what one of the numbers is so you replace it with a letter instead; the letter represents the unknown quantity. For example: 4 - x = 1 is an equation. (x would be 3 in this equation.)

equiprobable: Two outcomes are equally likely to occur. It literally means "having equal probability." Pronounced "equi - prob - able."

EXAMPLE: The sun rising and sun setting are equiprobable.

erase: To remove stored data from a computer.

EXAMPLE: If you erase an electronic document, that document is removed from your computer's memory and is no longer available for use.

ergonomics: See "computer ergonomics."

ERP: Stands for "Enterprise Resource Planning." This is a business management program that a company can use to collect, store, manage and interpret data from many business activities including: product planning, cost, manufacturing, marketing and sales.

EXAMPLE: IBM Maximo Asset Management is an ERP that tracks the operation, maintenance and disposal of assets.

error: A difference between the desired performance of a computer and the actual performance or behavior of a computer. An error is an unexpected occurrence – a mistake.

EXAMPLE: If you tell the computer to give you the answer to "4 + 7" and it gives you "12," that is an error.

error term: See "epsilon."

escape character: A letter or symbol (typically a backslash – \\) that changes how the computer handles a character that would normally be interpreted as an instruction. They are often used in working with text.

EXAMPLE: In the Python programming language, you print `Hello, World!` as follows: `print("Hello, World!")`. But what if you wanted the words `Hello, World!` to be displayed with quotation marks on either side? The quotation marks are normally an instruction – they tell the computer, treat everything inside these quotation marks as a connected set of characters. If you wanted to display the quotation marks, you'd use an escape character and write it as follows: `print("\"Hello, World!\"")`. Then, instead of displaying `Hello, World!`, the output would be "`Hello, World!`" What's happening here precisely is this: the first quotation mark is treated as an instruction – it won't be displayed. Then the escape character (the backslash) tells the computer to treat the next character it encounters as NOT an instruction, but simply as text.

Esc key: Short for "Escape key." It is used to stop a computer action. This can take many forms, depending on how the computer programmer decided to make use of the Escape key (yes, programmers can instruct computers as to what effects various keys have when pressed inside their program).

EXAMPLE: You may be using a computer program to connect to another computer so that you can access the files on the remote (separate; located at a distance) computer and could use the Escape key to stop the connection process.

(Esc key)

escape sequence: The use of a symbol in front of a character for a specific purpose. Here are some examples of Python escape sequences:
- "\t" to create a tab
- "\n" to start a string on a new line
- "\r" for a carriage return

EXAMPLE: The following Python code, when "printed," will display three separate lines of text.

```
myString = ("This is my string. \n This is my string on a new line.\
            \n \t This is my string on a new line and using a tab")

print(myString)
```

(escape sequence)

ES6: See "ECMA."

ES2015: See "ECMA."

ES2016: See "ECMA."

Ethernet: A set of technologies for creating computer networks that rely on physical wires to connect computers to the network. Ethernet was developed in the late 1970s and it refers to computers linked together with a special type of cable called an Ethernet cable. An Ethernet cable is able to have information traveling in both directions simultaneously. The plug looks like this:

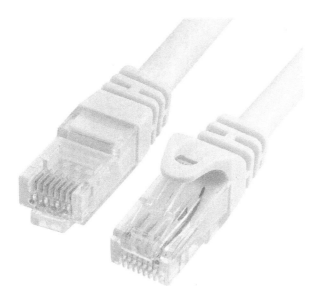

There are different "categories" of ethernet (abbreviated "cat" – like "cat 6"). Simply put, the higher the number, the newer the version, and so the faster the data transmission is, the higher the capacity is.

EXAMPLE: Many computers use Ethernet to connect to a network.

(Ethernet)

ETL: See "data pipeline."

event: "Things" that happen to elements (pieces of a web page). Events include actions the browser takes or actions the user takes. The JavaScript programming language can be used to "react" to HTML events (such as having a pop-up close when the user clicks outside of its box).

EXAMPLE: A mouse click on a submit button is an event.

event-driven programming: A programming paradigm where the flow of the program is controlled by events, like user actions (key presses, mouse clicks, etc.), a sensor interacting with something, messages from other programs, etc.

EXAMPLE: You might use event-driven programming when creating an app that allows you to send money back and forth between you and your friends. Each time you hit the send button, an associated event occurs.

event handler: An "event" is something done by the user or an action taken by a different source than the program itself. Common examples of events are a mouse click or keystroke (pressing a key on the keyboard). An "event handler" is code that processes events (like mouse movements, keystrokes, etc.). They are reactions to actions taken by the user. JavaScript is the most common language used for website event handlers.

EXAMPLE: The mouseover effect (an effect that takes place when you put the mouse pointer over an element) is an event handler.

event trigger: See "trigger."

evolutionary development: An iterative (repeating a sequence wherein each step in the sequence brings one closer to the end goal) and incremental approach. This approach breaks tasks down into "bite size" chunks and progresses projects forward in small steps. This is as opposed to knocking out the whole project in one big push.

EXAMPLE: Agile utilizes an evolutionary development approach.

exception: In normal English, an exception is a person or thing which does not behave in the expected way. In programming, an exception is something that disrupts the flow of execution of a program. "Exception" is short for "exceptional event." The primary difference between an error and an exception is: 1. An error cannot be recovered from. The only "solution" to an error is to terminate program execution and then attempt to fix it. 2. An exception can be recovered from. This is done by designing a program to catch (notice; observe) exceptions during program execution and to pre-program how to handle them. This is referred to as "exception handling" – how to address exceptions as they come up.

EXAMPLE: Let's say a user misspells a word that they input. With an exception handling, you could design the program to display: *Oops! This search term cannot be located. Please check the spelling and try again.*

execute: To perform a specific task or action. You are putting something into action. In computers, you are telling the computer to start performing a set of instructions. It means the same thing as "run."

EXAMPLE: To execute something in a computer, you can click on it with a mouse.

executive summary: A short document that is created for various business purposes. Executive summaries can be used to outline longer reports or to summarize large proposals. The purpose of executive summaries is to provide brief overviews that allow readers to become familiar with the overall data rapidly (as opposed to reading longer reports in full). The origin of the term comes from the fact that they originally referred to summaries provided to executives for rapid decision making and approvals. Executive summaries are still commonly used for this purpose. Also called a "management summary."

EXAMPLE: When submitting a proposal to your boss, you could attach an executive summary on top of it so they had a concise explanation of the project.

expansion card: See "card."

export: See "import."

Express: Short for "Express.js" – a web application framework that is free and open-source. Express is a "layer" built over the top of Node.js that assists in managing servers and routers. It can be used to develop web applications and mobile apps.

EXAMPLE: Express is used mainly to build web applications and APIs

expression: Numbers and symbols and operators grouped together that show the amount of something. An expression is a written math problem. In computers, an expression is a combination of values that are computed by the computer. There are different ways to write out expressions depending on which language you are programming in.

EXAMPLE: `Name = "What person types in the name box,"` could be an expression. Also: `x + 5` is an expression.

extensible markup language: See "XML."

extension: Metadata (data that provides information about other data) about an electronic file; it tells what type of information is contained in the file. As a reminder, the extension usually goes after the name of the file. An extension is also an optional feature that extends the abilities of a computer program. Something added onto a working program that makes it perform better or adds features is considered an extension.

EXAMPLE: If you have a file called "SoupRecipe" that is a written document, you might have "txt" (short for text) added to the name. This would be written "SoupRecipe.txt." Here, "SoupRecipe" is the name of the file, and ".txt" is the extension.

F

Facebook: One of the most popular websites in the world. People use it mainly for connecting to other people who use the site, and for consuming (reading or viewing) content shared by people who use the site. On Facebook you put in information about who you are, what things you like, and where you are from. You can connect with friends, send them messages, write things so that others can see them, etc. Facebook has over one billion users.

EXAMPLE: You might access Facebook to share with your friends and family something about a nice vacation you had.

FaceTime: A method of calling someone using your smartphone or computer where your face is shown on the screen. The person can hear your voice and see your face when you use FaceTime. FaceTime is similar to video chat. It was developed by Apple and is available on devices from Apple like the Macintosh computer, the iPhone, and the iPad.

EXAMPLE: On some iPhones, you can call someone using FaceTime. You hold your phone in front of your face – the person at the other end can see your face and hear your voice. If the other person's phone is capable of FaceTime, you will be able to see their face and hear their voice on your phone.

false: Not true. This is an important element of how computers work because they are often used to make decisions based on information. They need to be able to evaluate whether a certain condition is true or false, and then perform certain other actions depending on the answer. False (also referred to as "off" or "no") is represented as "0" inside a computer.

EXAMPLE: The computer is asked to evaluate a list of students and determine whether or not each student has a grade point average above 3.2. The computer would look at each student in turn, and determine whether it was TRUE or FALSE that their GPA was above 3.2.

fatal error: When a computer is executing instructions that a person entered into the computer, something might go wrong with the instructions as those instructions are executed. If this error is so severe that the computer can't continue to execute any instructions at all, that would be described as a fatal error. This is because the error effectively "killed" the actions the computer was attempting.

EXAMPLE: A fatal error could occur in a game you were playing and make it freeze.

FCD: Stands for *Fabric, Ceramic, Doping*. Fabric refers to a lightweight fabric that is used when creating certain speakers. A ceramic coating is also applied, heated, and hardened to add stiffness to the speaker. A slightly sticky plastic coating (called *doping*) is also used in the creation of the speaker that helps increase bass and add warmth to the overall tone of the speaker.

EXAMPLE: The "cone" of a speaker is the portion of the speaker that moves and vibrates to produce sound waves. FCD is a trademarked term used in the creation of a lightweight, yet extremely rigid cone, that sounds smooth and warm and does not exhibit any of the harshness or ringing often associated with metal cones.

F drive: See "floppy disk."

feasibility testing: "Feasible" means "workable; realistic; possible." A feasibility study is a review of how practical a proposed project is. The purpose is to analyze the strengths and weaknesses of a project. This includes confronting the various opportunities and threats, the required resources and how likely success is. The primary points that are reviewed in feasibility testing are: 1. The required cost of the project, and 2. The value attained by completing the project. Feasibility tests are supposed to be unbiased and provide a realistic view of the potential of success.

EXAMPLE: Feasibility studies can provide a historical background of the company or project, a description of the proposed project or service, financial information, details about various activities, market research and legal requirements.

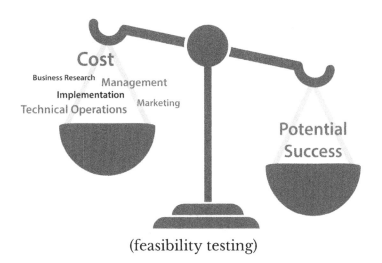

(feasibility testing)

feature extraction: In normal English, a *feature* is "a distinctive aspect or characteristic of something." In tech, a *feature* is a notable property of a program or device. *Feature extraction* is the process of taking the elements in data that are important for a machine to learn from. It is the process of extracting features of data – only the features you want – and it does not have to be all of the data. Feature extraction is also referred to as *feature recognition*.

EXAMPLE: Feature extraction for image recognition is the grouping of pixels and points and color combinations to work out the patterns on each picture.

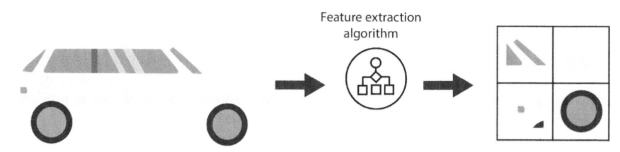

Feature extraction
algorithm

(feature extraction)

feature recognition: See "feature extraction."

feed: A flow of individual information items, either continuously flowing or arriving intermittently. Feeds are often used for news, and the software that manages them will usually notify a person that something new is available in the stream.

EXAMPLE: A news feed would be information sent to your computer giving current news. You might set up your feed to only present news related to a certain subject; for example, only news stories concerning auto racing.

fiber: See "fiber optics."

fiber optics: *Optics* is the study of visible and invisible light. *Fiber optics* is a term for a physical cable that can be used to transfer information over long distances. It is made out of glass or plastic, formed into threads (fibers). These fibers can carry pulses of light (which can represent information). You can see inside a fiber optic cable here:

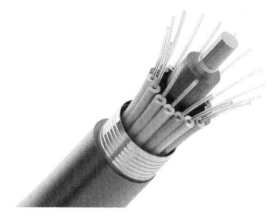

Obviously, these pulses of light move at the speed of light (which is 186,000 miles per second). In theory, nothing can travel faster than light. And so, when computers are connected by fiber, data transfer between them happens very quickly. Other forms of physical wire that are used to transfer information usually use electricity, which travels slower than light.

EXAMPLE: Currently, fiber optics allows for the fastest possible internet speed.

field: 1. Space in a data structure that is reserved for particular information. It is the smallest unit of information a user can access. Fields have certain attributes associated with them (numbers, text, etc.)

EXAMPLE: In a spreadsheet, fields are called cells. Another example: when you are filling in a form on your computer, each box where you enter in data is called a field.

2. See "database field"

FIFO: Stands for "First-In, First-Out." See also "stack." A method of handling information stored in a computer. The first piece of data put into the computer will then be the first piece of data that can be taken out.

EXAMPLE: In FIFO, if you entered: 1, then 2, then 3, into a list of numbers, and then retrieved a number from the list, then the number 1 would be the first retrievable piece of data.

fifth generation: See "generation."

file: See "folder."

file format: See "format."

file path: The route to a file. The "file path" is the address of a file and specifies the exact location of a file. It provides a "path" to the file. File paths say things like, "You can find the file named 'Winter' inside the folder named 'Poems', which is inside the C drive." The various components of a path are separated by a text character that is unlikely to be used in the name of a directory or a file. Usually this character is a slash, backslash or colon ("/," "\" or ":" respectively). The "\" (backslash) symbol separates the different parts of a collection of electronic documents in computers and it has been used for a long time. It was created as an aid to organizing and finding the various files you might store on a computer.

EXAMPLE: In a file path, backslashes are used to show that one item is below another (in terms of hierarchy). The item on the left is above the one on the right. Our earlier example a file path would be written as: C:\Poems\Winter

filter: See "image filter."

File Transfer Protocol: See "FTP."

finger stick: See "USB drive."

firewall: A port is a non-physical connection that is used in relation to connected computers. Different types of information can be sent between these computers – electronic documents, electronic messages, web pages, etc. Computers in the network can specify an exact computer to request information from or send information to. But the information is not just sent to "the computer" – rather, it is sent to a specific, numbered connection on that computer. There may be hundreds of such connections, or "ports," on a computer. It is important to understand that a port in this instance does not correspond to any specific physical connection to the computer. The physical connection has already been set up by this time, through a wired (or wireless) connection to a device like a router. All the communication to and from the computer will of course travel through this connection. But, there are other factors involved when we are sending information between computers. For example, just because the information arrives at a computer does not automatically mean the computer will accept it – it may need to verify the identity of the computer that sent the information. And even if the computer does accept it, the computer needs to know where to send it (i.e., what program needs the information). To accomplish this, the operating system controls communication on these ports. It monitors communication being sent to and from the computer and controls the routing of that communication. Because we now are tracking each separate port, we can set up rules around how each port works. These are things like, "What program do I route incoming communication to on this port?", "Will I allow outgoing communication on this port?", or "What protocol is being used for communication traveling through this port?" The part of the operating system at work here is called a "firewall." It is the area in the operating system program where the ports are maintained. The term "firewall" comes from the automobile industry. When building a vehicle, a wall is put in place between the front of the car (called the engine compartment, because that is where the engine typically is located) and the interior of the car (called the passenger compartment, because that is where the driver and passengers sit). This wall is there, among other reasons, to protect the people in the vehicle if a fire should break out in the engine compartment – that's why it is called a firewall. You can see a firewall protruding up between these two buildings here:

In a computer, the "firewall" is there for protection as well – it allows control over what information goes in and out of the computer. In a vehicle, these firewalls have many holes built into them where wires and other parts can go through to connect the parts in the engine compartment with the parts in the passenger compartment. This corresponds to the ports in a computer – they are places where a data connection is allowed into or out of a computer.

EXAMPLE: A low-quality firewall can be bypassed by hackers.

firmware: Permanently stored programs inside computers. The firmware is the software that controls the computer's hardware. An example of firmware is Basic Input/Output System (BIOS). It is a combination of the words "firm" (unmoving; solid) and "software." Firmware is also called "embedded software." Embed means to "firmly fix something inside another thing." Firmware is stored in ROM (Read Only Memory – permanent memory, as opposed to RAM).

EXAMPLE: Another example of firmware is in printers. Printers have small computers inside them that control their operation. These computers do not have storage drives that you can install programs on; they come with firmware built in.

first generation: See "generation."

5G: 1. See "G (cell phone)." 2. See "G (wifi)."

flag: A predefined bit or sequence of bits that holds a binary value. Flags are commonly used in a computer program to store settings or to leave a sign for another program.

EXAMPLE: In a system designed to handle various aspects of the font used to display text data, an 8-bit data sequence could be set up like this:

- `0001` (meaning "Text is normal")
- `0010` (meaning "Text is italic")
- `0100` (meaning "Text is bold")
- `1000` (meaning "Text is underlined")

You can see from this that a piece of text could have two or more properties that apply to it:

- `0110` would mean the text is both italic and bold
- `1010` would mean the text is both italic and underlined
- `1100` would mean the text is both bold and underlined

If you associate this data structure with a piece of text, you can check its properties and even change them with binary mathematics. As you can see, in certain programming situations, the ability to understand binary data structures and perform mathematics with that data will be valuable in your career as a technology professional.

F key: Short for "Function key." Many keyboards have several Function keys, and they are usually numbered – that is, one key is the F1 key, the next is the F2 key, and so on. These are used to provide keyboard shortcuts. Shortcuts are not always two keys – a shortcut can also be just one key that you press for quick access to something. It is common for one computer program to make use of the Function keys in a different manner than another program.

EXAMPLE: In a program for writing documents, the F3 key might be used to search a document for a specific word or phrase. In a video game, that same F3 key might be used to pause the game. Occasionally, a keyboard might have a single, non-numbered Function key in addition to the numbered Function keys; this usually operates as a modifier key (a key used in combination with other keys to perform various actions) in the same manner as the Alternate key, which is described next.

flag: See "command-line option."

Flash: A tool (discontinued in 2020) that was used to create web pages that have an interactive aspect. Flash was created by the technology company Adobe. It was discontinued because the things created using Flash are easily used to install harmful instructions on computers. See also "FLV."
EXAMPLE: Popular uses might be a video game or a business tool for maintaining financial records in a table structure.

flash drive: Another word for "USB drive."

flash memory: A type of computer memory that retains data in the absence of a power supply – meaning, it can store data even when power is off.

EXAMPLE: A flashdrive (see "USB drive") utilizes flash memory.

flash video: See "FLV."

Flask: A flask is literally a container for liquids. Flask is a Python web application framework that contains the tools and libraries needed to make building web applications easier. Flask is arguably the most popular web development framework written in Python.

EXAMPLE: Flask was used in the creation of Pinterest and LinkedIn.

(Flask)

Flexbox: Short for "flexible box." It is a tool in CSS that allows for a flexible website layout structure.
EXAMPLE: You can use Flexbox to make websites more responsive.

float: A data type that represents fractional numbers. This could be numbers like `5.3`, `-8.92`, `1024.00`, `3.14159625`, etc. The behavior of this data type includes mathematical operations like addition, subtraction, etc. A float variable would be declared and assigned like this: `float [variable name] = [fractional number]`. See also "floating point."

EXAMPLE: You could have a computer keep track of the width of the crack in a metal shield over a radioactive material using a variable called "`crackWidth`." You could set it to `2.43437` like this: `float crackWidth = 2.43437`

floating point: A specific way of representing large numbers. Instead of writing out the entire number, you can write the first part of it and then a factor to multiply it by – such that performing the multiplication will get you pretty much the same number you would have written out in full. When you do this, you move the decimal point in the number – hence the name "floating point."

EXAMPLE: Take the number three thousand, four hundred and twenty-five. Written normally it would be: `3425`; written in floating point notation, it could be: 3.425×10^3. Since `10` to the `3rd` power is `1000`, this means "`3.425` times `1000`," or `3425`. `10` to the `3rd` power is one thousand – which means: "Take the number `3.425` and multiply it by one thousand." That would, of course, give you `3,425`. This is called floating point because you do not HAVE to have the decimal point in the same place when using floating point representation. For example, you could use this floating point representation for the exact same number above: 34.25 X 10². Or you could use this: 0.3425 X 10⁴. These all resolve to the same amount: 3,425. This method of writing and storing numbers is especially useful when dealing with very large numbers. For example, if you were dealing with this number: 4,275,982,213,844. Storing this number in a computer would take up a lot more memory than storing a smaller number like 3,425. As a trade-off between the magnitude of the number represented, and the accuracy of the number represented, you can use floating point representation. For example, the above large number could be represented as: 4.275982 X 10¹². This would be the same as: 4,275,982,000,000 (the original number was 4,275,982,213,844). You would lose some accuracy, but use much less memory to store the number. There are times when utilizing a floating point is useful; depending on the situation.

floppy disk: The hard disk drive is differentiated from a similar type of storage device called a *floppy disk.* In a floppy disk, there is only one disk, and it is made of a flexible magnetic material. These floppy disks were popular in the past and were used for portable data storage. A floppy disk was contained in a hard plastic case. In order to be used by a computer, that computer must have a special component installed that can hold the floppy disk. This component is called a floppy disk drive. Once the floppy disk is inserted into the drive, the drive can spin the disk as needed in order for the computer to retrieve or add information to the disk.

Note the difference here: a hard drive contains a disk as well as the motor and arm used to rotate the disk and read or write to the disk. A floppy disk, on the other hand, only contained the storage disk; the floppy drive installed on the computer contained the motor and arm needed. Floppy disks are nearly obsolete. There are newer portable storage technologies that can hold much larger amounts of information and that can operate at much higher rates of data transfer. Years ago, if you were to purchase a computer game, it might come on several floppy disks. In order to install the game on your computer, you would have to put the disks into the drive, one after the other, until all the program information was loaded into the computer. The floppy disk was developed at IBM by a man named Alan Shugart in 1967. As you can see, IBM has been involved in many major computer developments.

EXAMPLE: Computers used to have a floppy disk drive, usually called the F drive. These drives were used to read, store and delete data on floppy disks. In the image below, the floppy disk is beneath the floppy disk drive:

(floppy disk)

floppy drive: See "floppy disk."

flow: The movement of something at a certain rate, from one point to another. In computer science, when discussing the flow of something, it is referring to the sequence in which computer instructions are executed. Every computer program is different in some form, and certain instructions can change the flow of execution of instructions from start to end. Simply put, flow is the path the computer's instruction execution follows as a computer program is run.

EXAMPLE: Opening a new message, typing the message, entering in the address it is being sent to and clicking send could be considered the flow of sending an email.

flowchart: A diagram that shows how to achieve a solution to a problem. Typically, a flowchart is created at the beginning of a project. They are a means of breaking down problems bit by bit in order to facilitate understanding of a problem or a complicated task. Very often, a flowchart helps to convey ideas to others in a way that is easy to understand. Just as an architect will create a blueprint for a project, a programmer should also create a blueprint before starting his or her project. Here are some common symbols used in flowcharts:

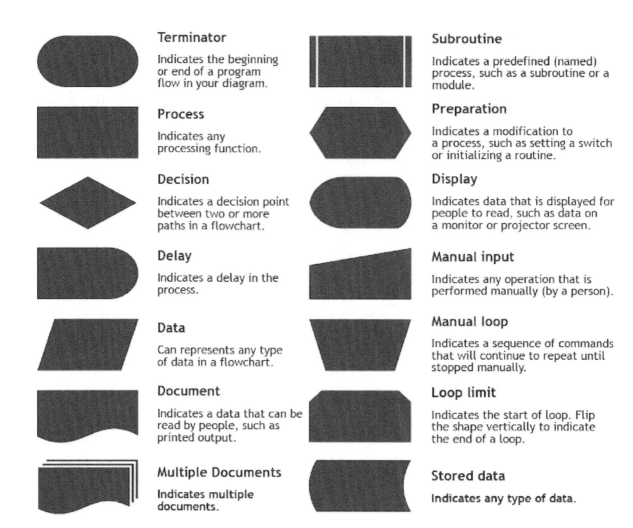

Terminator

Indicates the beginning or end of a program flow in your diagram.

Process

Indicates any processing function.

Decision

Indicates a decision point between two or more paths in a flowchart.

Delay

Indicates a delay in the process.

Data

Can represents any type of data in a flowchart.

Document

Indicates a data that can be read by people, such as printed output.

Multiple Documents

Indicates multiple documents.

Subroutine

Indicates a predefined (named) process, such as a subroutine or a module.

Preparation

Indicates a modification to a process, such as setting a switch or initializing a routine.

Display

Indicates data that is displayed for people to read, such as data on a monitor or projector screen.

Manual input

Indicates any operation that is performed manually (by a person).

Manual loop

Indicates a sequence of commands that will continue to repeat until stopped manually.

Loop limit

Indicates the start of loop. Flip the shape vertically to indicate the end of a loop.

Stored data

Indicates any type of data.

EXAMPLE: Here is an example flowchart:

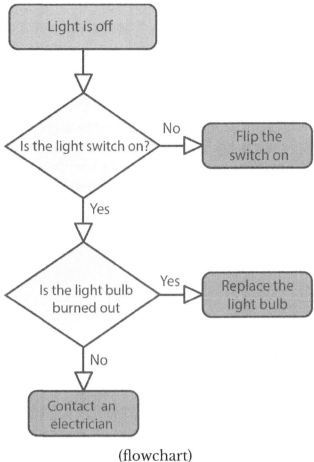

(flowchart)

fluid design: See "liquid design."

FLV: Stands for "flash video." A type of video that you can save and/or play on your computer. Flash videos are very common and are an exact format to store, transfer, and display videos on a computer. This technology is nearly obsolete; it was popular in the early 2000s, but has fallen out of use.

EXAMPLE: If you save a video of a horse race on your computer, it could be saved as "horserace.flv" – which means it is a flash video.

focus: The thing on a computer display where the attention of the computer program is currently placed.

EXAMPLE: If you have a collection of documents displayed on the screen, and the computer program is set up so you can select which document you want to do some action to, that document has the computer's "focus" – that is, the next action you take will usually affect that document.

folder: Data on computers are usually organized in files and folders. Files are collections of data stored on a computer. The data in a file is organized in a specific manner, usually based on how that data is going to be used by the computer. Files each have their own name and contain their own data. They often have a related thing, which is a folder. Folders are a way of organizing files on a computer. They are a sort of "container" where one or more files are stored and are usually given a descriptive name. Folders are also called "directories."

EXAMPLE: Let's say you want to write Christmas greetings to all of your relatives. You could save your letter to your grandma as "Grandma," within a folder called "Christmas Greetings." Other letters to relatives could be stored there as well, such as "Aunt Karla," "Father," etc. In the image below, the folder is on the left and file is on the right:

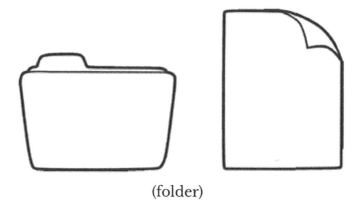

(folder)

F1 score: A measure of test accuracy. It uses precision and recall to find the score. F1 score is also simply called an *F-score*.

EXAMPLE: Let's take a precision value of 88% and a recall value of 40% as follows:

$$F1 = 2 \times \frac{Precision * Recall}{Precision + Recall} \qquad Precision = 0.88$$
$$Recall = 0.40$$

| Precision * Recall
0.88 * 0.40 = 0.352 | $\frac{Precision * Recall}{Precision + Recall}$ | F1 = 2 x 0.275 |
| Precision + Recall
0.88 + 0.40 = 1.28 | 0.352 / 1.28 = 0.275 | 2 * 0.275 = 0.55

F1 = 0.55 |

(F1 score)

font: A style used in displaying and printing text. As you're familiar with, there are many different types of fonts. The word font comes from the Latin word *fundere* which means "to pour." This refers to the idea of casting letters – i.e., pouring molten (liquified by heat) metal into a mold.

This sentence is written in Calibri font.

This sentence is written in Arial font.

This sentence is written in Times New Roman font.

EXAMPLE: Font refers to the weight (how thick the text is), width (how wide the letters are) and style of characters. Technically speaking, any variance in the styling of characters indicates different fonts – e.g., italicized Times New Roman is a different font than bolded Times New Roman.

font family: A set of fonts with a common design. For example, here is the Times New Roman font family:

Times New Roman
Times New Roman Italic
Times New Roman Bold
Times New Roman Bold Italic

Whereas each one of these is a font, the whole group of the related fonts is the font family. Another word for font family is "typeface." And so, a typeface is the overall design of lettering.

EXAMPLE: Here is the Calibri typeface:

Calibri

ABCDabcd - Regular
ABCDabcd - Bold
ABCDabcd - Italic
ABCDabcd - Bold Italic
(font family)

footer: Text that appears at the foot (bottom) of each page in a book or document. A footer typically contains: authorship information, terms and conditions, copyright information, contact information and links to a company's social media accounts. The bottom of most websites is the footer. It is an important part of a webpage because it is usually used to give the user information needed to contact the primary owner or manager of the website.

EXAMPLE: Here is what the footer on The Tech Academy's website could look like:

```
© Prosper Consulting Inc.
The Tech Academy
Phone: (503) 206-6915
Email: info@learncodinganywhere.com
Login
Contact
```

foreign key: A column in one table that holds the data from a primary key in another, related table. This is how the relationships between different tables are established.

EXAMPLE: The following diagram shows the relationship between a primary key and foreign key on two separate tables:

Customer

FirstName	LastName	CustID
Elaine	Stevens	101
Mary	Dittman	102
Skip	Stevenson	103
Drew	Lakeman	104
Eva	Plummer	105

Primary Key

Contact

CustID	ContactInformation	ContactType
101	555-2653	Work
101	555-0057	Cell
102	555-8816	Work
104	555-0949	Work
103	555-0650	Work
101	555-8855	Home
105	Plummer@akcomms.com	Email
101	Stevens@akcomms.com	Email
101	555-5787	Fax
103	Stevenson@akcomms.com	Email
105	555-5675	Work
102	Dittman@akcomms.com	Email

Foreign Key

(foreign key)

for loop: A type of loop used to repeat a section of code a number of times. For loops are used when the number of iterations (repetitions of a section of code) are known. See also "loop."

EXAMPLE: Take a look at this statement:
`For each student in the class (25), provide a grade.`
The for loop repeatedly executes instructions as long as a particular condition is true.

form: A visual representation of a document that prompts a user to fill out information.

EXAMPLE: The following image displays a very basic form:

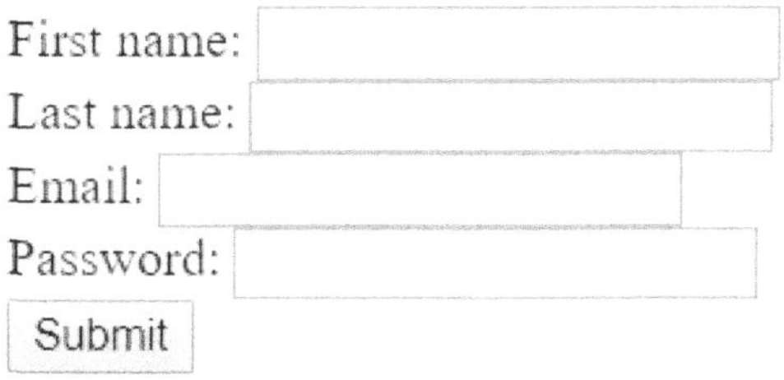

First name:	
Last name:	
Email:	
Password:	

Submit

(form)

format: The way that something is laid out, designed, and put together. In computers, format can mean two things:

1. The type of data you're dealing with. Information can be created and saved in different formats. Format is not the data itself; it's information ABOUT the data – how it's arranged, what the computer can do with it, etc.

EXAMPLE: If you have a file called "SoupRecipe" that is a written document, you might have "txt" added to the name. This would be written "SoupRecipe.txt." Here, "SoupRecipe" is the name of the file, and "txt" is an extension (information that tells what type of information is contained in a file – the extension usually goes after the name of the file) that tells you the data in the file is formatted as text.

2. Formatting means preparing a computer's memory device (a place where data can be stored) for use by erasing all the information on it and dividing it up into sections for the information to go when it is eventually used as a storage device.

EXAMPLE: If you format a hard drive (the main place on a computer where permanently stored data is kept), you erase everything on it before you save anything new on it.

forum: See "online discussion forum."

forward slash: See "slash."

4G: See "G (cell phone)."

4K: See "resolution, levels of."

FORTRAN: Two extremely popular programming languages that existed in the 1950s and 1960s were *FORTRAN* (FORmula TRANslation) and *COBOL* (COmmon Business Oriented Language). FORTRAN was invented by IBM (International Business Machines) in 1954. It was mainly developed for scientific use. FORTRAN can perform complex calculations and solve math, physics and engineering problems. For example, it has been used to predict weather based on various numeric equations (math problems). COBOL was designed by Grace Hopper (a famous American female programmer that contributed greatly to the field of computer science) and a team in 1959 as part of an effort to create one programming language that could work on several different types of computers. Up until that point, each manufacturer of computers often had designed their own programming language for their computers. COBOL was quite popular, and is still in use in certain industries today. For example, it is used in the financial analysis area of business. COBOL and FORTRAN sped up coding and made it accessible to more people.

EXAMPLE: With COBOL and FORTRAN, programmers could instruct the computer to perform a basic equation by inputting something like this: 5 + 5 and the computer would calculate 10. This is opposed to having to write a series of binary instructions like this in machine language: 0010 0001 0000 0100 0001 0001 0000 0101 0011 0001 0000 0110 0111 0000 0000 0001 0000 0000 0000 0101 0000 0000 0000 0101 0000 0000 0000 0000.

fourth generation: See "generation."

fragmentation: The breaking up of files on your computer into multiple storage locations. During the normal operation of a computer, as it is asked to store electronic files on the hard drive, it may have to break up the file and store it in two or more physical locations on the drive, simply because no one physical area on the device contains enough available storage space for the entire file to be recorded as one set of information. While this does not prevent the file from being used, it does mean that computer operations on that file take longer, as the computer has to manage the multiple locations of the file's information. See also "defragmentation."

EXAMPLE: Fragmentation can slow down how fast your computer operates because it has to dig around to find things since the pieces are spread out over a wide distance.

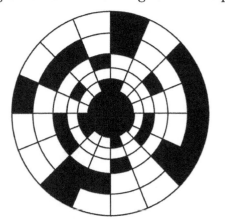
Fragmented Files

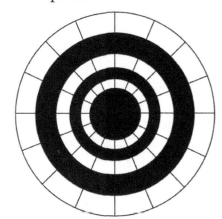
Defragmented Files

(fragmentation)

framework: A pre-made set of computer code that can be used in creating programs, along with documentation on how to use that code.

EXAMPLE: Microsoft offers a framework called the .NET Framework. It is a popular tool for creating business programs and other types of computer programs.

Usage note for framework and library:
The terms library and framework are often used interchangeably. They are similar, but not identical. Let's examine those differences and similarities. A library is a collection of pre-made resources used to create computer programs. Most often, these take the form of a package of code with built-in functions that all relate to a specific area. They are usually used by adding them to a software project already being created, and then having code in that project make use of the various functions in the library. A framework is similar in nature to a library, in that it is made up of pre-made resources, which are usually computer code. The framework is usually a fully-functioning system that provides a complete set of generic functionality as is, and it can be modified by the programmer to fit their needs. Examples: A library might exist for performing complex calculations that are common in scientific research. A programmer, wishing to create a program for scientific researchers, might add this library to the program they are creating. The action of adding the library would not modify how the program ran; rather, the programmer would have to modify their program to call certain functions now available from that library before their program would have modified behavior. On the other hand, we could look at a framework for creation of web applications. This framework would actually provide generic functionality from the moment the programmer installed it – in fact, the framework would likely be the web application in its initial form. The programmer would add to and modify the code in the framework to meet the specific requirements of the final application. In this way, a framework is a reusable "starting point" for a programmer to create programs with greater complexity. The difference could be summarized this way: a library is code that can be called by another, primary program. A framework is itself a working program that can call other code.

frequency: 1. A wave is a flow of energy that has a low point and a high point. Energy moves through space in waves. The space between one point in a wave and the next exact same point in the wave is called a wavelength.

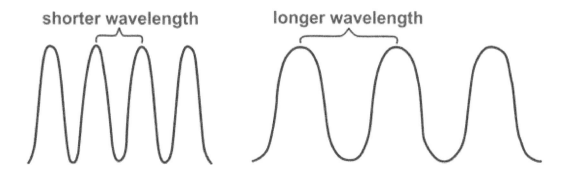

Frequency is how many wavelengths occur within a specified amount of time – the higher the frequency, the more wavelengths; the lower the frequency, the fewer the wavelengths. You can see this here:

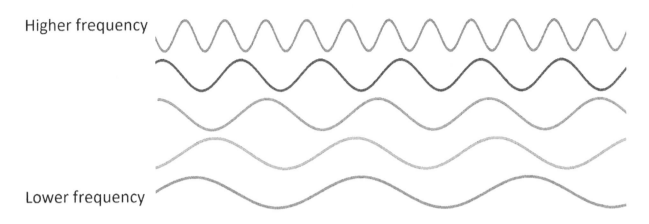

EXAMPLE: AM radio waves are sent using a medium level of frequency, whereas FM radio waves are sent at a very high frequency.

2. The number of occurrences of a repeating event per unit of time – how often or how little something is observed.

EXAMPLE: Consider the following list of ages: 24, 23, 30, 45, 41, 24 and 23. How many times did you see the age 23? It appeared twice, and so did 24. But some of the other numbers only appear once each. In this example, the frequency of age 30 is one.

front end: See "back end."

F-score: See "F1 score."

F#: A popular functional programming language.

EXAMPLE: F# was one of the programming languages used to create Microsoft Office.

FTP: Stands for "File Transfer Protocol." A protocol is a set of rules governing the exchange of data between devices. FTP is the standard protocol used to transfer files from one computer to another computer, using the Internet. It is mainly used for the transfer of information (in the form of files) from one computer to another over the Internet.

EXAMPLE: If you were maintaining a website, you might be creating some of the electronic files that make up the website on a computer at your office, but you'd need to send those files to the web server. You could send those files from your computer to the web server using an FTP client program. That program would copy the files, format them to conform to the File Transfer Protocol, and then send them to the web server. The web server, itself equipped with FTP client software, would receive the files and store them in its memory storage.

full adder: See "adder."

FULL OUTER JOIN: See "join."

full stack: A stack is a set of software systems that requires no other support and can operate on its own. Full stack refers to people trained in all the components of a stack, which include:
- An operating system (the main program on a computer that oversees and manages all other programs),
- A web server program (software used on a computer that is used as the source of data and/or services by one or more other computers [called a server]),
- A database management system (software used to operate the database; it is not the database itself), and
- A programming language (an organized system of words, phrases and symbols that let you create programs).

EXAMPLE: A full-stack developer can create virtually any type of software.

function: 1. Work performed by something. A function is an action taken to get something done. In computers, a function is a command put into a computer that makes the computer complete an exact task or series of tasks. A computer function is a procedure the computer performs. There are thousands of functions entered in your computer behind the scenes that instruct your computer how to operate. This also refers to the various actions available in a computer program – for example, in a word processing program, you might talk about the "print" function; this is the action available to the user to print the document they have created.

EXAMPLE: When you erase a file on a computer, the file is removed by a delete function.

2. A function is a block of organized, reusable computer instructions that is used to perform a specific action or set of actions. Please see the usage note below.

EXAMPLE: You can often find pre-made functions that can be copied and pasted for use in your own computer programs. This helps prevent "reinventing the wheel" by eliminating the need to create functions for commonly-used actions.

Usage note for function, method, routine, subroutine, subprogram, callback and procedure:
There is a set of terms that can be confusing in learning computer programming. These terms all relate to a fundamental element of all computer programs:

subprograms. A subprogram in the most basic sense is this: a set of computer instructions, separate from the main program, that can be executed on demand by the main program. Subprograms were an early development in computer programming, and their creation was driven by one basic factor: Programmers quickly found that they were often having a program do certain exact things many times as the program was being executed. This meant that the exact same set of programming instructions had to be entered in the computer program every time that thing was needed. This activity had two fundamental weaknesses. First, the process of typing the same exact instructions over and over again was time-consuming and error-prone for programmers. Second, if a programmer wanted to make a change to how that thing was done, they had to find every place in the program where they had entered the duplicate instructions and make the change in every one. In other words, these commonly-used chunks of computer code were hard to create and maintain. The answer to this problem was a subprogram. Here, the programmers would type in the set of instructions that performed the needed action, and give that set of instructions a unique name. This set of instructions was called a subprogram, and was not considered part of the main program that the computer was going to execute. Instead, the main program was modified so that it would just execute that subprogram whenever that particular action was needed. This is indeed a basic concept. In the early years of computer programming languages, where programmers worked with various low-level languages barely a step removed from machine language, the actual implementation of the concept stayed quite simple and very much as described above. However, as higher-level programming languages were developed, this concept began to develop variations and nuances. The central concept of pre-made sets of code that can be used as needed has remained, but the designers of the various languages have often implemented the concept in different ways, depending on the design objectives of the language. Because of this, you will find many related terms in this area. Some of the terms in use are:

- Functions
- Methods
- Routines
- Subroutines
- Subprograms
- Callback
- Procedures

If you try to clear up the definitions of these various terms, you can quickly become confused. Some sources will tell you that they are all basically the same thing. Other sources will articulate specific differences and similarities between two or more of the terms. It can be difficult to nail down. This is because of a few factors. First, some programming languages use the same term to mean slightly different things. Second, some programming languages are designed to implement this concept in two related ways, so the language designers needed two different terms. What this means in terms of your study of various computer programming languages is that you'll often have to research what a specific term means in that language, ignoring source data that's related to other languages. This concept is best illustrated through an example. We'll use the popular programming language JavaScript to do this. JavaScript uses two related terms: function and method. They are very similar, in that they both involve the creation of a pre-made set of instructions that can be made use of by other program elements. They do have some subtle but important differences, however. Let's explore them. First, some basic definitions – and remember, these definitions are for the use of these terms in JavaScript. We'll start with the definition for the term "object," as a clear understanding of this is needed in order to understand the other two terms. In JavaScript, an object is a type of data that represents a thing through its various properties (characteristics – what it looks like) and behavior (what it can do). An example of an object would be a "vehicle." Thinking of this common real-world thing as an "object" that will be stored in computer memory and kept track of as a program is executed, we can think of various properties and behavior for it. Under properties, we could have things like "chassis type," "engine type," "number of doors," "speed," etc. Under behavior, we could have things like "accelerate," "deccelerate," "turn right," "turn left," etc. An example of creating an object in JavaScript might look like this:

```
ar student = {
firstName: "Jane",
lastName: "Smith",
age: 28,
gradeAverage: 3.5
};
```

In this example, we have only specified properties for the "student" object, and not specified any behavior. We will look at that in a moment. So let's look at how this applies to methods and functions in JavaScript. Function: In JavaScript, this is simply a block of code designed to perform a particular task. This block of code gets executed when another piece of code calls it. An example could look like this:

```
function add(num1, num2) {
      return num1 + num2;
}
```

Other JavaScript code elements could call this "add" function by specifying its name and passing it two numbers. That could look like this:

```
var sum = add(5, 7);
```

Here, the code would create the variable called "sum," call the function "add" and pass it the two numbers 5 and 7, and take the result (12) and assign that value to the variable "sum." Method: In JavaScript, a method is a set of code associated with an object that is designed to change the state of that object when it executes. In other words, the method is performed on the object. You create these methods when you create the object. Let's look at how we might do that with our previous example of a "student" object:

```
var student = {
firstName: "Jane",
lastName: "Smith",
age: 28,
gradeAverage: function(avg) {
```

```
        return avg;
    }
};
```
Here, we are not setting the property "gradeAverage" to a fixed number of 3.5. Instead, we are setting that property to the value returned by a set of code. Specifically, that code will take in a number (the variable "avg") and set the value of the "gradeAverage" property to the value of that variable. Executing that code could look like this:
```
student.gradeAverage(3.4);
```
Here, we are telling the computer to make use of the object called "student." Specifically, the computer is to run the function "gradeAverage" that is defined in the "student" object. Since that function needs an input (the variable "avg"), we give it the number 3.4. So here's the distinction: In this specific situation, that function "gradeAverage" is called a method. Yes, it is confusing – until you recall that in JavaScript, a method is a set of code, associated with an object, that is performed on the object itself. So we have the confusing situation of a property of an object that we are defining using a function – but we're calling the action performed by the function a method. In actual practice, there is very little danger in using these terms interchangeably – and you'll often find technical sources will do so. But occasionally you'll find a source that uses the terms in their strictest sense. The lessons here are these: First, there are many varied terms in use for the concept of "a block of code that can be executed on demand by other code." Second, in order to clarify any potential difference between these various terms, you'll need to investigate their exact meaning in the language you're concerned with. Any attempt to give them a blanket, universal meaning ignores the subtleties described here.

function key: See "F key."

functional programming: A programming paradigm that uses what are called "pure" functions. A function is just a mathematical operation. It might take in some data to use, and it might give back some data to whatever computer instruction directed that it be used. Not all functions behave the same way. Specifically, when you give a function the exact same data as you've given it before, it may or may not give you the same result. This is because sometimes, functions can check the current condition ("state") of a piece of data, and use that data in its operation, therefore (potentially) giving back a different response each time it is used. This is not a "pure" function, as the function's results can differ based on the state of data that the program is keeping track of. A "pure" function, on the other hand, will always give you the same result when given identical data.

EXAMPLE: Functional programming languages make use of these "pure" functions. This changes how the program has to work with data that changes state, but it results in a program that is often easier to understand and modify than it might otherwise be.

G

g, G: Stands for "giga," which means billion. See also "byte."

EXAMPLE: 2GB is about two billion bytes.

G (cell phone): "G" stands for "generation." "Generation" means "a level or stage of development of a cell phone or device." Here is each generation defined:

- 1G: This refers to cell phones that could only make phone calls.
- 2G: Cell phones that had other functionalities on top of being able to make calls, such as text messaging.
- 3G: A major advance in cell phones and devices that allowed internet usage. This is when smartphones came out. 3G devices can email, browse the web, download videos, send pictures, etc. 3G devices transmit data at speeds up to around 10 Mbps (10,485,760 bits transferred each second – see "byte").
- 4G: This refers to devices that can do all that 3G devices can do, but that are able to transmit data at a rate of up to 150 Mbps.
- 5G: Devices that can do all that 4G devices can, with speeds that sit around 20 Gbps.

As a note on this: just because a device is 4G does not mean it operates at that speed because it needs an internet connection that allows for that level of speed. It does not matter how fast your phone can operate in accessing the internet if the connection to the internet is slow. Your mobile devices can connect to the internet in two main ways: 1. Using wifi, 2. Via a cell tower (also referred to as a "cellular network"). When you use a cell tower to connect to the internet, this is referred to as a "data connection" or using your phone's data plan (a cell phone coverage plan that allows a certain amount of internet usage, in terms of total transmitted data). A data connection is not wifi. Wifi connects you to the internet via a router. Again, a data connection occurs via cell towers. Cell towers also have the same generations as cell phones. Meaning, a 2G cell tower only allows calls and texts (no internet access), whereas a 4G cell tower allows up to 150 Mbps internet connection. Your data speed and mobile device capabilities are determined by: the generation of your mobile device and the generation of the nearest cell tower. Your connection is as fast as the lowest generation out of the mobile device and cell tower – meaning, you are limited by whichever is slowest. If you have a 4G smartphone, but are connected to a 3G internet connection, you will be connected to the internet at 3G speeds. No matter how good your device is, if you are out in a rural area with a 2G network, you won't be able to access the internet via your device without wifi, since 2G equipment does not access the internet! As a note of interest, when 4G first came out, cell phone networks weren't all set up to accommodate. That has since been fixed. "LTE" stands for "Long Term Evolution". You sometimes see this on your phone – for example: 4G LTE. This is actually a step between 3G and 4G – it is faster than 3G and slower than 4G. Simply put: the higher the generation, the faster the speeds. But keep in mind that the speed of your device is limited by the generation of the network and the generation of the device.

EXAMPLE: A 4G device will operate at 4G speeds, even if connected to a 5G network.

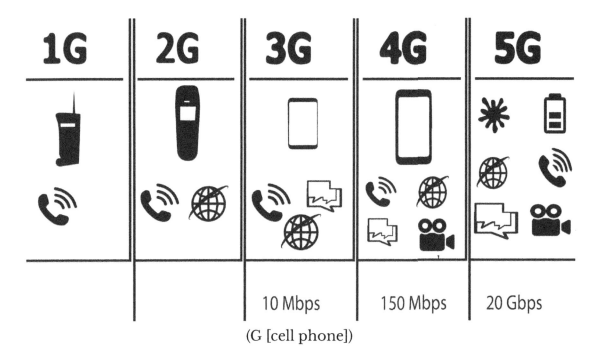

10 Mbps   150 Mbps   20 Gbps

(G [cell phone])

G (wifi): The G that follows numbers in wifi networks (such as "5G") is short for GHz (GigaHertz – which is a wave [a flow of energy which changes over time; it has low points and high points] containing a billion frequency [the rate of vibration of a wave] cycles per second – see "hertz" for more information). Frequencies have various bands, which are different ranges of frequencies:

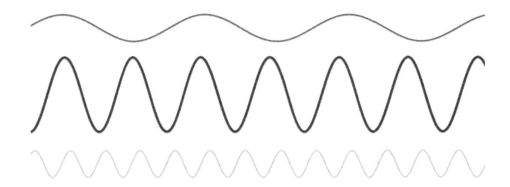

Wifi equipment passes digital information back and forth between the various computers and devices on a network. To do this, it is sending and receiving beams of energy. These beams are vibrating at a certain frequency, and they contain the actual information being sent back and forth. Most wifi equipment sends and receives signals that are either 2.4GHz in frequency or 5 GHz in frequency. Here are the primary differences between the two:

1. 2.4G wifi can support up to 450-600 Mbps (see "mbps") in data transfer speeds.
2. 5G wifi can support up to 1,300 Mbps.

3. 5G has a shorter range than 2G wifi, and the signal has more difficulty passing through solid objects (like floors or walls). So, if you're close to the wifi router (a machine that sends data between two or more computers), 5G is the better choice. If you're further from the router, such as in a bedroom, 2.4G is a stronger/faster internet (the largest and most-used computer network [connection that allows data transfer between machines] in the world, which is mainly utilized to access the World Wide Web) connection.

EXAMPLE: Most routers offer both the 2.4G and 5G connection.

gadget: A small machine or electronic device or tool.

EXAMPLE: A cell phone is a gadget.

gap analysis: See "business case."

garbage collection: A form of automatic memory management that occurs while a software program is running. The purpose is to reclaim areas of the computer's memory that are no longer needed by the program, so that memory is not tied up unnecessarily.

EXAMPLE: If you are using a computer program to manage students at a school. While viewing and modifying the data about a particular student, the program will store that student's data in memory so it is available to the program. Once you are done modifying the data about the student, and that data is stored on the hard drive of the computer (permanent storage device), the memory used to hold that data can be erased and used for other purposes.

gate: See "logic gate."

Gaussian blur: Also called Gaussian smoothing, this is an effect named after the French mathematician Carl Friedrich Gauss.

EXAMPLE: Gaussian blur creates an effect like this (left side is the original picture and right is with the effect):

(Gaussian blur)

Gb: See "byte."

GB: See "byte."

Gbps: See "byte."

GBps: See "byte."

generation: It is generally accepted that there are six generations of computers. A "generation" refers to the technology utilized by a computer to operate – particularly the hardware and software.

1. 1940-1956, First Generation: The first generation refers to computers that used vacuum tubes (tubes with all air removed) for their circuitry (electric circuits) and magnetic drums (memory stored on large metal cylinders that can be read and written on). These computers were enormous and took up entire rooms. They were also extremely expensive to operate. Programmers working on first generation computers used machine language (code written in as direct 1s and 0s) which was typically input with punched cards and tape.

2. 1956-1963, Second Generation: Computers utilized transistors instead of vacuum tubes. Even though transistors were invented before 1956, they weren't widely used until the late 1950s. Transistors were more efficient and cheaper to operate than vacuum tubes. Programmers working on second generation computers began utilizing assembly language (a language that replaced the numbers used in machine

language with easily-remembered English words and phrases that people can understand). The second generation moved away from drum memory to magnetic core memory (wires run around a magnetic ring used to store data).

3. 1964-1971, Third Generation: Computers started utilizing silicon chips (semiconductors – inexpensive material that through a small application of electricity can turn "on" and "off"). This led to a major increase in speed and reduction of cost. The third generation also saw the arrival of using keyboards and monitors as interfaces, and started to move away from punch cards and printouts. Computers in this generation were smaller and cheaper than their predecessors, and could run multiple programs at once.

4. 1972-2010: Fourth Generation: The microprocessor arrives, allowing CPU, memory, input/output (I/O) controls (the component that controls peripheral devices, like the keyboard) and other components to exist on one chip. This further reduced the size of computers and increased their speed. You could now have the abilities of a computer that in the past would have filled an entire room, but in a device so small you could hold it in your hands. At the beginning of the fourth generation, chips contained thousands of integrated circuits (circuits formed by tiny semiconductors made of silicon). The fourth generation saw the arrival of the GUI (Graphical User Interface), mice, consoles (electronic devices for playing video games), laptops and hand-held devices.

5. 2010 forward: Fifth Generation: This is the generation of artificial intelligence. AI (such as facial or voice recognition) exists in many modern computers.

EXAMPLE: While there is no sixth generation yet, quantum computers and nanocomputers could fit in that category.

generics: In normal English, *generic* means "characteristic of or connected to a class or group of things; not specific." Generic programming is an approach to software development where algorithms are written without specifying the data type (a specific category of information handled by a computer – such as numbers or comparisons) – instead, this is left open as "to be specified later." Such algorithms are instantiated (prepared for use) when needed for specific types provided as parameters. In coding, generics enables types (such as classes and interfaces) to be used as parameters when defining classes, methods and interfaces. These parameters provide programmers with a way to reuse the same code with different inputs and data types. Generics refers to reusable components – being able to create a component that can work over a variety of types rather than a single one.

EXAMPLE: Generic programming allows programmers to write a general algorithm which will work with all data types and eliminates the need to create different algorithms for each data type.

Gestalt principle: *Gestalt* is a German word meaning "form" or "shape." The *gestalt principle* is a design concept that embraces *similarity, proximity, symmetry* and *continuation.*

EXAMPLE: Here is the gestalt principle visualized:

Good Figure

Objects when grouped together are normally perceived as a single figure. Tendency to simplify.

Proximity

Objects that are near each other tend to be grouped together.

Similarity

When objects are similar they tend to be grouped together.

Continuation

When objects intersect one another they are normally perceived as being a single uninterrupted object.

Closure

Objects that appear to connect between different sets of elements but do not actually touch each other.

Symmetry

When the objects are perceived as symmetrical meaning both sides are equal in shape and size.

(Gestalt principle)

GHz: See "hertz."

GIF: Stands for "Graphic Interchange Format." GIFs are 8-bit images (each pixel takes up a byte of memory and only 256 colors are available). Compared with other modern image formats, GIFs are relatively low quality. As you've probably seen, GIFs are mostly used to show animations – low resolution "movies." These GIFs are actually a series of images displayed as a sort of "flip book."

EXAMPLE: There are actually varying opinions on how to pronounce "GIF" – some say "jiff" and some say "giff." In fact, in 2013, the creator of GIFs (Steve Wilhite) stated this, "It's pronounced JIF, not GIF." Most of us here at The Tech Academy go with the "g" pronunciation – considering the first word in GIF is "Graphic."

gigabit: See "byte."

gigabyte: See "byte."

gigahertz: See "hertz."

Git: A specific example of version control. It is a popular version control system. You can use Git to manage the versions of your computer programs and work on programs in conjunction with other developers. Git is itself a computer program. A computer programmer can install the Git program on their computers, and then use that program while creating software and websites.

EXAMPLE: Git is free software, and is used by millions of computer programmers around the world.

(Git)

GitHub: A popular web site owned by Microsoft. It can be used to store source code, accomplish version control on that source code, track defects in that source code and manage work tasks for the computer programmers working on that source code.

EXAMPLE: GitHub is the largest host of source code in the world.

(GitHub)

glitch: An error or mistake in a computer. Many things can cause glitches, including mistakes in code or manufacturing, or even external issues such as heat or magnetism.

EXAMPLE: Some video games have glitches that players can use to their advantage.

global scope: See "scope."

glyph: A picture that represents a word or concept (pronounced "glif"). For example, Egyptian hieroglyphics are glyphs.

EXAMPLE: Here are some example glyphs and their corresponding keyboard keys:

(glyph)

goodness of fit: Goodness of fit is a type of statistical hypothesis test to see how well the observed data fits the expected data. In other words, it asks the question, "Are there any discrepancies between the two?" Goodness of fit tells you if the statistical distribution of a sample accurately represents the population distribution.

EXAMPLE: It is assumed by a store manager that the day of the week will determine how busy he is with customers. Monday and Tuesday are considered the busiest days while Wednesday, Thursday, and Friday are moderately busy. Saturday and Sunday are the slowest two days of the week. So, the store manager staffs and stocks the store according to those days. Then, the store manager observes that he is losing business due to being out of stock of items and store associates not available to help customers when needed. So, he calculates the actual volume of customers that come into the store each day to see if his assumption (or expectation) of which days are the busiest or slowest is correct. He can then compare his findings to his expected values and what he observes. He finds that (actually) Friday, Saturday, and Sunday were his busiest days, but because he only restocks Sunday nights, the store is out of stock on most items when his busiest days arrive and he has much fewer staff available. Based on his findings, he changes how many staff work each day and when to order more stock.

Google: The most used website of all time. Google is used mainly to assist people with searching for things on the Internet (the largest and most-used computer network [connection that allows data transfer between machines] in the world, which is mainly utilized to access the World Wide Web). Google offers many other services, as well, and makes the majority of its profits from advertising. It was founded in 1998 and is based in California.

EXAMPLE: If you want to search for something on the Internet, people commonly refer to that as "Googling."

Gothic: See "sans."

gov (suffix): A suffix added to websites that only U.S. government entities are allowed to use.

EXAMPLE: The website for the State of Texas is texas.gov.

GPS: Stands for "Global Positioning System." This is a satellite-based system which (as long as some of the satellites can reach your device) can tell you exactly where you are in the world. It can also tell time and weather conditions, but it is mainly used for navigation purposes. The position and number of the satellites in orbit around the planet are such that they are effective over the entire surface of Earth; the only things that would make it so GPS would not be usable are, one (the device you have is not built to use GPS; and two) your device is physically obstructed from contact with the satellites in some way.

EXAMPLE: Most cell phones have GPS built in.

graceful degradation: The act of designing a computer so that a failure in a certain section or part, does not cause a complete breakdown of the computer. In graceful degradation, if one program does not operate, the computer will continue to operate at a reduced capacity.

EXAMPLE: If you had a computer program used for managing orders at a manufacturing plant, and the part of the program that allows you to print forms malfunctioned but you could still fill out the forms and store them for later use, that would be graceful degradation. The opposite of that would be if the failure of the printing section of the program caused the entire program to stop working.

graphic design: Graphics are art created on a computer by a person. Graphic design is a profession where people create graphics. Graphic design specializes in combining text, pictures and videos using a computer, especially as it relates to advertising, magazines and books.

EXAMPLE: Movie posters for upcoming releases are created by people trained in graphic design.

graphical user interface: See "GUI."

graphics: Images displayed on a computer, both still (pictures) or moving (videos). Graphics are visual content; they can be created by a person or by a device like a camera.

EXAMPLE: If you say a game has amazing graphics, you are saying the pictures and videos in the game look amazing.

grayscale: The range of shades of gray from white to black.

EXAMPLE: The following image displays several shades of a grayscale.

(grayscale)

grid: A framework consisting of spaced bars that cross each other and/or parallel (run even to) each other – like this:

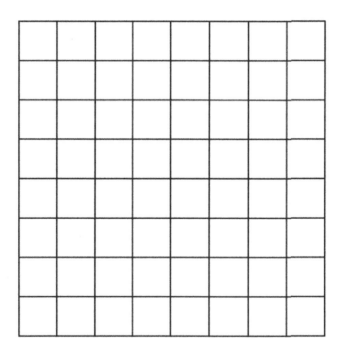

In design, a grid is a structure composed of intersecting (crossing) straight or curved lines used to arrange content.

EXAMPLE: The following image is an example of some grid website layouts:

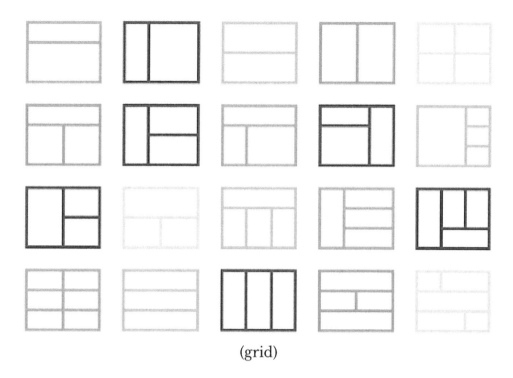

(grid)

grotesque typeface: See "sans."

GUI: Stands for Graphical User Interface (pronounced "gooey"). Graphical means having to do with images created on a computer screen. And an interface is a common point or boundary between two things. In the computer world, an interface is a device or program that enables a user to communicate with a computer. A "user interface" is the elements on a computer display that a user utilizes to interact with a computer program. It is where they type things in and click with the mouse, for example. This is where interaction between a machine and a user occurs. A user interface is important because a computer program usually needs some sort of user interaction in order to perform its function. When computers were first being developed, the interface between user and computer was entirely text-based – all input and output was done through typing. To access a file or program on the computer, the user would enter instructions, in text, that found that file or program and then opened or started the program. This was a challenging interface to use, as the user had to create a picture in his head of the arrangement of files and programs on the computer. The development of a graphical user interface was a major event in the history of computers. A Graphical User Interface is a representation of the various objects in a computer – files, programs, etc. – in a graphical form. That is, it presents the user with pictures and diagrams that communicate the things on the computer, and their arrangement. The pictures are not the things themselves; they are a graphical representation of the things. It is much easier for a new user to move a file from one location to another by dragging the picture of a file with the mouse than by having to remember and type complicated commands to accomplish the same task. GUIs have been used for decades now and are what you are familiar with.

EXAMPLE: If you have an image of a folder on your computer, and an image of files inside that folder, that is actually a graphical representation of how those files are stored in the memory of your computer. When someone refers to a graphical interface, they are referring to a GUI.

Guido van Rossum: See "Python."

Gutenberg diagram: Johannes Gensfleisch zur Laden zum Gutenberg was a German inventor who introduced printing to Europe with the printing press. The Gutenberg diagram refers to the natural direction that a user's eyes move through when viewing evenly-distributed information.

EXAMPLE: You can see the Gutenberg diagram below:

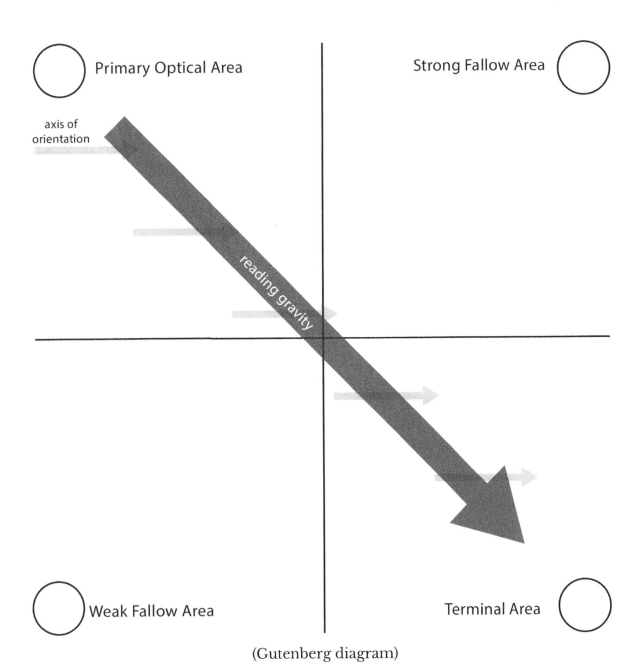

Primary Optical Area

Strong Fallow Area

axis of orientation

reading gravity

Weak Fallow Area

Terminal Area

(Gutenberg diagram)

H

H_a: See "hypothesis testing."

hack: To break into a computer without authorization. It can also refer to stealing someone's data. It is basically a form of digital trespassing. Some people also use the term to refer to coding (writing computer programs). In this case "hacking" is used to mean "the actions of a skilled computer expert." For example, computer programming competitions are sometimes called "hack-a-thons."

EXAMPLE: There are programs out there that are written to hack login forms (i.e., attempt to figure out user names and passwords so as to login without permission).

half adder: See "adder."

handshake: The act of two things (computers, machines, etc.) establishing a connection. Handshaking is used to mean that two computers are becoming linked. Essentially, this is a standardized way for two computers to establish a connection. It is basically each computer agreeing that they are in communication with the correct computer, and that they have agreed on the protocol they will use to exchange information.

EXAMPLE: Sometimes when you are connecting your computer to another computer, it will say "handshaking" until the connection is complete.

hard copy: A physical copy of something that you can hold in your hands. "Hard" literally means "tangible" (able to be seen, touched, felt, etc.). The opposite of a hard copy is something stored digitally on a computer – called a soft copy. Soft copies are viewed on a computer or device, instead of a physical copy of something that you can hold in your hands.

EXAMPLE: A printed book is a hard copy. If you create and save a document on a computer, that document would be considered a soft copy. If you print that document out, that would be a hard copy.

hard disk drive: See "hard drive."

hard drive: A drive is a device that the computer can use to store data for later use. The most important drive is the *hard drive*. The hard drive is a device used to store information that can be used by your computer. They're typically only slightly larger than your hand, yet can hold a massive amount of data. The data in a hard drive is stored on one or more disks that are mounted, in a stack, inside a solid case. A small "reader" is positioned over the disks so it can access the data stored on them. These disks spin extremely fast so that data can be accessed nearly immediately from anywhere on the drive. The data stored on the hard drive stays on the drive even after the power supply is turned off. When you wipe (erase) a hard drive, you are taking all the stored information off the drive.

Another term for this is "hard disk drive," so named because the disks were made of a rigid material. You'll sometimes see this abbreviated as "HDD." The first ever HDD was created by IBM in 1956. The hard drive weighed about one ton and stored about .01% of the memory that your average computer can store today. It looked like this:

On the surface of the hard drive disks is a layer of magnetic material. The way it works is that small pieces of the magnetic material can be changed so they point all in one direction, or all in another direction. One direction means a "one," and the other direction means a "zero." If you spin the disk and move the arm, you can reach any point on the disk. The tip of the arm can change the data at any place on the disk, or read the data at any place on the disk. You've now managed to store electronic data that a computer can use.

EXAMPLE: A drive will have an identifier (a "name") so users will know where to go to get stored data. Computers can have multiple drives installed. Drives are sometimes assigned letters as names (like A, B, C, etc.) For many computers around the world, the "C drive" is often the place on a computer where important data is stored (i.e., the hard drive is typically the C drive) – but other naming systems are used as well. "A drives" are typically reserved for floppy disk drivers and other types of disk drives. "B drives" are usually used as a second floppy disk drive. "D" and "E drives" are typically used as partitioned drives (i.e., part of the hard drive set aside for specific use) or as a second hard drive.

hardware: "Hard" means "solid" or "tangible" (able to be seen and felt), and "ware" means "something created." Hardware is the physical parts of a computer. It consists of the parts of the computer that you can touch, as opposed to the instructions stored in a computer, which you can't touch.

EXAMPLE: The computer screen, mouse, printer and keyboard are all hardware.

Harvard Mark I: See "Mark I."

hashtag: A symbol used to categorize written content. This is used mainly on social networking websites. The way it works is that a piece of content is created (say, an article about taking motorcycle trips in the American southwest) and then the creator adds one or more tags to the article. The tags are not added to the content of the article; rather, they are "attached" to the article. This is another example of "metadata" (data about data). In this example, the creator might add the tags "motorcycle," "Arizona" and "trip" to the article. Hashtags are used to make searching for content easier. You can search for all content on a certain subject by using hashtags – if you find all content that has the same hashtag attached to it, they should have a large quantity of related content.

EXAMPLE: If you search #TheOffice, content that has been tagged with #TheOffice will come up.

Haskell: A functional programming language used mainly in teaching, research and industrial application.

EXAMPLE: Facebook has used Haskell to help fight against spam.

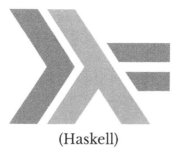

(Haskell)

HD: See "resolution, levels of."

HDD: See "hard drive."

HDMI: Stands for "High-Definition Multimedia Interface." HDMI is a specification (a standardized method of construction and operation) for equipment used in transferring high definition audio and video signals. It was created in the early 2000s. It is usually applied to cables that connect computers to televisions and other display devices.

EXAMPLE: HDMI cables are used to connect computers with certain advanced televisions. You would look at the television's manual to see if it could connect to another device using an HDMI cable.

(HDMI)

HD ready: See "resolution, levels of."

head: A drive is a device that the computer can use to store data for later use. Drives are often referred to as "disk drives," because the first designs of these devices made use of one or more metal disks that could be used to store computer data. The surface of these disks is magnetic, and can be modified so that it stores data for use in computers. When the computer needs to access data on the disk drive, the disk spins around quickly. As the disk spins, the data on the magnetic surface is read by the computer. The part of the drive that reads or sets this information is called the head.

EXAMPLE: When you save information on a disk, the head is moving rapidly around the disk to put that information on the disk.

heading: An element that allows for the placement of heads (titles) of sections. They're broken into a series of graduated sizes: <h1> through <h6>.

EXAMPLE: So that you can see how they work, on the left we have the code and on the right is the output:

CODE

OUPUT

```
<h1>Heading 1.</h1>
```
Heading 1.

```
<h2>Heading 2.</h2>
```
Heading 2.

```
<h3>Heading 3.</h3>
```
Heading 3.

```
<h4>Heading 4.</h4>
```
Heading 4.

```
<h5>Heading 5.</h5>
```
Heading 5.

```
<h6>Heading 6.</h6>
```
Heading 6.

(heading)

heat sink: The part of a computer that prevents overheating. As you know, computers use electricity. When they are doing lots of work, they use more electricity. When electricity flows, it generates heat. This means there are parts of a computer that can get hot when the computer is working a lot. A heat sink is something installed in a computer to keep it cool. A fan can also be used to help make the heat sink even more effective at removing heat from the computer; the fan blows air over the heat sink so heat is carried away more effectively.

EXAMPLE: Heat sinks are like the air conditioning for your computer. Here is a heat sink:

Here is a fan with a heat sink:

(heat sink)

hertz: A wave is a flow of energy that has a low point and a high point. Energy moves through space in waves. The space between one point in a wave and the next exact same point in the wave is called a wavelength.

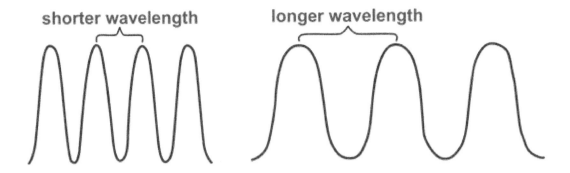

shorter wavelength   longer wavelength

Hertz (abbreviated "Hz") is a measurement that refers to how many wavelengths occur in one second – literally how many "ups and downs" occur in an electric flow per second. It was named after Heinrich Hertz, a German scientist who lived in the 1800s. Hertz did some of the early research that led up to the radio, and as part of this research he studied the behavior of electricity. Again, hertz means how many "ups and downs," or "cycles" in an electric flow that occur per second. Size and speed are measured in bits (see "bit" and "byte") using prefixes telling what magnitude (size) of number they are in. These are taken from Greek words. They are:

- Kilo, meaning "thousand";
- Mega, meaning "million";
- Giga, meaning "billion"; and
- Tera, meaning "trillion."

For example, "KHz" stands for "kilohertz." A kilohertz is one thousand hertz – literally 1,000 wavelengths in a second. The other common measurements of hertz are:

1. Megahertz – abbreviated as "MHz." MHz is 1,000,000 hertz.
2. Gigahertz – abbreviated as "GHz." GHz is 1,000,000,000 hertz.
3. Terahertz – abbreviated as "THz." THz is 1,000,000,000,000 hertz.

EXAMPLE: Hertz is one of the ways that CPUs are measured in terms of processing power. For example, when you see a computer advertised as having an 8GHz processor, what that means is that the CPU can perform operations at a rate of 8,000,000,000 instructions per second.

heuristic: Allowing a person to learn things for themselves – it comes from the Greek word for "find." This can apply to computer programs. Programs are written instructions, entered into the computer, that make it perform certain tasks. A heuristic program can progress toward a solution through trial and error. It "learns" from its mistakes to improve performance.

EXAMPLE: Some games are designed in a heuristic fashion wherein the computer "learns" from losses and plays better the next time around. It is important to note that the computer game does not actually learn anything. Like any computer program, the game can only do the actions that the creator of the program entered into the computer. The program creator can design the program to monitor how the user uses the program and then perform different actions when the program is used in the future. In every case, though, the actions are only those dictated by the instructions that are part of the program.

hexadecimal: *Hexa-* means "six; made up of six." *Decimal* literally means "ten" or "tenth." *Hexadecimal* is a base 16 number system. Meaning, it works out as follows (Hexadecimal/English):

```
0 = Zero
1 = One
2 = Two
3 = Three
4 = Four
5 = Five
6 = Six
7 = Seven
8 = Eight
9 = Nine
A = Ten
B = Eleven
C = Twelve
D = Thirteen
E = Fourteen
F = Fifteen
```

The place value of the hexadecimal number system can be diagrammed as follows:

65536	4096	256	16	1

EXAMPLE: Hexadecimal (abbreviated "hex") is used in computers to represent binary numbers, and is commonly used to specify the name of a computer memory address. It is beneficial for two main reasons: 1. You can display large numbers with relatively few characters, and 2. It is easily translatable into binary. 1B (hex) = 27 (decimal) (that is one "16" and eleven "1"s). 2AF3 (hex) = 10,995 (decimal). In binary, 2AF3 would be 0010101011110011.

\<h5>: See "heading."

\<h4>: See "heading."

high definition: See "resolution, levels of."

high-level language: A computer programming language that is designed to be easy for people to read and write. High-level languages look somewhat like English, and the words used have similar meanings to what they mean in normal conversation.

EXAMPLE: Code written as follows would be high level language:
```
print "hello";
```

Here, you are telling the computer to write out the word "hello" on the screen.

high resolution: See "resolution, levels of."

histogram: A diagram that is made of vertical rectangles used to show the frequency of variables and other data. It is similar to a bar graph.

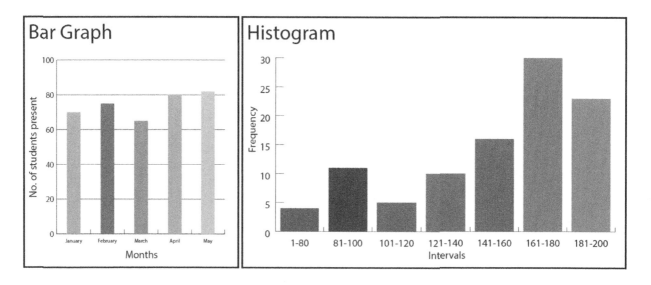

In histograms, data is stored in bins (buckets of data) – like 1-10 and 11-20. Histograms come in use when looking at how much or how little data there is in a range, rather than each individual piece of data. A histogram is commonly used to show the frequency distribution of data.

EXAMPLE: If we plot coffee sold by the hour, we can section the times from 7-9, 9-11, 11-1, and so on. Each of these sections is referred to as a "bin." You can see this here:

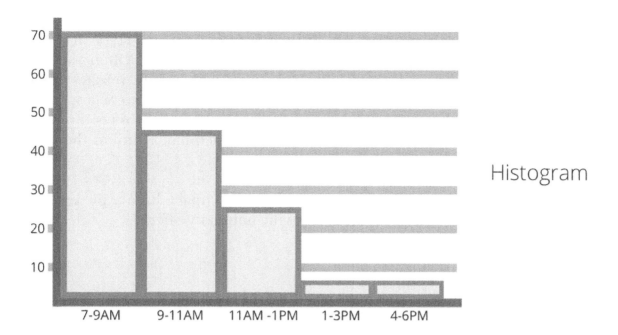

Histogram

In this image, the y-axis is the number of coffees, and the x-axis is the time range. This tells us that the most amount of coffee is sold between 7 am and 9 am and could probably close up shop at 1 pm. You can create a histogram to accommodate large amounts of data that would be too overwhelming for a dot plot, or for when a dot plot is not descriptive enough with too many single and empty dot points. The origin of the term *histogram* is uncertain. Some say that the word is derived from the Greek words *histos*, which means "anything set upright" (like the mast of a ship, or the vertical bars in a histogram), and *gramma*, which is a "drawing; record; writing." Others believe that Karl Pearson, who first used the term in 1895, stated that the word is a combination of "historical" and "diagram."

home: See "home page."

Home key: The keyboard key used to move the cursor (flashing bar on screen that indicates where to type) to the beginning of the current line of text. It is the opposite of the END key (which moves the cursor to the end of a line of text).

EXAMPLE: On some computers, the Home key can take you to the very beginning of a document when pressed in combination with another key.

(Home key)

home page: Also called "home" or "landing page." The main web page on a website. It is where you can navigate to other sections of the site from. When you type in a website name and go there, the first page you usually see is the home page. Often, the HTML (Hypertext Markup Language – the primary language used to create websites) file used to create this page is called "index.htm" or "index.html" because servers (a specialized computer used to store and transmit data, such as "serving up" websites through the World Wide Web) are programmed to utilize files named index.html as the landing page.

EXAMPLE: The home page for a university's website might have a picture of the university, and links to pages about the courses the university offers.

<h1>: See "heading."

host: A company that manages web servers. The data about all of your web pages (the written text, the pictures, all web pages and the website itself) are all kept with a host. There is a lot of information in one website. It is also a lot of work to have your computer sending information out to everyone trying to view your site. Using a host means you are basically renting someone else's computer(s) – a server – to store your website in so that your site is kept safe. They can then deal with all the work it takes to send your website to each person's computer that requests seeing it. Hosting is usually relatively inexpensive and allows you to set up a website with its own name and location on the web. The word comes from "host," which means to help and take care of someone.

EXAMPLE: You can design a website and then pay a company a monthly fee; they will save your website files somewhere on a server, and when people want to check out your website, their computer communicates back and forth to the host computer. You still have full control over your website and what happens with it.

(host)

hosting: See "host."

hot key: See "shortcut."

hover: See "mouse."

hover text: See "mouse."

<h6>: See "heading."

<h3>: See "heading."

HTML: A computer language that describes the appearance, content and behavior of web pages. It stands for "HyperText Markup Language." There are actually two concepts here: "hypertext" and "markup." Hypertext is a system for linking related electronic documents. It works by taking an item in the contents of one document and giving it a special property – it links to another electronic document. When that specific item is selected on the first document, the reader is taken to the linked document. Markup is the process of adding special data to the content of a document that dictates various changes to the appearance or format of that content. A typical example would be to make certain words bold or italic. You could even have them appear as a list. The electronic documents used to create web pages are written in a markup language called HyperText Markup Language (HTML). Files written in this language have the suffix

".html" after the file name – for example, "dogs.html." When we apply this to how a web page works, it looks like this:

1. The browser first requests the .html file from the web server.
2. The web server sends the requested .html file to the browser.
3. The browser then processes the HTML tags and the text in the file.
4. From there, it works out the visual appearance of the page that should be displayed on the screen.

The newest version of HTML is HTML5.

EXAMPLE: When you go to a website, you can find web pages that have words, pictures, sounds, and videos. The main language that is used behind the scenes to tell the computer to show you those words, pictures, sounds, and videos is HTML. There are other markup languages besides HTML. The one that applies to web pages is HTML. Like any markup language, HTML uses many different tags. These various tags handle things related to modifying the text displayed. They also handle things like displaying images, creating hyperlinks, etc. One common tag in HTML is the <title> tag. It tells a browser what to display in the tab in your browser. For example, if you go to the website for NBC, it might say "NBC TV Network" in the little tab in your browser where you see the NBC website. Here is an example of HTML:

```
<html>
    <title>
    Ninjas Everywhere!
    </title>
    <body>
    Ninjas are everywhere. There might be one behind you right now! Be sure to wear
    ninja-proof clothing at all times.
    </body>
</html>
```

Your browser would use this HTML to create a web page that looks like this:

The browser program on your computer uses the HTML commands to work out how to display the various parts of the web page on your screen.

HTML5: See "HTML."

HTML lists: In HTML (HyperText Markup Language – the primary language used to create websites), there are two main types of lists: 1. Ordered lists, and 2. Unordered lists. An ordered list is given in a sequence. An unordered list is not given a sequence and is usually bullet points. Here would be an example of an ordered list:

1. Bread
2. Milk
3. Eggs
4. Cheese

While this would be unordered:

- Cats
- Dogs
- Snakes
- Birds

EXAMPLE: To create an ordered list, we use the <ol> tag. Each item on the list is contained within the list element <li>. In the earlier example, this would be written as:

```
<ol>
   <li>Bread</li>
   <li>Milk</li>
   <li>Eggs</li>
   <li>Cheese</li>
</ol>
```

To create an underordered list, we use the <ul> tag. The earlier example would be written as:

```
<ul>
   <li>Cats</li>
   <li>Dogs</li>
   <li>Snakes</li>
   <li>Birds</li>
</ul>
```

(HTML lists)

HTTP: Stands for "Hypertext Transfer Protocol" and is one protocol (a standard way to format [arrange; structure] and pass data between computers), among others, for transferring information to and from computers over the internet. HTTP was devised many years ago. The type of information that HTTP is concerned with is the information on web pages – regular text, links, images, videos, etc. Most computers are designed so that they can read and understand HTTP, so HTTP is an important way of ensuring computers can communicate with each other via the internet and that the World Wide Web keeps working. If you try to request a web page without using HTTP properly, you won't be able to retrieve it. "HTTPS" stands for "Hypertext Transfer Protocol Secure" and it means the same thing as HTTP, except HTTPS is more secure. There are certain requirements one must meet in making a website compliant with the

HTTPS protocol. Many websites on the Internet are preceded with https, which shows that the information you're viewing used the Hypertext Transfer Protocol Secure as its method for being requested, being received, and being displayed. HTTPS is indicated by a lock symbol (🔒) in the address bar. Website addresses on the internet are preceded with http, which shows that the information you're viewing used the Hypertext Transfer Protocol as its method for being requested and received. http://www.facebook.com just shows that the Facebook website you're viewing was obtained using the Hypertext Transfer Protocol.

EXAMPLE: Another common protocol is SMTP, which stands for "Simple Mail Transfer Protocol." Whereas HTTP is used to transfer *websites* across the internet, SMTP is used to send *emails*. There are other protocols as well, but if you want to display a website, HTTP must be used.

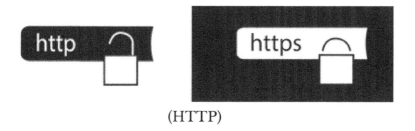

(HTTP)

HTTPS: See "HTTP."

<h2>: See "heading."

hub: A machine that relays information to the computers on a network. It does not matter which computer requested the information, the hub will send it to all of the computers. A hub can look like this:

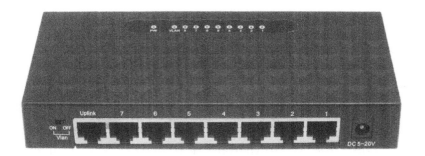

EXAMPLE: If your family had four computers on a network, the hub would send information to all four computers. If you were on the Internet and requested information, your request goes to the hub, the hub gets the information from the Internet, and then it passes the information to all the computers. That does not mean everyone else would see the information on their computer; it just means the hub sends out the data and then the computer that requested it knows to display it on the screen. The central computer in this picture is the hub:

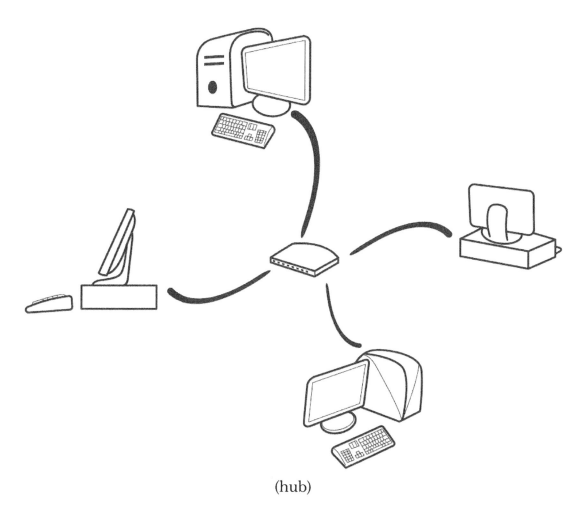

(hub)

hue: Refers to the color or shade of something. Such as, "Her eye shadow had a blue hue," or, "The hue of his shirt was a vibrant purple." The term originated from the Swedish word *hy*, which meant, "skin; complexion." When speaking of the wavelengths (i.e., color and light), hue is the wavelength of visible light measured in nanometers (nm). More specifically, hue is the main property of a color – the dominant color. Simply put, the terms "hue" and "color name" are synonymous.

EXAMPLE: You can see hues here:

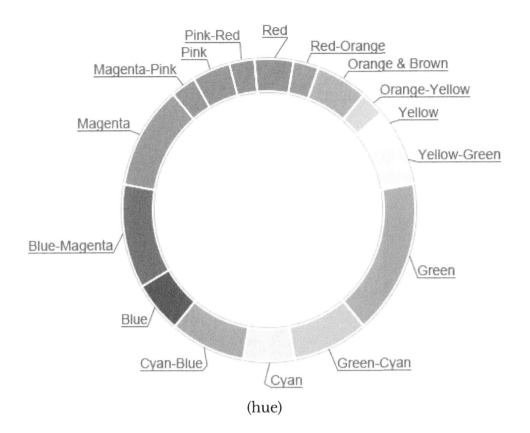

(hue)

hybrid: A computer program that was developed so it can operate on multiple mobile platforms (Apple, Android, etc.).

EXAMPLE: If you were creating a computer game and you wanted it to be available for both iPhones and Android phones, and you wanted to minimize your expenses, you might create the game as a hybrid application.

hyperlink: See "link" and "hypertext."

hypertext: A system for linking related electronic documents. It works by taking an item in the document (text, image, video, etc.) and giving it a special property – it links to another electronic document. When that specific item is selected, the reader is taken to the linked document. The origin of the term is taken from "hyper," which means "beyond." The special item is called a "hyperlink" because it links to a document that is "beyond" the one the user is reading.

EXAMPLE: Websites are composed of hypertext documents.

HyperText Markup Language: See "HTML."

hypothesis testing: In normal English, a *hypothesis* is the proposed explanation for something. It comes from the Greek word *hypothesis*, which means "foundation." In statistics, a hypothesis is a claim about something that we can test for validity. A *null* *hypothesis* (represented by the symbol: H₀) is when there are no major differences between specified populations (data sets as a whole). Technically, it is when there is no relationship between a dependent variable (data that has a name and a value [type/amount], and can be changed) and an independent variable. Loosely, a *null hypothesis* is something that is generally considered to be fact. An *alternative hypothesis* (represented by the symbol H_a – where H = Hypothesis and $_a$ = alternative) is the claim that the null hypothesis is incorrect. The alternative hypothesis is a new theory being offered over an old one. If a null hypothesis is found to be untrue (rejected), then the alternative hypothesis is accepted. On the other hand, if the alternative hypothesis is rejected, then the null hypothesis is maintained.

Alternative Hyposthesis	Null Hypothesis

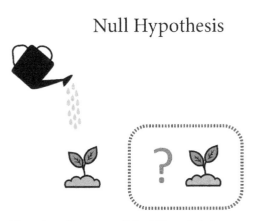

H_1 : Application of fertilizer 'x' increases plant growth.

H_0 : Application of fertilizer 'x' does not increase plant growth.

The alternative hypothesis is that which the researcher is trying to prove.

The null hypothesis is that which the researcher is trying to disprove or nullify.

EXAMPLE: You could have the hypothesis that students who get more than five hours of sleep a night before a test are likely to score 70% or higher.

Hz: See "hertz."

H₀: See "hypothesis testing."

I

IAR: See "instruction address register."

icon: A symbol or graphic (picture) representation on a screen of a computer program or option, especially one of several for selection.

EXAMPLE: If you want to look at what you have stored on your computer, you could click on the "My Computer" icon. You can see icons on a phone here:

(icon)

ID: 1. Short for "Identification." Identification is something that uniquely identifies a person or thing. IDs are used often in computers. Each user of a computer, for example, might need a unique ID so that the computer can store their files in an area only they can access. Pieces of computer equipment each have a unique ID as well. That way, when computers are connected together, each one knows how to connect to a specific computer in the network.

EXAMPLE: When you go on a website, you are often required to enter a user ID and password; for that website, no other user is allowed the same ID as you.

2. Short for "identity" and refers to a column or field in a database. Just like with the normal English meaning of ID (identification), an ID is a name assigned to something that can be used to identify (establish who or what something is) an item in a database.

EXAMPLE: You can see various IDs in these tables:

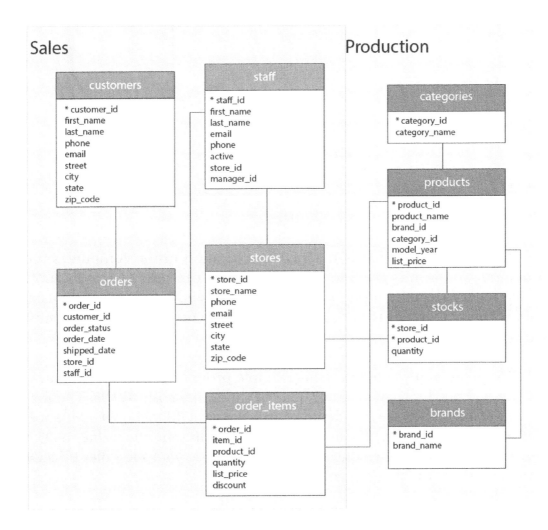

3. See "primary key."

IDE: Stands for *Integrated Development Environment*. A set of programming tools for writing software programs. IDEs are a great aid to computer program creation. An IDE often combines many available tools into one place. Essentially, an IDE is software that helps you make software.

EXAMPLE: Visual Studio, available from the technology company Microsoft, is one of the many IDEs available for software developers.

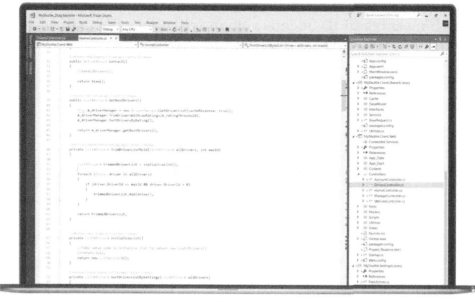

(IDE)

identifier: A descriptive name that is mapped to a location in the computer's memory. Once a memory location is given a specific name, we can refer to that location using the identifier rather than the numeric address. This system of associating a name with a memory location allows us to choose names that give meaning to the contents of the memory location.

EXAMPLE: Suppose you wanted to write a simple program to calculate the amount of sales tax you will need to pay on a new pair of shoes that costs $19.95. The first thing you will need to do is create an identifier called PriceOfShoes that is mapped to a particular memory location. Then you need to represent the value 19.95 in the computer at that location. Once this is done, you can use your identifier PriceOfShoes to refer to the price of the shoes in your program.

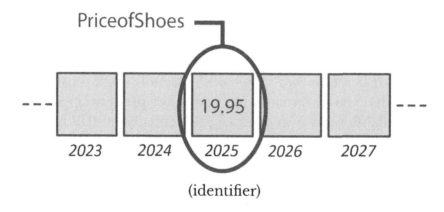

PriceofShoes

(identifier)

IDLE: An IDE (Integrated Development Environment) is a set of programming tools for writing software programs. Where most IDEs can be used to write programs in several different computer languages, IDLE is only used to write programs in the popular computer language Python. Guido van Rossum (the creator of Python) says IDLE stands for "Integrated Development Environment" – but since van Rossum named Python in honor of the British comedy group Monty Python, the name IDLE was probably chosen partly to honor Eric Idle, one of Monty Python's founding members. IDLE is intended to be a simple development environment suitable for beginners, especially in an educational setting.

EXAMPLE: You can get IDLE for free if you want to start creating computer programs using the programming language Python.

IIS: "IIS" stands for "Internet Information Services." IIS is a web server software created by Microsoft for use with the Windows operating system. It is a web server software package designed for Windows Server (brand name for a group of server operating systems released by Microsoft). It is used for hosting websites and other content on the Web.

EXAMPLE: IIS provides a graphical user interface (GUI) for managing websites and the various users.

IIS Express: "IIS" stands for "Internet Information Services." IIS is web server software from Microsoft that runs on the Windows system, and helps to store and transmit electronic files for a website over the internet. IIS Express is a version of IIS that was created to assist developers in creating and testing websites.

EXAMPLE: Visual Studio allows you to develop and test websites using IIS Express.

IM: Stands for "instant message." A message sent from computer to computer that immediately shows up on the screen of the computer of the receiver. It can also be used as a verb, "IMing," meaning "having a conversation using Instant Messaging." To send and receive messages in this fashion, both the sender and the receiver need to have compatible programs installed on their computer to manage the process.

EXAMPLE: In the 1990s, IMing was very popular among teenagers.

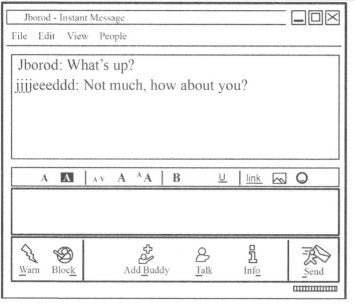

(IM)

image filter: As you may have come across, there are such image effects as "color filters." An image filter is software that alters the appearance of an image by changing the shades and colors of the pixels in some way. Filters can also be used to increase brightness or contrast.

EXAMPLE: Grayscale can be used over an image as a filter (The range of gray in each pixel can either highlight and intensify details of an image, or mute [reduce strength or intensity of] them), like this:

(image filter)

IMAP: IMAP ("Internet Message Access Protocol") and POP3 ("Post Office Protocol" version "3") are two popular email protocols (rules on how to transfer digital data). IMAP stores email messages on a server but allows users to view and handle the emails as though they were stored locally on the user's computer. With POP3, emails are moved from the server to the user's computer when they are opened.

EXAMPLE: The difference between IMAP and POP3, is that with IMAP, your messages remain on the server instead of deleting them. In POP3, the messages are deleted from the server (transferred to your computer) when read.

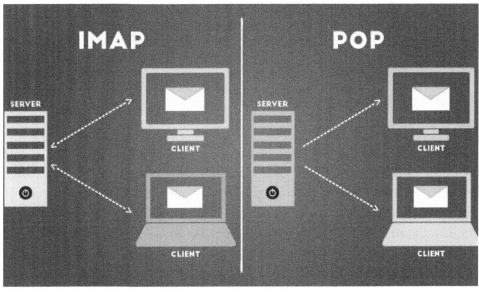
(IMAP)

immutable: Unchanging or not able to be changed. In programming, immutable refers to something that cannot be modified, updated, added to or deleted.

EXAMPLE: If you type an immutable list, the items on that list would be permanently stored that way.

impediment: Something that blocks or slows progress. In a literal sense, a tree that falls over and blocks a road is an impediment.

EXAMPLE: In Scrum, an impediment is anything that prevents the team from meeting their potential. This includes issues that could prevent a project from being completed on time or on budget.

implicit: implied; able to be understood but not directly stated. In SQL, implicit refers to a JOIN that is not clearly specified as a JOIN. I.e., it is code that functions as a JOIN but does not use the JOIN clause.

EXAMPLE: The following code is an implicit JOIN:

```
SELECT e.First_Name, d.Department_Name
FROM Employee e, Departments d
WHERE e.Department_Id = d.Id
```

This would return the following from the database:

e.First_Name	d.Department_Name
Hannah	Marketing
Jeff	Development
Adam	Development

We have "joined" two tables without using a JOIN clause. Again, this is considered to be an implicit join. "Explicit" means "in great detail; stated clearly." An explicit JOIN is the opposite of an implicit JOIN – you can clearly see that a JOIN is being performed because the JOIN clause is included in the code. To be clear: explicit JOINs and implicit JOINs perform the same functions (combine rows of tables based on related columns between them). Here is an explicit JOIN:

```
SELECT * FROM
table A INNER JOIN table B
ON A.Id = B.Id
```

As you can see, the explicit JOIN uses the JOIN clause and the ON clause. The same could be performed with the following implicit JOIN:

```
SELECT A.*, B.*
FROM table A, table B
WHERE A.Id = B.Id
```

Simply put: do not use implicit JOINs. Explicit JOINs improve code readability and are considered best practice. This is also mentioned here because, in the past, SQL Server (and other RDBMSs) used syntax such as IMPLICIT OUTER JOIN but this has been deprecated (usable but replaced by something better – therefore, best avoided) since 2005.

import: To bring something into something else. For example, you can import pictures by moving them in from one location to another. Importing refers to taking computer information from one location and placing it in another location. You can also import things onto a computer from a device (such as a camera or video camera). On the other hand, export means to take some data that is used by a computer program and send it somewhere else, usually so that the data can be used by another computer program.

EXAMPLE: If you had a program that kept track of all the customers at your bicycle manufacturing company, you might export all the data about your customers so it could be used by a computer program that prints customized holiday greeting cards.

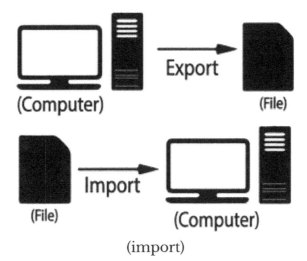

(import)

impressions: How many times a certain thing is seen by the members of an intended audience. This term is most often used in terms of advertising or content that people can view on their computers. Since you usually can't know with certainty that the content was actually read, you may need to rely simply on whether or not the content was on a display screen where a member of your audience could see it if they were looking. This is called a single "impression."

EXAMPLE: If your ad were displayed on the computers of 10,000 users, that would be 10,000 impressions.

inbox: The location where all electronic mail (email) messages are stored when they first arrive. It is essentially the "mailbox" on your computer.

EXAMPLE: Emails that you send are stored in the "sent folder," while emails that you receive are stored in your inbox.

increment: A mathematics term that means "to add to a number by a set amount." If you count by fours (4, 8, 12, etc.), the increment is four. An increment is one step, phase, or part of something. There is a corresponding (opposite) action called "decrement." This means "to subtract from a number by a set amount." If you count down by twos (20, 18, 16, 14, etc.), the decrement is two. Note that the increment does not need to be a positive number. You could count down from 10 (10, 9, 8, 7, 6, etc.) by using an increment of negative one. Nor does a decrement need to be a positive number. You could count up from 0 by twos (0, 2, 4, 6, etc.) using a decrement of negative two. Using negative numbers for increment and decrement is not recommended; it would be confusing – but you should know that it is possible.

EXAMPLE: Computers sometimes use increments when handling numbers and performing operations. If you have a computer mark every fourth employee in a list of employees for an internal survey, your increment is four.

incremental development: An *increment* is a small step. *Incremental* refers to moving forward in stages. *Incremental development* is a practice where software is designed, deployed and tested incrementally (a little bit more added each time) until the project is completed. Each step builds on the previous with additional advancements.

EXAMPLE: Agile is an incremental development approach.

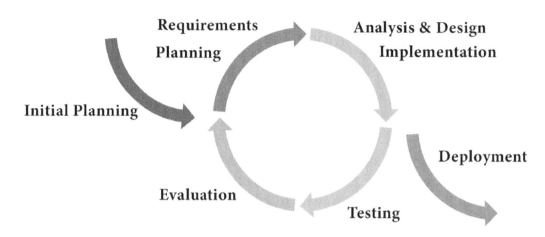

(incremental development)

indent: To set something apart from the edge or start of a page. A small space separating text, pictures, etc. from the side of a page. The TAB key moves the cursor (flashing bar on screen that indicates where to type) forward on the screen a set number of spaces – usually this is set to eight spaces – this is an indent. In coding, some languages require specific indentation of code, while others do not.

EXAMPLE: If you are typing a letter, the beginning of a paragraph is often indented. Here is an example of that:
Dear Elwood,

As you may recall, I placed an order with your firm for 437 brass statues of 'Joliet' Jake Blues. I have as yet not received them after a wait of 5 weeks. I would appreciate your prompt attention to this matter.

Here, the paragraph that begins "As you may recall" is indented.

index: See "array."

index (database): See "database index."

index (web): See "web indexing."

indexing: See "web indexing."

Individual: In data science, an object that makes up a set of data. Individuals have associated (connected; related) variables. Unlike conventional computer programming variables – here, a variable is a description of what the individual consists of. Using a spreadsheet as an example, an Individual would be one customer. The variable would be the data about each customer.

EXAMPLE: Let's say we have a property manager that oversees multiple apartment complexes. In this case, each complex would be considered the Individual of that data set, and the data about each complex would be the variables. The following sample of apartment complexes are examples of Individuals:

1. Ashwood
2. Hunters Glen
3. Tramor
4. The Grove

Examples of variables for these Individuals could be: Total number of tenants, landlord name, address, etc.

inferential statistics: In normal English, *infer* means to "conclude information from reasoning or evidence – as opposed to explicit statements." *Inferential* means "having to do with conclusions reached by reasoning and evidence." *Inferential statistics* are statistics that result from taking a sample of data from an overall population and making conclusions about that data as a whole.

EXAMPLE: Let's say you have a list of cars that have been bought over the course of a year – there are 200 sales on the list. Each sale has associated data, like: info about the buyer, car make, car model, car year, car color, etc. To obtain an inferential statistic, you would need to select at random a smaller portion of those sales – let's say 60. You then analyze the 60 sales and determine that people who bought a Nissan, were more likely to get the car in the color silver. You could then "infer" that same conclusion for the entire 200 sales.

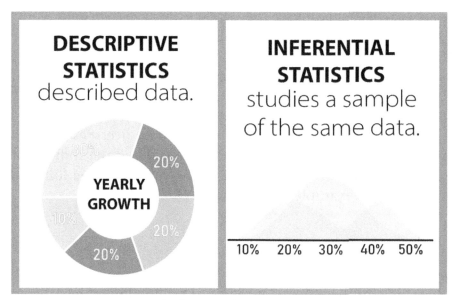

(inferential statistics)

information technology: See "I.T."

infrared: The color spectrum includes visible (able to be seen by the human eye) light and colors. There are others. The prefix *infra-* means "below." Infrared refers to light with wavelengths greater than the red end of the color spectrum. These wavelengths are not perceivable by the human eye. Infrared has a wavelength from about 800 nanometers to 1 millimeter. Infrared wavelengths can be emitted by heated objects.

EXAMPLE: You have probably seen infrared "goggles" or "scanners" in movies that show pictures like this:

(infrared)

infrastructure: The basic physical organization and arrangement of things that society uses to operate (like roads, bridges, etc.). In computers, infrastructure refers to hardware (the physical parts of a computer) and anything related to connecting computers.

EXAMPLE: The computer's hard drive (where electronic files are stored) is part of its infrastructure.

inherit: See "class."

inheritance: See "class."

INI (file format): "INI" is short for initialization. INI files are used by the Windows operating system, typically to lay out operating instructions for the OS and some programs.

EXAMPLE: Usually the instructions to the computer that enables the use of a mouse are stored in .ini files.

initialize: To prepare something for use for the first time. It means to put something in the proper format or condition for operation.

EXAMPLE: When you initialize something, sometimes it means that you wipe it clean so it can be used for the first time.

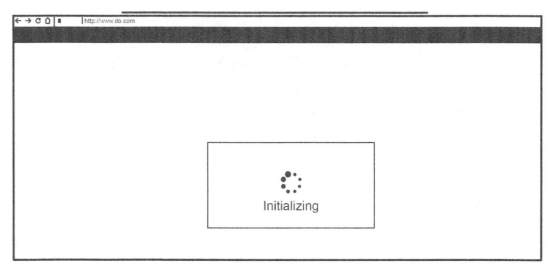

http://www.do.com

Initializing

(initialize)

injection: 1. See "SQL injection." 2. See "code injection."

inkjet printer: See "printer."

INNER JOIN: See "join."

input: Data or information that is collected by a computer. This can take many forms. It may be information a user has typed into a form on the computer. It may be electric signals sent to the computer by an attached device, like a mouse or a display screen that takes touch input. It may be a set of electronic data from another computer that is connected to the first one by wires. One of the most common ways to input data into a computer is through typing on a keyboard.

EXAMPLE: A customer service agent at a retail store takes down your information and types it into their computer; that information is input for the computer to use.

input device: See "I/O device."

input/output device: See "I/O device."

Ins key: "Ins" is short for "Insert key." It is used to change the text input mode. Before it is pressed, the computer is in "insert mode" – new characters (letters, numbers, etc.) that are typed are added to the right of the cursor (flashing bar on screen that indicates where to type), forcing any existing text over to the right.

EXAMPLE: If the Insert key is pressed, it puts the keyboard into "overtype mode" or "replace mode," where new characters will overwrite (delete and replace) the character(s) to the right of the cursor position. Pressing it again will return the computer to "insert" mode.

(Ins key)

Insert key: See "Ins key."

insertion sort: A type of sorting algorithm. In an insertion sort, the list of items is gone through, one item at a time, starting at the beginning. As each item is reached, the correct location earlier in the list is found for it, based on the desired outcome – for example, if the algorithm is meant to sort a list of numbers in ascending order, the current item would be inserted at the correct spot earlier in the list. When the end of the list is reached, the whole list is sorted properly.

EXAMPLE: You could use an insertion sort to sort a list of students alphabetically by last name. This is how most people sort playing cards when playing card games. Start at the first card, compare it to the second, move the second card where it should go depending on how you want the cards arranged, then go on to the third card, compare it to the two you've already inserted, put it where it goes, etc. and so on.

install: To put something inside a computer that the computer can then use. You can install both software and hardware.

EXAMPLE: When you are adding a new feature to your computer, your computer might display "please wait, installing…"

installer: Install means to put something inside a computer that the computer can then use. You can install software and you can install hardware. An installer is a specialized computer program that installs other programs on a computer.

EXAMPLE: When you put a new game on your computer, you use an installer.

instance: 1. An example or single occurrence of something. Often in computer programming, there will be part of a computer program that defines the concept of a thing. When the program needs to create one of those things, it looks to the definition and uses it in creating one of them. Another term for these things that can be created is "Objects."

EXAMPLE: A computer program for use in a school might have a definition for a thing called a Student. The program instructions in that definition are essentially answers to the question, "If I were a student, what characteristics and actions are available to me?" Characteristics of a Student object might be things like:

- Name
- Age
- Grade Point Average
- Areas of study

Actions available to a student might include things like:

- Calculate new Grade Point Average
- Add a new area of study
- Remove an area of study

This type of definition is often called an "Object definition" or a "Class." Here, we have an Object definition for an Object called a "Student." Until the computer program is directed to create an actual "Student" object, there are not any in the program. When the program is directed to create an actual Student object, the program looks to the Object definition of a Student and creates an actual Student.

To do so, the program will need the data for that actual Student – their name, their age, their GPA. It will then create a "Student." This "Student" is a collection of data, stored in the computer memory, that defines an INSTANCE of a Student. That is, it is a single occurrence of the type of thing defined by the Object definition called "Student."

EXAMPLE: If a 15-year-old student named Angela Smith enrolled at a school to study Physics and Computer Science, and her Grade Point Average was 3.25, the Student Object created in the computer program might look like this:

```
Object type:          Student
Name:                 Angela Smith
Age:                  15
Grade Point Average:  3.25
Major areas of study: Physics, Computer Science
```

The computer program will now maintain all the data about this instance of a Student object in computer memory, as long as it is instructed to do so. Now that we have an instance of a student that is being maintained by the computer program, we can do a couple of things: 1. We can modify the characteristics of that instance. For example, when the student turns 16, we can change the Age characteristic on that instance so it is set to 16. 2. We can execute the actions available to instances of the Student object. For example, if Angela dropped her focus on Physics and instead concentrated on Mathematics, we could use the "Remove an area of study" action to remove Physics from the characteristic "Areas of study," and then use the "Add an area of study" to add Mathematics to the characteristic "Areas of study." See also "class."

2. See "database instance."

instantiate: To create an instance of something. See "instance."

instant message: See "IM."

instruction: A command or set of commands entered into a computer that performs a certain operation(s). Instructions control a computer and tell it what to do.

EXAMPLE: You could make a computer draw a square by typing in instructions.

instruction address register: A register is a place in a computer where special types of information can be stored; registers are physically located in the computer. The instruction register is the part of a computer that stores commands that are currently being executed by the CPU. The "instruction address register" (IAR) stores the address of the next instruction that is to be moved over to the IR. The IAR points out the address of the next command to be done from the IR. The IAR helps store the address of upcoming instructions to be executed by the CPU and then passes them over to the IR at the proper time. The distinction here is: The Instruction Register holds the instruction to be performed by the CPU; The Instruction Address Register holds the location of the instruction to be performed once the one in the IR is done being executed.

EXAMPLE: When a computer is performing several tasks, the next one to be performed is stored in the IAR temporarily, but directly before being executed by the CPU.

instruction register: A register is a place in a computer's memory where special types of data can be stored; registers are physically located in the computer. A register will have an "address" – a unique identifier that the computer can use to locate that register. An Instruction is a specific action that a computer is directed to perform. There are many instructions available when programming a computer. The Instruction Register (IR) is the part of a computer that stores the instruction that is currently being executed by the CPU. The CPU only performs one instruction at a time; the Instruction Register is where that instruction is stored. See also "instruction address register."

EXAMPLE: If a computer is being directed to add two numbers together, the first step might be "read the number entered on the keyboard." That instruction would be in the Instruction Register. The CPU would do that action. Then the next instruction would be put in the IR. It might be "store that number in memory so you can use it later."

integer: Another word for "whole number." Integers are like whole numbers in that they do not include fractions, but technically, there is a difference between integers and whole numbers: unlike whole numbers, integers can be negative. -104, 45, -3, 555, 0 and 90,423 are all integers – but only 45, 555, 0 and 90,423 are whole numbers. And so, integers include all whole numbers (1, 2, 3, 4, etc.) and also all of their negative counterparts (-1, -2, -3, -4, etc.)

EXAMPLE: 56 is an integer. -78 is an integer. 9.368 is not an integer, as it has a fraction of a number in its value.

integrated circuit: Integrated means "linked" or "connected." A circuit is a complete path that electricity flows through. This is a very small piece of a computer that electricity flows through to perform exact functions. Integrated circuits are typically linked by an imprinted pathway of conductive material.

EXAMPLE: Integrated circuits can be around 450 millimeters in width.

integrated development environment: See "IDE."

IntelliSense: A feature in the Integrated Development Environment "Visual Studio" that helps aid rapid software development by helping to predict what you may want to type when you are writing computer code.

EXAMPLE: IntelliSense is similar to predictive text on your cell phone:

```
</handlers>
<rewrite>
  <rules>
    <rule name="MyRule" enabled="true">
      <match url="(.*)"/>
      <action type=""/>
    </rule>
  </rules>
</rewrite>
</system.webServer>

<runtime>
```

| None |
| Rewrite |
| Redirect |
| CustomResponse |
| AbortRequest |

(IntelliSense)

interactive: Refers to two things that influence one another and create effects on each other. In computers, interactive refers to a computer that is able to be communicated with and directed to perform activities by a human; these activities involve the person using the computer. An interactive computer (most computers you've handled, if not all, have been interactive) is a computer that you can affect in some way (like moving a pointer on a screen and selecting something) and which will respond in some manner. A non-interactive computer would be one that simply performed a specific, predetermined set of actions and did not respond to any user actions – for example, a computer that controlled the display of an electronic billboard. The computer has no method for receiving input, and as long as it is turned on, all it does is display the same images, one after the other.

EXAMPLE: An interactive computer might be a display at a mall that allows you to enter in a type of store or item, and which then shows you the name and location of any stores in the mall that matched the words you entered.

interface: A common point or boundary between two things. It is something that allows two things to interact smoothly and communicate with each other. In the computer world, an interface is a device or program that enables a user to communicate with a computer, or that enables one program to communicate with another program. A user interface is something that someone using a computer can use that makes the interaction with the computer easier or smoother.

EXAMPLE: Your web browser is an interface you use to access the Internet.

internal memory: See "main storage."

intermediary: Acting between two other things. In computers, intermediary things are machines that connect two other things so they can communicate. Intermediary machines link other machines together.

EXAMPLE: When you send an email (electronic message) to someone, it does not go directly to them. It typically goes to a special computer that can store it until that person checks for any new emails. That special computer is an example of an intermediary.

Internet: A combination of the words "interconnected" and "network." The internet is an interconnected network of many computers around the world. It is the largest network in existence and allows computers to pass data to one another. There are lots of different types of data that can be sent back and forth between computers connected to the internet – like electronic messages, electronic documents, healthcare records, etc. In addition to referring to the connected computers that make up this network, internet also means the set of agreements, or protocols, for how to transfer different types of data between those computers. A "protocol" is an official procedure. In technology, it is a formal description of how a certain type of information will be formatted and handled. Basically, it is an agreement that the various people who work with that type of information all adhere to. Protocols are usually described in written documents, and are very precise. They are created by experts in the applicable industry. An example of a type of data where a protocol would be valuable is healthcare information. If various organizations in the healthcare industry were to transfer healthcare data back and forth between computers as they perform their work, it would be important that they all agree about things like the exact format of the information, how to keep private data safe, etc. All of that would be laid down in a written protocol. Several such protocols do exist in the healthcare industry. One or more protocols have been created for each type of data that can be transferred around on the internet. Violation of these protocols results in an error and the data will not be transferred properly or at all. So to recap: the internet is an interconnected network of many computers around the world, and a set of agreements, or protocols, for transferring different types of data between those computers.

EXAMPLE: What is the difference between the internet and the World Wide Web? The internet is the hardware and protocols for exchanging information, whereas the web is one type of information that is accessed over the internet. The web is a collection of linked electronic documents called webpages. The internet is the infrastructure (physical framework), while the web is the code that is transmitted and displayed. In a way, the internet is the hardware and the web is the software. The web is the largest collection of data ever assembled by mankind. By far.

(Internet)

Internet bot: See "bot."

Internet exchange point: Abbreviated "IX" or "IXP." An IXP is a physical machine that different Internet Service Providers (ISP) use to exchange Internet traffic. An Internet exchange point is the connection point through which ISPs share Internet information with each other.

EXAMPLE: IXPs allow ISPs to team up and thereby increase Internet speed.

Internet forum: See "online discussion forum."

Internet of Things: "IoT" for short. IoT refers to connecting everyday objects to the internet. This allows control of and communication with all sorts of devices through the internet. IoT allows various machines to be controlled remotely (at a distance). An example of IoT would be controlling the locks on your house using your phone, via the internet. Other objects and devices that can be embraced by IoT (i.e. hooked up to and controlled through the internet) are thermostats, security systems, cars, refrigerators, lights, alarm clocks and more. The concept of IoT has been around for decades – the idea that you could control machines from a distance over a network. For example, Coca Cola did so in the 1980s. They connected to Coca Cola vending machines over a distance and were able to see if there were drinks available and if they were cold. In addition to the increased efficiency, IoT has as a purpose – "data gathering." Meaning, as all of these machines are connected to the internet, the data they all pass along the internet can be collected and analyzed. For example, a traffic light connected to the internet could automatically track how many cars pass by it every day. If this were expanded across the entire country, the data gathered by all of these traffic lights could be used to discover the most efficient traffic systems or rapidly isolate the most common causes of traffic accidents.

EXAMPLE: The term IoT was first used in 1999 by the British technologist (an expert in a particular tech field) Kevin Ashton during a presentation. He is the "inventor" of the term and had this to say about it during an interview in 2009: "The fact that I was probably the first person to say 'Internet of Things' doesn't give me any right to control how others use the phrase. But what I meant, and still mean, is this: Today computers – and, therefore, the internet – are almost wholly dependent on human beings for information. Nearly all … of data available on the internet were first captured and created by human beings – by typing, pressing a record button, taking a digital picture or scanning a barcode. Conventional diagrams of the internet include servers and routers and so on, but they leave out the most numerous and important routers of all: people. The problem is, people have limited time, attention and accuracy – all of which means they are not very good at capturing data about things in the real world… If we had computers that knew everything there was to know about things – using data they gathered without any help from us – we would be able to track and count everything, and greatly reduce waste, loss and cost. We would know when things needed replacing, repairing or recalling, and whether they were fresh or past their best. We need to empower computers with their own means of gathering information, so they can see, hear and smell the world for themselves, in all its random glory."

Internet Protocol address: See "IP address."

Internet server: See "web server."

Internet service provider: See "ISP."

interpreter: A special program that converts high level (similar to English) language instructions into low level language (designed to be easy for a computer to execute) instructions. An interpreter converts code for execution in this way one instruction at a time, rather than converting the entire set of instructions in the program prior to execution. In other words, the interpreter will read an instruction, convert it to language the computer can understand, have the computer execute that instruction, then go on to the next instruction in the program and repeat.

EXAMPLE: Interpreted computer languages use interpreters.

interval data: *Interval* literally means "the space or gap between two things." *Interval data* is a type of discrete data. It is also called *integer* data. Integers are like whole numbers in that they do not include fractions – but unlike whole numbers, they can be negative. Examples are -1024, 45, -2, 555, 0, 90004. Note that in these examples, the numbers 45,

555, 0 and 9004 are whole numbers as well as integers. More precisely, integers include all whole numbers (1, 2, 3, 4, etc.) as well as all of their negative counterparts (-1, -2, -3, -4, etc.). Interval data is equidistant. *Equidistant* means "equal distances between two or more points." For example, the points of this triangle are equidistant (A to B, B to C and C to A):

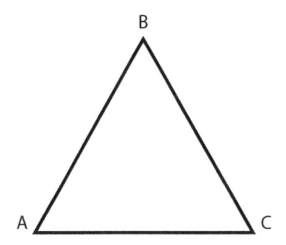

The discrete differences between the values in interval data are equidistant. Interval data refers to the distance between two values. In interval data, there is no zero – meaning, there is no such thing as no data. Interval data can be measured on a scale – like a thermometer. In the thermometer example, there is technically a "0 degrees," but it is not an absolute zero (meaning, it is not a complete absence of temperature). 0 degrees is still a temperature, and we can continue lower to -1 degrees, -2 degrees, etc. Zero can mean two things: 1. The number 0, or 2. A complete absence of anything – nothing. This is sometimes referred to as "absolute zero" or the "true value of zero." When we say there is no zero in interval data, we are referring to the second definition. While the number 0 can be used in interval data, the concept of absolute nothingness can't.

EXAMPLE: Altitude (the height of an object compared to ground level) – there can be negative and positive altitude. An airplane in flight would be in positive altitude, while the ocean floor would be negative. 0 altitude wouldn't mean "no altitude" – instead, it would be the ground. Because interval data is numerical, it can be added and subtracted. Because there is no absolute zero in interval data, you cannot multiply or divide it. To take our temperature example, 80° F is not twice as hot as 40° F. And 30° is not ⅓ of 90°. Interval data can be measured; it is ordered and the increments are equidistant. Meaning, the data can be measured equally from one point to another.

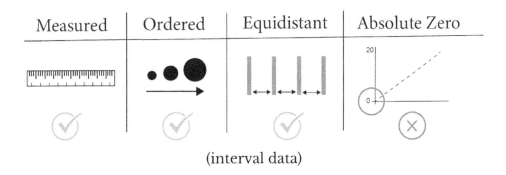

Measured	Ordered	Equidistant	Absolute Zero

(interval data)

introspection: See "code introspection."

intuitive design: Intuit means to use your instinct to understand something or work it out. It comes from the Latin words in- which means "upon" and tueri which means "to look." Intuitive means "based on or utilizing what you feel or your instinct, as opposed to conscious reasoning." In UI/UX, intuitive design has no formalized definition but is meant to refer to product design that seems to sense what the user needs and wants, and can be operated with relative ease. It is software that can "predict" how the average user will interact with an interface. Intuitive design typically conforms to common conventions that users are used to, so as to ensure consistency between applications and minimal "user training."

EXAMPLE: A developer creates a design so that the X in the right corner of their app opens a new window, instead of closing the application. Another example would be allowing a user to zoom in by pinching their fingers on a touchscreen.

I/O device: Short for "Input/Output device." Devices are machines with a purpose. An I/O device is a machine that people use to communicate with a computer. "Input" refers to putting data into a computer. "Output" refers to taking data from a computer.

EXAMPLE: A microphone connected to your computer is an input device. A printer is an output device because it receives data from the computer.

iOS: See "OS."

IoT: See "Internet of Things."

IP: Short for "Internet Protocol." 1. See "IP address." 2. See "protocol."

iPad: See "Apple."

IP address: Stands for "Internet Protocol address." An IP address is the numbered address of a machine, in the format used on the Internet. Each computer that uses the Internet is assigned its own IP address. IP addresses are written as a series of numbers with periods in between them and they designate an exact device that can be connected to the internet.

EXAMPLE: An IP address of a computer could be written as 128.192.12.9.

iPhone: See "Apple."

IR: See "instruction register."

ISP: Stands for "Internet Service Provider" and is a company that provides the devices and service that allows customers to access the Internet. They are an intermediary between the individual computer user and the network of computers that make up the Internet. ISPs exist because an extremely large set of physical equipment is needed to connect all of the many computers to the Internet. This is equipment like cable, telephone lines, wireless transmitters, etc. The companies that own this equipment are key elements of the Internet. The history of how these companies developed in each country on earth, and the technologies used or created along the way, could fill a book. However, this much should be known: The first large-scale computer networks made use of existing wiring that had been installed by telephone companies. Since telephone companies already had wiring installed that reached most houses and businesses in the various countries on the planet, it made sense to use that existing infrastructure to create the Internet. This meant that the earliest ISPs were the telephone companies. Later, television broadcasting companies installed specialized equipment and wiring ("cable") around the planet so they could offer television services to consumers. This equipment and cable was capable of much higher rates of data transmission, so the cable companies began offering access to the internet as one of their services. Today, most ISPs are cable companies – television broadcasters. In the future, it is likely that a network of satellites in orbit around the planet will be used to provide the connections for the computers on the internet.

EXAMPLE: Comcast is an Internet Service Provider.

I.T.: Short for "Information technology." The study and use of machines (especially computers) that store, send, and receive data. IT is mainly used when talking about computers, but technically other advanced machinery subjects, such as phones, fall under the category of IT, too. IT has to do with machines that handle information.

EXAMPLE: If someone says they are studying IT in college, they are essentially saying that they are studying computers.

item: See "PBI."

iteration: To iterate means to say or do something again – to repeat something. An iteration is the act of repeating. It means to go through a defined series of actions, repeating them a certain number of times. Usually this defined series of actions is repeated a certain number of times or until a condition is met.

EXAMPLE: Computer programs are usually created in iterations: Coming up with a basic working version, reviewing the program for mistakes to correct and improvements to make, doing that work, and repeating. This can be continued indefinitely.

iterative development: Iterative means performing repeatedly. Iterative development refers to developing software through repeated cycles (iterative). These cycles each accomplish some sort of a minimum viable product. Agile is iterative.

EXAMPLE:
1. First iteration: Create a basic HTML homepage.
2. Second iteration: Implement design plans on the homepage using CSS.
3. Third iteration: Add animations to the homepage using JavaScript
4. Fourth iteration: Create a basic About page using HTML. Etc.

IX: See "Internet exchange point."

IXP: See "Internet exchange point."

J

Java: An object-oriented programming language created in 1995 by a team of developers. Java has similarities to other languages but was simplified to eliminate common errors people were making with other languages. It is able to run on most computers and is a general-purpose language with a number of features that make it useful for use in making programs for businesses. Many people and companies use Java.

EXAMPLE: The popular free word-processing program OpenOffice was created in Java.

(Java)

JavaScript: Not to be confused with "Java," JavaScript is a computer language that is able to work on most computers. It was created in 1995 by an American named Brendan Eich and is particularly useful in making websites. JavaScript is used mainly to make websites more dynamic (describing websites that have content that changes based on user action or other factors, rather than being static in appearance and content). There are many other uses for JavaScript; it is used in the creation of many different types of computer programs. JavaScript can make programs and websites more interactive.

EXAMPLE: JavaScript can be used to make videos that start to play as soon as a user moves their mouse over the video.

(JavaScript)

JavaScript interpreter: JavaScript is an interpreted language, meaning it is a language that requires additional software to read and translate the instructions into code that the computer will understand. This process will be performed one line at a time within the JavaScript document until all lines of instruction have been completed. Knowing how JavaScript is interpreted is essential to writing effective code. Web browsers (the program people use to view web pages) come pre-installed with a JavaScript interpreter, often called an engine.

EXAMPLE: Some of the most popular JavaScript engines (interpreters) are: V8 (Google Chrome), SpiderMonkey (Firefox), JavaScriptCore (Safari) and Chakra (Microsoft Edge).

JIT: See "just in time."

join: A special operation in a database that lets you retrieve data from more than one table at the same time, using the relationships you've defined between your tables. A JOIN clause is used to combine tuples (rows) from two or more tables. The joining of these tables is based on a related attribute (column) between them. See also "implicit."

EXAMPLE: There are four types of SQL JOINs:
1. INNER JOIN: This returns records (rows) that have matching values in both tables.

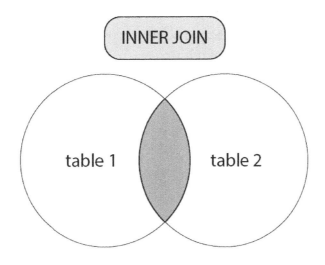

2. (FULL) OUTER JOIN: This returns all records where there is a match in either the left or right table.

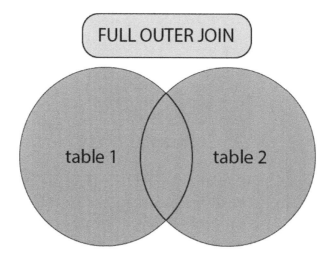

3. LEFT (OUTER) JOIN: This returns all records from the left table, and the records from the right table that match up.

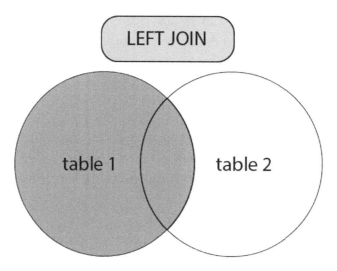

4. RIGHT (OUTER) JOIN: This returns all records from the right table, and the records from the left table that match up.

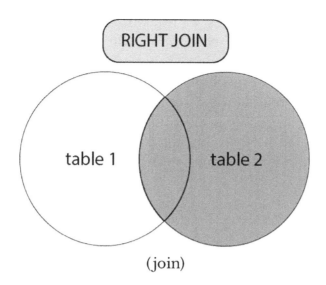

(join)

JPEG/JPG: Short for "Joint Photographic Experts Group" (a group of highly trained people who decided upon some standards required in the sharing of digital images). JPEG is also referred to as JPG – they're the same format and the only difference is the number of letters in their file extensions. A JPEG is a type of electronic file that holds images and is usually pronounced "jay-peg." Technically, JPEGs are a method for lossy compression (compression that results in a loss of information) of digital images – meaning, when the data is decompressed, the image is no longer an exact copy of the original but instead is an approximation. In JPEGs, the degree of compression can be adjusted which allows for tradeoff between storage size and image quality. The "original" image is usually referred to as a "raw" image.

EXAMPLE: You can see a JPEG next to a raw image here:

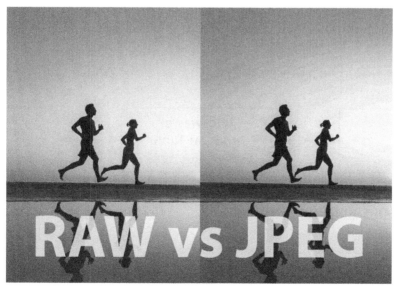

(JPEG/JPG)

J++: See "Visual J++."

jQuery: A library is a collection of files. In the world of computer programming, these library files are often made up of computer code (instructions). Programmers often make libraries of useful computer code so that others do not have to do all that work over when they need to do things that the code in the library does. JQuery is a JavaScript library used in creating web sites. It is pronounced "Jay-Query."

EXAMPLE: JQuery can be used to quickly add a feature to a website where a set of pictures is displayed, one after the other, on the screen.

J#: See "Visual J#."

JSON: (pronounced "JAY-son" or "Jason") Stands for JavaScript Object Notation. JSON is a system used for exchanging information between different computer programs. The format is relatively easy for humans to read and write, while also being able to be understood and handled by computers. JSON is mainly used to transmit data back and forth between a server and an internet application. JSON is compatible with many languages.

EXAMPLE: If you designed a website, you could use JSON to ensure your app smoothly exchanges information with the computers of people visiting that website.

jump drive: Another word for "USB drive."

junction table: A "junction" is literally a place where two items meet or are joined. A junction table maps tables together through referencing the primary keys of each table. A junction table contains foreign keys that have a many-to-many relationship between the junction table and individual tables. Another term for this type of table is a "lookup table," because you can use it to look up information in one table that is tied in some way to another table.

EXAMPLE: Here would be a junction table to track job applicants:

Here is another junction table example:

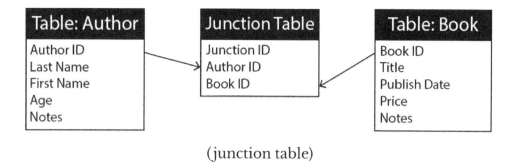

(junction table)

junior developer: Someone who has recently been trained in software development and does not yet have much experience. They may require assistance and will most certainly make mistakes. "Junior developer" is considered the lowest "rank" of software developer, and refers to someone newly trained in the area. Junior developers are also called "entry-level developers" or "junior-level developers."

EXAMPLE: A junior developer has the basic skill-set necessary to work as an entry-level technology professional.

Jupyter Notebook: An open-source web application that uses the python language to create and share documents that contain code, statistical equations, data visualizations and text. You can use Jupyter Notebook for working with data in a variety of ways.

EXAMPLE: Jupyter Notebook can be utilized in data science projects.

(Jupyter Notebook)

just in time: In manufacturing, just-in-time refers to a system where supplies and materials are delivered right before they'll be needed (as opposed to warehouses stored with all possible supplies and materials ahead of time). The purpose of just-in-time manufacturing is to reduce inventory costs.

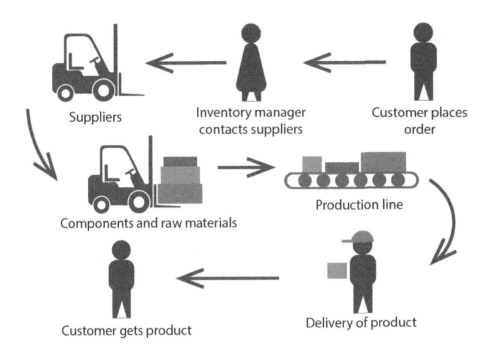

Suppliers

Inventory manager
contacts suppliers

Customer places
order

Components and raw materials

Production line

Customer gets product

Delivery of product

In software development, just in time (JIT) refers to compiling, executing or loading code only as it is needed. Meaning, instead of all of the data being processed at once, that which is needed is handled at the time it is needed.

EXAMPLE: Microsoft's software development framework (.NET) contains a vital component called the JIT compiler.

JVM: Short for "Java Virtual Machine." JVM is an engine that provides a runtime environment for Java code or Java applications. The JVM converts Java code into machine language.

EXAMPLE: At some point in the past you may have been prompted to download and install Java in order to run a program. Within that Java installation is found the JVM.

K

k, K: Stands for "kilo." This is a part of the Metric measuring system. Kilo means thousand. See also "byte."

EXAMPLE: $1K is $1,000.00.

Kanban: A project management methodology, and also software that implements that methodology. It is used to visualize tasks and workflows using columns and cards (squares containing various information). The cards represent tasks, and the columns organize those tasks by their progress or current stage in development. Kanban is the Japanese word for "billboard." This process was developed by the car manufacturer Toyota in the 1940s and was originally a scheduling system. The purpose was to improve efficiency by limiting supplies to just what was needed for the immediate task at hand.

EXAMPLE: Kanban was used by Pixar to manage projects.

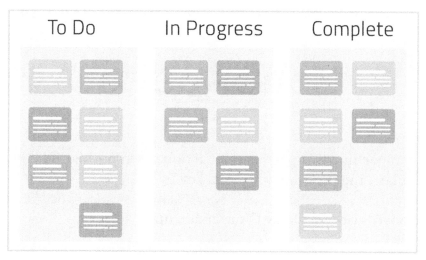

(Kanban)

Kb: See "byte."

KB: See "byte."

Kbps: See "byte."

KBps: See "byte."

kern: To adjust the spacing between letters and characters. The term comes from the Latin word cardo, meaning "hinge." The spacing of letters is referred to as *kerning*.

When the kerning is proportional to each letter, it appears more aesthetically pleasing, as well as more legible. Just like line spacing, if the characters overlap, the user will struggle to read the text properly. Also, switching around the kerning for every character could cause issues for readers.

EXAMPLE: Here are some examples of kerning:

Typography

T y p o g r a p h y

Typography

When letters are spaced so that they only take up the amount of space they need (not more or less) this is called proportional kerning:

Proportional

Monospace kerning is when the spacing for each letter is exactly the same, like this:

Monospace

(kern)

key: 1. A button on a machine that performs an action when pushed. The pushing of a key is called a keystroke – the pressing down of a key.

EXAMPLE: Keyboards (see "keyboard") are made up of keys.

2. A field or a combination of fields in a database table. Keys are used to retrieve (grab) and sort rows (records) based on specific requirements. Their purpose is to speed up data access and to create links between separate tables. Keys establish and identify relationships between tables. More precisely, a key is a piece of data that is used to uniquely identify a specific row in a table in a database. No two rows in a table can have the same key. If someone attempts to add a row to that table with a key that is the same as a key used in an existing row, the row will not be added to the table. In the real world this would be something like a Social Security Number – many people may have the same exact name, but no two people can have the same Social Security Number. The SSN is therefore a "unique identifier" for an individual citizen.

EXAMPLE: Review this image:

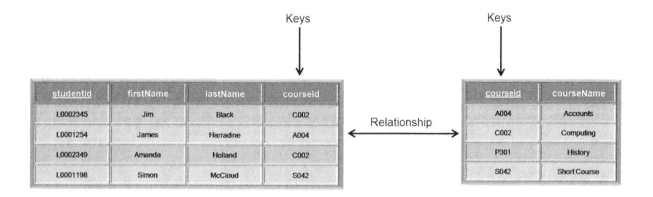

3. Another word for "password."

4. See "KVP."

keyboard: The main part of a computer keyboard is much like a typewriter – it has keys for alphanumeric (made up of a combination of letters and numbers) input. This includes keys for the letters A through Z, a Space bar to insert an empty space, the digits 0 through 9, and a Shift key to modify the output of the letter keys from lowercase to uppercase. Keyboards have been the primary input device (machine for putting data into a computer) used with computers nearly since computers were first created. This was a logical move, since typewriters were in common use in society at that time, and since alphanumeric data was a common type of data needed by computer programs. Keyboards can often have a "Caps Lock" or "Shift Lock" key that can toggle (switch) between two states. If the Caps Lock has not been pressed, the A-Z keys are lower case. If the Caps Lock key is pressed once, the keyboard is in a different mode, and the A-Z keys will be upper case without needing to use the Shift key. When the Caps Lock key is pressed again, the keyboard returns to the previous mode, and the A-Z keys are lower case again. The Caps Lock key does not affect how the number keys operate. Over the years, computer manufacturers have worked together with keyboard manufacturers to add additional keys to keyboards that provide certain functionality (actions able to be performed) beyond just input of alphanumeric data (text). Not all keyboards have these additional keys, and some keyboards can have others. Keyboards often come with a manual that describes the use of these additional keys. These additional keys are often used in combination with other keys to perform special actions. This involves holding down one key while pressing one or more other keys. This action is usually described as a "keyboard shortcut" because they're quicker than more complex interactions involving the mouse and the various programs on the computer.

EXAMPLE: The most common computer keyboard is called the "QWERTY" keyboard (which refers to how the keys are laid out – look at the letters on the top left of a keyboard). The placement of keys on the keyboard was based on feedback from telegraph (machines that send messages over long distances) operators in the past. Keyboards were incorporated into telegraphs to help type out messages.

(keyboard)

keyboard shortcut: See "shortcut."

key constraint: A constraint (see "constraint") that relates to keys (a piece of data that is used to uniquely identify a specific row in a table in a database).

EXAMPLE: The PRIMARY KEY constraint uniquely identifies each record in a table. It makes it so that primary keys must contain UNIQUE values and it does not allow NULL values for the column used as the primary key for a table.

key-value pair: See "KVP."

keyword: 1. An informative word used in an information retrieval system to indicate the content of a document. When you search for something in a collection of data, the keyword is what you type in as the thing to search for.

EXAMPLE: If you type the word "fish" into the search bar, that would be a keyword. Ideally, this would result in the computer returning a list of all content related to fish. You could then view that content.

2. There are certain words you can't use as variables. These are called reserved words or keywords. The reason you cannot use reserved words (keywords) is that they already mean something else – they are reserved for the programming language.

EXAMPLE: Examples of keywords in Python are: "True" and "False" – which are used to show the result of a comparison. For example, a comparison that checks "is 4 bigger than 2?" would result in True.

KHz: See "hertz."

kilobit: See "byte."

kilobyte: See "byte."

kilohertz: See "hertz."

KVP: Short for "key-value pair." KVPs are sets of two linked data items that consist of: 1. "Key" (a unique identifier for some item of data), and 2. "Value" (the data that is identified by the key). The key is the unique name, and the value is the content. Collections of Key-Value Pairs are often used in computer programs.

EXAMPLE: Here is an example of a collection of KVPs that might be used in a computer program for a school. Here, the KEY is used to store the name of a course, and the VALUE is the description of the course:

KEY	VALUE
ALG1	"Algebra 1"
ALG2	"Algebra 2"
HIS	"History"
PHYS1	"Physics 1"
PE	"Physical Education"

Note that in the above list, you could not have a second Key-Value Pair that used the Key "HIS," as the keys in a given collection of KVPs must be unique.

L

lambda: The eleventh letter of the Greek alphabet: Λ, λ. A lambda expression is a temporary function that does not have to be traditionally defined and named, and so it cannot be repeatedly called upon within the software. Lambda expressions are also referred to as *anonymous functions*. Using lambda expressions, you can write local functions that can be passed as arguments or returned as the value of function calls.

EXAMPLE: In C#, to create a lambda expression, you specify input parameters (if any) on the left side of the lambda operator =>, and you put the expression or statement block on the other side. For example, in the lambda expression **x** =>, x * x specifies a parameter that's named x and returns the value of x squared.

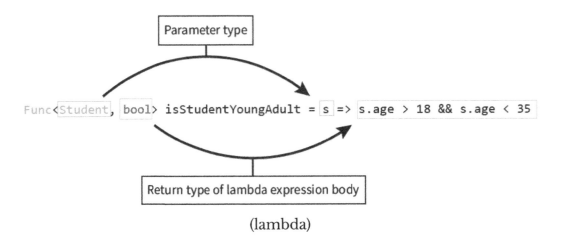

(lambda)

LAN: Stands for "Local-Area Network." A network of connected computers where the computers are located near each other (in the same room or building, for example). The fact that the computers are connected via the network allows them to share access to files and devices (such as printers). In the most basic sense, there is little difference between the internet and a smaller Local Area Network. Each is a set of computers that are connected through physical or wireless connections, and that uses a set of protocols to facilitate exchange of information between those computers. The difference is mainly that the internet is so massive. A LAN can connect to the internet. Specialized computer programs can be used to control whether the computers that are on the internet are allowed to access the computers inside a LAN.

EXAMPLE: There is an activity in the gaming community where gamers will bring their computers to a central location for a large gaming activity called a "LAN Party." All the computers will be connected together for the duration of the event, and the gamers can play multiplayer computer games.

landing page: See "home page."

language: A communication system that allows you to transfer ideas in written and spoken words. Computer languages are organized systems of words, phrases and symbols that allow you to communicate with the computer and tell it what to do. There are many different types of computer languages. See also "programming language."

EXAMPLE: A computer game could be written using one or more languages, depending on your skills, preferences and the type of game you wish to make.

laptop: A small, lightweight computer (usually under 8 pounds) with a screen you can flip up. Laptops are powered by rechargeable batteries and are easily portable.

EXAMPLE: A lot of students have laptops so they can carry their computer from class to class.

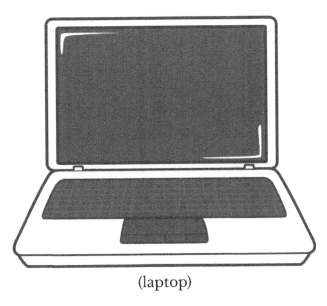

(laptop)

laser: A wave is a flow of energy that has a repeating variation in terms of how much energy is present at any one point in time. The energy amount will cycle from low to high, and back to low again – and so on. Waves come in all sorts of types, patterns, and sizes. Waves are how energy moves through space. The length of time between when the wave hits one point in its cycle and the next time the wave hits that exact same point in its cycle is called a wavelength. How many times this cycle repeats in a second is called the frequency of the wave. A laser is an extremely focused beam of light. The difference between a laser and normal light is this: Normal light sources, like light bulbs, emit (send out) light that has several different frequencies. In a laser, the light that is emitted is all the same frequency. Laser light contains a lot of energy, and that energy is absorbed by materials the laser hits against.

EXAMPLE: Lasers can be used for many purposes, including: cutting, scanning, burning and guiding machine operation by detecting very precise distances.

laser printer: See "printer."

layout: The way in which something is arranged or organized. For example, here is a house layout:

MAIN LEVEL FLOOR PLAN   UPPER LEVEL FLOOR PLAN

Software designers create layouts for apps and websites. These are specifications on where to place various elements.

EXAMPLE: Here are various website layout ideas:

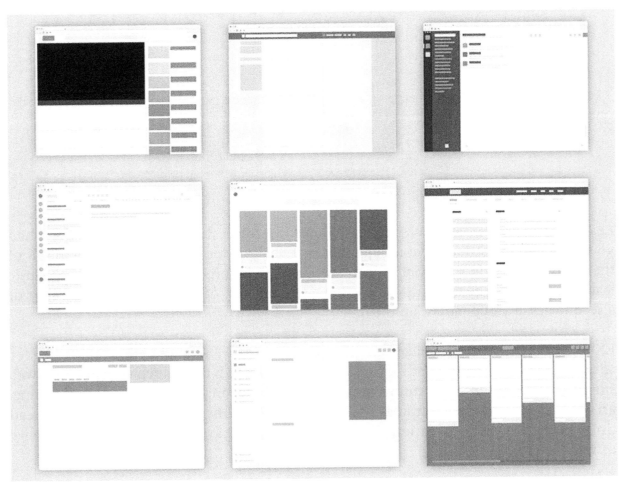

(layout)

leading: Pronounced "led + ing." This is the vertical distance between lines of text. It is typically used when referring to blank space in between lines of print.

EXAMPLE: Excess leading in a display screen can waste valuable space that could be used to promote one's products/services.

leading zero: The zeros you can add to the beginning of a binary number without changing the number.

EXAMPLE: 1010 is the same amount as 00001010 in binary, as the leading zeros are all "off."

lead time: How much time has passed since the client initially ordered the project and the completion of the project. It is the amount of time between project requirements and their fulfillment. Here's how lead time could apply to ordering food at a restaurant:

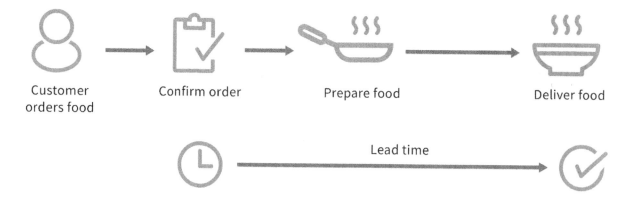

Lead time is used in another related manner in project management. It applies when you have two tasks that have a dependency – that is, one task requires some or all of the work involved in the other task to be complete before it can be started. In this use, lead time means "the amount of time between the start of one activity and the start of a second activity dependent on the first."

EXAMPLE: A project manager might use this idea in setting a time schedule for various tasks to be completed – they might need to push the launch date of a new web site two weeks out into the future because that is how long it will take for the shipping, arrival and setup of the computer that the web site will be installed on. Here, the "lead time" of the web site installation is two weeks, since we have to wait that long before we can start that task.

LED: Light-Emitting Diode. A small electronic device that can give off light. Emit means to send out. A diode is an electronic device that will allow electricity to pass through it in one direction only. When electricity passes through a light-emitting diode, the device itself gives off light. LED lights generally use less electricity than other types of lighting devices (such as light bulbs) and are usually less hot and therefore run a smaller chance of causing a fire. LED monitors use LED lights to display data.

EXAMPLE: Some flashlights use LEDs to create light. Here are some LED lights:

(LED)

left click: See "mouse."

LEFT JOIN: See "join."

LEFT OUTER JOIN: See "join."

left skew: In statistics, this is when the data is bunched up to the right on a graph with a long left tail. This indicates that the mean (average) is smaller than the median (the middle point in a set of values). The direction of the tail is key in determining the skew distribution. The left skew is also known as negatively skewed. See also "right skew."

EXAMPLE: The following image shows a left skew:

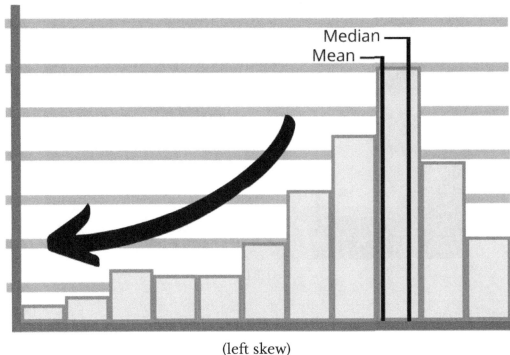

(left skew)

leg: See "path."

Leibniz, Gottfried Wilhelm (1646-1716): A German mathematician and philosopher.

EXAMPLE: In 1679, Leibniz perfected the two-digit numbering system now utilized in computers to count items and track information (binary).

(Leibniz, Gottfried Wilhelm)

Let: A command you type into a computer that tells it to do something. You are telling your computer to let something occur.

EXAMPLE: You could type "Let: Computer restart" to get your computer to turn off, then back on.

LF: Stands for "line feed." LF is a control character. Control characters are not printable characters and instead represent an action to be done by the computer for text files. The control character LF denotes a line break in a text file – the cursor moves down to the next line but does not move to the beginning of the line.

EXAMPLE: Here's an example of using the LF control character:

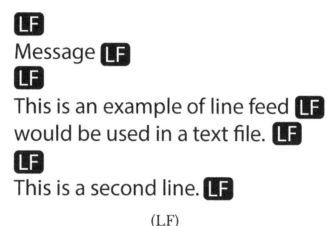

(LF)

library: A collection of files. In the world of computer programming, these library files are often made up of computer code (instructions). Programmers often make libraries of useful computer code so that others do not have to do all that work over when they need to do things that the code in the library does. See also "framework."

EXAMPLE: jQuery is a popular JavaScript library that can be used for such things as animations.

LIFO: See "stack."

light-emitting diode: See "LED."

linear data structure: Linear literally means "in a straight line." A linear data structure is a data structure where the data in the structure are organized one after the other – basically, a list. See also "nonlinear data structure."

EXAMPLE: A list of the states in the U.S. Each element of the structure, conceptually, comes right before or after another element.

line feed: See "LF."

linear regression: An approach which seeks to establish the relationship between a dependent variable and one or more independent variables, by using a straight line. This straight line is also referred to as the *line of best fit, trend line* or simply *best fit*. The best fit may pass through some points, no points or all of the points. It represents the trend of the data, as well as its direction.

EXAMPLE: If you were to track the scores in a game in terms of hours, you might see a linear regression line like this:

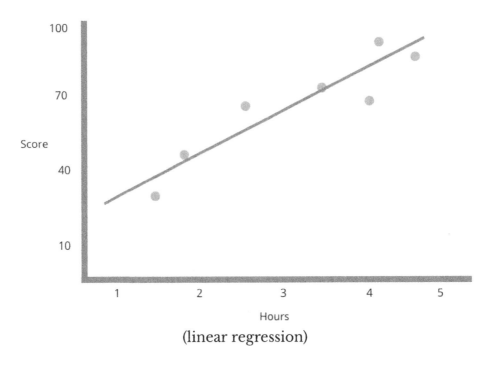

(linear regression)

line break: Starting text on a new line. It is like pressing "ENTER" in a word processor. In HTML, a line break is created by using what's called a <br> tag.

EXAMPLE: The following is an example of how line breaks are created in HTML.

```
<p>
   Two roads diverged in a yellow wood,<br>
   And sorry I could not travel both <br>,
```

(line break)

line chart: A chart used to display data over a period of time – allowing for a better understanding of trends. It is the most common method to display statistics. Line charts are also called *line plots* or *line graphs*.

EXAMPLE: A data scientist may need to analyze a chart that looks like this:

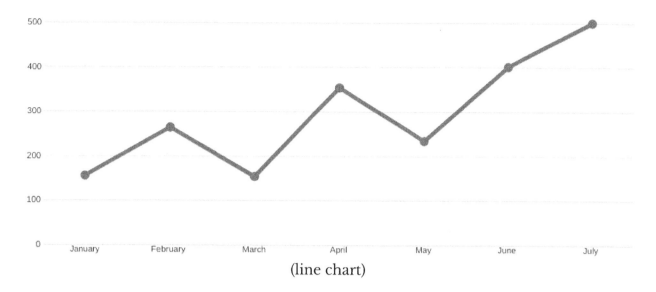

(line chart)

line graph: See "line chart."

line of best fit: See "linear regression."

line plot: See "line chart."

link: Any kind of communication path between two computers – a connection between two or more computers. A link is also something that you click on that takes you somewhere else. Links are often distinguished by <u>blue underlined text</u>. Also called "hyperlink." See also "hypertext."

EXAMPLE: You are looking at something on your computer and you see the words "<u>click here</u>," so you click on it and you are taken somewhere else. The words "<u>click here</u>" are the link.

LINQ: Stands for "Language Integrated Query." LINQ is a set of software libraries, as well as a specific system of syntax, that is used in conjunction with a programming language in the .NET Framework (such as C#) so that one can write queries against data sources – typically against databases. The syntax used to write the queries is similar to the syntax used in SQL (Structured Query Language – the most common language used to create, manage, interact with, delete and edit databases). The data source does not have to be a database – it can be an array (a list of values), an XML document or another LINQ-compatible data format. LINQ is a feature added to the .NET Framework that adds enhancements to C# and other .NET-compatible languages. LINQ is mainly used when writing queries and allows developers to interact with data stored in many common data structure formats. The advantage of it is that the way you write the queries against the data source does not change depending on the type of data source, so you can switch out the data source and not have to worry about then having to rewrite the code that queries the data source.

EXAMPLE: You could use LINQ in a program to write code that queried a database hosted by SQL Server; then, at some point in the future you might find yourself having to use a completely different system for hosting your databases. You wouldn't have to change the code that queried the data source; you'd just have to change the code that specifies what source of data to use. This is a very small change to make.

Linux: An operating system created in 1991. There are free versions of Linux available. It is based on an earlier, proprietary (owned by a particular person or company that has all the rights regarding its use) operating system Unix.

EXAMPLE: Linux is often used as the operating system for specialized computers called servers (computers that act as a central repository [storage location] of data that will be used by many other computers).

(Linux)

liquid design: *Liquid* refers to layouts that use relative font sizes and widths based on percentages. It is liquid because the website is meant to "flow smoothly" across all devices, in terms of UI (user interface) and UX (user experience). Liquid websites and software use relative fonts and images (i.e., content that changes with the display area). Liquid design is also referred to as "fluid design." Liquid and fluid design are responsive. A key element of fluid/liquid design is that the same proportions are maintained across screen sizes.

EXAMPLE: The following image shows how a liquid web page is different from a static page.

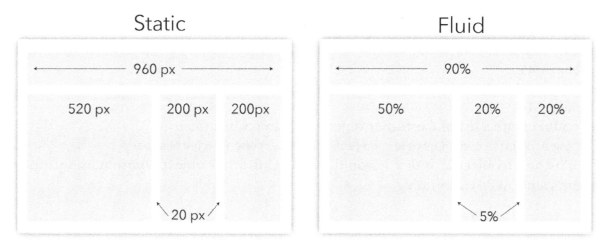

Static   Fluid

(liquid design)

list: 1. A collection of objects, where the objects are of a specific type, organized as a list of one object after another. A common example of this is a list where the objects in the list are decimal numbers. Usually, a list is written out using square brackets at the beginning and end of the list:

`[4.5, 3.14159265, 234.789]`

This list has three 'elements' – that is, three distinct objects in the list. One important thing about lists is that each object in the list has two things about it that are kept track of by the computer – its value, and its position in the list. Each object in a list is called an 'element.' The position of an element in a list is noted using what is called an 'index.' This is a number that tells where, in the order of the elements in the list, that particular element can be found. Usually, these index numbers start at the number zero, and count up from there. That is, the first element in the list would have an index of 0, the second would have an index of 1, and so on. Index numbers are often written in square brackets, much as the entire list itself can be written between square brackets. In our example above, the element at index [0] has a value of 4.5. Lists are very useful. The objects stored in a list can be objects of any type that the computer can keep track of. This means that you can have a list of where the objects stored are of type string:

`["cat", "bird", "chicken hawk", "Sylvester"]`

You can have a list where the objects are of type integer:

`[65, 2, 333, 678, 49, 19435]`

EXAMPLE: As a software developer, you will create objects. These can be put in a list. As an example, let's say you've created a class of objects that's meant to represent customers of a business. You've called this class 'Customer.' To refresh what this means: You'll have defined the properties of the Customer class ('name', 'customer type', 'standard discount', etc.); you'll also have defined the actions that can be performed on a Customer('Activate', 'Deactivate', 'Create', 'Delete', etc.). As your program is used, new objects of type 'Customer' will be added. You could have three 'Customer' objects, for example. They could look like this:

```
Customer    object    one:    name='John    Jones'    customer    type='Retail'    standard
discount='10%'
Customer    object    two:    name='ACME    Plumbing'    customer    type='Wholesale'    standard
discount='45%'
Customer    object    three:    name='Sheryl    Anderson'    customer    type='Retail'    standard
discount='14%'
```
You could create a list of Customer objects that looks like this:
```
[Customer object one, Customer object two, Customer object three]
```
The Customer object at index 1 would be the Customer object whose name property has the value 'ACME Plumbing'.

2. See "HTML lists."

literal: Something that represents a value within source code (the original code of a program as written by the program's creator[s]). Normally, when a programmer is done making a program, he has the computer convert the code he wrote the program in (the "source code") to another format that is easier and faster for the computer to use. In that new format, the program can't be easily understood by people – but it is very useful to the computer. It also can't be modified by other programmers at that point.

EXAMPLE: In programming, when you assign the number 7 to the variable (data that has a name and a value [type/amount], and can be changed) "myNumber," 7 is considered a literal.

live: Able to be seen in the real world; published. In the computer industry, this term is used to describe the point where a computer program or system has moved from a state of being in development to a state where it is in use in its final state and environment. The term is often used with the verb "go" – as in, "our new banking software has a go-live date of 1 October."

EXAMPLE: If a computer programmer was finished creating and testing a new computer program and she installed it on her client's computer and verified it was operating as expected, that computer program would then be "live."

liveware: A slang term for the people who run computers. Alive beings such as programmers, administrators and technicians. This is a play off the words "hardware" and "software," where hardware is the physical equipment of a computer and software is the computer programs that run on those computers. Other slang terms for this are "wetware" and "meatware."

EXAMPLE: A computer programmer is liveware.

load: 1. To transfer memory from one location to another (usually the original memory is kept intact).

EXAMPLE: When you load a file, it usually means that you are opening one from memory and viewing it on your screen.

2. The amount of demand on a computer program or computer system.

EXAMPLE: If you had a computer network where one of the computers held information that all the other networked computers needed to access, and one hundred other computers were consumers of that data where, at any one point in time, 80 of those computers were trying to access the computer that had the information, you could say that the load on that "data computer" was 80%.

load testing: You can run tests on a program or website where you simulate it being used by many individual users at once in order to see how it performs under those conditions. This is called "load testing."

EXAMPLE: There are many companies that offer load testing as a service.

local area network: See "LAN."

localhost: The shorthand way of typing the IP address of your local computer. If you type "localhost" into a browser, the browser knows to look at what is located on the current computer's web-facing directory (typically this location: c:\inetpub\wwwroot). Localhost is used when a program is running locally on a computer.

EXAMPLE: You could create an entire website on your computer, then run it from "localhost" in your browser.

local scope: See "scope."

location: An exact spot in the memory of a computer. The computer can use that location to retrieve data it needs at a later time. The location will have a unique number that identifies it; that number is called an address. The word location can refer to the actual physical location, or the numbered address of that memory storage spot.
EXAMPLE: A computer might store the user name "Bob Smith" at location 123456 in a memory device. Later, when the computer needs that user name, it would retrieve it from that same location.

lock: A mechanism for controlling access to something. In programming, locks are often used so that multiple programs or sections of a program can share a resource – for example, access to a file for updating it – on a one-at-a-time basis. This is done so that the data being accessed by one program is not changed by another program in between the time the data is acquired and when it is used.

EXAMPLE: Typically, a lock is of temporary duration and when the resource is no longer required, it is freed for locking and use by the next sharer in line.

logic: Actions, behavior and thinking that makes sense. When speaking about computers, logic is the rules that form the foundation for a computer in performing certain tasks. An example of computer logic is the guidelines the computer uses when making decisions, such as:

- If the maximum number of students has not been enrolled in the class, then allow another student to be added.
- If the maximum number of students has been enrolled in the class, then do not allow another student to be added.

George Boole (English mathematician) developed Boolean logic. "Boolean logic" is a form of logic in which the only possible results of a decision are "true" and "false." There are not any vague or "almost" answers to a calculation or decision – black or white, no gray. An example of Boolean logic would be answering questions with only "yes" or "no." Computers "think" this way:

5 is larger than 3 = TRUE
3 is bigger than 5 = FALSE

EXAMPLE: Boolean logic relates to digital in that digital devices only allow for one of two states. These terms both relate to the binary number system because 1 can be used to mean "true," while 0 can be used to mean "false" (two distinct states). And so, Boolean logic is the foundation for the construction and operation of computers. Boolean logic uses certain kinds of comparisons that revolve around something being true or false.

logical operator: See "operator."

logic gate: Also called a gate. A logic gate is a switch (a physical device that can be used to control whether or not electricity is passed through) that implements one of several different types of Boolean logic (the "logic" a computer uses to make comparisons, where only one of two possible outcomes is possible: true/false, yes/no, on/off, etc. – which is based on a system of logic developed by English mathematician George Boole) operations. It takes one or more "true/false" inputs and produces a single "true/false" output. In computers, if electricity is allowed to flow, that is considered "true"; if it is not allowed to flow, that is considered "false." Gates are part of how we can use computers to make decisions based on the results of analyzing data. A conceptual diagram of a gate could look like this:

Here, the two lines on the left represent the input bits; the single line on the right represents the output bit. The part that looks like a large letter "D" represents the actual gate itself – the electronic components that do the work of analyzing the input bits and determining what output bit to create. The inputs on the left are commonly labeled "Input A" and "Input B." One of the most common types of gates is called an "AND gate." Let's use that as an example to illustrate how gates work. An AND gate takes two "true/false" inputs and produces a "true" output ONLY if BOTH of the inputs are "true." Here is the symbol used for an AND gate:

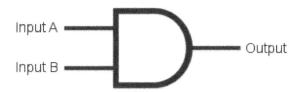

Here, the inputs are the two lines on the left, and the output is the line on the right. The inputs on the left are commonly labeled "Input A" and "Input B." To show how the AND gate works, we will use a truth table. Truth tables are mathematical tables laying out the possible inputs for a logic gate, along with their corresponding output. Here is a truth table for an AND gate:

INPUT A	INPUT B	OUTPUT
FALSE	FALSE	FALSE
FALSE	TRUE	FALSE
TRUE	FALSE	FALSE
TRUE	TRUE	TRUE

EXAMPLE: You are in charge of controlling who can access a final exam summary page in a computer program for college students. Access is based on two factors: age and Grade Point Average (GPA). The page is intended for use by students who are adults and have good performance in their studies. In this instance, you might want to allow access ONLY if the student is above 18 years of age AND has a GPA above 3.20. When you put instructions in a computer program to this effect, the computer could use an AND gate to decide whether or not to allow the student to access the summary page. The truth table for that AND gate would look like this:

Input 1: Age > 18?	Input 2: GPA > 3.20?	Output: Allow access?
FALSE	FALSE	FALSE
FALSE	TRUE	FALSE
TRUE	FALSE	FALSE
TRUE	TRUE	TRUE

logistic distribution: A method to model the representation of growth. Its application is used in real-life data, such as sports and finance. Logistic distribution provides insight into the likelihood of extreme events occurring.

EXAMPLE: Logistic distribution could give us an accurate picture of how likely it would be for a baseball player to hit five home runs in a game.

logistic regression: In statistics, *logistic regression* is used to find the probability of success or failure in an event or events. It is used when the dependent variable (a variable is data that has a name and a value [type/amount], and can be changed) is binary in nature. Meaning, the dependent variable is represented by true/false, 1/0, etc., while one or more of the independent variables is either:
- Nominal (named data),
- Ordinal (data that is both categorical and statistical),
- An interval (ordered data that can be measured), or
- A ratio (data that has an absolute zero, that can be added, subtracted, multiplied, and divided, but cannot be negative).

EXAMPLE: Let's say we wanted to predict if an email is a scam: [1] yes, [0] no.
Here are some independent variables that could determine if the email is a scam:
- Starting the email with "Hello customer," instead of your name.
- Multiple typos.
- Asking for money.
- Asking for personal information.
As a graph, logistic regression can be displayed like this:

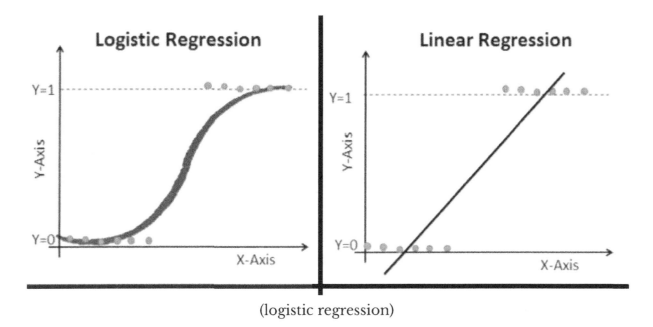

(logistic regression)

log in: See "log out."

log off: See "log out."

log out: To disconnect from a system, computer, or program. Often, this refers to the situation where access to the computer or program requires providing certain credentials, or where the computer or program needs to keep track of who is using it. Also called "log off." The opposite of logging out would be logging in. Logging in typically requires a username and password.

EXAMPLE: If you do not log out of Facebook, then people can read your messages, comment for you, etc.

lookup table: See "junction table."

loop: A sequence of instructions that are continually repeated until an exact condition is achieved. A loop works this way:
First, a series of instructions is created that is intended to be performed repetitively.
Second, a condition is defined that will mean that the series of instructions can stop being performed.
Finally, the loop is started – the series of actions is done, and the condition is checked.
If the condition is met, the loop ends – that series of instructions is no longer performed. If the condition is not met, the series of instructions is performed again. This is something we do in life all the time, though we may not think of it the same way. For example, let's say you are washing dishes. You have a set series of actions you take to wash a dish. This real-world "loop" could go like this:
1. Scrape excess food in the garbage.
2. Wash the dish with warm soapy water.

3. Rinse the dish in warm clean water.
4. Place the dish on a drying rack.

While doing the dishes, you would repeat this series of actions over and over until you were "done." Typically, this would be when you have no more dirty dishes to wash. So, this is basically a loop – the steps to wash a dish are your series of instructions, and "no more dirty dishes" is your condition for no longer repeating the loop. Loops are used very often in computer programs. Here, a loop is where a certain set of instructions are performed by a computer program, then the program checks to see if it has reached the condition required for completion. If not, it starts over and repeats the set of instructions. If so, it exits the loop and moves on to the next consecutive instruction in the computer program.

EXAMPLE: Loops are an example of the difference between humans and machines because if you do not tell the computer when to stop the loop, it will continue looping (repeating) forever. Loops that incessantly repeat are called "infinite loops." Computers have to have every step, including "begin" and "end," spelled out to them. A person would lose their mind adding 1 forever, but computers are machines – they have no mind, and cannot feel – they are inanimate objects made up of plastic, metal, electricity, etc.

Lovelace, Ada (1815-1852): In 1833, an English mathematician named Ada Lovelace met Charles Babbage (an English mathematician, philosopher, inventor and mechanical engineer). Babbage had invited her to see an early design for his Difference Engine (automatic mechanical calculator). She was fascinated with it and in 1842 ended up writing her own computer program to run on his machine. You can see a copy of the original here:

Diagram for the computation by the Engine of the Numbers of Bernoulli. See Note G. (page 722 et seq.)

Her program was designed to run on one of Babbage's computers – it accurately calculated a sequence of numbers. Though she is sometimes referred to as the first person to ever write a computer program, that is not technically accurate because Babbage had written programs about seven years before. But while Babbage's programs were found to have some errors in them, Ada's code was verified as being able to operate flawlessly – when actual Difference Engines were eventually constructed from Babbage's design, Ada's code was tested on Babbage's computer and her program ran correctly with no errors. So, in truth, Ada was the first computer programmer to write a perfect program. She was also one of the first to view computers as more than just a calculator. She even mentioned the possibility of using computers to create art and music. One of her inventions includes the "loop" – a sequence of instructions that are continually repeated until an exact condition is achieved.

EXAMPLE: Ada Lovelace is justifiably revered as one of the most influential figures in the history of the computer. Not only did she break down gender barriers in the male-dominated field of scientific research, but her breakthroughs in some of the core principles of computing laid the foundation for work done nearly a century later when electronic computers became a reality. She has been honored in many ways, not the least of which was the creation of a computer language called "Ada."

(Lovelace, Ada)

low definition: See "resolution, levels of."

low-level language: A programming language (a system of specialized words and symbols used to communicate with a computer and to create programs) that is designed to be efficient for a computer to execute. This is called a low-level language because it is brought close down to the computer's level of physical construction. A person attempting to read a low level language may become confused because the lower the language, the less it is like English. The opposite of this is a high-level language (one written in a similar way to English). Most people find that a low-level language is more difficult to learn than a high-level language.

EXAMPLE: Computer instructions in a low level language can look like this: `MOV AL, 61h`. Here, you are telling the computer to store a number in a specific location in the computer's memory. An instruction in a high-level language, however, might look like this: `age = 18;`. Assembly language and machine language are low-level languages.

LTE: See "G (cell phone)."

lurker: A person who hangs out in a chatroom or on a message board and just lurks (remains "hidden" to just watch; spectates) and does not participate.

EXAMPLE: In a chatroom, if you just watch and do not chat, you are a lurker.

M

m, M: Stands for "mega." This is a part of the Metric measuring system. Mega means million. See also "byte."

EXAMPLE: $1M is $1,000,000.00.

Mac: See "Macintosh."

MacBook: A laptop computer created by the technology company Apple. Macbooks were first introduced in 2006. Their screens range from 11-17 inches in size. The "Mac" part of the name is short for "Macintosh," which is a variety of apple. See also "Macintosh."

EXAMPLE: A Macbook can be used to record and edit music.

machine: A device (equipment with a purpose; tools) made by humans to get work done. Machines are usually made out of durable materials like wood, plastic and metal. Normally they have some parts that move and some parts that do not; sometimes they have no moving parts at all. They receive some kind of energy that they use to do their work. One of the things that makes people different from animals is their ability to create complex machines. Usually people create machines because there is some work they want to do that the machine could help them with. The help the machine provides could be to get the work done faster, to do the work with less chance of errors, or to do the work nearly continuously, without the need to stop for food or sleep. There are other reasons people make machines, but it usually comes down to getting more work done in a given amount of time with fewer errors. As time goes on, machines often get improved or changed to make them more effective or to respond to changes in the area of society where they are used.

EXAMPLE: Cars, computers, planes, telephones and ovens are all machines.

(machine)

machine code: See "machine language."

machine cycle: Several steps for completing a computer instruction. When computers are manufactured, the CPU (Central Processing Unit – the "brain" of the computer; a physical piece within the computer that processes [handles; performs actions with and on] data) is made so that it will obey certain instructions and perform exact actions when given those instructions. The machine instructions (a command given in a way the computer "understands" and that reflects the construction of its components – 1s and 0s) are available from the manufacturer of the computer. To complete an instruction, the CPU does a series of steps called a machine cycle. This cycle is often called the "fetch-decode-execute" cycle. The machine cycle is composed of:

1. "Fetch": Getting the next instruction to be executed
2. "Decode": Translating the instruction from a coded form into a form the computer can understand
3. "Execute": Performing the instruction

One of the primary performance ratings of a computer will be how many machine cycles it can perform per second.

EXAMPLE: Most actions you do with a computer require hundreds or thousands of machine cycles per action. However, most computers are able to perform billions of machine cycles per second.

machine instruction: See "machine language."

machine language: Also called "machine code," "native code" and "computer language." Computers have their own language called "machine language." Computers are designed to perform actions based on instructions written in machine language. The only two symbols used in machine language are 1 and 0. What this means is that by typing these 1s and 0s into a computer, we can make it operate. For example, by typing

1100 0111, you could change the color of the text on the screen. But wait – when was the last time you typed 1s and 0s into a computer to get it to do something? Probably never. Fortunately, the people who designed computers worked out how we can write the instructions for the computer in a language that looks a lot like English – and inside the computer those instructions are translated into machine language that the computer can understand. Commands written in machine language are called "machine instructions." When computers are manufactured, they're made so that they obey machine instructions. Some machine instructions are already built in and they automatically run so as to enable your computer to perform basic actions, such as starting up when you turn on the computer.

EXAMPLE: For example, every letter you type has its own series of binary 1s and 0s assigned to it so the computer can "understand" what to display. The letter "A" could be binary number 01000001, and the binary number for a lowercase "a" could be 01100001. Here's an example illustration:

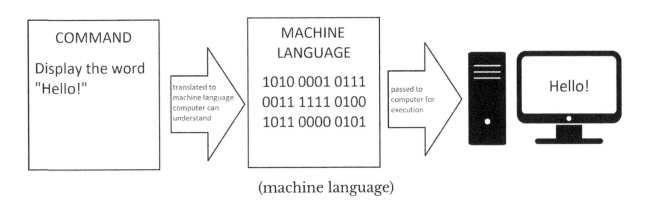

(machine language)

machine learning: "Machine learning" is sometimes used interchangeably with "AI," but there is a slight difference between the two terms. Machine learning is using AI to allow computers to "learn" based on data. It is a subcategory of AI that specifically relates to computers using data to make predictions or decisions without being specifically programmed to make those exact predictions or decisions.

EXAMPLE: Let's take a concept called "image recognition." You could program a computer to "recognize" which pictures contain cats. You wouldn't have to program every cat picture that ever existed into the computer but instead give exact parameters (instructions; boundaries that define the scope of a particular activity) that lay out what the computer is to look for when scanning images. Then a computer could recognize that an image it never saw before contained a cat.

Macintosh: Mac for short. The main computer line (a range of various products that are all related in some way) produced by the technology company Apple. The first Mac was introduced by Apple's co-founder, Steve Jobs, in 1984. Macs operate on a different operating system (OS – the main program within a computer that manages all other programs and external devices [e.g., keyboards, mice, displays, etc.]) from other computers. An operating system is a special-purpose computer program that supports the computer's basic functions, such as scheduling tasks, running other computer programs, and controlling peripherals (external devices, such as keyboards, mice and displays). At the time of this writing, the operating system used by Macintosh computers is called macOS. Macs come in different forms, mainly laptop and desktop computers.

EXAMPLE: Macintosh computers were the first computers to popularize a graphical user interface, in which visual images are used to represent the various elements of the computer system that the user interacts with (files and their storage arrangement, computer programs that are installed on the computer, etc.).

macOS: See "OS."

macro: A single computer programming command that actually contains a series of instructions, with the purpose of performing a certain task. This is especially valuable when a repetitive task needs to be performed. Often, a computer program that utilizes macros will have a "macro recorder" that can be used to create these macros. Essentially, the recorder tracks each action the user takes in performing a certain task with the program and then saves that series of steps as a macro. Later, the user can just run that macro, and that series of steps is performed automatically by the computer program. Sometimes a computer program will come with certain macros already installed in the program.

EXAMPLE: If you had a computer program used to resize photographs and add a border to the photos, and this took several individual steps in the computer program, you might make a macro called "ResizeAndBorder" that contained each of the steps needed. Later, you could just run that macro instead of having to manually perform every step.

mainframe: A large central computer that can maintain and process a lot of information and is very secure. Mainframes hold massive bodies of information and provide information to other computers. A mainframe can support hundreds to thousands of computers. It is a very powerful computer. These came before the smaller "personal computers" that we are all used to working with today. The word actually comes from the early days of the telephone industry. There were places where many telephone wires could all come together so that phone calls could be connected to various places around the country. These were called telephone exchanges. The wires and equipment for a telephone exchange would all be contained in a large metal frame. These came to be called mainframes. When the computer industry formed, the terminology started being used to describe the large frames that contained the parts of a large computer.

EXAMPLE: A company that handles gigantic amounts of data, like a huge bank, might have mainframe computers.

(mainframe)

main memory: See "main storage."

main storage: The only memory storage directly accessible by the CPU. It is the area the CPU uses for its main activity – processing data. If the CPU needs data that is stored in another data storage device (the disk drive, for example) it gives that device an instruction to move data into main storage. At that point the CPU can operate on that data. Also called "primary storage," "main memory," or "internal memory."

EXAMPLE: If you had a text document stored on your disk drive containing a list of students, and you wanted to sort the list alphabetically, the CPU would put that list into main memory, where it could process the data into the alphabetical list and then store it in the document back on your disk drive.

management information system: Abbreviated "MIS." 1. A set of systems and procedures that gather information from a range of sources, compile it and present it in a readable format.

EXAMPLE: A large corporation could use an MIS to track important company data.

2. An academic discipline involving the study of people, technology, organizations, and the relationships between them.

EXAMPLE: Someone with interest in technology and how people interact with it might study MIS in college.

many-to-many: In the area of databases, many-to-many relationships can connect multiple rows in one table (a set of rows and columns) to multiple rows in other tables.

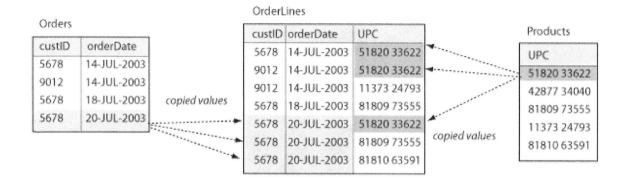

EXAMPLE: Let's say there's a list of authors and a list of books. Each book could have one or more authors, and each author might have written multiple books – many authors related to many books.

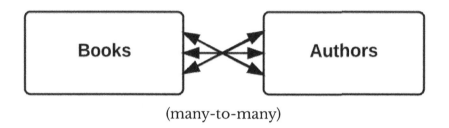

(many-to-many)

mapping: The creation of a system that connects one thing to another – essentially, it answers the question "how do I get from here to there?" In computers, this can take on any one of several different meanings or applications, including: 1. Establishing a connection from one computer to another computer or device in a network.

EXAMPLE: In a small business, you might have three computers, a printer and a fax machine. If you connected all of these physically using computer cables, you would still need to go to each computer and establish a connection so that the computer programs on each computer could locate the other computers, the printer and the fax machine. That way each computer could transfer information back and forth between itself and the other computers or devices. The process of establishing that connection to another computer or device is called "mapping" the computer or device.

2. Creating a table that shows how the elements of one set of data correspond to the elements of another set of data.

EXAMPLE: Let's say you had two schools that were going to start sharing performance data in order to increase their effectiveness. School A has a set of data with the following categories:
StudentNameFirst
StudentNameLast

```
GradeLevel
GradePointAverage
```
School B has a set of data with the following categories:
```
FirstName
LastName
GradeLevel
GPA
```
Even at a glance, you can see the two schools are tracking the same types of data; they just have different names for some of the categories of data. A "mapping table" could be created that looks like this:

SchoolA	SchoolB
StudentNameFirst	FirstName
StudentNameLast	LastName
GradeLevel	GradeLevel
GradePointAverage	GPA

You could say that "SchoolA.StudentLastName maps to SchoolB.LastName." This mapping table is an example of an *associative array* (an array that describes the association between two different sets of data).

mapping table: See "mapping."

MAR: See "memory address register."

marketing automation: The utilization of online services or software to perform marketing functions. These are tools that can be used to measure marketing efforts and automate various marketing functions.

EXAMPLE: Software that automatically sends out emails to all your customers would be marketing automation.

Mark I: The Harvard Mark I was an early general-purpose electromechanical computer. It operated similarly to a calculator. It was also called the Automatic Sequence Controlled Calculator (ASCC). It was designed and built by IBM (International Business Machines – a major technology company) and delivered to Harvard University in Cambridge, Massachusetts in 1944. It was fifty-five feet long and eight feet tall – about the size of a room. It contained around 760,000 individual parts and five hundred miles of wire.

EXAMPLE: Complex addition and subtraction problems could be performed on the Mark I.

(Mark I)

markup: See "markup language."

markup language: "Markup" is an old term used in making books and other printed things. When someone was writing a book or other text, they would do so by hand – literally writing it on paper with a pen or other writing implement. Then, when they were preparing it for a printer to use in creating a printed version of the book or text, they would literally "mark up" the pages. This would involve writing instructions on the paper. These instructions would say what size they wanted the words to be, or different things they wanted done to the text when the book was printed, etc. They are basically instructions to the next person that will be involved in the creative process to manipulate things OTHER THAN the text content itself. These instructions are called annotation. When the document is printed, whether on a piece of paper or on a computer display screen, these annotations are not shown – instead, they are used to determine the appearance of the text, images, etc. that are displayed. A markup language is a specialized computer language used to modify the appearance and format of written documents. Markup transferred over into use in computer programs that display or print electronic documents. The way to do this is with a type of computer language called a markup language. Using instructions written in that language, you are telling the computer something like "hey, this is what size text to use here," or "hey, please make all my chapter titles 50% larger than the rest of the text in the chapter." Markup languages are languages that can be understood by people as well as computers. You can use them to make certain text in a written document behave differently than the rest of the plain (not marked up) text in the document.

EXAMPLE: When creating a fiction book, you could receive the written document from the author and give that document to a designer. The designer would use markup to set various presentation elements, such as the size of the text used for chapter headings and regular text, the border to be used for any photographs or images, etc. The document, along with its markup, would be given to a printer who would produce the finished book.

mathematical object: Anything that can be used to do equations or math operations on. Each branch of mathematics has its own set of objects. Common mathematical objects are numbers, integers, and variables.

EXAMPLE: In algebra, letters are mathematical objects.

matrix: An array of numbers. The plural is *matrices* (may-tris-sez).
- A *scalar* is a number (such as 10 or -25.3).
- A *vector* is a list of numbers. These *can* be in a row or column, but do not have to be.
- A *matrix* is an array of numbers. Matrices have one or more rows, one or more columns.

EXAMPLE: You can see the above diagrammed here:

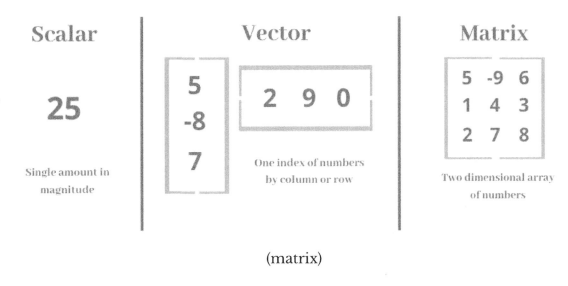

(matrix)

Mb: See "byte."

MB: See "byte."

Mbps: See "byte."

MBps: See "byte."

mean: The average of the sum. The *sum* is the total amount resulting from the addition of two or more amounts, numbers, or items. Here it is as a math formula:

$$\text{Mean} = \frac{\sum x_i}{n} \qquad \text{Mean} = \frac{27 = {\scriptstyle 1+5+6+7+8}}{5}$$

Σ is the Greek letter *sigma*, which means "sum of the total amount." In this case: $\Sigma = 27$. x_i is pronounced "zi" and is a representation of the individual data points. Σ (sigma) is the sum of x_i (zi). In this case: $x_i = 1 + 5 + 6 + 7 + 8$. n is the count of how many data points there are. In this case: $n = 5$

EXAMPLE: $1 + 5 + 6 + 7 + 8 = 27$. 27 is the sum. To get the mean, you divide the sum by the number of data points– like this: $27/5 = 5.4$

meatware: See "liveware."

media: Refers to communication of information to large quantities of people. Radio, Internet (the largest and most-used computer network [connection that allows data transfer between machines] in the world, which is mainly utilized to access the World Wide Web), newspapers, music, and magazines are all considered media. A medium is something used to relay media over.

EXAMPLE: The Internet is a medium.

median: The absolute middle of a data set. To get the median, you can rearrange the values from lowest to highest.

EXAMPLE: Let's take a set of numbers:
1. 4, 5, 10, 6, 7, 3, 2, 1, 9.
2. Rearranged, these are: 1, 2, 3, 4, 5, 6, 7, 9, 10.
3. 5 is the median because there are exactly four numbers to the right and four to the left.

This data set was an odd amount of numbers. If there were an even amount, the median would be the average of the middle two data points. Let's take an even amount of numbers:
1. 5, 4, 2, 6, 7, 6.
2. Rearranged, these are: 2, 4, 5, 6, 6, 7.

3. 5 and 6 are in the middle. So we add them (5 + 6 = 11), then we divide them in half (11 / 2 = 5.5).
4. 5.5 is the median.

megabit: See "byte."

megabyte: See "byte."

megahertz: See "hertz."

megapixel: 1. "Mega" means one million. A "pixel" is the smallest single component of a digital image. It can be thought of as a small dot that, together with many other similar dots, helps to make up an image on a computer display, television, or similar display device. Each pixel gets set to display a specific color; when many pixels are arranged together, an overall image is displayed that is a composite of the individual pixels. A megapixel is a unit of measurement equal to 1,000,000 (one million) pixels. Megapixels are used to indicate the density of pixels in a specific display screen. 5 megapixels = five million pixels. The larger the physical screen, the more important it is that the density of pixels be high. Density is a measure of how many items you have in a given area. If you had a screen that was around 3 inches wide and 5 inches tall (like that of a typical smartphone), 10 million pixels (10MP) would produce images that were sharp and clear. If you had a screen that was 40 feet wide and 20 feet tall, 10 MP would produce a very poor image.

EXAMPLE: A display screen that measured 100 pixels tall by 150 pixels wide would be a 15000-pixel screen. This example serves the purpose of showing the math involved; actual display screens are often in excess of one million pixels.

2. There is another use of the term pixel that applies to modern digital cameras: an image sensor element in a digital camera. A digital camera contains sensors that record the image the camera is pointing at. The sensors can be thought of as a grid of many tiny image detection points. Camera image detection accuracy is given in terms of pixels – here, pixel is used to describe those individual image detection points that make up the grid. This is usually given in megapixels – how many millions of pixels there are in the sensor of that specific camera.

EXAMPLE: A 3.2 megapixel (3.2 MP) camera has 3.2 million image sensor elements.

memory: A computer makes use of physical data storage devices in order to do its job of processing data. A data storage device could be thought of as a collection of boxes. Each box can contain one piece of data. Each box has an individual identifier so that the computer can keep track of it. These "boxes" are called memory locations. The individual identifier for a memory location is called an address. The computer can "read" or "write" to these memory locations – read means to get the value of the data in the location, and write means to set the value (type; characteristics) of the data in the location. Memory storage devices are either *volatile* or *persistent*. In normal English, volatile means "likely to change quickly." In computing, volatile refers to devices that lose their data when they are not powered on, while persistent devices maintain their data even when they are not powered.

EXAMPLE: When you save a file, it is stored in the persistent memory of the computer.

(memory)

memory address register: "MAR" for short. The MAR is part of the CPU and it holds the addresses for where various data can be found in a computer. The computer looks at the MAR to find out: a. the address where it can read certain data from, or b. The address where the computer wants to write information to.

EXAMPLE: If you were having the computer do addition, the MAR would store the addresses that contained the two numbers you wanted to add together, as well as the address where the answer would be stored.

memory allocation: The action of setting aside computer memory for a specific purpose or function. When you "release" this memory back, this is referred to as deallocating.

EXAMPLE: Let's say you are creating a new Twitter account. In order to complete the process, you need to provide a name and password. The fact that there is even an area for you to provide those pieces of information means that twitter has "allocated" memory for someone like you to come along and use for your name and password.

memory stick: Another word for "USB drive."

merge: Merging is the action of combining various versions of a file or folder (a location where a file or files are stored within a computer). In version control, it means to combine changes in files that exist in two or more different locations (or being handled by two or more developers). It is combining changes in data.

EXAMPLE: If a developer wanted to explore an alternate method for sorting a large collection of financial records, they could create a branch (a duplication of code or a portion of it, so that changes can be made to it without affecting the original code) of the original code and work on that alternative sorting approach while they, or other developers, continued to do other work on the original code. Then, when they had perfected the new approach to sorting the data, they could merge the changes they made back into the original code, which now had additional functions due to the continued work on that original code. When the two sets of code do not merge properly, this is referred to as a "merge conflict." For an example: If you attempt to merge code stored on your laptop with source code (the original code of a program as written by the program's creator[s]) elsewhere, but someone had made changes to the exact section of the code you had been working on, you might have a merge conflict.

merge sort: Sort means "to arrange as to sort, kind or class." An example might be dividing dirty clothes into two piles – whites and colors. An algorithm is a mathematical term. It is a plan for solving a problem. Algorithms consist of a sequence of steps to solve a problem or perform an action. Computers use algorithms. An algorithm is a set of instructions that is used to get something done. A sorting algorithm is an algorithm that arranges a list of items in a certain order. There are different methods one can use to sort things. Sorting algorithms are ways to sort through data. One such method is called a merge sort. It is a type of sorting algorithm. In a merge sort, the list of items is divided into many smaller lists. Each of these lists is merged with another list, sorting them at that point according to the desired outcome. This is repeated, with larger and larger lists, until the entire original list is sorted.

EXAMPLE: You could use a merge sort to sort a list of numbers in ascending order.

meta-: A prefix that indicates a concept which is an abstraction behind another concept. An abstraction, as it is used here, is a set of general rules or principles that have been derived from the usage and classification of actual specific examples. Abstraction can also be thought of as the process of moving from a specific idea to a more general one. An example would be the abstraction of a car as "a motor-operated vehicle whose usual purpose is the personal transport of an operator and a small number of other people for routine transportation uses." Many concrete, specific examples that fit this general principle could be thought of: sedan, truck, limousine, convertible, etc. As a prefix, meta- is added to other words in order to modify their meaning.

EXAMPLE: Metaconflict is a conflict about whether or how to engage in conflict. It is not any specific conflict itself.

In recent years, the use of the word "meta" on its own has arisen as a slang term. Here, it means "something that is self-referential."

EXAMPLE: A film that was about people who were making a film could be described as "meta," as the film references films in its content.

metadata: Meta is data about data. Here, meta- is a prefix that indicates a concept which is an abstraction behind another concept. An abstraction, as it is used here, is a set of general rules or principles that have been derived from the usage and classification of actual specific examples. Abstraction can also be thought of as the process of moving from a specific idea to a more general one. An example would be the abstraction of a car as "a motor-operated vehicle whose usual purpose is the personal transport of an operator and a small number of other people for routine transportation uses." Many concrete, specific examples that fit this general principle could be thought of: sedan, truck, limousine, convertible, etc. As a prefix, meta- is added to other words in order to modify their meaning. The term "metadata" means "data that describes other data."

EXAMPLE: An example could be the printing of a word on a page in bold. The fact that the word is bold is not part of the data on the page; the data on the page is just the word "data" itself. Rather, the fact that a specific word should be printed in bold is metadata – data that describes other data. Here, it describes the visual character of the word "data."

In computers, there is another common usage: Metadata is the data that describes the characteristics of an electronic file. One of the primary purposes of computers is the creation, maintenance and storage of electronic files. A common type of file you would find on a computer is a written document – a file containing text. A written document might have a file type of "txt," indicating that the type of data in the file is alphanumeric text. The file type is metadata – it is data about the data in the file.

EXAMPLE: You use a computer to create a written document about elephants. You might name this document "ElephantReport." The actual electronic file that would be created on your computer would be called "ElephantReport.txt." The ".txt" is the metadata for the file that shows what type of data the file contains.

method: See "subprogram." Also, see the usage note under "function."

methodology: A way to do something. Methods, techniques and approaches to getting something done.

EXAMPLE: There are several different methodologies used for managing projects in a professional organization. One of the most popular is called "Agile."

MHz: See "hertz."

microchip: See "chip."

microcomputer: A long time ago, computers were very big and filled up entire rooms. Micro just means "very small." Microcomputers came around in the 1970s and were basically small computers (small compared to the huge ones that people were used to).

EXAMPLE: Nowadays most computers are "microcomputers" because they are small, but we just call them computers.

microprocessor: 1. See "CPU."

2. The circuit containing the CPU, millions of transistors, sound card, network card and more. It basically puts the most important electronic parts of a computer all in one place. It looks like this:

EXAMPLE: Not only computers contain microprocessors, modern household appliances (such as ovens and refrigerators) have them as well.

microservices: A style of software architecture that structures applications as collections of services that are:
- Able to be maintained
- Highly testable
- Independently deployable
- Organized in accordance with the capabilities of a business

Microservices have the purpose of enabling quick, frequent and reliable delivery of complex applications.

EXAMPLE: Netflix has adopted microservices.

Microsoft: Microsoft stands for "microcomputer software." Many years ago, computers were very large and filled entire rooms. *Micro* means "very small." Microcomputers began to appear in the 1970s and were essentially small computers (small compared to the huge ones that people were used to). Nowadays most computers are "microcomputers," because they are small, but we simply call them *computers*. Microsoft is a computer company founded by Bill Gates (one of the richest men on Earth) that makes software and electronic devices. Microsoft also delivers consulting and other services.

EXAMPLE: Windows is a well-known software program created by Microsoft.

(Microsoft)

Microsoft Web API: A framework that allows you to build HTTP services for a broad range of clients including browsers and mobile devices. It is an ideal platform for building RESTful applications, which is a system that can use the HTTP protocol to monitor and control the state of various resources.

EXAMPLE: Let's say you wanted to create a database of world records that can be accessed by any websites that are interested in displaying the information on their site. You could use Web API to accomplish this.

Microsoft Windows: See "Windows."

middleware: Software that connects the operating system to applications. It can also connect databases to programs and applications. Some refer to middleware as "software glue." An example of middleware would be software that allowed communication into a database (such as putting data in, extracting data, etc.). Devices with varying levels of processing power and bandwidth need to access a network and communicate data in near-real time. Middleware provides a unified way for these systems to talk to each other. However, an operating system and other applications do not all use the same programming language (a system of specialized words and symbols used to communicate with a computer and to create programs). Middleware is compatible with multiple programming languages. Middleware became popular in the 1980s as it allowed for newer applications to be run on older systems without having to replace everything.

EXAMPLE: Here are some services offered by middleware:
- Transactional management: Manages and controls individual transactions and ensures that the integrity of a system or database is not corrupted.
- Directory: Enables client programs to locate other servers.
- Security: Authenticates client programs and confirms that the program is what it claims to be.
- Message queues: Passes messages between different systems or software that can trigger a transaction or other action.

- **Web server:** Accepts client requests from web browsers (the program people use to view web pages) and channels them to the main server database and then delivers the response to the browser.

migrate: See "database migration."

migration: See "database migration."

minimum viable product: See "MVP."

mintty: A terminal emulator. A terminal is a text-based console interface – like the windows command line. An emulator is software that imitates a computer program and can perform the same kinds of tasks. For example, there are video game console emulators (such as Sega Genesis or Nintendo 64) that allow you to play video games from these systems on a computer. The mintty terminal emulator provides an environment to run on the Windows operating system.

EXAMPLE: mintty looks like this:

(mintty)

MIS: See "management information system."

mobile: This means "not requiring a physical connection or a fixed location in order to operate." This term usually describes devices such as cell phones, handheld digital devices or similar devices, where part of the functionality of the device requires a wireless connection to a communications network like a telephone system, etc.

EXAMPLE: A smartphone is a mobile device.

mobile phone: See "cell phone."

mode: The value that occurs most in a set of data.

EXAMPLE: Let's take this set: 1, 2, 2, 2, 4, 8, 7, 5, 4, 2. 2 is the highest frequency in this list of numbers and so, in this case, 2 is the mode. There can be no mode, one mode, or multiple modes in a data set. No mode would be a rare circumstance where we had values that were consecutive and never repeating, like: 1, 2, 3, 4, 5, 6, 7. Multiple modes occur when there is more than one value with the highest frequency. For example: 1, 2, 1, 5, 8, 5, 1, 6, 5. 1 and 5 both occur three times, so they are both the mode.

model: In an MVC (see "MVC") application, a class that represents a specific element or thing (object) with which your program is interacting. Many times it corresponds exactly to a table in the database: each property of the class has a corresponding column in the table.

EXAMPLE: If you were building a program for a Bike Shop, possible Models would be Bike, Customer and Order.

modem: The word "modem" comes from these two terms: "modulate/demodulate." To *modulate* a thing means to change it. To *demodulate* means to reverse that change. Modem is short for "modulator-demodulator." In the area of computer technology, this means you take a stable electrical signal and change it (modulate it) so that it now carries information along with the stable signal.

EXAMPLE: You could have a machine that puts caps on soda bottles at a soda plant. The machine could output a stable, unchanging sound – it has a constant volume level – when no bottles are being capped. This is the output signal of the machine. A visual representation of the sound, over time, might look like this:

————————————————————————

The way modulation works is that we modify that stable signal to indicate the data we want to communicate. In this case, we want to communicate the capping of bottles over time. Here's how we could do that: When the machine starts to operate and cap bottles, you could then cause that sound to spike up in volume for a split second every time a bottle was capped. You have now modulated (changed) the output signal so that it carries information (in this case, the information it carries is the rate at which bottles are being capped). A visual representation of the signal, over time, might look like this:

Here, the "_" character represents the constant-volume, steady sound emitted by the machine, and the "|" character represents the spike in volume of that sound whenever a bottle is capped. Now you have taken the output signal from the machine and changed (modulated) it so it carries information. Since it would be easy to lose track of the count just by listening to the changing sound, it would be good to have another piece of equipment that could keep track of the spikes in the sound signal. That would be a demodulator. The way it would work is this: It would listen to the sound produced by the machine (the signal). It would ignore any sound that was at the stable, low level, and only register (count) times when the sound jumped up in volume. It would be extracting the data from the signal. This is "unmodifying" the signal – demodulating. This is just an illustration. In practice, the signal that is used to send information is not sound – it is electricity, traveling over a wire between the two devices – the modulator and the demodulator. The signal works the same way, though – it is a stable signal, modified such that it carries the data we want to send. A common type of modem is one that converts data from a computer into a signal to be transmitted over telephone lines, or vice versa. Most computers have a modem installed inside them. Here, the modem does two things, depending on whether it is receiving information or sending information. When a computer has information it wants to send to another computer, it gives that information to the modem. The modem takes that information and uses it to modulate a constant signal that can be sent over phone lines. When the destination computer is receiving the information, its modem extracts the information carried on that constant telephone signal and turns it into computer information. Here is what it might look like:

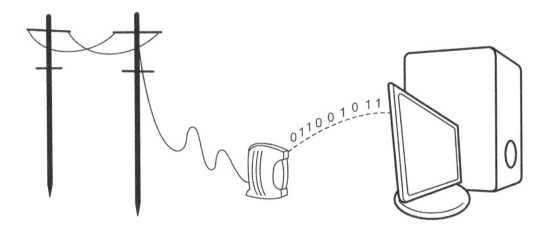

On some modems, you can plug your phone line directly into it for internet access.

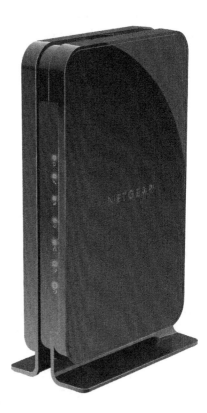

An internet connection is the primary use of a modem. But wait, isn't that a router? Well, nowadays, most routers have modems built in them. The modems within routers perform the functions covered in this definition for the router.

modulate: See "modem."

module: An individual part of a complex system. The term module can apply to several things in the computer industry: 1. A computer program may have two or more "sections" that the user can operate in, where each section is centered around a certain task or set of tasks. These "sections" are commonly called modules.

EXAMPLE: A computer program that helps maintain records for a warehouse might have a "Receiving" module and a "Shipping" module.

2. A machine may be built so that it can receive one or more physical devices that add to the functionality of the machine. These devices are often called modules.

EXAMPLE: A machine that accesses radio signals from countries around the world may have a separate device that can be attached to the main machine which can record the sound of the station being listened to. This device might be called a "recording module."

3. A module is a piece of code for a specific purpose of functionality. Each module is a file that can be edited separately, allowing you to keep your code and files organized.

For example, in building a game, one file would be responsible for gathering player-information while another would give dice outputs after each roll. These files are then imported whenever their specific functions are needed during the game making process. A module in Python is a code library that can be used to do specific tasks. A module can define functions, classes and variables and can also include premade executable code.

EXAMPLE: There is a Python module for decompressing zip files or manipulating HTML.

MongoDB: A document-oriented database program. It is cross-platform and runs on NoSQL.

EXAMPLE: Many major companies have used MongoDB, including Toyota, Verizon and Forbes.

(MongoDB)

monitor: See "screen."

Moore's law: Moore's law is the observation that (over the history of computers) the number of transistors in a computer chip doubles approximately every two years. The observation is named after Gordon E. Moore, co-founder of Intel (the world's largest manufacturer of computer chips).

EXAMPLE: If you buy a new computer to replace your two-year-old computer, it is a good rule of thumb that it can process information at a rate approximately double that of your old computer.

(Moore's law)

motherboard: Boards are thin plates with many little parts attached that electricity flows through; boards help machines perform certain functions. "Mother" is used to refer to something that protects or cares for other things. The motherboard is the largest board in a computer. It contains the most important electronic parts in the computer. Lots of things are placed on top of and as part of the motherboard. Every part of the computer is connected in some way to the motherboard (either by direct connection or via cables or other connectors). The motherboard can be considered the "glue" that holds all sections of the computer together.

EXAMPLE: More individual parts of the computer are stored on the motherboard than any other part of the computer. You can see a motherboard here:

(motherboard)

motion design: Motion (moving elements) can be very useful in design. Motion design simply refers to the usage of animations, moving effects, videos, etc. in order to impart your message. Motion attracts attention and can convey emotion. It can also signal a user to click on or interact with a particular element, without having to give any instructions. These are the four pillars in which temporal behavior is expected in motion design:

1. Expectation: The user can perceive what an object or element is by how it behaves.
2. Continuity: The flow and consistency of the user experience.
3. Narrative: The linear progression of events which becomes a series of moments for a user.
4. Relationship: Spatial, temporal and hierarchical representations guide the user through the interface.

EXAMPLE: When you see a carousel of images moving across your computer screen, you are witnessing motion design in action.

mouse: One of the primary I/O devices is a mouse. As you know, it is a device that allows the user to interact with the visual display screen of the computer. A mouse is a moveable device about the size of a small hand. There is a pointer on the computer's display screen that moves in unison with the movement of the mouse. This allows the user to specify an item or items on the screen that they want to interact with. They do this by moving the pointer to the desired location on the screen. Once the pointer is in the desired location, the user will want to take some action with the item or items that are at that screen location. A mouse has one or more buttons that can be used to control the action to be taken. The common physical actions you can perform to control actions are:

- Click (press the button down and release it right away),
- Double-click (perform two clicks in rapid succession), and
- Drag and Drop (press the button down and hold it down while moving the mouse pointer; then release the button when you want).

The mouse is one of the primary devices used to control the focus of the computer – again, that means that the "attention" of the computer is on a selected item. By moving the mouse pointer over the item and taking an action (typically, clicking on one of the mouse buttons), you can put focus on the item.

EXAMPLE: Click and Double-click operations are often used to start programs on the computer. They are also sometimes used to select an item on the screen that you wish to do some sort of work on. Drag and Drop is often used to move various items around on the screen. Most mice have two buttons side-by-side – the left button and the right button. Each of the two buttons can do those same operations (Click, Double-click, Drag and Drop). The terminology used is [Right or Left] [Action]. For example: "Left Click"; "Right Double Click." As the left button is the primary button, you will often see an instruction that neglects to specify which button – for example, "Click the picture on the screen." As you know, this means to move the mouse pointer over the indicated picture and then click the left button. There are many ways to configure (set up in an exact way) how the mouse and its buttons can be used, and they vary based on the manufacturer of the mouse or the computer, as well as the way a specific computer program is created. Programmers can actually specify what mouse actions they will use, and what will happen in the program based on those mouse actions. They can even make the program make use of a combination of key presses on the keyboard with a simultaneous action of the mouse. For example, "Hold down the Shift key and double-click the image." Another thing that can be specified by a programmer is what will happen, if anything, when a mouse pointer is positioned on an item on the screen but a mouse button is not being clicked. This action is called "hovering." A common possibility here is that some short text item might be displayed when the mouse pointer is hovering over an item. You have seen this. For example, if you hover over a picture of a bird, the programmer might have set it up so that some text appeared near the mouse pointer that said, "American Eagle in a nest" or similar text. This text is called "hover text." Some mice have a scroll wheel. *Scroll* means to move text or pictures in a particular direction on a computer screen. It comes from the idea of rolling or unrolling a scroll (a roll of paper).

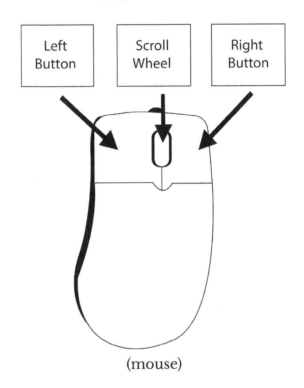

(mouse)

MP: See "megapixel."

MP4: Stands for "Moving Pictures Experts Group-4." The Moving Pictures Experts Group is a group of people chosen to determine standards for how video and audio content will be transmitted, shown, etc. The -4 refers to the type of file it is and that there were three earlier formats before this one. MP4 is a specific format (exact kind) for a type of file that contains information about videos, sounds, subtitles, etc. This kind of file can be used to play videos on computers and other devices. An MP4 is a video and audio recording, such as a movie, put into a form which a computer can process, and which uses much less computer processing and storage than the original video and audio recording.

EXAMPLE: Many YouTube videos were uploaded in the MP4 format.

MP3: Stands for "Moving Picture Experts Group Audio Layer III." The Moving Picture Experts Group is a group of industry experts chosen to determine the standards for how video and audio content will be transmitted, shown, etc. Layer 3 is one of the seven "layers" used in one method of transmitting messages between points in a network of computers. Layer 3 handles how to address and route data to the correct destination. MP3 is a specific format for a type of file that contains information about sounds; this kind of file can be used to play songs and other audio content on computers and other devices. An MP3 is an audio recording – such as a song – put into a form which a computer can process, and which uses much less computer processing and storage than the original audio recording. The information that makes up the song is organized in a specific format. There are other formats besides MP3 that are used to store audio files, but the term "MP3" has come to mean any music or audio file. An MP3 player is any handheld device used to store and play audio files.

EXAMPLE: The iPod, manufactured by the technology company Apple, is a popular MP3 player.

MS-DOS: Stands for "Microsoft Disk Operating System." One of the early popular operating systems for personal computers was MS-DOS. This was an operating system that Microsoft created for the multinational technology company International Business Machines (IBM) in the early 1980s. MS-DOS was initially used for personal computers manufactured by IBM; later, many computer manufacturers began creating computers based on the IBM design, and these computers usually used MS-DOS as their operating system.

EXAMPLE: MS-DOS is not in use any longer but if you bought a computer in the mid 1980s, it would likely have MS-DOS installed.

(MS-DOS)

MVC: Stands for "Model – View – Controller." MVC is a pattern of organization for a computer program. It is designed to divide a computer program into three interconnected parts. These parts provide separation between the three common elements in computer programs, so that the program can be modified easily over time. These three elements are referred to as "concerns" – as in, areas that the program concerns itself with. They are:

1. Presenting data to the user (VIEW)
2. Managing the data, logic and rules of the program (MODEL)
3. Taking in user input and passing commands to the MODEL and the VIEW based on that user input (CONTROLLER)

This separation can be helpful over time, since changes in one area are less likely to make changes necessary in the other areas of the program. Probably the most common design pattern out there is the Model-View-Controller pattern. It involves putting most of your code in one of three folders: The Models folder, the Views folder, or the Controllers folder.

EXAMPLE: If you wanted to change the way the program presented data to the user, you would only have to make changes to the part of the program that was the View; little or no changes would be needed in the Model or Controller. The MVC pattern is very popular, and is used in several different types of programs. Many MVC frameworks exist, for a variety of types of programs. The programmer would start with the framework and then add to the programs in the framework to customize the overall program for their needs. Let's say you write a computer program using the MVC pattern, and want to change your presentation of data to the users. You'll find that relatively easy to do without impacting the rest of your program, as you'll likely only have to change the views in the program.

MVC

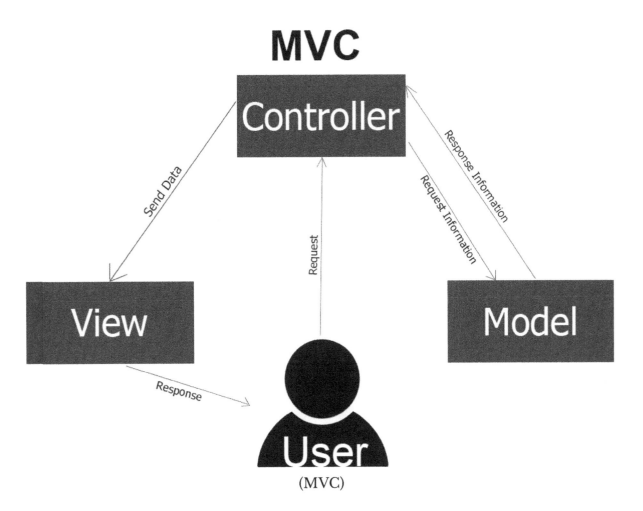

(MVC)

MVP: Viable literally means "able to survive." It refers to something that can operate successfully. A *Minimum Viable Product* (abbreviated *MVP*) is a version of a product with just enough features to satisfy early customers and provide feedback for future product development. It is not a completed project but can be used to show basic functions.

EXAMPLE: An MVP app may be able to produce some basic actions but might not look aesthetically pleasing yet.

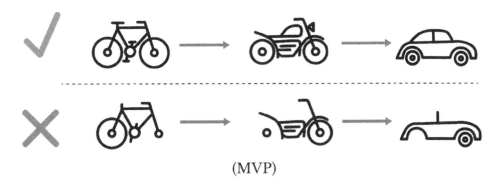

(MVP)

MySQL: One of the most popular RDBMSs out there. MySQL is a free and open-source database management system, meaning that the actual computer program instructions (the "source code") is available to the general public for use and/or modification from its original design. MySQL can be used for many purposes. Many websites use MySQL to link their web site to a database. This is pronounced "My-SEE-kwull" or "My-S-Q-L." The version of SQL that MySQL uses to operate databases is also called MySQL. It has some minor variations from the standard SQL language.

EXAMPLE: When you use the popular content management system WordPress to create a web site, your site uses MySQL to store the data needed to create the site's web pages when page requests come in for your site.

(MySQL)

N

namespace: A group of related elements that each have a unique identifier (name). A namespace is an agreed-upon system used for ensuring that all of the names for objects (individual units in a computer program that represent real-world things – such as "customer," "employee," "player," etc.) within a program are unique and to avoid code conflict.

EXAMPLE: In the image below, each last name is a namespace for each group of names:

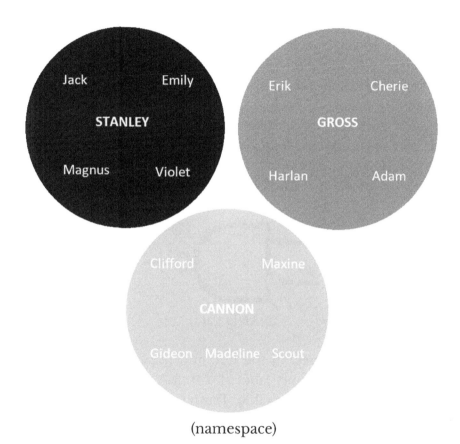

(namespace)

naming convention: A "convention" refers to "the way in which something is usually done." In programming, a naming convention is a set of rules for choosing the wording and/or format for variables (data that has a name and a value [type/amount], and can be changed), functions and other written code. One of the primary purposes of naming conventions is to improve code readability. Naming conventions are fairly arbitrary (based on opinions).

EXAMPLE: We could use letters from the alphabet to represent variables:
```
A = B * C;
```

(In this code, we are saying that variable B multiplied by variable C equals variable A.) While the syntax is correct, it does not convey a clear purpose. Here would be a better naming convention:

```
weekly_paycheck = hours_worked * hourly_pay_rate;
```

Here, we are using names for our variables that have significance, or meaning, related to what the code is doing. We have now made it clear that the worker's paycheck each week is based on the total number of hours worked and their hourly pay rate.

NAND gate: A logic gate is a switch (a physical device that can be used to control whether or not electricity is passed through) that implements one of several different types of Boolean Logic (the "logic" a computer uses to make comparisons, where only one of two possible outcomes is possible: true/false, yes/no, on/off, etc. – which is based on a system of logic developed by English mathematician George Boole) operations. It takes one or more "true/false" inputs and produces a single "true/false" output. In computers, if electricity is allowed to flow, that is considered "true"; if it is not allowed to flow, that is considered "false." Gates are part of how we can use computers to make decisions based on the results of analyzing data. There is a type of logic gate called an AND gate. An AND gate takes two "true/false" inputs and produces a "true" output ONLY if BOTH of the inputs are "true." A NAND gate is different – it actually stands for "not and." A NAND gate takes two "true/false" inputs and produces a "false" output ONLY if BOTH of the inputs are "true." Here is the symbol used for a NAND gate:

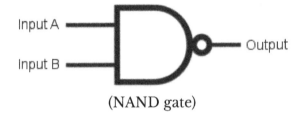

(NAND gate)

Here, the inputs are the two lines on the left, and the output is the line on the right. The inputs on the left are commonly labeled "Input A" and "Input B." To show how the NAND gate works, we will use a truth table. Truth tables are mathematical tables laying out the possible inputs for a logic gate, along with their corresponding output. Here is a truth table for a NAND gate:

INPUT A	INPUT B	OUTPUT
FALSE	FALSE	TRUE
FALSE	TRUE	TRUE
TRUE	FALSE	TRUE
TRUE	TRUE	FALSE

EXAMPLE: You are in charge of controlling who can access a "remedial study" page in a computer program for college students. Access is based on two factors: age and Grade Point Average (GPA). The page is intended for use by students who are above the usual age for college, and who have poor performance in their studies. In this instance, you want to deny access if the student is under 21 years of age AND has a GPA above 3.20 – the remedial training is not for them. When you put instructions in a computer program to this effect, the computer could use a NAND gate to decide whether or not to allow the student to access the summary page. The truth table for that NAND gate would look like this:

Input 1: Age < 21?	Input 2: GPA > 3.20?	Output: Allow access?
FALSE	FALSE	TRUE
FALSE	TRUE	TRUE
TRUE	FALSE	TRUE
TRUE	TRUE	FALSE

nanometer: "Nano-" means one billionth. A meter is about 3 feet and 3 inches. For reference, some examples of things that measure about one meter are chairs (from ground to top of the back of the chair) and guitars (measured from the bottom to the top). Doorways are around .8 or .9 meters wide. There are 100 centimeters in a meter (centi- means "hundredth" or "hundred," and there are 1,000 millimeters in a meter (milli- means "one of a thousand equal parts of something"). And so, a nanometer is one billionth of a meter, or one millionth of a millimeter (a pencil eraser is about five millimeters). Here is an illustration:

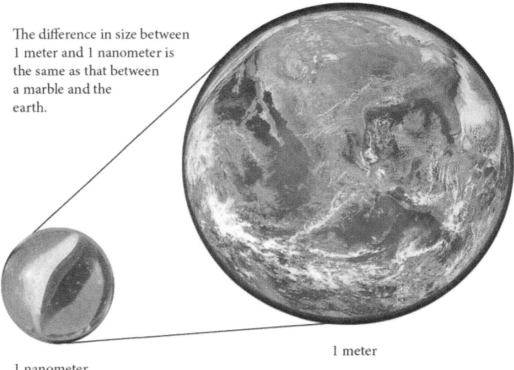

The difference in size between 1 meter and 1 nanometer is the same as that between a marble and the earth.

1 nanometer

1 meter

(not to scale)

EXAMPLE: In modern day, computers have some individual parts that are as small as 14 nanometers. Considering a human hair is about 75,000 nanometers, and a human red blood cell (tiny entities that carry oxygen through your blood) is about 7,000 nanometers, we've gotten computer components down to a microscopic size.

native: When creating a computer program (a set of written instructions, entered into a computer by people, that make it execute [perform] specific tasks) for a mobile device (called an "application," or "app"), you have two broad approaches: 1. You can write the application in such a way that it only works on a specific platform (a specific combination of hardware and an operating system), or 2. You can write it in such a way that it can easily run on multiple platforms. The first approach is called a "native" application; the second is called a "hybrid" application. There are usually strong advantages to creating a native application – they generally perform faster than hybrid applications, and they generally have greater access to the hardware features of the device (camera, motion sensors, buttons, etc.). This is because the computer programming language (a system of specialized words and symbols used to communicate with a computer and to create programs) used to create those native applications was purpose-built for that exact platform. When creating hybrid applications, the goal is to use one computer programming language to create an application that can run on multiple mobile platforms. This can greatly reduce the time and money needed to get an application into the market that can be used by multiple mobile platforms. In order to create a hybrid application, though, you usually have to rely on special computer programs that can translate your program into a form that works on the platform your application is actually running on. This has many challenges, including the fact that device manufacturers often make changes to their hardware or operating systems that can make it so a hybrid application no longer has the full functionality it once did. A native application can usually make better use of the specific features of a particular hardware/operating system combination than a hybrid app can. See also "cross-platform."

EXAMPLE: A native iPhone app would only work on iPhones.

native code: See "machine language."

near field communication: See "NFC."

negative: See "circuit."

nested: Something contained within something else. In computers, this can apply to many things. At the heart of the concept, though, is the hierarchical relationship between various types of objects. An example might be "a list of lists" – there is a top-level list, and each item in that list is itself a list. Those lists are lower in the hierarchy (an arrangement of items in terms of rank, so that some are "higher," "below," or "at the same level as" one another) than the top-level list.

EXAMPLE: A nested list of class offerings at a school might look like this:
```
Science classes
        Physics
        Chemistry
Math classes
        Algebra
        Geometry
```
Here, there is a top-level list with the items "Science classes" and "Math classes." There are two nested lists as well. The first one, nested under "Science classes," has the items "Physics" and "Chemistry." The second one, nested under "Math classes," has the items "Algebra" and "Geometry."

net (suffix): .net is short for network. .net was originally a suffix added to websites used to designate a website that oversaw a network – meaning, websites ending in .net used to only be websites that acted as the central point in a network for computers to give and receive information from; a website ending in .net meant that the owners of that site were the bosses of a network. Nowadays, anyone can choose to call their website such-and-such.net.

EXAMPLE: The website for the popular tool "SpeedTest" is "speedtest.net." This site can be used to check the speed of a computer's connection to the Internet (the largest and most-used computer network [connection that allows data transfer between machines] in the world, which is mainly utilized to access the World Wide Web).

network: A system where two or more computers are connected to each other. The computers can be connected by a cable (i.e., a wired connection) or connected wirelessly. When the connection covers a long distance, often it goes through more than one type of connection – both wired and wireless. Network is the word used to describe the link between things that are working together. Networks are used in many different ways with computers.

EXAMPLE: Information can be shared from computer to computer through the use of a network.

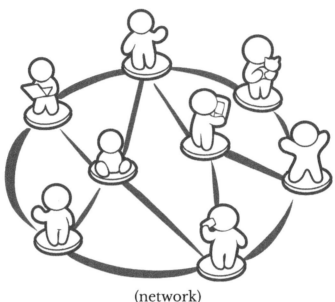

(network)

network backbone: A backbone is a part of a computer network that interconnects various pieces of a network, providing a path for the exchange of information between different subnetworks. This is part of a computer network that connects various sections of the network. It provides a path for information exchange between the various networks integrated into it. It is essentially a "senior" network containing a high capacity connection that forms the main link to various "junior" networks.

EXAMPLE: If several offices were connected to a network, the network backbone would be the main link connecting all of the offices. If this connection were a wireless connection, one would say, "Our company uses a wireless network backbone."

network card: Cards are computer parts that perform specific functions. "Card' is short for "expansion card." Often, certain types of cards come built into your computer but you can also purchase better cards to upgrade them, or different types of cards than your computer comes with. One of the cards built into most computers is a network card (also called network interface card). A network card is a physical card that enables computers to connect to and operate on a network (i.e., the Internet).

EXAMPLE: Without a network card, your computer could not connect to the internet.

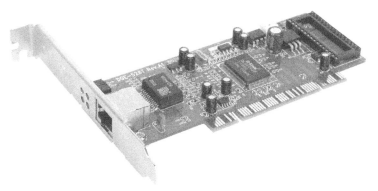

(network card)

network server: When several computers are joined together and share information, the main computer that stores the information is called the network server. The network server "serves up" (sends and receives) requested data to the various computers on the network. See "server" for more information.

EXAMPLE: If you had an office with nine computers and wanted to make it into a network, you would turn your best computer into the network server. That computer would send and receive information between the computers.

neural network: In normal English, *Neural* means "having to do with a nerve or the nervous system." Nerves are the part of your body that transmit sensation to your brain or spinal cord, and impulses from these to muscles and organs. *Neural network technology* (also known as *artificial neural network* or *ANN*) is an attempt to reproduce the human brain in a computer. The purpose of neural network technology is to try to create computers that can learn from experience – like humans do. Basically, a neural network is a type of machine-learning that attempts to imitate the human brain by recognizing things through patterns.

EXAMPLE: In science fiction, some robots use neural networks to imitate human intelligence.

NFC: An abbreviation for "Near Field Communication." NFC is a protocol (a formal agreement about how to format and send a particular type of data) for establishing communication between electronic devices that are in close proximity. If two devices have NFC equipment installed and they are placed within about 1.5 inches of another, the devices can establish a connection and send information back and forth. NFC is used for services like sharing files, wireless payments, connecting with other devices, etc.

EXAMPLE: Using NFC, your cell phone could connect to a debit card machine and send your debit card information to that machine. This can be done wirelessly.

nm: Abbreviation of "nanometer."

node: A point where lines meet; it is where paths intersect. In computers, a node is something connected to a network. If several computers are joined together, each computer is considered a node. In a computer network, the various connected devices send signals to each other. This sometimes requires the use of electronic equipment that is not the final intended device for the signal to arrive at, but is instead, a device that simply helps route the signal to the destination. A node is any device in the network that can send and receive those signals – so it includes the actual computers and devices that are communicating with each other, as well as the various devices that can receive the signals as they travel and send them on to the intended recipient.

EXAMPLE: A printer hooked up to a network is a node.

Node.js: A runtime environment that lets you run JavaScript code outside of a web browser – typically on a web server. To illustrate this: consider how JavaScript is used in a browser. The basic job of a browser is to retrieve HTML files and render a user-interface (UI) based on those files. However, nearly all browsers have a sub program in them that can read JavaScript code and execute it. That sub program is commonly called the "JavaScript Engine." Web servers do not automatically allow JavaScript code to be executed on the computer. In order to do so, you need a program like the "JavaScript Engine" that is in a browser. To set up a system like this, you install the Node.js program on the server and start the Node.js program. As long as the Node.js program is continually running, it allows JavaScript code to be executed on the server. This means you can write a computer program in JavaScript, install it on the web server and it will work. One advantage of this is that a programmer can write their code in JavaScript, whether that code is to be used in the browser or on the server.

EXAMPLE: Many major companies, such as Netflix and LinkedIn, utilize Node.js.

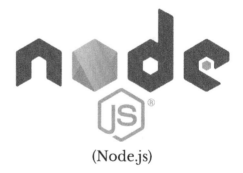

(Node.js)

noise, colors of: Noises can be assigned arbitrary colors based on the types of frequencies that make them up. The practice of assigning colors to names started with "white noise." White noise is a combination of many frequencies that have equal intensities (power). Television static and a whirring fan are examples of white noise.

EXAMPLE: Pink noise is a combination of frequencies that are all the same note (pitch) but different octaves. Leaves rustling in the trees, waves crashing on a beach, and rain falling are all examples of pink noise.

nominal data: "Nominal" literally means "in name only." A type of qualitative data is *nominal data*. Nominal data is descriptive. It is data that is used for naming qualitative variables. Nominal data is sometimes called "named" data. For example, if you had a list of stores in various U.S. states, and one of those states was New York, New York would be the nominal data type. With nominal data, there is no sequence or ranking; it can not be measured.

EXAMPLE: The following are examples of nominal data:

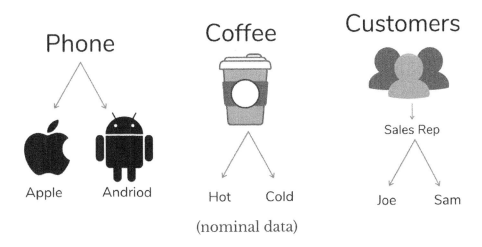

(nominal data)

non-breaking space: A common character entity used in HTML is the non-breaking space – written like this: A non-breaking space is a space that will not break into a new line. Two words separated by a non-breaking space will stick together. This can be useful when breaking the words might be disruptive. For example:

```
<p>3:11 p.m.</p>
```

would ensure that the output is:
```
3:11 p.m.
```
As opposed to:
```
3:11
```
```
p.m.
``` (or something)
Additionally, browsers automatically default multiple spaces down to 1. For example: if you write 12 spaces, the browser will delete 11 of them. You can try it out for yourself but here's an example:

```
<p>      Here's                    Johnny            !</p>
```

will display as:

Here's Johnny !

  can tell the browser to leave extra spaces in place.

EXAMPLE: If we wanted to start every sentence with two spaces, we would write:

```
<p>  Sentence.</p>
```

nonlinear data structure: A data structure where the elements (items; parts) of the data do not necessarily follow one after the other.

EXAMPLE: A common example is a family tree; parts of it might seem linear, for example, when it lists the children of two parents – but others are not linear. This is clear when you consider the children from two different branches of a family. Conceptually, two pieces of data that represent children from different branches of the family tree do not follow one to the next.

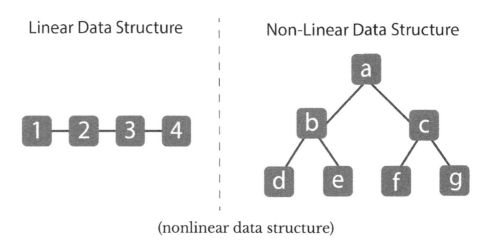

(nonlinear data structure)

non-responsive: See "responsive."

non-volatile: Cannot change. In computers, we use non-volatile when talking about a certain type of information stored in a computer. It simply means that when the power is turned off, the information is preserved so that it can be used the next time the computer is turned on. Another term for this type of information is "persistent." Information that is stored in a computer that does erase when you turn the computer off is called "volatile" information.

EXAMPLE: You have an alarm clock plugged into the wall. That alarm clock has the time set into it by you. Someone unplugs the alarm clock. You plug it back in and now the time displays: 12:00:00. The time setting on an alarm clock is volatile.

NOR gate: A logic gate is a switch (a physical component) that implements one of several different types of Boolean logic (the "logic" a computer uses to make comparisons, where only one of two possible outcomes is possible: true/false, yes/no, on/off, etc. – which is based on a system of logic developed by English mathematician George Boole) operations. It takes one or more "true/false" inputs and produces a single "true/false" output. In computers, if electricity is allowed to flow, that is considered "true"; if it is not allowed to flow, that is considered "false." Gates are part of how we can use computers to make decisions based on the results of analyzing data. There is a type of logic gate called an OR gate. An OR gate takes two "true/false" inputs and produces a "true" output if EITHER or BOTH of the inputs are "true." A NOR gate is different – it actually stands for "not or." A NOR gate takes two "true/false" inputs and produces a "false" output if EITHER or BOTH of the inputs are "true." Here is the symbol used for a NOR gate:

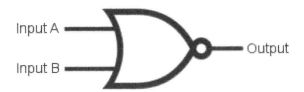

Here, the inputs are the two lines on the left, and the output is the line on the right. The inputs on the left are commonly labeled "Input A" and "Input B." To show how the NOR gate works, we will use a truth table. Truth tables are mathematical tables laying out the possible inputs for a logic gate, along with their corresponding output. Here is a truth table for a NOR gate:

INPUT A	INPUT B	OUTPUT
FALSE	FALSE	TRUE
FALSE	TRUE	FALSE
TRUE	FALSE	FALSE
TRUE	TRUE	FALSE

EXAMPLE: You are in charge of controlling who can access a "remedial study" page in a computer program for college students. Access is based on two factors: age and Grade Point Average (GPA). The page is intended for use by students who are above the usual age for college and who have poor performance in their studies. In this instance, you want to deny access if the student is under 21 years of age or has a GPA above 3.20 or both – the remedial study materials are not for them. Only those students who are 21 years of age or above AND who have a GPA of 3.20 or below will be allowed to access the page. When you put instructions in a computer program to this effect, the computer could use a NOR gate to decide whether or not to allow the student to access the summary page. The truth table for that NOR gate would look like this:

Input 1: Age < 21?	Input 2: GPA > 3.20?	Output: Allow access?
FALSE	FALSE	TRUE
FALSE	TRUE	FALSE
TRUE	FALSE	FALSE
TRUE	TRUE	FALSE

normalization: When working with databases, database normalization is the process of organizing the tables in the database to eliminate data redundancy. Data redundancy in a database refers to a situation where you're storing the same data in more than one table in the database. This leads to problems in using the database – not the least of which is the fact that when a particular piece of data changes, you now have to change it in two or more places in the database. Normalization can be done on a gradient basis. This means that there is a minimum arrangement in order to consider a database normalized, and there are increasingly efficient ways of organizing and using the data, leading to a fully-optimized database. The minimum level of normalization is called "First Normal," or "1NF." What this basically means is that the tables you have created in your database separate out the various types of data you are tracking in the database so that each field in a table will only hold one piece of data.

EXAMPLE: For example, if you've been tracking a field called "telephone number" for a customer, and you then learn that a customer might have two phone numbers, you wouldn't want to store two phone numbers in one field. This would make it difficult to use the data in the table, and the table could be described as violating "normal" form.

NoSQL: NoSQL originally stood for "non-SQL" or "non-relational." More recently it has been used to stand for "not only SQL." A NoSQL database stores data in a way that is different from tables (rows and columns). NoSQL refers to data storage mechanisms that are not relational and, therefore, do not require using SQL (a language used to monitor and operate databases) to access their data.

EXAMPLE: An example of NoSQL are document databases (also called document-oriented databases). Document databases allow users to store, manage, and retrieve data that is in the form of documents. Document databases store the data as documents instead of tables. Here it is visualized:

Client Table

Key	Name	Company	Units
1167	Ale C	Miller	570
3424	Beerio	Ians	340
5612	Amstel	Amtel	121
2409	Colt's	BeerCo	98

Client Document

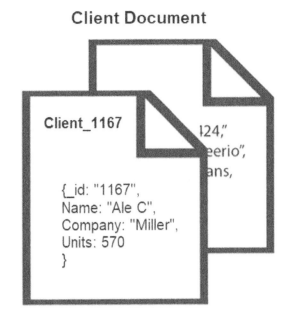

Client_1167

```
{_id: "1167",
Name: "Ale C",
Company: "Miller",
Units: 570
}
```

(NoSQL)

NOT gate: A logic gate is a switch (a physical device that can be used to control whether or not electricity is passed through) that implements one of several different types of Boolean logic (the "logic" a computer uses to make comparisons, where only one of two possible outcomes is possible: true/false, yes/no, on/off, etc. – which is based on a system of logic developed by English mathematician George Boole) operations. It takes one or more "true/false" inputs and produces a single "true/false" output. In computers, if electricity is allowed to flow, that is considered "true"; if it is not allowed to flow, that is considered "false." Gates are part of how we can use computers to make decisions based on the results of analyzing data. A NOT gate takes a single "true/false" input and switches it to its opposite – i.e., for a "true" input it outputs a "false"; for a "false input it outputs a "true." Here is the symbol used for a NOT gate:

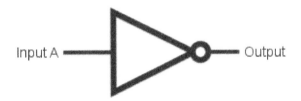

Here, the input is the line on the left, and the output is the line on the right. The input on the left is commonly labeled "Input A." To show how the NOT gate works, we will use a truth table. Truth tables are mathematical tables laying out the possible inputs for a logic gate, along with their corresponding output. Here is a truth table for a NOT gate:

INPUT A	OUTPUT
FALSE	TRUE
TRUE	FALSE

EXAMPLE: You are in charge of controlling who can access a final exam summary page in a computer program for college students. When the instructor gives you an order, you can switch whether or not a particular student has access. In our example, let's assume a student starts out by not having approval to access the page. In this instance, you might have a computer program that shows you a profile for an individual student, along with a button that lets you switch the access status of a student. When you put instructions in a computer program to make the button perform that function, the computer could use a NOT gate to switch the access permission for a particular student. The truth table for that NOT gate would look like this:

Input 1: Access allowed?	Output: Access allowed?
FALSE	TRUE
TRUE	FALSE

nth: Denotes an unspecified number in a series of numbers. It refers to an unspecified item or instance in a series. Sometimes the term is used as slang to mean you are emphasizing the number of times something has occurred. Like, "My two-year-old son asked for candy for the nth time."

EXAMPLE: If you performed testing on a group of people, you could refer to this as, "systematic testing by taking every nth name from a list."

null: Having the value of zero; nothing. In databases, null (or NULL) indicates there is no data in that particular field of the database table. It essentially indicates "nothing present." This is different from the value 0, in the same way that a lack of an answer is not the same thing as an answer of "no."

EXAMPLE: Think about this question, "How many college students have graduated in the last 60 seconds?" The answer, "Zero," *is* data. The answer would be "null" if no answer was given. Null is a complete lack of data – no data was given or specified.

null hypothesis: See "hypothesis testing."

number system: A system for naming and representing quantities. Some of the digits you're used to using are 2, 3, 7, etc. A number system is concerned with how many digits will be used in counting, doing math, etc., and what symbols will be used to represent those digits. Digits are the fundamental part of any number system. There are many different number systems. The one we are accustomed to using uses ten digits: 0, 1, 2, 3, 4, 5, 6, 7, 8, and 9. Other number systems exist that even use letters (such as: A, B, C...) in addition to digits.

EXAMPLE: Binary is a number system that only utilizes the digits 1 and 0. Any number can be represented in binary using 1s and/or 0s. For example, one thousand is represented in binary like this: 1111101000.

number: See "numeral."

numeral: A symbol, word, figure or letter that expresses a number. A number is an amount – the numeral is how we write that amount (the number). Basically, a number is technically an idea of a total quantity and we communicate that quantity (number) with numerals.

EXAMPLE: 1,001 is a numeral. Here are some various types of numerals:

NUMERALS

	0	1	2	3	4
English	0	1	2	3	4
Arabic	.	١	٢	٣	٤
Bengali	০	১	২	৩	৪
Chinese (simple)	〇	一	二	三	四
Chinese (complex)	零	壹	貳	參	肆
Ethiopic		፩	፪	፫	፬

(numeral)

O

object: 1. See "OOP." 2. See "mathematical object." 3. See "database object."

object-oriented programming: See "OOP."

object relational mapping: See "O/RM."

ODD: See "optical disk drive."

off: No electricity is running through a device that operates using electricity. This can apply to an overall system, like the monitor, keyboard and computer of a computer system – or it can apply to one part of a system or device – like just a monitor.

EXAMPLE: Just like if a light is off, there is no electricity flowing through the bulb = no light.

offline: Also written off-line. Offline means that a machine is not connected to electricity and is turned off. Offline is also used to say that a computer is not connected to a network (most commonly, the Internet). If you are offline, your computer is not giving and receiving information from a network it is attached to. The opposite of offline is online.

EXAMPLE: If a printer is offline, it means that there is no connection going to and from other devices to the printer. This could mean that the printer is not connected to a computer network (you can connect to printers using a network) or that the printer is turned off, etc.

OLAP: See "OLTP."

OLTP: Stands for "Online Transactional Processing." It is a category of data processing that focuses on transaction-oriented tasks. Transaction-oriented refers to an approach that is built around transactions (units of work performed), as opposed to objects. OLTP consists of inserting, updating and deleting small amounts of data in a database. It is an approach for dealing with many transactions from a large base of users. OLTP is sometimes contrasted with OLAP (online analytical processing), which is a computing method that enables users to view data from various points of view. It allows users to analyze database information from multiple database systems at one time.

EXAMPLE: Here is a diagram showing the differences between these approaches:

OLTP vs OLAP

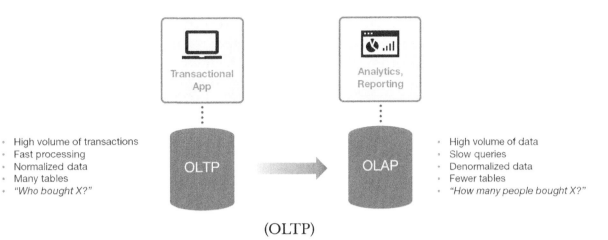

- High volume of transactions
- Fast processing
- Normalized data
- Many tables
- *"Who bought X?"*

- High volume of data
- Slow queries
- Denormalized data
- Fewer tables
- *"How many people bought X?"*

(OLTP)

on: Electricity is running through a device that operates using electricity. In a computer, this can apply to the entire computer, or it can apply to individual parts inside the computer. Many of the parts inside a computer are used to represent one or the other of two opposite states – true/false, yes/no, one/zero. The terms "on" and "off" apply here as well – if there is electricity running through that part, it is considered "on" – and that is used by the computer to represent the "true," "yes" or "one" that it needs to do its job. Conversely, if there is no electricity running through the part, that represents "false," "no" or "zero," depending on what kind of work the computer is doing.

EXAMPLE: An oven that is on when it has electricity flowing through it and therefore can heat up and cook food.

OneDrive: A service provided by Microsoft for storing files online.

EXAMPLE: You could back up your hard drive on OneDrive and share the data with other people.

(OneDrive)

1G: See "G (cell phone)."

one-to-many: One of the most common types of relationships in a database is called "One-to-Many." One-to-many refers to how a particular row on one table can be related to multiple rows of data on another table. In relational databases, a one-to-many relationship exists when a parent record in a table can potentially reference child records in another table. This relationship does not require that a parent record has child records – there can be no (0) children records, one, or many. In the one-to-many relationship, the child record(s) can only have one parent – therefore, one (parent) to (potentially) many (child records).

EXAMPLE: The following diagram shows how one table's customer ID is related to other tables with the same ID.

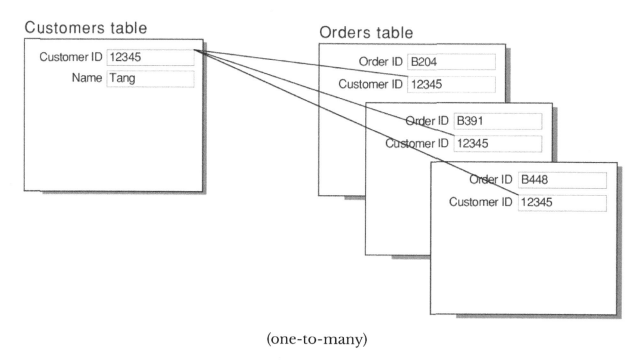

(one-to-many)

one-to-one: Within a database, there is sometimes a relationship called "one-to-one." A one-to-one relationship between two tables means that a row in one table can only relate to one row in another table (the table at the other side of the relationship) and vice versa.

EXAMPLE: Each country in the world has only one capital city (the most important city in a country – usually where the top of its government is located), and the capital city is only the capital of one country:

A one-to-one relationship ensures that only one record from each side of a relationship will ever point to a single corresponding record in another table.

Employees_table

EmpID	EmpFirst Name	EmpLast Name	Home Phone	<< other fields >>
100	Zachary	Erlich	553-3992	......
101	Susan	McLain	790-3992	......
102	Joe	Rosales	551-4993	......

Compensation_table

EmpID	Hourly Rate	Commission Rate	<< other fields >>
100	25.00	5.0%	......
101	19.75	3.5%	......
102	22.50	5.0%	......

(one-to-one)

online: Also written "on-line." Online means that a machine is connected to electricity and is turned on. Online is also used to say that a computer is connected to a network (most commonly, the internet). If you are online, your computer is capable of giving and receiving information from a network it is attached to. The opposite of online is offline.

EXAMPLE: If a printer is online, it means that there is a connection going to and from other devices to the printer.

online transactional processing: See "OLTP."

OOP: Short for "Object-Oriented Programming." Objects are items that can be represented in a computer program. They are often meant to represent real-world things. In the world around you, you are surrounded by objects – your dog, the tv, etc. Objects have *state* and *behavior*. The state of an object would be the size, color, etc., at any point in time. The behavior of an object would be what the object does (the actions it can take).

EXAMPLE: A race car could be an object. Things that describe its state at any point in time could be: engine type, engine horsepower, wheel size, gas tank capacity, etc. Things that describe its behavior could be: accelerate, decelerate, turn right, turn left, etc.

Objects are parts of computer programs.

EXAMPLE: A program might work with a Customer object. Again, the state of an object would be the characteristics and attributes of the object, and the behavior would be what the object could do. In our example, our Customer object could have states like active or deleted. It could have behavior like Upgrade Rewards Level or Add to Family Account.

Objects are often one of the first things you think about when designing a program.

EXAMPLE: Let's say you had a computer program that let you design and order a bicycle from a custom bicycle company. That program would have a written description of the state and behavior of a bicycle. Once you started designing and ordering an actual bicycle, the program would create an actual bicycle object within the computer, and its state and behavior would be affected by the choices you made in designing and ordering the bicycle.

There are different approaches you can take to programming. Object-oriented is an approach to programming that focuses on objects and data (as opposed to consecutive actions or some other approach). The first step in OOP is determining what types of objects you are going to be dealing with and how all the objects relate to each other. In particular, you would look at how some objects might be created that were based on state and behavior of other objects. OOP is a popular approach to programming computers that is used in many languages.

EXAMPLE: If you were creating a program designed to help people operate a school, you would likely make a list of the different types of objects you'd need to work with in the program: Student, Teacher, Class, Exam, Classroom, etc. You might then start describing the behavior of each object, and whether there might be other objects that could be created which would depend on one of those main objects for their state and behavior – for example, you might need a Full-time Student object and a Part-time Student object; they could inherit their state and behavior from the Student object.

Objects are created by creating *classes*, using one of many specialized computer programming languages. Classes are used to describe one or more objects. This would be created by creating (or "declaring") a class called a Customer class. It is important to know that when you first create this class, you are describing the POTENTIAL characteristics and behavior of that TYPE of thing. You will still need to create an actual one of those things. That process is called "creating an INSTANCE" of the class, where "instance" means "an actual one" of the things described when you declared the class. When you do this, the data that makes up the object is kept in the computer's memory.

EXAMPLE: In a computer program designed to track pay records for all employees, you could have a class called "Employee." Each program element representing an actual employee (John Smith, Sally Jackson, etc.) would be an instance of the "Employee" class. You would have one instance for each employee you entered into the computer. Each time you created an "employee" object, the computer would first find the "employee" class, and use the definition of that class in creating that particular "employee" instance using the data for the actual employee. See "class" for more information.

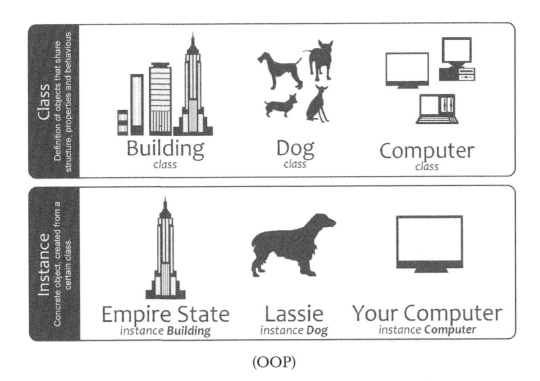

(OOP)

online discussion forum: Also just called "forum" or "Internet forum." A forum is a meeting of people on a website where ideas and viewpoints are shared about a particular issue. Online discussion forums are places on the Web where people discuss certain subjects. It usually consists of people writing messages on a "board" that can be seen by all of the other people having the discussion. These messages can be organized in many ways; typically they are listed chronologically, or by subject.

EXAMPLE: You could join a political forum and either engage in the conversation or read what other people are saying to each other about politics.

opcode: Short for "operation code." An opcode is part of a machine instruction (a command given in a way the computer "understands" and that reflects the construction of its components – 1s and 0s). Opcode specifies the exact operation that is to be performed. It is a series of binary numbers that the CPU (Central Processing Unit – the "brain" of the computer; a physical piece within the computer that processes [handles; performs actions with and on] data) is set up to understand, that tell the CPU the exact action it should take.

EXAMPLE: If a machine instruction looked like this: 0111011010, the first three digits ('011') would be the opcode. For a certain brand of CPU, this opcode could mean 'Add a number to an earlier number.' The other part of the machine instruction could give the actual number to be added to the earlier number.

open-source: Short for "open-source software." It literally means "a type of software in which the source code (the original code of a program as written by the program's creator[s]) is available (open) for use, study, alteration and distribution by anyone for any purpose." Often, in order to protect the intellectual property contained in their programs, companies will not release the source code for their software programs. On the other hand, companies can decide to make the source code for a program freely available. This is open-source software development. In the open-source community, code is typically created as a collaborative effort in which programmers improve upon the code and share the changes within the community. Open-source usually means the software is free and you can modify and use it without cost.

EXAMPLE: OpenOffice is a very popular open-source program and operates similarly to Microsoft Word.

open tag: See "tag."

operand: This is the number that is being dealt with in a mathematical operation. It is not the action being taken with the number, it is the number itself.

EXAMPLE: In 5+6, the operands are 5 and 6. The "+" is the operator.

operating system: See "OS."

operation: 1. Something a computer is designed to do. An operation is an action or set of actions created by a person that makes a computer do something.

EXAMPLE: If you set your computer to turn the screen black every five minutes the computer is undisturbed, the computer performs an operation to dim the screen each time five minutes pass where the computer is untouched.

2. In math, an operation is a process in which a number is changed or handled by addition, multiplication, division, etc.

EXAMPLE: 5 X 5 = 25 and 20 ÷ 5 = 4 are math operations.

operations environment: See "environment."

operator: A symbol used to carry out a computation. There are several different kinds of operators. Arithmetic operators such as +, -, /, *, % are used to perform math functions. Operators such as >=, ==, != are used to compare values. Logical operators like "and," "or," and "not" are used to evaluate whether an expression is true or false.

EXAMPLE: In creating programs, instructions like "AND" and "OR" are considered operators. For example, an instruction might specify:

`If someone types in both "John" AND "Sally," then turn the screen blue`

(Here, AND is an operator. It is a symbol for the action of comparing whether two things are both true.) Another instruction might specify:

`Total price = base price + tax`

(Here, + is an operator. It is a symbol for addition). Other common operators are the mathematical actions for multiplication or division. The symbols used for these operations are usually an asterisk (*) for multiplication and a forward slash (/) for division. Additional examples:

`AgeInMonths = Years * 12`

(* is an operator).

`PricePerItem = TotalPrice / NumberOfItems`

(/ is an operator)

optical: Relating to vision and sight of the human eye and how the eye perceives things.

EXAMPLE: Take a look at this optical illusion. It can make the eye perceive that there are moving black dots when in fact all the dots are actually white and the image is completely static.

(optical)

optical disk drive: Abbreviated "ODD." A device that can read or write information to and from optical disks. Optical disks are flat, circular disks that can store digital information such as audio files, video files, or computer programs. The information is stored and retrieved using a laser, which is a high-energy light – hence the name "optical" disk. CDs are an example of optical disks.

EXAMPLE: A CD player is an example of an Optical Disc Drive.

optimization: The act of making something more optimum (ideal; close to a perfect state). So it is with computers – optimization means to make a certain aspect of the computer, or something contained in the computer, perform better and accomplish things more efficiently. Optimization is an attempt at doing something as near to perfect as possible. The term "optimize" is used most often in reference to making sure that the web pages on a website will operate well and have a pleasing appearance when the device that is displaying the web pages is not a normal computer display. Specifically, there are many devices today that are capable of displaying web pages that have displays that are much smaller than a full-size monitor. Since there is much less display space available, the designer of the web page often sets the page up so that it displays differently on smaller screens. This process is called optimization.

EXAMPLE: If you looked at a website using your computer's regular display, and then looked at that same website using a smartphone, they would probably look different – possibly there might be a different arrangement of the elements on the page so that they were in one long stack, rather than being broken into two or three side-by-side columns. If so, the website has been optimized for mobile devices.

option: See "command-line option."

OR gate: A logic gate is a switch (a physical device that can be used to control whether or not electricity is passed through) that implements one of several different types of Boolean logic (the "logic" a computer uses to make comparisons, where only one of two possible outcomes is possible: true/false, yes/no, on/off, etc. – which is based on a system of logic developed by English mathematician George Boole) operations. It takes one or more "true/false" inputs and produces a single "true/false" output. In computers, if electricity is allowed to flow, that is considered "true"; if it is not allowed to flow, that is considered "false." Gates are part of how we can use computers to make decisions based on the results of analyzing data. An OR gate takes two "true/false" inputs and produces a "true" output if EITHER or BOTH of the inputs are "true." Here is the symbol used for an OR gate:

Here, the inputs are the two lines on the left, and the output is the line on the right. The inputs on the left are commonly labeled "Input A" and "Input B." To show how the OR gate works, we will use a truth table. Truth tables are mathematical tables laying out the possible inputs for a logic gate, along with their corresponding output. Here is a truth table for an OR gate:

INPUT A	INPUT B	OUTPUT
FALSE	FALSE	FALSE
FALSE	TRUE	TRUE
TRUE	FALSE	TRUE
TRUE	TRUE	TRUE

EXAMPLE: You are in charge of controlling who can access a final exam summary page in a computer program for college students. Access is based on two factors: age and Grade Point Average (GPA). The page is intended for use by students who are adults OR who have good performance in their studies, or both. In this instance, you might want to allow access EITHER if the student is above 18 years of age OR has a GPA above 3.20, or both. When you put instructions in a computer program to this effect, the computer could use an OR gate to decide whether or not to allow the student to access the summary page. The truth table for that OR gate would look like this:

Input 1: Age > 18?	Input 2: GPA > 3.20?	Output: Allow access?
FALSE	FALSE	FALSE
FALSE	TRUE	TRUE
TRUE	FALSE	TRUE
TRUE	TRUE	TRUE

Oracle: One of the largest software companies, whose primary business is database products. Oracle was the first company to support SQL (Structured Query Language – the most common language used to create, manage, interact with, delete and edit databases).

EXAMPLE: One of the most popular software programs sold by Oracle is called Oracle Database. It is used by many companies around the world.

(Oracle)

ordered list: See "HTML lists."

ordinal data: *Ordinal* literally means "relating to an item's position in a series." *Ordinal data* is data that is both *categorical* and *statistical*. For example, *over $30,000 annual salary* would be ordinal data. *Ordinal numbers* are numbers that describe an item's position in a series. You have used ordinal numbers many times in life. Common examples of ordinal numbers are: first, second, third, etc. In ordinal data, the variable name indicates that the value has some sort of order to it. For example, *low income, middle income* and *high income* are ordinal data. With ordinal data, it can be difficult to measure the "distance" from one piece of data to another because that info may not be known or subject to opinion.

EXAMPLE: Peppers can be: mild, medium, and hot. This is ordinal data on a scale of "not so spicy" to "really spicy."

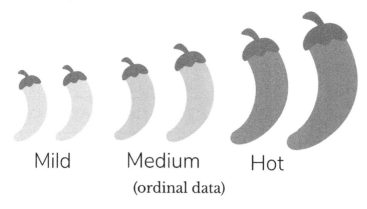

Mild   Medium   Hot
(ordinal data)

org (suffix): .org is short for organization and is a suffix added to websites for nonprofit organizations. It has also gradually become a general-purpose domain (a section of the internet indicated by a suffix, such as: .com, .org, .gov, etc.), with websites of nearly any type of entity represented.

EXAMPLE: The website for the popular web encyclopedia Wikipedia is wikipedia.org.

organic search results: The results of searching the index of web pages available to the search engine, as opposed to promotion or advertisements provided by the search engine company based on the search terms entered by the user. When a search engine returns its search results, it gives you two types of data: organic and paid. Organic search results are simply the search results that most closely relate to your keywords. SEO is meant to increase how high a website is displayed in organic search results (see "SEO").

EXAMPLE: When you search for something on Google, all the search results (except paid ads) are organic search results. Usually, the paid advertisements are clearly labeled as such.

ornamental typeface: See "decorative typeface."

OS: Stands for "Operating System." An OS is a special-purpose computer program that supports the computer's basic functions, such as scheduling tasks, running other computer programs, and controlling peripherals (external devices such as keyboards, mice, and displays). Most computer programs need an operating system to be already installed on the computer in order to function on that computer – install means to put something inside a computer that the computer can then use. Nearly all computers available today come with an operating system already installed on the computer. Computer manufacturers install the operating system before they sell the computer. Some operating systems are free; others are available for a fee. The most popular operating system in the world is called Windows. It is sold by Microsoft. Other popular operating systems are macOS (created by Apple and installed on their desktop computers and laptops), Linux (a family of operating systems; there are free and paid versions available), Android (owned by Google and installed on mobile devices, such as smartphones), and iOS (created by Apple and installed on their iPhone, iPad, and iPod mobile devices).

EXAMPLE: Windows 10 is a popular operating system.

OS X: Stands for "Operating System Ten." OS X is an operating system (the main program within a computer that manages all other programs and external devices [e.g., keyboards, mice, displays, etc.]) created by the technology company Apple; it is used on their desktop computers and laptops. Apple changed the name of the operating system in 2016. It is now called macOS.

EXAMPLE: If you buy an older laptop computer from Apple called a MacBook, it may have the operating system OS X installed on it.

OUTER JOIN: See "join."

output: The data sent out from a computer to other devices. It is electronic data, meaning it is composed of electrical signals representing the data as a series of ones and zeroes. Data displayed on a screen and printed data are both examples of output.

EXAMPLE: When you play a video game on your computer, the signal sent to your computer display to show the game is an output signal.

output device: See "I/O device."

overhead: The base cost it takes to operate an activity. This term applies to the business world, but also to computers – but in different ways. Your business overhead is the price of rent, electricity etc., as opposed to things like paying for marketing. In computer terms, overhead can have a number of meanings. For example, you might have an electronic document stored on your computer – say, a letter to a friend. In looking at the data for that document that is stored on the computer's storage device, you would see the actual data of the letter – the words you wrote. You would also see data apart from the actual words. This is data that the computer uses to do its job as far as that electronic document is concerned. It might be data such as: when the file was created, who was using the computer when it was created, who last changed the document, how much space the document took up on the storage device, where the document was stored on the device, etc. This type of data is called "overhead" – it is the data you need to have just to have an electronic document on a computer. Another example might be the routine tasks the computer does as it is sitting unused – it is periodically checking the keyboard to see if the user has typed anything; it is continually sending information to the computer display, etc. These tasks require work on the part of the computer – therefore, if you give the computer other tasks to do (such as printing a document), it will still need to do those basic tasks in addition to the new task you gave it. The work done by the computer on those basic tasks is called overhead.

EXAMPLE: If you design a computer program that continually places news headlines at the bottom of the computer screen, you have added to the overhead of the computer.

P

PaaS: Platform as a service (PaaS) is a cloud computing model in which a third-party provider delivers hardware and software tools – typically those needed for application development – to users over the internet.

EXAMPLE: Microsoft offers Azure Paas to clients that need a platform for publishing web applications and other software projects.

package: See "software package."

package manager: A set of software tools that automates the process of installing, configuring, upgrading, and removing computer programs for a computer's operating system in a consistent manner. Package managers deal with packages (a package contains all the files you need for a module). Package managers usually maintain a database of software dependencies and version information to prevent software mismatches and missing prerequisites. One of their main uses is to eliminate the need for manual installs and updates.

EXAMPLE: NPM is a package manager for JavaScript.

padlock icon: See "certificate authority."

paradigm: A typical example of something; something that can be used as a model for other things. In programming, there are different approaches to building software. These approaches are called paradigms.

EXAMPLE: Object-oriented programming is a programming paradigm.

parameter: Sometimes the subprogram needs some information from the main program in order to perform its tasks. When the subprogram is created, its description might include this information. That information is called the "parameters" of the subprogram. Often, the subprogram will do its work and then provide the main program with some information derived from its work. That is called returning information to the main program.

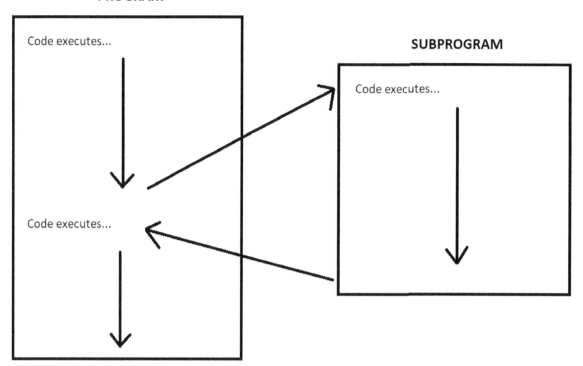

PROGRAM

Code executes...

Code executes...

SUBPROGRAM

Code executes...

EXAMPLE: You might have a subprogram that adds two numbers. It could look like this:

```
subprogram AddTwo(x, y)
{ return x + y }
```

Here, the name of the subprogram is "AddTwo." The parameters of the subprogram are two numbers called x and y. The subprogram will return the sum of those two numbers. The creation of a subprogram, as shown above, is called "defining" the subprogram. The above is an example of a subprogram definition. Let's look at how that would be used in a main program. Say you had a school with two Physical Education classes per day, and you wanted to have the program calculate the total number of students in those classes. You could make a main program that made use of our "AddTwo" subprogram. It might look like this:

```
classSizePE1 = 25
classSizePE2 = 43
totalSize = AddTwo(classSizePE1, classSizePE2)
print("The total number of students in the PE classes is: " + totalSize)
```

Let's look at this program one line at a time.

1. Line 1: The main program created a variable called "classSizePE1" and gave it a value of 25.
2. Line 2: The main program created a variable called "classSizePE2" and gave it a value of 43.
3. Line 3: There are five things happening here.
   A. First, the main program created a variable called "totalSize."

B. Second, the main program called the subprogram "AddTwo." That subprogram was given the values 25 and 43 since those are the values of the variables "classSizePE1" and "classSizePE2."

C. Third, the subprogram "AddTwo" performed its work, taking the values 25 and 43 and adding them together to create the value 68.

D. Fourth, the subprogram returns that value to the main program.

E. Fifth, the main program gave that value to the variable "totalSize."

4. Line 4: The main program then continued running. Here, the program used the value of the variable totalSize to display this text on the screen:

`The total number of students in the PE classes is: 68`

This brings us to the concept of arguments. Arguments are the actual data passed to a subprogram when it is called. In the above example, the arguments are the numbers 25 and 43. This comes from mathematics. In mathematics, there are formulas. These are exact math operations that are done in an exact order. Typically, these math formulas need to be given some initial values to start processing the math steps. Those initial values are called arguments. A subprogram does not necessarily need any arguments. Some subprograms may take one argument; some may take more than one. To clarify: when a subprogram is defined, any data items it will need are called parameters. When the subprogram is actually used, the actual data passed to it at that time are called arguments.

parent class: An object is an item within a computer program that has state and behavior and a class is a description of an object. A parent class is a class that other classes (referred to as child classes) derive properties and behavior from. See also "class."

EXAMPLE: A parent class could be "Insect," with the following states and behaviors: awake, asleep, move and eat. You could then create a child class called "Ant," which automatically would contain the states and behaviors contained in the parent class (awake, asleep, move and eat).

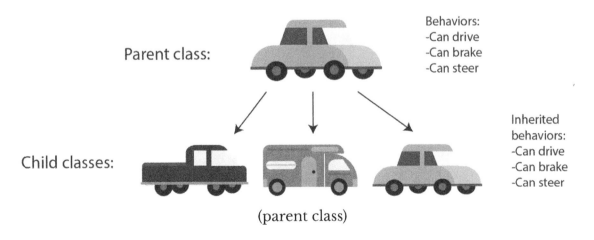

(parent class)

Pareto principle: The Pareto principle (also called the 80/20 rule) is the idea that about 80% of an outcome results from 20% of the effort. Some say this concept was named after the Italian economist Vilfredo Pareto.

EXAMPLE: When it comes to websites and software, about 80% of users will use about 20% of the features.

parse: To break something up into its parts and analyze it. In computing, it means that the program code is analyzed and read.

EXAMPLE: If you write code for a web site, the web server parses the code and then outputs the correct HTML code to the browser.

Parsing can also refer to the process of scanning ordinary text to apply logic to it. For example, search engines typically parse search phrases entered by users so that they can more accurately search for each word.

Pascal: A computer programming language released in 1970.

EXAMPLE: Many other programming languages were derived from Pascal (such as Macintosh Programmer's Workshop Pascal – which was used to create the program Photoshop).

Pascal, Blaise (1623-1662): A French mathematician, writer, physicist and inventor. He contributed many things to mathematics and other fields. There is a computer programming language (a system of specialized words and symbols used to communicate with a computer and to create programs) named after him: Pascal.

EXAMPLE: He is considered one of the inventors of the first mechanical calculator.

(Pascal, Blaise)

password: A set of letters, numbers and symbols used to verify one's right to access controlled data, devices or computer programs (a set of written instructions, entered into a computer by people, that make it execute [perform] specific tasks). Passwords are also called "keys."

EXAMPLE: The simpler (and easier-to-guess) one's password is, the less secure their use of the associated data, device or program, as they are at risk of someone else figuring out their password.

patch: A piece of code added to a software program in order to fix a defect or add additional functionality, especially as a temporary correction. It is called a patch because it is a small set of instructions, meant to handle a specific, tightly-defined part of the program. It is contrasted with a full version of the program, in which many areas of the program might have new functionality.

EXAMPLE: If there was a tax-preparation software, and a defect was discovered that could cause incorrect calculations of individual tax refunds, a patch might be sent to users of the software. Once installed, the patch would correct the defect in the program.

path: Also called a leg. A path is one of two or more possible series of actions that may be performed in a computer program. A fundamental aspect of computer programs is the idea that the computer can have multiple possible actions it can perform. That is, the computer can be told to perform one of two or more available actions depending on the state of certain data. As an example, the computer might be told to check the test scores of a student, and, depending on whether or not the student's test scores were above a minimum level, send them a message inviting them to an advanced class. This type of operation would require two important elements: an instruction to evaluate data for the purpose of determining what to do, and the actual instructions to be performed once that determination has occurred. This is basically the concept of "if this, then that," applied to computer programming. The first part, the evaluation instruction, is called a "conditional statement" – because the step the computer will take next is conditional, and is based on the evaluation of the data given to the conditional statement. An example might be, "if age is greater than 19," or "if the number of items in the order is equal to or less than 10." The second part, the actual instructions to be executed based on the evaluation of the conditional statement, is called "paths." There are always at least two paths; there can be more. Based on the result of the conditional statement, one of the sets of instructions is performed. An example might be "mark this student as an adult learner," or "apply 10% discount to the order." Each of these possible sets of instructions is called a "leg."

EXAMPLE: If you are using a computer program to order food from a restaurant, and the restaurant has a different procedure for ordering if you want the food to be delivered instead of being set aside for you to pick up, there will be a point in the computer program where the user will be prompted as to whether their order is for pickup or delivery; the computer will have two possible legs it can perform. The conditional statement in the computer program will take in the choice the user made, evaluate that data, and execute one or the other of these legs based on the user's choice.

PATH (environment variable): See "environment variable."

PBI: "Product backlog" is a list of products that need to be gotten; tasks that need to be completed. A "product backlog item" (also called PBI, backlog item or item) is a single task that is to be completed. It is simply breaking a backlog down into items. PBIs are all the small things that need to happen for production to be completed.

EXAMPLE: In creating a website composed of ten web pages, each web page could be considered a PBI.

PC: Stands for "Personal Computer." A PC is the same as a computer; it is a computer that is typically used by one person at a time. The computer itself (as opposed to the screen) is usually in a box made of metal and/or plastic. This box is sometimes called a "tower," since they often stand upright like a tower. When you say "PC," you can be talking about the computer all by itself, or you can be talking about the computer AND all the parts that are needed to use it (monitor, keyboard, etc.). Usually these other parts are physically separate from the computer itself. Sometimes, manufacturers make machines that have the monitor and the computer all in one container; this is still called a PC. An important note: While the term "personal computer" can be used to apply to any computer that is intended for use by one person at a time, there is another use of the specific acronym "PC": As the personal computer evolved and became more popular, a few major manufacturers became dominant. The majority of computers in those early years, and still today, are modeled from a design created by the technology company International Business Machines (IBM). IBM called their first personal computer the IBM PC – so the term "PC" can refer to a personal computer, or more specifically to a computer whose design is based on that early design from IBM. Like any computer, these machines needed an operating system (a special-purpose computer program that supports the computer's basic functions, such as scheduling tasks, running other computer programs, and controlling peripherals [external devices, such as keyboards, mice and displays]). The early IBM PCs (and most personal computers over time that use designs based on those early IBM PCs) use operating systems from the technology company Microsoft. As you probably know, this operating system from Microsoft is called Windows and it is the most popular operating system used on personal computers. Therefore, any personal computer that uses the Windows operating system is often referred to as a *PC*. Another popular operating system is macOS. It comes from the technology company Apple. Since the most popular line of personal computers manufactured by Apple have been marketed under the name "Macintosh," or "Mac," computers manufactured by Apple that use the operating system macOS are often referred to as "Macs." A Macintosh is a fruit; it is a variety of apple, like Red Delicious or Granny Smith. You will often see comparisons between PCs and Macs. The distinction made above is what they are referring to.

EXAMPLE: Most companies provide their employees a personal computer to work on when they are at the office. Some of these may be PCs; some may be Macs. In this picture, a PC is on the left and a Mac is on the right:

(PC)

PCB: Abbreviation for "printed circuit board."

peer: A person or thing that is considered equal to another person or thing in some regard. In computers, a peer is a computer that is considered at the same functional or hierarchical (rank) level as another, connected computer. This is compared to the earlier network concept of a client/server system, in which the server is considered "above" the clients, in that it is the source of the data or service needed by the client computers. Establishing a *peer-to-peer* relationship means directly joining computers together so that they can all provide data or services to each other. This activity is often abbreviated as *P2P*. In a peer-to-peer system, two or more computers can act as either client or server, so each one can provide information to the other in response to requests. Each computer has a special program (P2P software) running on it that helps coordinate the work of each connected computer. This is best illustrated by explaining the first popular use of P2P technology: sharing audio (music) files. P2P technology was developed around the year 2000, and was used in music search software. The software was free and was easily obtained, and many people installed it on their computers. Let's say you wanted to download the song "The Star Spangled Banner" to your computer. The P2P software would check all the connected computers that also had that P2P software installed, seeing if they had that song stored in their hard drive. The software would then start sending that song to your computer. But here is where P2P technology became valuable: Each computer that had that song would not be sending you the entire song. Instead, each computer would send a different small portion of the overall song to you, all at once – and the P2P software on your computer would use those portions to assemble the full song and save it on your hard drive. This had a couple of advantages over the conventional client/server system. First, the download would happen much faster. This is mainly because each part of the song would not take long to arrive at your computer. The second advantage is also related to speed: in a client/server system, the server might suddenly receive a huge number of requests for the same song, from a huge number of computers. It would not be able to service each of those requests all at the same time, so the process could take a long time. This is not a factor in P2P systems. There is also a negative aspect to this technology: it is very difficult in such a system to ensure that people are not allowed to access information they are not legally allowed to obtain. Let's use that example of wanting to download the song "The Star Spangled Banner." If that song were under copyright protection, the owner of the copyright might want to control access to the song. Typically, this would mean that the owner would want you to pay for the song in order to download it. In a client/server system, this is easy to implement: You would have to pay for the song before your request to download was approved. In a P2P system, however, no such controls are implemented. This means that one person might pay for the song and obtain it legally, but after that, if they were using P2P software, other people would be able to obtain the song without paying for it. This is what happened in the early 2000s.

EXAMPLE: A free computer program called Napster, which used P2P technology, allowed people to search for and download songs from other Napster users who had those songs on their computers. Many people used this to obtain songs they had not paid for. The various music publishers, who owned copyrights on those songs, objected to this and mounted legal attacks against some people who used Napster to obtain songs for free; they even mounted legal attacks against the creators of Napster, Shawn Fanning and Sean Parker. The Napster service was ultimately shut down. There are many legitimate uses for P2P technology, as well.

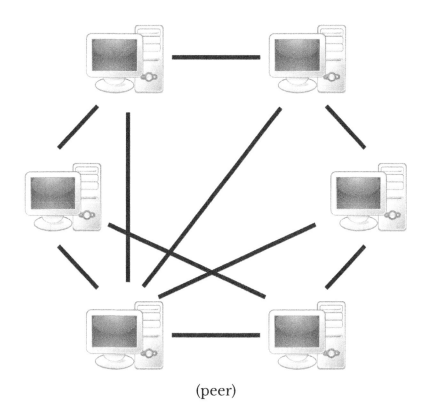

(peer)

peer-to-peer: See "peer."

pen drive: Another word for "USB drive."

percentile: The value below which a percentage of data falls. It is a measurement in statistics that indicates the value below which a given percentage of data falls.

EXAMPLE: Let's say there is a group of 20 people and you are the 4th tallest. That means 80% of the people in the group are shorter than you. This puts you in the 80th percentile. Here is an image showing this:

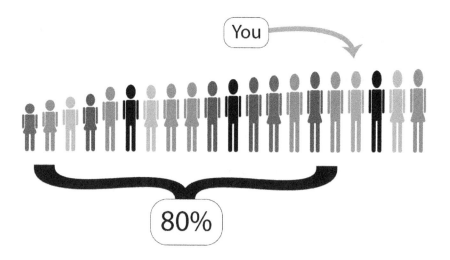

As another example, let's look at test scores. A student in the 66th percentile means that she scored better than 66% of the other students.

peripheral: These are things that can be hooked up to a computer, including external devices. Peripherals include mice, keyboards, external drives, displays, etc. Peripherals are often used to get data into a computer, or to receive data from the computer.

EXAMPLE: A printer is a peripheral.

Perl: A popular computer programming language (a system of specialized words and symbols used to communicate with a computer and to create programs) developed by Larry Wall in the 1980s.

EXAMPLE: Perl has been referred to as the "Swiss Army Knife of programming languages" because of its flexibility.

persistent cookie: See "session cookie."

persistent data: See "memory."

persistent data store: See "memory."

personal computer: See "PC."

phishing: a scam where someone pretends to be an official company or someone trustworthy in order to steal information like your credit card number or anything else. This is called "phishing" because it is a variant of "fishing." The implication is that you are the "fish," and when you take the bait, the "fisher" gets your information. These are also called "phishing attacks."

EXAMPLE: The following email would most likely be phishing: "This is Mr. Adams. I am from your bank, Acme Bank. I need you to send me your account information so I can wire you funds." If you were to actually reply to this email and give them your bank account information, you might get money stolen from your bank account.

PHP: Originally, PHP stood for Personal Home Page. Currently, it is short for PHP: Hypertext Preprocessor. PHP is a scripting language designed for web development. This means that you could have an HTML page, and you could put a script inside it that performed some function; this script would be executed by the computer that was hosting the web page files (the server). The script could be written in PHP. The code written in PHP is stored on a web server with the HTML pages it's meant to work with. PHP can also be used as a general-purpose programming language, not just for adding functionality to web pages. The main use of PHP is to create interactive websites and web applications.

EXAMPLE: PHP is one of the languages utilized by Facebook.

PID: Short for "process identifier" or "process ID." PID refers to the number assigned to a process by the operating system. The PID uniquely identifies each process that is running on the system.

EXAMPLE: PID 1 is typically the initialization process responsible for starting and shutting down the system.

pin: A thin piece of metal. In computers, pins are used to transfer electricity. One use for pins in a computer is to plug one part into another part of a computer. The pins are inserted into another part of the computer to connect them together. Because we can represent data in a computer using electricity, pins are where the data can pass from one point to another once a connection has been made.

EXAMPLE: Data can be transferred through a computer by passing electricity through pins.

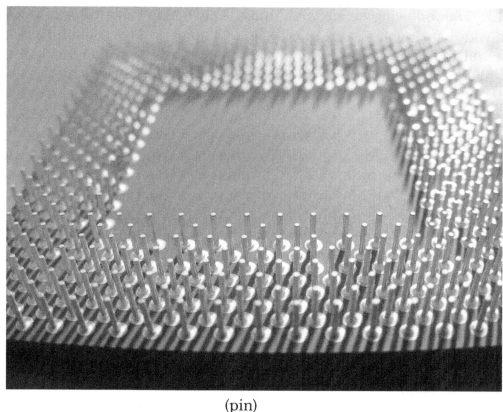

(pin)

pink noise: See "noise, colors of."

pip: The most popular Python package manager. It is used to manage and install software packages written in Python.

EXAMPLE: If you were coding in Python, and wanted to analyze some data, you might download the popular package, NumPy.

pixel: The smallest single component of a digital image. It can be thought of as a small dot that, together with many other similar dots, helps to make up an image on a computer display, television, or similar display device. Each pixel gets set to display a specific color; when many pixels are arranged together, an overall image is displayed that is a composite of the individual pixels.

EXAMPLE: If you are looking at a picture on a computer, that image is actually made up of many small pixels of different colors. Together, they combine to form the picture.

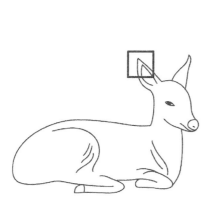
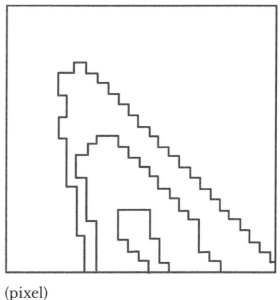

(pixel)

pixel density: See "PPI."

pixel per inch: See "PPI."

place value: When you write a number (a series of digits, like "327"), each digit in that number has its own *place value* based on where it is placed in the written series of digits. If you write 7, there is only one place value. If you write 327, there are three different place values. The places are counted starting from the right. The quantity that each digit represents changes, depending on the position of that digit in the series of numbers (how many spaces over from the right). There are many different number systems, so the exact quantity represented by each place varies – but as you move to the left, the quantity increases.

EXAMPLE: In the decimal system (a counting system using ten digits; 0-9), the first place represents how many "ones" there are in terms of quantity. The second place represents how many "tens" there are; the third represents how many "hundreds," and so on. So the number 327 would be read as "seven 'ones' plus two 'tens' plus 3 'hundreds'" – or 7 + 20 + 300.

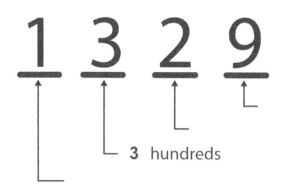

1329 : one thousand, three hundred and twenty-nine
1329 = (1 x 1000) + (3 x 100) + (2 x 10) + (9 x 1)

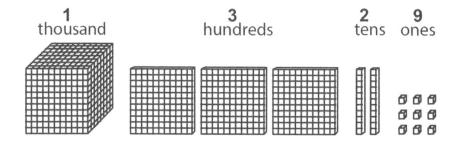

Here is the place value of each of the numbers in this picture:

- 1 = thousands
- 3 = hundreds
- 2 = tens
- 9 = ones

placeholder: A person or thing that occupies the position or place of another person or thing. In coding, a placeholder is a character or string that temporarily takes the place of the final value.

EXAMPLE: If you are writing code and need to assign a variable but you do not know what to input, you can use a placeholder until the correct value is assigned.

platform: A computer's operating system and hardware combined. When you speak of a platform, you are talking about what kind of hardware composes the computer and what operating system (the major part of a computer that helps all the programs in it to work together) it uses. There are many different types of platforms. A computer with really nice hardware and a slick operating system (top of the line platform) will do everything better than a computer of lower quality. It is called a platform because everything else rests on top of it and depends on it. You build off of your platform.

EXAMPLE: If you buy a computer with the Windows operating system on it, the computer and all its physical components and software, including Windows, is a Windows platform.

(platform)

platform as a service: See "PaaS."

plot: In statistics, plotting is the action of taking data and marking where the data would be located visually on a graph. 2D plotting is data visualization in two-dimensional form, on an x and y axis – this is usually done with two different variables (data that has a name and a value [type/amount], and can be changed) to see their relationship. 3D plotting is similar to 2D plotting, except now there is a third axis called the z axis which is used to display a third variable and its relation with the variables on the y and x axis.

EXAMPLE: You could make a data plot in order to visualize the demographics of a city.

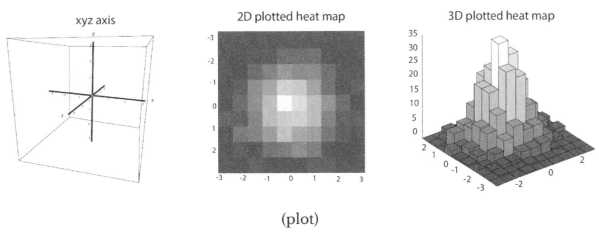

(plot)

PLUGE: See "calibration."

plugin: A small computer program that you can add to a larger computer program that adds new functions to the larger program. It's basically an optional set of functionality that can be added to a program.

EXAMPLE: You could add a plugin to a sales-tracking program that could keep track of commissions to be paid based on various sales factors.

podcast: A series of regularly-created audio recordings that are available for users to download from the web and listen to whenever they want. It can be thought of as "radio on demand." Creators of podcasts can record the actual content of the podcast at any point in time. When they want to release it for people to listen to, they take the recording and put it on a web server (a specialized computer used to store and transmit data, such as "serving up" websites through the World Wide Web). At that point, people who want to listen to the podcast can request a copy of the recording to be sent to their computer or smartphone. When they get the recording, they can listen to it whenever they want. Specialized computer programs exist that help people search for, store, and listen to podcasts – these are called podcatchers.

EXAMPLE: There are many podcasts available to entertain you with stories, news, music, etc. If you had a particular popular TV show you were a fan of, like Star Trek, chances are you could find many different podcasts related to that TV show to listen to.

podcatcher: Specialized computer programs that help people search for, store, and listen to podcasts.

EXAMPLE: There are many podcasts available to entertain you with stories, news, music, etc. If you had a particular popular TV show you were a fan of, like Star Trek, chances are you could find many different podcasts related to that TV show to listen to. The program you would use to find, store, and listen to those podcasts would be a podcatcher.

pointer: 1. The various symbols used to show where the mouse is on the display screen.

EXAMPLE: Here are some pointers:

See also "cursor."

2. Usually the "=" symbol is used to set the VALUE of a variable. When the "=" symbol is used to set the value of a variable, it is usually used like this:

`[NAME of the variable] = [VALUE that is being assigned to that variable]`

EXAMPLE: fabricColor = "blue." Here, there is a piece of data that the computer is keeping track of that has been given the name "fabricColor." By using the "=" symbol, we can set the value of the piece of data called "fabricColor." In this case, we are setting that value to the series of letters "blue." A pointer is a variable whose value is the address of another variable. The pointer "points to" another value stored somewhere else. Basically, it is a link.

EXAMPLE: Let's say that Y has the address "0003" in memory. Then we assign X the value 0003. X would "point" to Y's address (0003). In this case, X is the pointer.

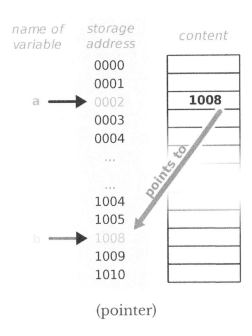

(pointer)

Poisson distribution: Named after the French mathematician Siméon Denis Poisson, the Poisson distribution tells us the probability of a given number of occurring events that will happen in a fixed interval of time or space, given that the mean (average) rate of occurrences is known since the last event.

EXAMPLE: Let's say a sales representative selling a skin care product in a busy store stops 10 people per hour on average and makes a sale to at least 3 of those people. Each instance of a person stopping to talk to the salesperson happens independently from each other. And at the rate the sales person stops these 10 individuals on average per hour, the distribution of people stopping to talk to him would follow the Poisson distribution.

polymorphism: The condition of occurring in several different forms. In Object-Oriented Programming, polymorphism means that you can assign a different meaning or usage to something, depending on various conditions. It can mean to allow code you've typed to act in different ways depending upon the situation. Polymorphism is the ability of an object to take on multiple forms.

EXAMPLE: If you typed in a class "shape," polymorphism would allow you to enter whatever type of shape you wanted: a circle, square, triangle, etc. Overriding is one of the commands that can be used in programming to bring about polymorphism. As an example, let's say you have a class called "Automobile" and from that class another class was derived called "Truck," and the "Automobile" class had a method called "Accelerate" with max speed 100. Using override for the "Truck" class, you could change the accelerate method to a max speed of 70.

pop: Remove an item from a list of items being handled by a computer. There are many different ways of representing data in a computer. One of the main concepts used is collections of data – say, a list of students in a list of classes. Often the uses we have for computers make it necessary to add or remove items to lists like this. When a computer is directed to add an item to a list of items, that is called a "push" operation. When a computer is directed to remove an item from a list of items, that is called a "pop" operation.

EXAMPLE: If you are using a computer to grade a set of student exams, and you retrieve an exam from the list of exams so you can grade it, you are "popping" an exam off the list.

POP email: See "IMAP."

port: A specific location or device for the input and output of information. There are a couple different uses of the word port in computers:
1. A physical location on a computer that is used to connect some sort of input/output device.

EXAMPLE: There is nearly always a port on a computer that can be used to connect some sort of display device, so that users have a display screen for use of the computer. You can see some computer ports here:

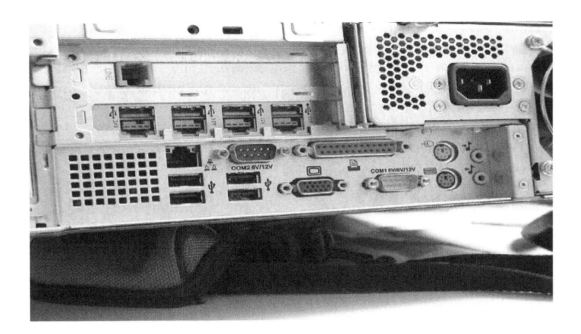

Here are some laptop ports:

2. A port is a non-physical connection that is used in relation to connected computers. Different types of information can be sent between these computers – electronic documents, electronic messages, web pages, etc. Computers in the network can specify an exact computer to request information from or send information to. But the information is not just sent to "the computer" – rather, it is sent to a specific, numbered connection on that computer. There may be hundreds of such connections, or "ports," on a computer. It is important to understand that a port in this instance does not correspond to any specific physical connection to the computer. The physical connection has already been set up by this time, through a wired (or wireless) connection to a device like a router. All the communication to and from the computer

will of course travel through this connection. But, there are other factors involved when we are sending information between computers. For example, just because the information arrives at a computer does not automatically mean the computer will accept it – it may need to verify the identity of the computer that sent the information. And even if the computer does accept it, the computer needs to know where to send it (i.e., what program needs the information). To accomplish this, the operating system controls communication on these ports. It monitors communication being sent to and from the computer and controls the routing of that communication. Because we now are tracking each separate port, we can set up rules around how each port works. These are things like, "What program do I route incoming communication to on this port?", "Will I allow outgoing communication on this port?", or "What protocol is being used for communication traveling through this port?" The part of the operating system at work here is called a "firewall." It is the area in the operating system program where the ports are maintained. The term "firewall" comes from the automobile industry. When building a vehicle, a wall is put in place between the front of the car (called the engine compartment, because that is where the engine typically is located) and the interior of the car (called the passenger compartment, because that is where the driver and passengers sit). This wall is there, among other reasons, to protect the people in the vehicle if a fire should break out in the engine compartment – that's why it is called a firewall. You can see a firewall protruding up between these two buildings here:

In a computer, the "firewall" is there for protection as well – it allows control over what information goes in and out of the computer. In a vehicle, these firewalls have many holes built into them where wires and other parts can go through to connect the parts in the engine compartment with the parts in the passenger compartment. This corresponds to the ports in a computer – they are places where a data connection is allowed into or out of a computer.

EXAMPLE: If your computer was receiving an electronic file from another computer over the Internet, your computer might use port 80 to input the data.

port address: The unique identifier for a port on a computer. A port is a non-physical connection that is used in relation to connected computers. Different types of information can be sent between these computers – electronic documents, electronic messages, web pages, etc. Computers in a network can specify an exact computer to request information from or send information to. When a computer sends or receives information in this manner, it uses a special computer program to control the process. Part of this process is the creation of uniquely-named connections called "ports" that send or receive information. These ports are given unique numbers. A computer can manage the creation and operation of many different ports at once.

EXAMPLE: If your computer was receiving an electronic file from another computer over the Internet, your computer might use port 20 to input the data.

positive: See "circuit."

POST method: POST is a keyword in the HTTP protocol and is used to send data to a server in order to create a resource. The data needed by the server in order to do the creation is stored in the request body.

EXAMPLE: Given the URL (address) http://www.exampleschool.com/adminportal/createStudent?studentId=23&firstName=Harry&lastName=Potter, the actual HTTP request would look something like this:
```
POST /adminportal/createOrUpdate_student
Host: www.exampleschool.com
Accept-Language: en-us
studentId=23&firstName=Harry&lastName=Potter
```

power supply: "Power" or "power source" is where a machine receives its energy (usually electricity) from. A "cable" is a wire or wires, wrapped in a protective casing (container), that are used to transport electricity. A power cable is the cord that provides electricity to something. Computer power cables look like this:

The power cable plugs into the power "supply" (the part of a computer that manages the electricity that is passed into the rest of the computer). A power supply converts the power coming through the power cord into various different levels of electricity needed by the computer. It looks like this:

That picture shows the power supply of a computer separated from the main computer. Here is what it looks like as part of the whole computer:

You can see the power supply at the top of the picture; it has a place to plug in the power cord (on the left), and a vent to allow air flow (on the right). The power supply performs important functions: The first thing it does is to lower the amount of the electricity that goes into the rest of the machine. Without getting buried in a bunch of electronics terminology, you should know this: you measure how much "force" electricity has by what's called "voltage." Higher voltage means more "force" in the electricity available to move through a machine. When electricity moves through things, it produces heat. The higher the voltage, the more electricity is moving. Therefore, the temperature rises. The parts in a computer can't tolerate a lot of heat. In fact, if we did not use the power supply to drop down the voltage of the electricity that goes to the rest of the computer, we could break or melt those parts and the computer would be damaged. A common source of electricity is a wall socket (a device you plug cords into). A computer's power supply takes in the electricity that comes from the wall socket, through that power cord. The voltage that comes out of a wall socket is around 110 "volts" (measurement of voltage). This is way too high a voltage for the parts in a computer, so the power supply drops it down to a much lower level: 5 volts. As a note: 5 volts is not enough to even noticeably shock someone – it is very little electrical force. That 5 volts is what comes out of the power supply and gets distributed to the parts inside the computer that need electricity. The other thing the power supply does is to "regulate" (control) the electricity that it sends into the computer. This means keeping the level of the electricity constant. Even if the level of the electricity coming from the wall socket into the power supply varies a bit, the power supply keeps the electricity level it sends out constant at 5 volts, no matter what. This is very important, because the computer relies on exact levels of electricity to represent data, and if the voltage level varies, the computer gets incorrect data and provides us with wrong answers. Electricity is the source of "life" for computers.

EXAMPLE: In some laptops, the power supply and power cable are connected together as one unit, like this:

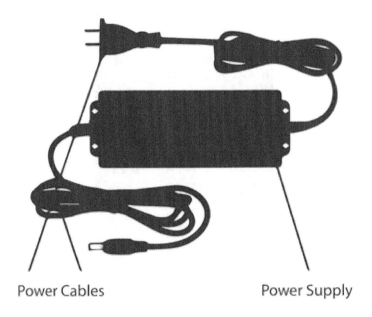

Power Cables   Power Supply

Here, the power cable delivers electricity from the wall to the power supply at 110 volts and the power supply passes electricity to the laptop at 5 volts. As a note, the process of dropping the voltage down from 110 volts to 5 volts produces a good amount of heat. You may notice the power supply on a laptop gets warm. The power supply will have a vent and a fan to get rid of this heat.

PPC: Stands for "pay per click." Pay per click refers to a type of paid advertising on the web. PPC is an advertising model used to direct traffic to websites, in which advertisers pay the publisher (typically a website owner) when the ad is clicked.

EXAMPLE: Google Ads is the most popular PPC provider.

PPI: Stands for "pixels per inch" (also called "pixel density"). A pixel is the smallest single component of a digital image. It can be thought of as a small dot that helps to make up an image on a computer display, television or similar display device. Each pixel gets set to display a specific color; when many pixels are arranged together, an overall image is displayed that is a composite of the individual pixels.
PPI (pixel density) is how many dots are displayed or printed in a square inch. The higher the PPI, the sharper the picture or image.

EXAMPLE: Typically, with each new smartphone that comes out, the PPI of the display screen is increased.

precedence: Importance; rank. In CSS, inline CSS always overrides (takes priority over) internal and external CSS. This topic is referred to as "CSS precedence." For example, if an external stylesheet instructs the browser to display fonts inside the paragraph element in red, but inline styling instructed the browser to display fonts inside the paragraph element in blue, the fonts would be displayed in blue. The inline styling would take precedence over the external stylesheet. CSS code inside the <style> tags in the HTML head is granted equal importance to CSS in an external stylesheet. So, what happens when there's conflicting CSS code between these two placements of CSS? The browser chooses whatever code came later in the sequence. Let's say you have an external CSS file entitled test.css and it contains the following:

```
body {
background-color: black}
```

And in your HTML file, you have the following code within the head element:

```
<head>
    <style>
        body {
          background-color: lightblue;
        }
    </style>
    <link rel="stylesheet" type="text/css" href="test.css">
</head>
```

As you can see, we have a conflict (the body is assigned black in the external stylesheet but blue within your HTML file). The browser will make the background color black in this case simply because the link is referenced later in the code than the style element – if these two were reversed, the background would be blue. If an element is targeted by multiple CSS declarations, the most specific selector will override the rest.

EXAMPLE: The order of specificity (least specific to most) goes as follows:
1. Type selectors: selectors that target an element by its HTML name. Such as:

```
p {
  background-color: skyblue;
}
```

2. Class selectors: selectors that target an element by its class name are more specific than type selectors. Such as:

```
.class_Name {
  background-color: red;
}
```

3. ID selectors: selectors that target an element by its ID are more specific than the other two selectors.

```
#id_name {
  color: teal;
}
```

4. Style attributes: Special words used inside an opening tag to control the element's behavior. Such as:

```
<p style="background-color:seagreen;">Paragraph</p>
```

or

```
<title style="color:gray;">Title</title>
```

Meaning, if we have an ID selector specifying a particular font family, with a type selector specifying a different one, the font family named in the ID selector will be displayed. This is yet another aspect to CSS precedence.

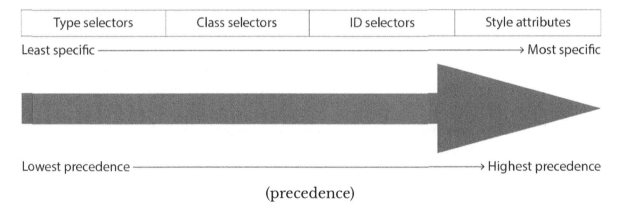

| Type selectors | Class selectors | ID selectors | Style attributes |

Least specific ———————————————————————→ Most specific

Lowest precedence ———————————————————————→ Highest precedence

(precedence)

predictive analytics: Describes the use of a statistical model or models to determine a future event or occurrence based on current and historical data. It looks for patterns to see the likelihood of those events and occurrences happening again. Some of the techniques used in predictive analytics include machine learning and data mining.

EXAMPLE: A grocery store can use predictive analytics in order to forecast the quantity of groceries in stock.

primary key: A column (attribute) or a combination of columns that is used to uniquely identify all the records (rows; tuples) in a table.

primaryKey	firstName	lastName	scheduleID
L0002345	Jim	Black	C002
L0001254	James	Harradine	A004
L0002349	Amanda	Holland	C002
L0001198	Simon	McCloud	S042
L0023487	Peter	Murray	P301
L0018453	Anne	Norris	S042

There are certain rules regarding primary keys: 1. It must contain a unique value for each row of data, and 2. It cannot contain null values. As a note: primary keys are also sometimes referred to as "candidate keys." You can define primary keys or they can be auto-generated by the RDBMS. In database tables, primary keys are often numbers – for example, "32546" or "33298." The important thing is that no two primary keys are ever identical. Often, these primary keys are called "ID"s, where "ID" stands for "Identification." This is because the primary key "identifies" the unique row in the table.

EXAMPLE: In the table below, the Customer ID column in the table below would be the primary key:

Customer ID	First Name	Last Name	Date of Birth
1	Patrick	Caudle	07-14-87
2	Derek	McCrea	02-13-69
3	Brett	Meyer	04-05-73

(primary key)

primary optical area: In design, this is the upper top left portion of a web page or on a piece of paper it is the top left corner. It is called the primary optical area as most humans read from left to right from top to bottom. So it inherently would be the first place a person would place their focus when looking at a design.

EXAMPLE: Consider the below web page. The user will more than likely see different navigation options to choose from, the author of the blog post and a part of the title of the post. The primary optical area is where you would want your important elements to be.

primary optical area

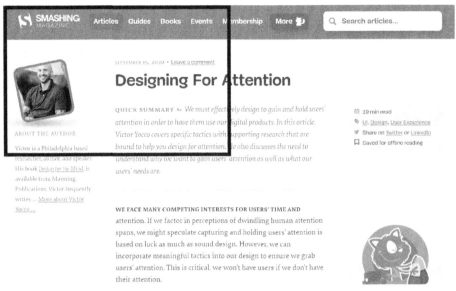

(primary optical area)

primary storage: See "main storage."

primitive: In computer programming, every data type besides objects (i.e., numbers, strings, booleans, functions, undefined values and symbols) are primitive – "primitive" refers to types of data that are built into (automatically included in) a programming language. Primitive data types cannot be broken down or simplified more than they already are. See also "class."

EXAMPLE: Primitive data types are immutable (cannot be altered).

printed circuit board: A circuit is a path that electricity flows along from beginning to end. In that path, there might be certain components that do work, control the flow of the electricity, etc. A circuit board is a thin, flat board that contains complex electronic circuits. They are also called "printed circuit boards." "Printed" refers to the fact that someone initially designs the circuits for the board and then the metal tracks that comprise the circuits are printed by a machine onto the board – similar to how you could type a document and then print it out using a printer.

EXAMPLE: If you opened up a printer at your office, somewhere inside you would find a printed circuit board that contained the important electronic circuits that controlled the printer's operation.

printer: A machine connected to a computer that takes blank paper and prints documents, pictures, etc. on the paper. Printers are useless without ink. The two most popular types of ink are: 1) Liquid, and 2) Toner. Liquid ink is typically used by "inkjet printers" which are printers that literally spray the liquid ink from tiny jets inside the printer.

Toner is ink in the form of powder or powder suspended in liquid. Another type of printer is a "laser printer." The first thing to understand about lasers is frequency. A wave is a flow of energy that has a repeating variation in terms of how much energy is present at any one point in time. The energy amount will cycle from low to high, and back to low again – and so on. Waves come in all sorts of types, patterns, and sizes. Waves are how energy moves through space. The length of time between when the wave hits one point in its cycle and the next time the wave hits that exact same point in its cycle is called a wavelength. How many times this cycle repeats in a second is called the frequency of the wave. A laser is an extremely focused beam of light. The difference between a laser and normal light is this: Normal light sources, like light bulbs, emit (send out) light that has several different frequencies. In a laser, the light that is emitted is all the same frequency. Laser light contains a lot of energy, and that energy is absorbed by materials the laser hits against. A laser printer is a printer that prints using toner and lasers. The lasers fix toner on the page with a high degree of accuracy through a heating process.

EXAMPLE: Printers can be connected to a computer wirelessly or with a wire.

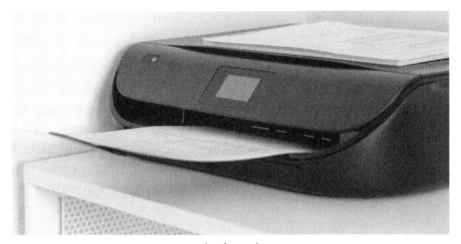
(printer)

private: In the popular programming language C#, "private" is used to protect some section of code from random access so it can't be damaged or changed by other parts of a computer program. The word private is an access modifier. An access modifier is something that modifies what parts of the program can access a particular thing. Access modifiers are usually applied to variables and methods in a class. Specifically, it means that if something is marked "private," only the things in that class can access it.

EXAMPLE: If you wanted a class to have a method that could change a tax rate, and you wanted to protect that method from being executed by another part of the program, you could set the method to "private," and only other methods in that class could use that method.

probability distribution: A way to display statistics that shows all the possible values and likelihoods that a random variable can take within a specific range. This range has minimum and maximum possible values.

EXAMPLE: There are various ways to show probability distributions. The following image illustrates this:

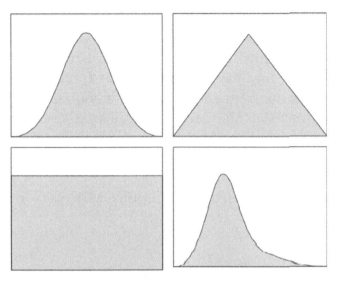

(probability distribution)

procedural programming: A computer programming paradigm where the code is written as a list of actions that tells the computer what to do, step by step, to finish a task or series of tasks. Procedural code instructs a device how to complete tasks in a series of logical steps. This paradigm uses a linear top-to-bottom approach. In procedural programming, code is divided into procedures – meaning, code is divided into chunks of subprograms that are executed in sequence.

EXAMPLE: JavaScript can be used as a procedural language.

procedure: See "subprogram." Also, see the usage note under "function."

process: To handle something through use of an established (and usually routine) set of procedures. When a computer displays the word "processing," it is saying, "Hold on while I perform some pre-established procedures." Processing refers to "taking actions with data." When data is being processed by a computer, you sometimes see a "progress bar" (a symbol that shows how far along something is) like this:

Processing...

Or you may see this symbol when data is being processed:

This circular symbol is called a "throbber" due to the fact that they originally expanded and contracted in size – i.e., the symbol "throbbed."

EXAMPLE: Searching through words to locate typos would be an example of "processing data."

process ID: See "PID."

process identifier: See "PID."

processing: See "process."

processor: See "CPU."

prod: See "production code."

product backlog item: See "PBI."

production: See "production code."

production code: The live code that users interact with. This is also referred to as simply production or prod. When someone says, "Release it to prod," they are saying, "Publish the code for public use." See also "environment."

EXAMPLE: The Facebook app you see on your phone is production code, as opposed to code that is being tested or has not been deployed yet.

production environment: See "environment."

product owner: The person who has final authority in representing the customer's interests. This person is available to the project's team at any time (even though they are not involved in the actual creation of the project) and is present at most meetings. They are the "boss" of the project, but they allow the members to make their own targets and manage themselves.

EXAMPLE: The product owner is typically the person who meets regularly with the client.

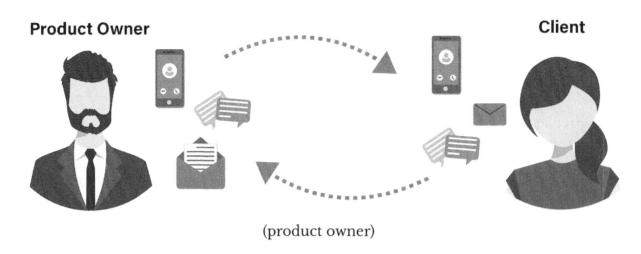

Product Owner

Client

(product owner)

profile: A short description written about a person or organization.

EXAMPLE: Your profile on a website would tell people things about you like what city you live in and what your interests and hobbies are. It is common for users to have a profile on social media websites (like Facebook).

program: This is a written instruction, entered into the computer, that makes it perform certain tasks. Programs are the things on a computer that you interact with to get things done. You use a program of one sort or another for basically everything you do on your computer, whether it is checking the weather or looking up banking information. There are countless programs that people have created over the years that can do any number of things. Programs are also called "applications" or "software." Programs are also called "apps" – though, an app typically refers to programs run on a mobile device, such as a cell phone.

EXAMPLE: "Paint" is a program on many computers that allows users to draw and color.

programming language: A language used to write a computer program. There are many different types of programming languages that you can learn and use, depending on what kind of programs (sets of written instructions, entered into a computer by people, that make it execute [perform] specific tasks) you want to write and what your tastes are. The most basic computer language used in a computer is called machine code (data given in a way the computer "understands" and that reflects the construction of its components – 1s and 0s). These instructions are built into the CPU (central processing unit – a tiny internal device that is the "brain" of the computer; it is responsible for processing data and directing the operation of all other parts of the device) at the time of manufacture. These instructions control the various actions the CPU, and therefore the computer, can take. If an instruction is not built into a CPU for what you want to do with the computer, you can't do it. It is inconvenient to program a computer using machine code. Many other languages exist that use instructions that are words. These are called "higher-level" languages. An example of an instruction in one of these "higher-level" languages might be:

```
sum = num1 + num2
```

Programming languages are also called "coding languages," "computer languages" or just "languages."

EXAMPLE: There is a common programming language called C. It has been used for several decades to create millions of computer programs.

project: An undertaking that typically has exact requirements and specifications. Projects are usually created following a plan. Within code editors (programs that developers use to write their code) websites and programs are typically saved as projects.

EXAMPLE: If you were creating a portfolio website to showcase your accomplishments as a developer, the code for this site would be referred to as, and saved as, a project.

project management: A "project" is something taken on with some sort of an end goal in mind. It comes from the Latin word *proiectum,* which meant "something thrown forward." "Management" means to organize, coordinate and control something effectively. It comes from the Latin word *maneggiare,* which meant "to handle; touch." Project management is the practice of starting, planning, completing and controlling the work on a coding project. Typically, project management relates to coordinating the actions of an entire team – from the client the project is being done for, to the developers, to the actual work. Project management includes formulating plans, assigning roles, acquiring appropriate tools and materials, developing and managing schedules, conveying information, promoting good communication, meeting milestones, and exhibiting strong leadership skills to ultimately resolve and complete the project within the agreed-upon deadline. In fact, the purpose of project management is to ensure that projects are accurately completed on or ahead of schedule.

EXAMPLE: A popular project management approach is called "Agile" (a type of project management that focuses on teamwork and rapidly adjusting to circumstances).

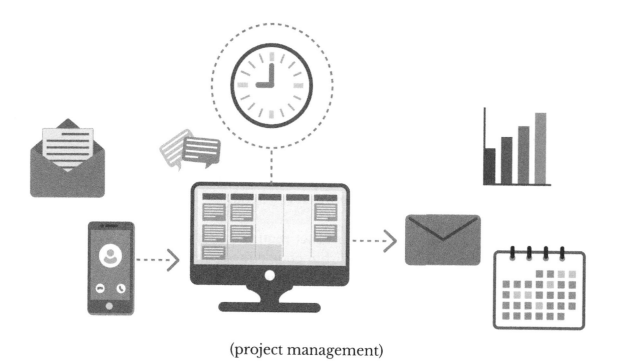

(project management)

project management lifecycle: "Life cycle" literally refers to the stages of one's life – from birth to death. The project management life cycle are the various phases that software development goes through, including:
1. Initiation (start),
2. Planning,
3. Execution,
4. Monitoring,
5. Closure (completion).

EXAMPLE: The project management life cycle includes such actions as:
- Keeping documentation,
- Working to meet deadlines,
- Obtaining compliance,
- Reducing overall production time,
- Maintaining support,
- Improving product quality and reliability,
- Avoiding expensive issues through improved forecasting (future prediction),
- Lessening production costs.

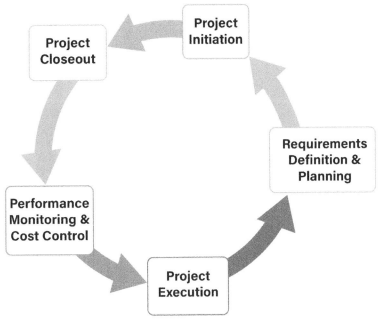

(project management lifecycle)

project manager: The person responsible for leading a project from the starting till the end, which includes planning of a project, execution of a project, delivering the project on time, on a schedule and on a budget as well as manage the people and resources. They work with the team to ensure that the desired outcome is achieved and ensure that work is completed in the correct sequence.

EXAMPLE: Project managers commonly coordinate with clients, direct the overall plan, define the scope of the project, set milestones, monitor progress, evaluate performance and attempt to complete projects on or ahead of schedule and on or under budget.

(project manager)

project team: The people involved in working together on a project to achieve its goals. Project teams are composed of the project manager, all project management staff, the development team and any one else involved in work related to the project. The project manager is the boss over the project team and is ultimately responsible for the project's success and quality. Some of their duties include:
1. Developing the overall plan,
2. Leading and managing the team,
3. Figuring out the project schedule,
4. Assigning tasks to other team members,
5. Providing regular updates to upper management.

Project team members have a wide range of duties and responsibilities – again, they're just any one else involved in the project. This includes employees and even outside consultants. The typical duties of project team members include:
1. Contributing to the project's objectives,
2. Completing individual assigned tasks,
3. Providing advice and feedback,
4. Working with users to determine their needs,
5. Documenting all work done.

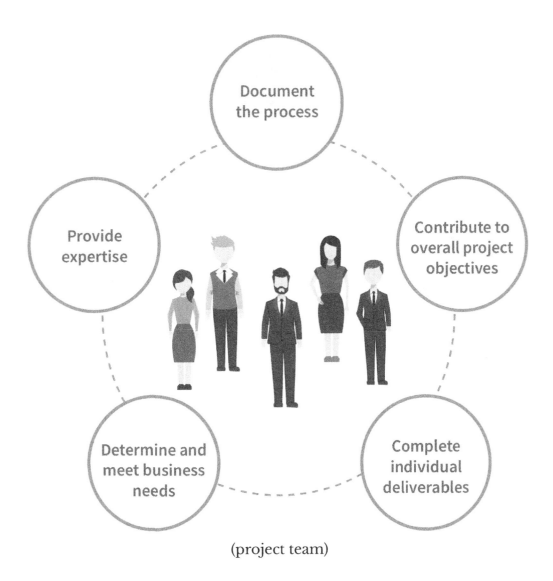

(project team)

property: See "class."

protocol: The rules and regulations computers have to follow to be able to transfer various types of data between each other. One such protocol is the set of behind-the-scenes rules that determine exactly how an internet (the largest and most-used computer network [connection that allows data transfer between machines] in the world, which is mainly utilized to access the World Wide Web) document gets sent to your computer screen and displayed. Protocols are the rules that people are required to follow when telling a computer what to do (such as creating something that is going to be on the world wide web). This is a common thing in the real world as well. In a bank, for example, there are rules in place that keep your money safe. These rules, or protocols, are enforced out of sight but you know that your money will be there in a predictable fashion.

EXAMPLE: If you do not follow protocols when creating a website you intend for other computers to display, the website will not display correctly on other computers.

pseudocode: You put "pseudo" in front of a word to show that you are describing something that is pretending to be something it is not. Pseudo means false or "not really that way." Pseudocode is a way to describe a set of computer code or coding without using the actual code itself. It is an informal way of describing the programming code you will use, and what it will tell the computer to do, in words that read very much like regular English.

EXAMPLE: Pseudocode might look like this:
```
If the user is younger than 18
Print that they are a minor
If the user is 18 or older
Print that they are not a minor
```
Depending on the programming language a programmer used to actually write this as code, it might look like this when turned into an actual program:
```
if(age < 18)
{
        print("User is a minor);
}
if(age >= 18)
{
        print("User is not a minor");
}
```

P2P: See "peer."

public: Open to or shared by all the people of an area. In the C# programming language, public is an access modifier used to denote that a particular piece of code is available to any other part of the program. See also "private."

EXAMPLE: Open-source software is public.

push: 1. When a program is being created, the creator will eventually get to a point that they think the program is ready to be given to the users. Informally, push means to make a program available, or to add one part of a program to the overall program that is under construction. When you push a product, you make it "live" and available for public use.

EXAMPLE: If you added a feature to a program that made a new logo appear at the top of the program, you could push that new feature to the program. That feature would now be present when the program was used.

2. Adding an item to a list of items being handled by a computer. There are many different ways of representing data in a computer. One of the main concepts used is collections of data – say, a list of students of a list of classes. Often, the uses we have for computers make it necessary to add or remove items to lists like this. When a

computer is directed to add an item to a list of items, that is called a "push" operation. When a computer is directed to remove an item from a list of items, that is called a "pop" operation.

EXAMPLE: If you are using a computer to grade a set of student exams, and you add an exam to the list of exams so you can grade it, you are "pushing" an exam to the list.

3. To send out information to a user (person utilizing a computer, software, etc.) without them needing to request the data first.

EXAMPLE: Sending out emails to all customers informing them of a discount would be a push.

PUT method: Within the HTTP protocol, PUT is used to replace a resource. In effect, this ends up editing the resource, as the old data associated with the resource is replaced with the new. The request needs to contain the location where the resource should be placed, and any needed data about the resource.

EXAMPLE: Given the URL (address) http://www.exampleschool.com/adminportal/editStudent?studentId=23&firstName=James&lastName=Potter, the actual HTTP request would look something like this:
```
PUT /adminportal/createOrUpdate_student
Host: www.exampleschool.com
Accept-Language: en-us
studentId=23&firstName=James&lastName=Potter
```
This would result in the name for student 23 being changed from Harry Potter to James Potter.

Python: A popular computer programming language created in the late 1980s by Dutch computer programmer Guido van Rossum. Born in 1956, van Rossum worked for Google from 2005 to 2012, where he spent half of his time developing the Python language. In the Python community, Van Rossum is known as the "Benevolent Dictator For Life" (BDFL). BDFL refers to the fact that he continues to oversee the Python development process, making decisions where necessary. Due to the fact that Python resembles common English words and speech, it is considered by many to be one of the easier languages to learn. Python can be used to create apps, websites, games, and many other things. It is a very versatile language with many uses. Python was named after the famous British TV show Monty Python, which aired from 1969–1974.

EXAMPLE: Python is used to build many popular web applications, e.g., Dropbox and BitTorrent. Python was even put to use in developing the search engines of YouTube, Yahoo, and Google.

(Python)

p value: *P* is short for *probability*. In statistics, a *p value* (or *p-value*) indicates the probability that a null hypothesis (the expected result) of a data set is true. The higher the p-value, the more likely the null hypothesis is true.

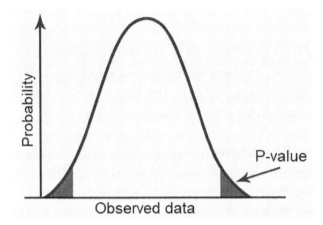

EXAMPLE: Let's say that we want to find out if a coin has equal physical proportions. If we flip it 1000 times, the final outcome will give us a pretty good indication of whether or not it is proportioned equally. Our null hypothesis is that the coin is, in fact, proportional. If we set a p value of .05 (5%), that means that if we find the results to be wider than a 55-45% split, we conclude that the coin is probably not proportional, and we reject the null hypothesis.

Q

QA: See "test."

QA environment: See "environment."

QA testing: See "test."

QR code: Stands for "Quick Response Code." A unique image that contains encoded information. It is a type of barcode; instead of a series of vertical lines like the barcodes on items in a grocery store, it is a square image made up of many small square dots in a unique pattern. QR codes originated in the automotive industry in Japan; they were used to identify unique automobile parts and keep track of where and how those parts were being used in the manufacturing process. At various points throughout that process, a device might read the QR code on the part and then update a computer as to where the part was and what had just been done with it. However, their most common use now relates to the Web. QR codes can be created with encoded information linking it to a specific web page. When you take a picture of the image with your smartphone, it takes you to that web page. A special computer program is used to read the QR code; it needs access to a camera in order to view the QR code for analysis. On most modern smartphones, the camera has this program built into it, so you can just point your camera at a QR code in order to read it.

EXAMPLE: QR codes can be used to promote a music concert. Using a smartphone, someone can take a picture of a QR code on a poster advertising the concert, and their phone will open up a web page with information about the concert.

(QR code)

quad-core: See "core."

quality assurance environment: See "environment."

qualitative variable: A variable that is not numerical. It is a variable that describes data that fits into categories. This is as opposed to a "quantitative variable."

EXAMPLE: Hair colors are qualitative – brunette, blonde, red, etc.

quality assurance testing: See "test."

quantitative variable: A variable that represents a measurable quantity. This is as opposed to a "qualitative variable."

EXAMPLE: The number of planets in our Solar System is quantitative – 8 (or 9, if you include Pluto).

quantum computer: A theoretical machine that can perform calculations based on the behavior of particles at a subatomic level. Such a computer could be capable of processing far more instructions per second than any existing computer. This advance in processing capability would be based on the fact that the data units in a quantum computer can exist in more than one state at a time. In computers today, the data units can only exist in one state – "on" or "off." The field of quantum computing is rather new and no actual quantum computers have been created, though some people claim they have done so or have gotten close. Quantum refers to "the smallest possible discrete unit of a physical property, such as matter or energy."

EXAMPLE: An example of this can be found here: en.wikipedia.org/wiki/Sycamore_processor

quartile: Each of four equal groups that a population can be divided into.

MILLENNIAL POPULATION QUARTILES

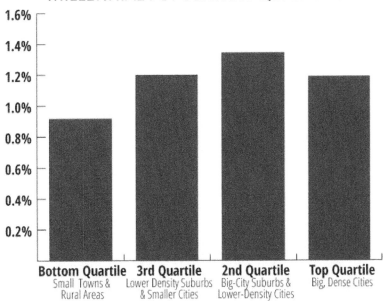

In statistics, *quartile* refers to one of three markers (dividing points) in a data set.

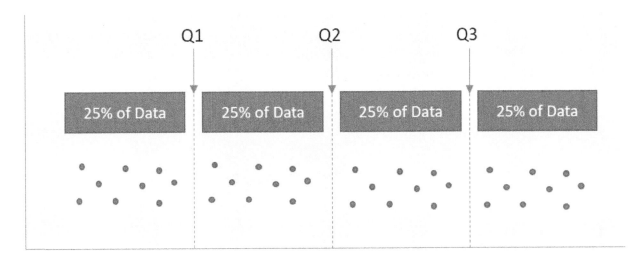

Quartiles are divided into: 1st quartile (lower quartile), 2nd quartile (called middle or median quartile) and 3rd quartile (called higher or upper quartile).

EXAMPLE: Let's take this set of numbers: 6,5,6,8,2,4,7,6,7,6,9. We can sort the numbers in order like so: 2,4,5,6,6,6,6,7,7,8,9. We now find the median in the set. There are eleven numbers, so there should be five numbers on either side of the median. Here's what it looks like: 2,4,5,6,6 | 6 (median) | 6,7,7,8,9. Again, the median is referred to as quartile 2 (Q2). Then we split the remaining numbers on either side of Q2 and find the median in those halves. Here it is diagrammed out:

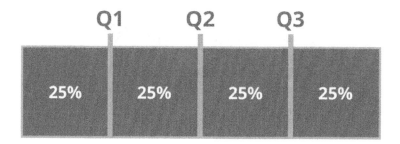

5 is the median of Q1, 6 is the median of Q2, and 7 is the median of Q3. Now we cut the data into 4 parts.

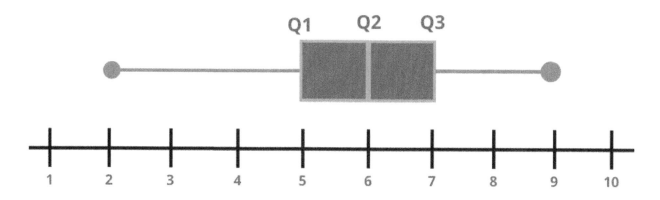

Each of the four parts represents 25% of the data. Interestingly enough, a quartile refers to both one of the three divisions in a data set *and* one of the four areas in a data set. These four areas do not always look as even as the 25% boxes, as some values are larger than others. There is a name for displaying quartiles: *box plot*, *boxplot* or *box and whiskers plot*. Here is a box and whiskers plot:

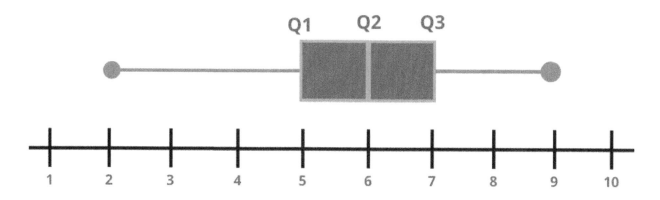

Either end shows the lowest and highest value, and will always give the exact median. Box plots typically have lines extending out from the boxes (as you can see above) that indicate the variability outside of the lower and upper quartiles – hence the name "box and whisker" (the box being the "boxes," and the lines being the "whiskers"). The above box plot shows the interquartile range – which is the distance between Q1 and Q3. In other words, Q3 – Q1. The Interquartile Range (IQR) tells us where the bulk of our data is. Out of our earlier-listed eleven numbers, a majority were from 5 to 7, with a mode (most occuring value) of 6.

query: A question that is usually expressed in a formal way. In coding, a query is a way to ask a database to bring up specific data from the full set of data in the database. Queries are utilized in SQL. A query is a specific instruction to a computer to search through a database and collect all data that matches a certain set of criteria.

EXAMPLE: Say you had a database that stored sales data for a bicycle manufacturer. If you were trying to analyze sales trends for the company, you might want to create a query that searched the database and gave you "all sales since the beginning of the year where the retail price was above $400 and the bicycle color was red." You would create a query to perform that search. You would need a special computer language in order to create that query. Structured Query Language is one such language. SQL is a language used to monitor and handle databases. SQL can edit, change, modify, delete, etc. data in a database.

EXAMPLE: An example of a query in SQL might be this:
```
SELECT Price, ItemName FROM Products WHERE Price < 10.00
```
This would look in a database and find all the products in the table "Products" that cost less than $10.00. It would then make a list that had the price and name of each of those products.

query language: See "data query language."

queue: (Pronounced "Q") A line of people or things waiting to be served or worked with. You have seen queues at the Department of Motor Vehicles (DMV), a grocery store, or an amusement park. In computers, a queue means a sequence of information or tasks that are waiting to be handled. The computer (or other device) takes one item from the queue and handles it. It then handles another item. This process continues until all items are handled. Meanwhile, the information is stored so that things in the queue are not forgotten.

EXAMPLE: When you try to print five different documents at once, these are placed in a queue, and your printer then prints them one at a time.

quick key: See "shortcut."

QWERTY: See "keyboard."

R

RAM: Stands for "Random Access Memory." In order to understand Random Access Memory, you should first understand the concept of *storage hierarchy*. A *hierarchy* refers to arranging things according to rank or status. It refers to arranging items according to their relative importance or characteristics. A common example of hierarchy would be how most companies are arranged: there are bosses and functions are compartmented. For example: there's a Chief Executive Officer (CEO; boss) over the company, and a Chief Financial Officer (CFO) that oversees the accounting department. Storage hierarchy refers to a system where various data storage devices are given a hierarchical importance ranking as far as how they are used by the CPU. The primary factor influencing a given device's ranking is its response time – how long the device takes to read or write a piece of data when the CPU requests such an operation. Faster response times are ranked higher. Memory storage devices are either volatile or persistent (volatile devices lose their data when they are not powered on; persistent devices maintain their data even when they are turned off). The most common type of volatile memory is RAM. RAM has very fast response times, so it is ideal for meeting the CPU's need to rapidly manipulate data during computer operation. *Main storage* (also called *primary storage, main memory* or *internal memory*), is the only memory storage whose data is directly accessible by the CPU. It is the area the CPU uses in its main activity – processing information. If the CPU needs data that is stored in another data storage device – a disk drive, for example – it gives that device an instruction to move data into main storage. At that point, the CPU can operate on that data.

EXAMPLE: If you had a text document stored on your disk drive containing a list of students and you wanted to sort the list alphabetically, the CPU would put that list into main storage, where it could process the data into an alphabetical list and then store it in the document back on your disk drive. The most common devices used for main storage in modern computers are Random Access Memory devices. This is called "random access" because any particular piece of data stored in the memory can be retrieved just as quickly as any other piece of data in the memory – that is, if you choose a piece of data at random that you wish to retrieve, it can be accessed just as quickly as any other. The development of random access memory was a big step forward in the speed of computer operations. The reason for this is that previous forms of volatile memory were NOT random access – that is, if you were to choose any piece of data at random that you wished to retrieve from memory, it would take a longer or shorter time to retrieve that piece of data than to retrieve another piece of data. This is because previous forms of volatile memory were based on a physical design that wouldn't allow access to individual points of data with the same length of time between "request" and "response." As an example, a common type of persistent memory was magnetic tape. These were basically very large versions of the common cassette tapes that are used to store pre-recorded music. The data on magnetic tapes was stored on a strip of magnetic material that was wound around two wheels. To get to a specific piece of data on the tape, a motor had to turn the wheels until the exact point on the tape was reached that contained that exact piece of data.

You can see then, that any particular piece of data on the tape would be reached in a length of time that was different from that needed to reach any other piece of data on the tape. Therefore, any two randomly-selected pieces of data would have different access times, so this was not "random access" memory. Here is what RAM looks like:

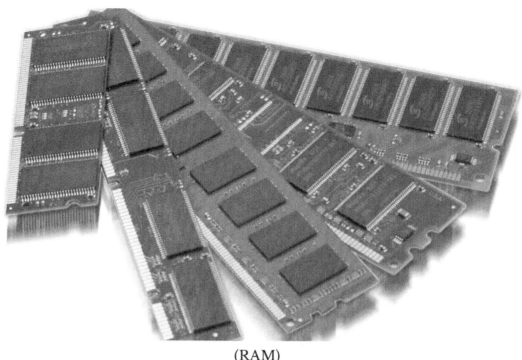

(RAM)

random access memory: See "RAM."

random error component: See "epsilon."

random variable: A set of possible values from an experiment that can be repeated numerous times under the same conditions.

EXAMPLE: Let's say we toss a coin: we could get heads or tails. Consider this image:

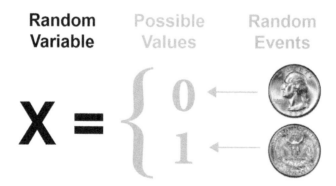

In this image: $X = \{0, 1\}$

range: This is the difference between the highest and lowest values in a data set. A range gives you a rough idea of how spread out your data is. Sometimes the range can be incredibly misleading due to extreme outliers, so be sure to look out for those. Calculating the range can help you map out your data visualization on your x-axis.

EXAMPLE: Review this image:

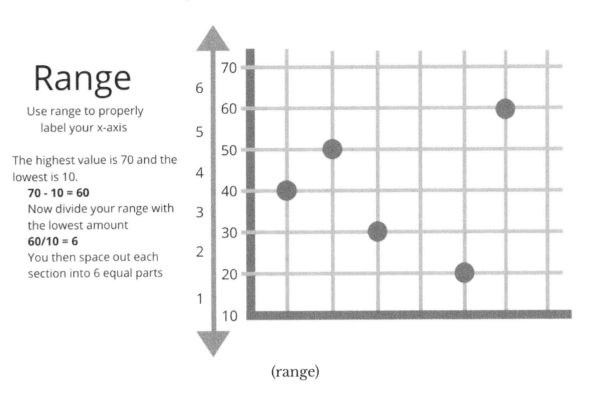

Range

Use range to properly label your x-axis

The highest value is 70 and the lowest is 10.
70 - 10 = 60
Now divide your range with the lowest amount
60/10 = 6
You then space out each section into 6 equal parts

(range)

Raspberry Pi: Raspberry Pi is an affordable, small computer that can be connected to monitors and television. Just like a computer, you control it with a keyboard and mouse. It can perform a wide range of functions, from allowing users to play classic video games to providing an educational platform.

EXAMPLE: Many people use a Raspberry Pi to play old Nintendo games.

(Raspberry Pi)

raster graphics: A type of electronic image made up of many dots. A raster is a dot matrix (a grid of dots which are filled selectively to produce an image on paper or a screen) image. "Raster" comes from the German word for "screen."

EXAMPLE: The larger a raster image is displayed, the less clear it becomes.

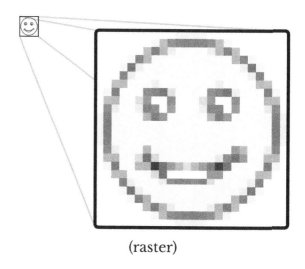

(raster)

ratio data: You're probably familiar with ratios, like: there were two girls in the class to each boy (2 to 1 or 2/1), or there were five monkeys in the zoo for each two ducks (5 to 2 or 5/2). Ratio data has all the same characteristics of interval, except that it has an absolute zero value *and* it cannot have negative values. Ratio data can be added, subtracted, multiplied and divided. It is a subcategory of continuous data.

EXAMPLE: If someone has $20, then another person with $100 would be considered to have five times the amount of the first person. The amount of money can be added, subtracted, multiplied and divided. $20 - $30 is not the same as $50 - $60 since $50 and $60 are values higher than $20 and $30. Some other examples of Ratio Data include:
1. Height
2. Weight
3. Number of items of objects
You can see in each of these examples that there are absolute zeros and there can't be a negative.

raw data: In normal English, "raw" refers to substances and materials in their natural state – things that have not been purified or processed. Raw data is information that has not been evaluated, analyzed, or processed for use.

EXAMPLE: If someone emailed you an unorganized spreadsheet that listed all customers of a company – that would be raw data.

raw input: In normal English, "raw" refers to substances and materials in their natural state – things that have not been purified or processed. In programming, raw input is the input from a user which usually acts as information about the user (e.g., their name or age) and then converting that input into data that can be processed.

EXAMPLE: When you enter your name into a text box online, you are entering a raw input.

Razor: A markup syntax that lets software developers create web pages utilizing C# and HTML in the same file. It was released by Microsoft in early 2011 as part of ASP.NET MVC. Files that contain Razor syntax will have the file extension .cshtml, which is C# HTML. Razor syntax is indicated by an @ symbol at the front of the code.

EXAMPLE: The .cshtml file could look something like this:

```
@{ var age = 18;}
<html>
  <body>
    @if (age > 18)
    {
    <p>You need to be 18 or older to create an account.</p>
    }
  </body>
</html>
```

The Razor syntax is telling the HTML file what parts of it are actually C# and that it should take the complex task written in C# and render its output to the browser.

RDBMS: DBMS stands for "DataBase Management System." DBMS is software that handles data storage, retrieval and updating. An RDBMS (Relational DataBase Management System) is a type of a DBMS that is used for relational databases. A relational database is a type of database where the data in it is organized into collections called "tables," and where the data in one table can have some sort of relationship to data in other tables. An RDBMS is a type of program that lets you manage relational databases – it is not the databases themselves; it just helps you run the databases.

EXAMPLE: The primary differences between a DBMS and an RDBMS: DBMSs store data as files and RDBMSs store data as tables. Also, DBMSs do not provide a way to define relationships between different sets of data; RDBMSs do.

React: Short for "React.js." React is a JavaScript library mainly used for building user interfaces. It was created by developers at Facebook and is currently maintained by Facebook and a community of developers and other companies. React lends itself to single-page or mobile applications, as it is optimal for rapidly fetching and changing data.

EXAMPLE: Facebook's current software was built with the help of React.

(React)

read: To view something and then understand it. In computers, reading is when the computer acquires information from a storage device and is then able to use the information. When a computer reads something, it takes in information from somewhere and is able to operate with it. If a computer is given data that is not in the format the computer expects it to be or is given data from a device that is broken or somehow faulty, the computer can't "read" it.

EXAMPLE: If you put a music CD into a computer, it reads the CD and plays the music. If the CD is badly scratched, the computer may not be able to read the CD and play the music.

reader: Reading is when the computer acquires information from a storage and is able to perform with that information. A reader is something that obtains and looks at stored information from another thing.

EXAMPLE: A CD reader would be the part of a computer that reads CDs.

readme: A text file containing useful information about a program (a set of written instructions, entered into a computer by people, that make it execute [perform] specific tasks). It is often entitled "READ ME" or "README" so as to get the user's attention. Readme files sometimes contain instructions on how to install the software, and how to perform basic functions with the software and a description of what it does.

EXAMPLE: On GitHub (a website where you can store and display your code), READMEs are quite common and can be used to tell people about each project.

reading gravity: Gravity in physics is a physical force that pushes things down. Gravity is all around you, it's why the objects and people around you stay down (not floating in the air) and have weight or feel heavy. Reading gravity in design refers to how a user reads down a page. Typically, a user would start in the primary optical area and move over to the strong follow area (right side of the page). In most design principles the reading gravity of a user moves from left to right in a diagonal line like so:

EXAMPLE:

Notice how the designer placed some of the most important aspects at the beginning of the reading gravity line such as "Quick summary" to give the user a brief overview of what the article contains so as to peak their interest. This line is used to indicate a reading pattern that users do not actually read; they briefly scan it looking for information that sticks out to them.

read-only memory: See "ROM."

read-write memory: Memory is a physical device used to store information on a computer. It holds recorded electronic data that can be accessed in the future. Read-write memory is memory in a computer that can be changed. You can erase it, alter it, save over it, etc. See also "ROM."

EXAMPLE: Documents are usually saved with read-write memory.

Really Simple Syndication: See "RSS."

real time: Refers to a data transmission in which there is no delay between the production of the data and when the data is actually received and/or viewed. It literally means "completely up to date; current; live." This applies in any situation where the stream of information that is produced can be accessed as it is produced – that is, in "real time."

EXAMPLE: This is best illustrated by the concept of watching a sporting event on TV. The cameras at the event are capturing the game play and broadcasting it to televisions around the country. In one scenario, there is little to no time lag between when an event occurs at the game, and when the viewers at home see that event. This is "real time." In another scenario, the events of the game are recorded, and then viewed at another time. This can be called "delayed playback." The delay can be a few seconds, an hour, a day or any other length of time.

record: In a database, a record is a row.

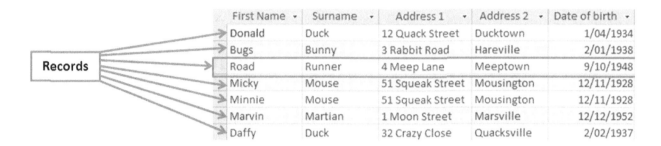

Records are a group of fields within a table that reference a particular object. In the example table above, the outlined row represents the object "Road Runner" – a cartoon character. A record is also referred to as a tuple (pronounced: TOO-pull). A tuple is an ordered list of things. In a database table, a row is a list of data items, in the order of the columns of the table.

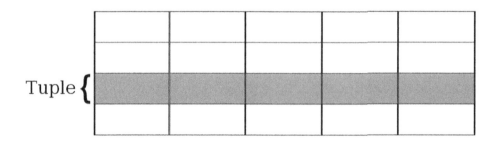

EXAMPLE: A record might contain the following information: Arya, Stark, 11/24/1990.

redress: To go back and make something right again. To remedy something.

EXAMPLE: If an addition to your code had an error in it when you attempted to run it, redress would consist of fixing the error so the code would run properly.

refactor: To rewrite code with the purpose of improving its structure and readability, without changing its behavior. Streamlining your code, cleaning it up or making it more concise could all be considered refactoring.

EXAMPLE: Let's say you created a script that scanned websites for company phone numbers. Your program is made up of 250 lines of code. You go through your code and through intelligent use of functions you're able to decrease your total lines of code to 100, while still maintaining the initial purpose of your script, and possibly getting it to perform faster – that would be refactoring.

reference: To refer to or mention. In computer science, a reference is a data type that refers to an object elsewhere. References can be used to construct data structures – such as by linking lists. In databases, it refers to data in one section referring to data in another section. References link to data in other areas.

EXAMPLE: You can see references here:

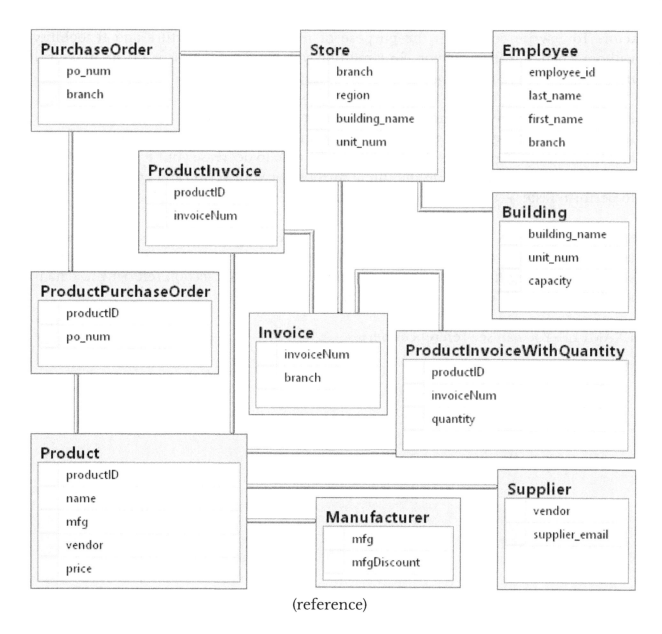

(reference)

referential integrity: The special specifications and rules that a database must abide by in order to ensure that the data assigned within the particular field is always related with the values assigned within the field that has referenced it. It is a process where the database is designed to ensure that all table (made up of rows and columns) relationships remain consistent. If you attempt to provide instructions to a database that violate referential integrity, there would be an error (i.e., the instruction wouldn't execute).

EXAMPLE: The blue line in the table below shows referential integrity – the red line shows a lack of referential integrity:

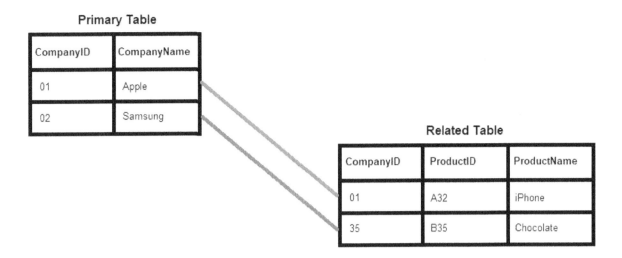

Primary Table

CompanyID	CompanyName
01	Apple
02	Samsung

Related Table

CompanyID	ProductID	ProductName
01	A32	iPhone
35	B35	Chocolate

In this example, attempting to add the data in row two of the Related Table would result in failure – no row would be added, because the "CompanyID" column in that table is a foreign key to the "CompanyID" column in the Primary Table. Because adding this second row would violate referential integrity, or "the integrity of the reference," the operation is not allowed.

refine: To make something more pure or precise. In computers, it often means to make an operation more accurate or efficient, or to make a set of data more precisely organized and displayed.

EXAMPLE: You can refine search results to more precisely find what you are looking for.

refraction: Refract means to alter or distort something. It comes from the Latin word *refractus*, which means "to break open" or "break up." Refraction refers to the bending of the path light follows as it passes from one material into another. Literally speaking, refraction is *the change of direction of a wave caused by a change in the wave's speed through space.*

EXAMPLE: When a light wave passes through air and then hits water, refraction occurs.

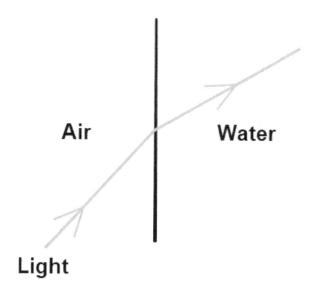

Air　　**Water**

Light

EXAMPLE: This relates to colors because different colors have different wavelengths and refraction (by changing wavelengths) affects the color you perceive. A common example of refraction is sending white light through a prism (an object with equal sides):

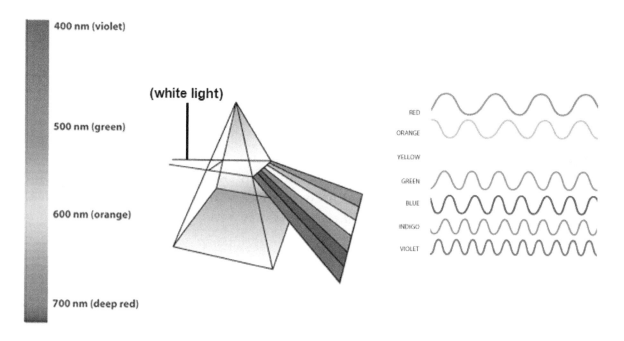

This separation of colors is also referred to as "dispersion."

register: A place in a computer where special types of information can be stored. Registers are physically located in the computer. There are different types of registers, each with their own name, inside your computer. They are not complicated – in fact, they are just memory locations that can store binary information. These locations are set aside for specific uses by the CPU.

EXAMPLE: When the computer is performing one specific instruction it has been given, it might store the next instruction it will execute in a specific register.

registry: A place where records are kept. In Windows computers, the registry is a database that stores the settings of the operating system and some applications. The registry contains data, options, settings, and other information for hardware and programs installed on the Window operating system.

EXAMPLE: When a program is newly installed, instructions related to the program (such as how to start the program and which version of the program it is) are stored in the registry.

regression: In statistics, this is a form of statistical modeling which attempts to provide information about how one or more independent variables relate to a dependent variable in a given data set.

EXAMPLE: Statistical regression can give an entrepreneur a good idea about the relationship between advertising and products sold.

relational database: A database is an organized collection of related data, typically for use on a computer. Other computers might connect to a database that is stored on another computer in order to access the data in the database. Usually, the data in a database is organized into tables. Tables are a data structure made up of rows and columns. Each column would represent a type of data that could be stored in the table; each row would represent one entry into the table. What makes a database "relational" is when various tables in the database are related to each other in some way, and when those relationships are somehow defined and when they affect how the data in the tables is used.

EXAMPLE: A typical relationship might be like this: One table holds data about students. Another table holds data about addresses. The relationship between Students and Addresses is that one or more students can live at a given address. A relationship is defined between the two tables, tying one or more students to addresses.

relational database management system: See "RDBMS."

release: Passing over a finalized product to the general public. A release is done after the product has been created and tested and is ready for the client to put it to use.

EXAMPLE: A test version of a product would not be a release.

remote: Something that is located far from the main area. Things that are remote are distant. If you are working remotely, it means you are far away from headquarters. A remote computer refers to one other than your own.

EXAMPLE: You can work on creating a website remotely, which means you are working from home or at a personal office as opposed to working in the building of the company paying you to do the work.

render: To take the HTML code and translate them into commands the Operating System can execute. Remember, at the end of the day, everything displayed on your screen is controlled by the hardware on your computer and your OS. When we say "render a web page," we mean: The web file is received by the browser and processed, the rendering engine (see "rendering engine") then "translates" and passes the data to the OS in a way it can understand and execute, your computer then processes the data and displays the resulting output. Simply put: rendering a web page is displaying a web page.

EXAMPLE: If a web page does not render properly, it either will display with errors present or not display at all.

rendering engine: The engine that displays what you see on your screen. It receives HTML code and other items passed from a server and then creates the Document Object Model (DOM).

EXAMPLE: The rendering engine creates a DOM tree like this from code received:

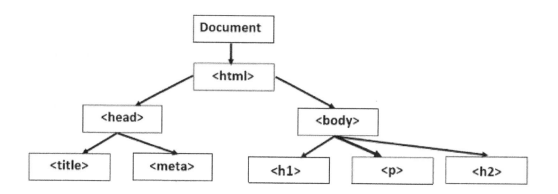

Though, technically, the DOM (render tree) would look like this:

```
<!doctype html>
···<html lang=""en""> == $0
  ▼<head>
     <title>This is the title</title>
     <meta name="author" content="Jack Reacher">
  </head>
  ▼<body>
     <h1>This is heading 1</h1>
     <p>This is a paragraph</p>
     <h2>This is heading 2</h2>
  </body>
</html>
```

NOTE: In this image, $0 is included. That is a command specific to Google Chrome. The $0, $1, $2, $3 and $4 commands work as a historical reference to the last five DOM elements inspected within the Elements panel or the last five JavaScript heap objects selected in the Profiles panel. $0 returns the most recently selected element or JavaScript object, $1 returns the second most recently selected one, and so on. In the following example, an img element is selected in the Elements panel. In the Console drawer, $0 has been evaluated and displays the same element.

render tree: See "rendering engine."

REPL: Short for "read-eval-print-loop." A REPL is a simple, interactive computer programming environment that allows developers to write code and see a near-immediate result. The REPL takes input, evaluates (executes) it, and returns the result to the user.

EXAMPLE: W3schools (an online coding education website) provides a REPL to its users for test-running code.

repository: A main location where data can be stored and handled.

EXAMPLE: There are online repositories to store one's code.

requirements: The things needed in a project. The requirements are what your customer needs and wants and what needs to be completed for a project to be considered done. Emergency requirements would be sudden unexpected things that come up that need to be done or handled in a project.

EXAMPLE: Requirement gathering sessions would be a meeting between the customer and company(s) to establish the full scope of work.

reserved word: See "keyword."

resident: A program that stays in the memory of the computer the entire time the computer is turned on. It refers to data that is immediately accessible and does not have to be loaded up from elsewhere.

EXAMPLE: A computer's operating system (OS – the main program within a computer that manages all other programs and external devices [e.g., keyboards, mice, displays, etc.]) is a resident.

residual: In normal English, *residual* refers to leftover amounts; the remainder. In statistics, a *residual* is the measure of how well a data point matches its predicted value. We do this by measuring the distance of a data point to the line on the graph.

EXAMPLE: The data point for (3,4) has a residual of 2, and the data for (3,1) has a residual of -1.

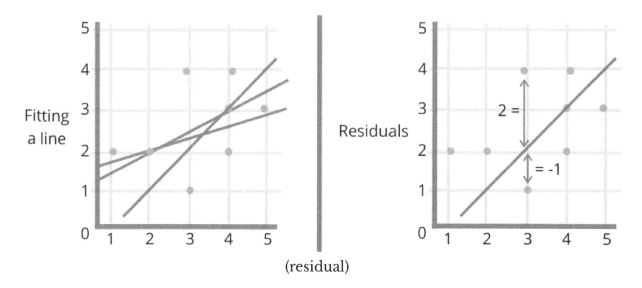

resolution: How clear an image is. On a computer or TV, pictures are made up of many tiny little dots, arranged in a grid. A higher resolution means there are more of these little dots in a given area (a higher density) so a higher level of image clarity will be present. At low resolution, you can actually see these dots (the dots are bigger) and the image would be relatively unclear. At high resolution, you can't identify the individual dots. These individual dots are called "pixels" and the higher the resolution, the smaller the pixels are. See also "resolution, levels of."

EXAMPLE: A modern television will have a much higher resolution than one which is ten years old.

resolution, levels of: The terms *definition* and *resolution* mean the same thing (how clear an image is). On a computer or TV, pictures are made up of many tiny little dots, arranged in a grid. A higher resolution means there are more of these little dots in a given area (a higher density) so a higher level of image clarity will be present. At low resolution, you can actually see these dots (the dots are bigger) and the image would be relatively unclear. At high resolution, you can't identify the individual dots. These individual dots are called "pixels" and the higher the resolution, the smaller the pixels are. Here are the most common levels of screen resolution:

- **144** – this refers to 144 total pixels from top to bottom on a screen. This is considered very low definition – the image would be pixelated and blurry. From here forward on the list, the number written indicates how many vertical (up and down) pixels there are on a screen – i.e., the total number of pixels top to bottom.
- **240** – Though it is almost double the number of pixels contained in 144, 240 is also considered low definition.
- **360** – this is the next step up in resolution/definition and is also low definition.
- **480** – this is the first level of what is considered "standard definition" or "standard resolution."
- **720** – this is the first level of "high resolution" or "high definition." Again, like all numbers before, this simply refers to a total of 720 pixels running from the bottom of a screen to the top.
- **1080** – this is also high resolution/high definition. To differentiate it from 720, 1080 is sometimes referred to as "HD ready" or "standard HD."
- **4K** – now we shift from vertical (up and down) to horizontal (left to right). 4K refers to about 4,000 pixels running left to right across a screen. 4K is also referred to as Ultra HD (UHD).
- **8K** – this is currently the highest possible definition – like 4K, this refers to the total horizontal pixels, which in this case is about 8,000.

EXAMPLE: To be clear: screens and monitors are designed to display up to a specific one of the levels of resolution covered above; this usually means they are capable of displaying the levels below the one they were designed for. There are Full HD screens, 4K screens, etc. Separately, videos have their own level of resolution. The resolution is established when they're recorded, saved or uploaded. For example, a 4K video camera can record 4K videos and video editing software allows users to choose what level of resolution they'd like to save the file as. Of course, a video is recorded so it can be watched later – so with video, we are concerned with resolution during both the recording process and the playback process (the point where the recorded video is later displayed on a screen of some sort). The resolution/definition of a displayed video is established by the resolution level at which the video was recorded, and the resolution level of the screen the video is being displayed on – whichever is lower. For example, a 4K video would not display as 4K on an HD (1080) screen – it would be displayed as 1080. Additionally, some video players allow users to choose the level of definition of the video. This is also limited by the level of definition of the original video and the user's display (screen).

responsive: Having to do with or indicating a website or application whose design automatically changes according to change in screen size.

EXAMPLE: The following depicts the difference between responsive and non-responsive:

Non-Responsive   Responsive

(responsive)

Retina display: The retina is the third layer of the eye which is sensitive to light. A retina display is a term (trademarked by Apple) for a type of display that is so sharp and clear that dots (called pixels) cannot be seen with the human eye.

EXAMPLE: Modern iPhones have retina displays.

return key: One of the most important keys on most computer keyboards. It is also sometimes called the "enter" key. This key performs various functions, such as: executing a command or starting a new line when typing. The name of this key comes from mechanical typewriters. A typewriter has a printing mechanism that actually imprints the letters on the paper. It also has a part called a carriage that moves the printing mechanism from left to right. When the typist wants to end off typing on the current line and move down one row and start a new line of writing, they press the return key. This makes the carriage move down one row and back all the way to the left. In other words, the carriage returns to its default position.

EXAMPLE: When going through an options menu, you could press the return key to choose a specified option.

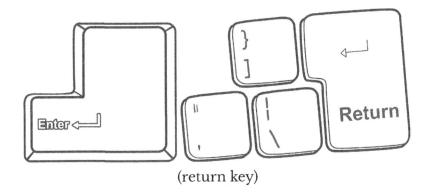

(return key)

RGB: Stands for "Red, Green and Blue." These are the primary colors for light, and are used in digital publication since computer screens emit light. These colors are additive, meaning the colors get lighter as you blend them.

EXAMPLE: Here is an RGB color wheel:

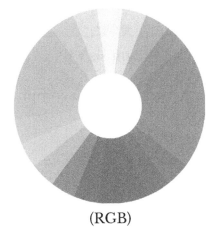

(RGB)

Rich Site Summary: See "RSS."

right click: See "mouse."

RIGHT JOIN: See "join."

RIGHT OUTER JOIN: See "join."

right skew: In normal English, *skew* means "crooked; not straight." When something is skewed, it deviates from a symmetrical form. A right skew is where a distribution is higher on the right of a statistic (also known as positively skewed). Meaning, the data is mostly bunched to the left with a long trailing tail skewed to the right. With a right skew distribution, you will normally find the median to the right of the mode, and the mean to the right of the median. See also "left skew."

EXAMPLE: The below graph shows a right skew:

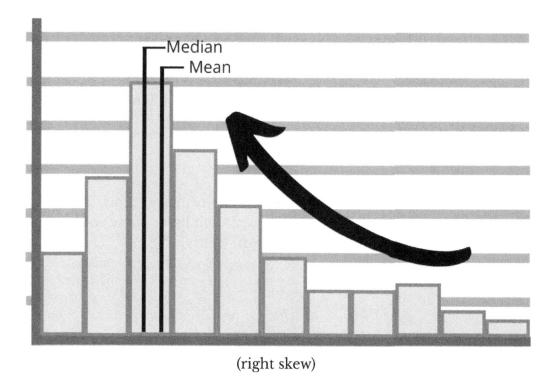

(right skew)

ring network: A type of computer network wherein computers and devices are connected in a loop (ring). To pass information along the network, the information is passed in a circle until it arrives at its destination.

EXAMPLE: A ring network could be utilized in an office wherein employees share data with each other.

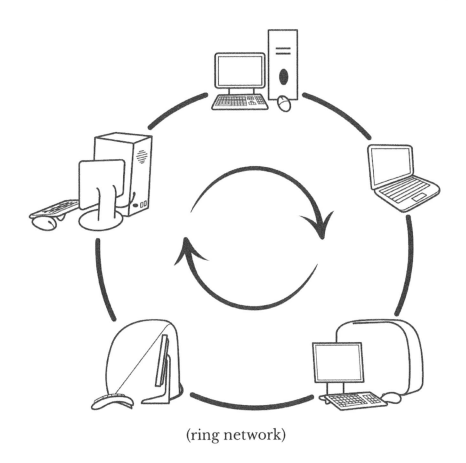

(ring network)

robot: 1. A machine that resembles a human and can perform some similar movements to a human. You've probably seen these in movies:

A robot can also be used to refer to a machine that automates various functions. In this definition, robots do not particularly look anything like humans. Here are robots building a car:

Robot comes from the Czech word *robota* which means "forced labor" or "slave." Even though that may sound dark, keep in mind that robots are simply machines – they are not people and they have no soul. All machines, from your car to your phone, are technically slaves. One should feel no different towards using these than one would feel about using a pen or a hammer.

EXAMPLE: Roomba is a robot that vacuums floors.

2. See "bot."

ROM: Stands for "Read-Only Memory." Read-only is a computer term that means that what you are viewing is not meant to be edited or changed. It means that you can only read (view) the information there. ROM is memory containing important information that the computer uses every time you turn it on and every time the computer performs any function. ROM is meant to be left alone and not fiddled around with, because changing it could make it so that a part of your computer or a particular computer function does not work anymore.

EXAMPLE: The instructions on what exactly the computer should do from the point it is turned on until it is ready for user input are stored in ROM.

(ROM)

router: A machine that sends information to two or more locations. A router is most commonly used to transfer information to various computers in a network. Modern routers contain parts that connect computers to the internet. They typically look like this:

EXAMPLE: If you had a network where one computer had a set of information that was commonly accessed by the other computers in the network, a router would help manage the requests by those computers for that information. This would be especially important in the event that two simultaneous requests were given for the same exact information – the router would make sure that the requests were both handled.

routine: Another word for "program" or "subprogram." Also, see the usage note under "function."

row: A horizontal (left to right) arrangement of numbers or information. The opposite of a row is a column (up and down).

EXAMPLE: Spreadsheets have rows and columns.

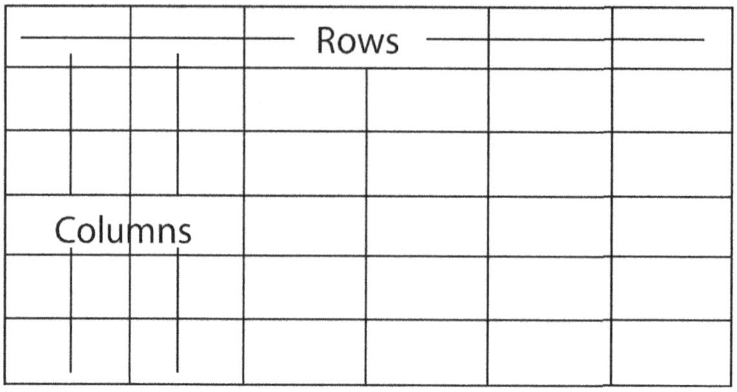

(row)

RSS: Stands for "Rich Site Summary" or alternatively, "Really Simple Syndication." RSS is a tool that allows things to automatically be sent to you so that you are kept updated on your favorite subjects. RSS sends information to you as you request it. That way you do not have to go to several different places to get the information you want. Instead, the information from all those different places gets sent to you. RSS requires use of a specialized program called an "aggregator." It maintains the connections to the websites you have subscribed to, and periodically checks to see if those websites have published any new content in a format that it can use. If so, it downloads the content and you can then view it. This type of program is also called an "RSS reader."

EXAMPLE: If you like The New York Times, you could use an RSS reader to go to their website and click on an RSS button on the site. This is called "subscribing" to the RSS feed. Then you would regularly be sent articles from The New York Times, which you could read using your RSS reader.

RSS reader: See "RSS."

Ruby: A popular programming language (a system of specialized words and symbols used to communicate with a computer and to create programs). It was created in the early 1990's in Japan, and started to become popular in America in the late 2000's.

EXAMPLE: You could create a program to monitor and maintain the inventory of a library in Ruby.

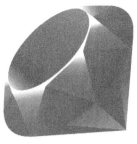
(Ruby)

Ruby on Rails: A web application framework (code written by others [and documentation on how to use it] that can be used by developers to enhance their programs) that is written in the Ruby programming language. It is popular and has been used to create many different websites and web applications.

EXAMPLE: Groupon, Shopify and Airbnb are built on the Ruby on Rails framework.

(Ruby on Rails)

rule set: A block of CSS code that contains: 1. Selector – this points to the HTML element that you want to style, and 2. Declaration – a statement that consists of a property and a value.

EXAMPLE: This is a CSS rule-set:

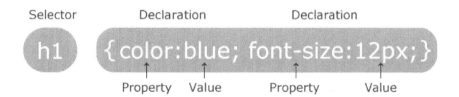

As a note: px stands for CSS pixels. For example: a 96px line would be one-inch long. Font size 10 in a word processor is about 13pxs. It is a unit of measurement to define size (width, length, etc.) in CSS. The declaration block contains one or more declarations separated by semicolons. Each declaration includes a CSS property name and a value that is separated by a colon. A CSS declaration always ends with a semicolon. Declaration blocks are surrounded by curly braces.

run: To start or perform something. By running something, you are putting it into action to perform a specific task or procedure. Essentially, you are pressing the "go" button.

When you run something on a computer, you are telling the computer to perform a series of instructions. It means the same thing as "execute."

EXAMPLE: If you pressed "run" on a coffee maker, it would make coffee for you.

runtime: The time when something in the computer is running – the time when the program is run. You can say something happens at runtime instead of happening at compile time. The term "runtime" also describes software or instructions that are being continuously executed in the background while your program is running – especially those instructions that you did not write explicitly, but are necessary for the proper execution of your own code. This is actually called a "runtime library," but is often shortened to simply "runtime." The reason runtime programs were developed is that the programs you create will often need to interact with features in the computer that are very common and which you would not want to have to recreate in every program you create – things like accessing the files on the computer, managing where the program stores data in the computer's memory, etc. So these special computer programs – runtime programs – were created so your programs can access these features when they are running.

EXAMPLE: Let's say you create a program that manages information about the students in a class. The runtime would take care of designating areas in the computer's memory to store that information.

runtime environment: The set of computer processes related to a specific computer program that are in use by the computer as that program is running. These processes handle such things as memory allocation for the program's data, access to the program's variables, the passing of needed data between various subprograms, interfacing with the operating system of the computer and more.

EXAMPLE: When you open an app on your phone, its runtime environment becomes active.

runtime library: See "runtime."

RYB: This stands for "Red, Yellow and Blue." RYB color models are the colors that are subtractive (i.e., they absorb light from the visible spectrum and reflect back the color we actually see). When you blend RYB colors, they get darker, due to their absorbent nature. The RYB color model is used by painters as a basis for creating various paint colors.

EXAMPLE: Here is an RYB color wheel:

(RYB)

S

sampling error: A situation where a population sample results and characteristics actually vary and differ from the entire population. This can occur when the researcher does not select an accurate representation of the population.

EXAMPLE: Let's say you wanted to find the average height of High School students, but the sample chosen only included basketball players. As you know, on average, basketball players are taller than the typical person. Therefore, your sample result might erroneously state that the average high school student's height is 6 feet and 4 inches tall – when the actual population height is 5 foot 8 inches. That's a nine-inch difference which can cause a very inaccurate generalization of the population data set.

sandbox: A digital environment where new or untested software can be run securely. Sandboxes are where developers can play around with their code and do development work without affecting the live website/software.

EXAMPLE: Let's say you were creating a video game. You implemented a large amount of features, but are unsure which to keep in the game. A sandbox would allow you to create different versions of the game, each with different features to try out.

sans: Without. And so, when you see "sans serif," it means the font has no serifs. Sans-serif typefaces (font families) are also referred to as *grotesque* or *Gothic* typefaces.

EXAMPLE: The "F" on the left is serif, and the "F" on the right is sans serif:

(sans)

SAS: Stands for "Statistical Analysis System." SAS is a statistical software suite used for data management and analysis reporting.

EXAMPLE: You can use SAS to display and compare statistics.

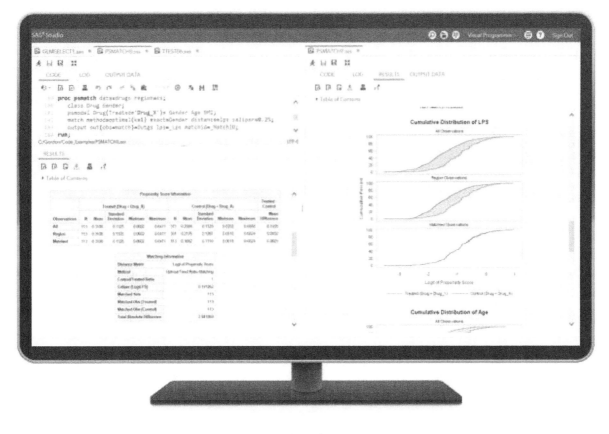

(SAS)

Sass: Stands for "Syntactically awesome style sheet." It is a style sheet language that can be used in conjunction with or independently from CSS. It has its own syntax and performs the same functions as CSS.

EXAMPLE: You can use Sass to style your website.

(SASS)

saturation: To soak or drench something. It is to fill (something or someone) with something until no more can be absorbed or held. When speaking of colors, saturation refers to the intensity or purity of hue. The lower the saturation, the weaker (less intense) the hue is. Whereas, a high saturation removes almost all color dullness and brings it to a purer hue. The terms *tone* and *saturation* are sometimes used interchangeably because lowering saturation mixes gray in with the original hues.

EXAMPLE: Here are examples of low and high saturation:

High Saturation   Orginal   Low Saturation

(saturation)

scaffolding: Visual Studio has built-in templates for different types of applications. When you start a new one, Visual Studio builds the basic framework of it so that you can focus on just adding features. This process is called scaffolding.

EXAMPLE: When scaffolding an MVC application, Visual Studio generates 8 folders (a location where a file or files are stored within a computer), including folders for Models, Views, and Controllers.

scalar: An amount that has only magnitude. Scalars do not have direction. The word comes from Latin *scala*, meaning "ladder."

EXAMPLE: Time is an example of a scalar quality.

schema: A representation of something in the form of an outline or model. It comes from the Greek word *skhēma* which means "form" or "figure." A data schema is a structure for organizing and classifying data in a database. It defines both the data contents and relationships.

EXAMPLE: Here is an example of a data schema:

NOTE: "Int" refers to integer (whole number) and "varchar" is short for Variable Character Field. A varchar is a data type that can contain any type of data, including: characters, numbers, punctuation or spaces.

scope: Code can have "scope." In programming, the scope is the code you have access to. Scope can be limited. Variables have scope in that they can either be accessed by one, more than one, or all functions in a program. The scope of variables is either "local" or "global." In the programming language JavaScript, a global variable can be accessed from any function within the program, whereas a local variable is only accessed by the function it is assigned to. Global variables are declared outside of functions, while local variables are declared inside of functions.

EXAMPLE: In JavaScript, a global variable would be written as follows:

```
var X = 10;
function Add_numbers_1() {
    document.write(20 + X + "<br>");
}
function Add_numbers_2() {
    document.write(X + 100);
}
Add_numbers_1();
Add_numbers_2();
```

This code would return "30" and "110." The variable X was assigned the value 10 outside of our function, but we still accessed it – therefore, the above is an example of a global variable. The following would be an example of a local variable:

```
function Add_numbers_1() {
    var X = 10;
    document.write(20 + X + "<br>");
}
function Add_numbers_2() {
    document.write(X + 100);
    }
Add_numbers_1();
Add_numbers_2();
```

This time, the code would only return "30" because the variable was local – meaning it was written within the function Add_numbers_1 and couldn't be accessed outside of it. Let's say you wrote the above code and did not understand why Add_numbers_2 did not display a result. We could use the console.log() method to help us debug our code as follows:

```
function Add_numbers_1() {
    var X = 10;
    console.log(15 + X);
}
function Add_numbers_2() {
    console.log(X + 100);
}
Add_numbers_1();
Add_numbers_2();
```

If you executed this code in the browser, no result will be shown. But if you open the console, you'll see the error "X is not defined."

scrambling: The act of making something jumbled. Scrambling takes information sent from one computer to another and changes the binary characters being sent. The characters are then changed back at the receipt point for security purposes. An important point to bring up here is that the information sent between computers is always sent as binary data – ones and zeroes. The receiving computer will use whatever protocol is in effect to convert that binary data into the needed format. The tools you may use in the future as a technology worker may not show you the data in binary form, but you should know that the information is converted to binary before it is sent.

EXAMPLE: If a criminal stole credit card numbers online, but the information was scrambled, they wouldn't be able to utilize the information.

Scratch: There are many different types of programming languages (a system of specialized words and symbols used to communicate with a computer and to create programs), each of which was created to fill a specific purpose. Usually a language is created in order to make the creation of certain types of computer programs easier. Scratch is a simple computer programming language that is used mainly for designing interactive stories, games, and animation. It is often utilized to teach young people how to create programs.

EXAMPLE: Scratch can be used by dragging and dropping chunks of simple instructions together. You could use it to make a simple game where you move through a park, making choices as you go about whom you interact with and what you do.

imagine • program • share

(Scratch)

scatter chart: See "statistical modeling."

scatter graph: See "statistical modeling."

scatter plot: See "statistical modeling."

screen: A TV screen is the part of the TV that shows the pictures. It is the same thing with a computer – the computer screen is the part of a computer where you can view things. It is also called a monitor or a display.

EXAMPLE: Some screens house the computer inside them, while others are a separate component (such as external monitors) that you connect to your computer with a wire or wirelessly.

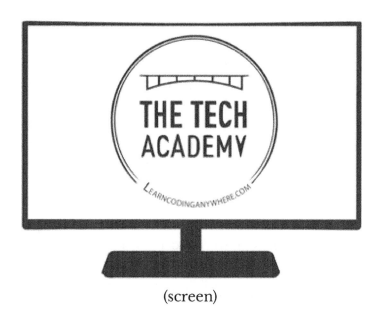

(screen)

screen sharing: A way to duplicate your screen on another computer and vice versa. You can literally share your screen with others. Also called "desktop sharing." This is similar to video conferencing where people hold meetings online. Some video conferencing allows for screen sharing.

EXAMPLE: If you wanted to help a friend fix their computer, but you were stuck at home, you might consider doing a screen share.

script: A set of computer instructions that automates a task so that a multi-part task can occur without your involvement. The origin of the term is similar to its meaning in "a movie script tells actors what to do," in that a script tells a computer what to do.

EXAMPLE: A script could be created that checks for new orders created at a manufacturing company every ten minutes, and prints them off on a printer.

scripting language: A computer language used to make scripts (sets of computer instructions that automate tasks, so that multi-part tasks can occur without user involvement). Often the tasks these scripts accomplish are valuable to automate, so that the task steps do not have to be entered into the computer again every time you want to do those tasks. Scripting languages have some of the following characteristics:

a. The code is written in a similar way to English – meaning, it is easier for people to read and understand than some more highly technical languages.

b. You use a scripting language to program automatic functions into a computer that are performed without the person using the computer to type out every instruction.

The origin of the term is similar to its meaning in "a movie script tells actors what to do": a scripting language controls the operation of a normally-interactive program, giving it a sequence of work to do all in one batch. For instance, one could put a series of editing commands in a file, and tell an editor to run that "script" as if those commands had been typed in the moment by a human being.

EXAMPLE: If you wanted to make it so that every night at midnight, a list of all the people who signed up for your school classes was printed, you could use a scripting language.

scroll: See "mouse."

scroll wheel: See "mouse."

Scrum: The most popular branch of Agile (a project management methodology that is popular in the computer industry). The term "scrum" comes from a rugby term that consists of teammates interlocking their arms and pushing forward into opponents. In the technology world, Scrum is a method of project management that consists of tightly coordinated teamwork, strong organization and completing projects according to client demands. Most software development projects use Scrum nowadays. There are a set of terms and techniques that are used in Scrum but it all centers around teamwork.

EXAMPLE: An element of Scrum is to hold daily meetings with the entire development team.

Scrum board: In Scrum (a project management system for software development that focuses on collaboration and teamwork), this is a physical surface that can be used to visualize information and manage the sprint backlog (tasks assigned to project members within a specified period of time). Scrum board is also referred to as the taskboard.

EXAMPLE: When working on a software development project, you could use a Scrum board to keep track of individual assignments.

Scrum Board

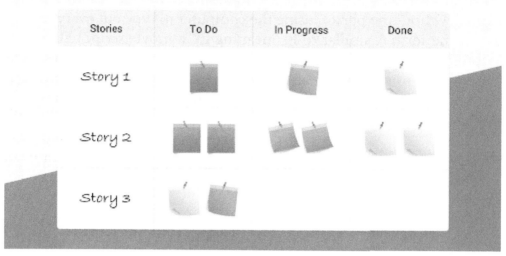

(Scrum board)

Scrum Master: Scrum is a project management system for software development that focuses on collaboration and teamwork. In software development, the Scrum Master is the person actually involved in the computer programming/software development, who coordinates the group activities and runs them. The Scrum Master is there, on the ground, performing work and helping their fellow teammates. The same person need not be the Scrum Master over a long period of time; some teams have each team member take on this role in turn over time.

EXAMPLE: The Scrum Master typically oversees daily meetings.

(Scrum Master)

SD card: Stands for Secure Digital card. A card is a physical component that you can put inside your computer or other electronic equipment to have it perform better or perform additional functions. An SD card is a portable memory storage device. It is a small card that has electronics inside it. You can record electronic information on the card; the information can be accessed by computers.

EXAMPLE: A very common use of SD cards is to save photos from a digital camera.

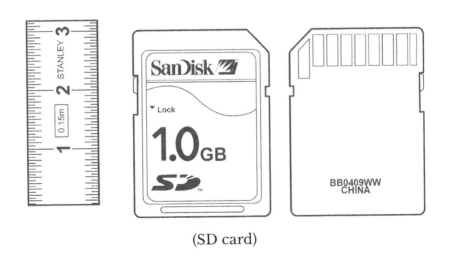

(SD card)

SDK: Stands for Software Development Kit. SDKs are sets of tools that can be used to create various types of software (programs). They are useful tools that make software development easier.

EXAMPLE: PayPal offers SDKs that help developers integrate online payments into their website.

search engine: A special program that can access an index (searchable information about a collection of data) containing data about many of the web pages from websites around the world. Using a search engine, you can enter descriptive search terms and get back a list of all the web pages that contain those search terms. This is valuable because there are now billions (or even trillions) of web pages available through the Web. Search engines are very popular tools used by nearly every user of the Web. In fact, the most popular website in the world is google.com, the search engine owned by the U.S. technology company Google.

EXAMPLE: Microsoft Bing is a search engine.

(search engine)

search engine optimization: See "SEO."

secondary key: A column or set of columns that can be used to find a row in a table. It is a key (a piece of data within a record [row] in a database that is used to uniquely identify that record) which can be used in addition to the primary key (an attribute [column] or combination of attributes, within a database table, that uniquely identifies each record [row] in the database table) to locate specific data.

EXAMPLE: Here is an example of the relationship between a primary and secondary key.

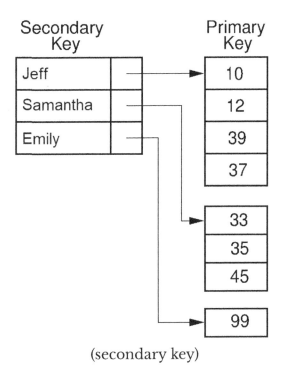

(secondary key)

second generation: See "generation."

Secure Sockets Layer: See "SSL."

secure password: A password that is hard for other people or computers to guess.

EXAMPLE: "Password" is not a secure password, but "Z$7f!k25@" could be.

security certificate: See "certificate authority."

security (computer): See "computer security."

security (cyber): See "cyber security."

selection sort: A type of sorting algorithm. In a selection sort, the list of items is divided into two lists: a list of sorted items (initially empty), and a list of unsorted items (initially this has all the items in the list). The unsorted list is then gone through, one item at a time. Each item is placed in the sorted list at the correct point, according to the desired outcome. Once all items in the unsorted list have been handled, the sorted list is the final product.

EXAMPLE: You could use a selection sort to sort a list of students alphabetically by last name.

semiconductor: A conductor is something that allows electricity to flow through it. A semiconductor is a substance (most commonly a material called silicon) that can conduct electricity under certain conditions, but not others. Semiconductors are a good way to control electricity. If you increase the temperature of a semiconductor, it will allow more electricity to pass through it; if you decrease the temperature of a semiconductor, it will allow less electricity to pass through it. This is one way that semiconductors can be used to regulate electricity. There are many semiconductors inside a computer that help control the electrical flow throughout the computer.

EXAMPLE: Computer chips (small components that transmit, store and process data) contain semiconductors.

semi-structured data: See "structured data."

senior developer: A senior developer (or senior-level software developer) is a master software developer and is the highest "rank" one can achieve in this area. A senior developer is trained in several languages and has vast experience. Software development teams and projects are usually run by a senior developer.

EXAMPLE: The main thing that determines whether someone is a junior or senior developer is their competence level. A senior developer might have 5 to 20 years of experience in software development.

SEO: Stands for "Search Engine Optimization." The process of setting up a website so that it is more likely to appear near the top of search results for specific search terms. There are many factors involved in where a website might rank in a particular search result, and those factors change fairly often. The basic elements, though, are related to how much the website really aligns with a particular search term. As an example, consider the website that sells antique bicycles. The content and images on the site probably relates to the sale of antique bicycles. Because of this, a search for "lawn mower repair" would probably not even have the antique bicycle website in the search results.

EXAMPLE: It is usually considered good practice to update the content of a website often, and to ensure that the new content accurately represents the purpose of the website. That action is one aspect of search engine optimization.

separation of concerns: In programming, this refers to splitting your project into sections for usability or where a user would be concerned. The idea is to focus on how a single piece should function or what kind of data it should contain. You'll see code files that contain a single block of code or just a few lines, and their file names would be relevant to what that code is used for.

EXAMPLE: If you were building a large piece of software, you may want to use a framework (code written by others [and documentation on how to use it] that can be used by developers to enhance their programs) that allows a separation of concerns.

serif: A *serif* is literally a small line or stroke (mark) attached to the end of a larger stroke in a character. It comes from the Latin word *scribere* which means "to write." Serif typefaces (font families) are also sometimes referred to as *roman* typefaces.

EXAMPLE: You can see serifs circled in red below:

(serif)

server: A computer that is used as the source of data and/or services by one or more other computers. In this case, the computers are connected into a network, and are equipped with specialized computer programs (a set of written instructions, entered into a computer by people, that make it execute [perform] specific tasks) that allow them to communicate with each other over that network. A common design for a computer network is to designate one or more of the computers in the network as a "server," and all the other computers as "clients." The servers contain important data and computer programs needed by the client computers. Using those specialized computer programs, clients request data or services from the servers. The servers get the needed data from their storage devices and send it to the requesting client computer. There are many different types of servers, depending on the needs of the computer users.

EXAMPLE: The technology company Google has over 1,000,000 servers in various locations around the world. Here is a picture of the first ever Google server:

(server)

server side: A web server is a specialized computer used to store and transmit data, such as "serving up" websites through the World Wide Web. "Server side" is one of two broad areas of the internet (the largest and most-used computer network [connection that allows data transfer between machines] in the world, which is mainly utilized to access the World Wide Web). Server side deals with computer operations on servers, while computer operations on computers with browsers for using the internet are called clients. These two areas are called "server side" and "client side." When the web server receives a request for a web page, the server may have several computer operations it needs to do in order to retrieve, format and send the web page. These operations are called "server side" operations. Similarly, on the client computer, the web browser (the program people use to view web pages) may have several operations it needs to do in order to receive, format and display the web page. These operations are called "client side" operations.

EXAMPLE: If you requested to view a web page about the top 10 most popular news stories of the week, the server would likely have to execute a computer program that could search through a stored collection of news articles and their accompanying popularity rankings, retrieve the top ten articles, insert the text of those stories into the web page data it was preparing, and then send the web page data back to your computer. Those operations are all server side operations.

session cookie: See "cookie."

Set: A collection of things. In math, sets are groups of numbers listed together. Sets are used in computers as well. The type of data in a set might be numeric, or text, or another type of data. Sets might contain items that are all the same type of data (all of them are numbers or all of them are text), or they might contain items of different types of data.

EXAMPLE: Each of these are sets:
- 2,4,6,8
- 12423, 4, 54, 943
- "Bob," "James," "Tim," "Charles"
- 2, "dog," 5, "cat"

There does not have to be a pattern to the items in the set. Usually a set has these symbols at the beginning and the end, so you can easily tell what is in the set: [ ]. Additionally, the items in the set are separated by commas to make the set easier to understand. So the format is this: [item1, item2, item3] for example. Another example would be: You could write a set that has the first five letters of the alphabet as ["A," "B," "C," "D," "E"]. Each individual thing in the set is called an element – that is, a set has multiple elements.

settings: Options on a device (machine – such as a computer) or in a program (a set of written instructions, entered into a computer by people, that make it execute [perform] specific tasks) that customize how you want the device or program to operate.

EXAMPLE: You can adjust your ring tone sound or volume within the settings in your phone.

720: See "resolution, levels of."

SharePoint: A Microsoft program that you use over the Internet (the largest and most-used computer network [connection that allows data transfer between machines] in the world, which is mainly utilized to access the World Wide Web). It is used to have a central place for a business's employees and clients to access websites and documents for that business. It can also show each employee's calendar for coordinating meetings, etc. It basically keeps everyone in an office or on a project, on the same page, with all the newest information available.

EXAMPLE: You can coordinate all project meetings through the SharePoint calendar.

(SharePoint)

shell: A computer program (a set of written instructions, entered into a computer by people, that make it execute [perform] specific tasks) that provides an interface (a device or program that enables a user to communicate with a computer) between the user and the operating system (OS – the main program within a computer that manages all other programs and external devices [e.g., keyboards, mice, displays, etc.]). You can use the shell to locate files, start and stop other programs, etc.

EXAMPLE: Some shells provide a graphical interface, where visual objects on the screen are used to represent the files and programs on the computer. Other shells provide a text-only interface.

shift: A key on the computer keyboard typically used to make capital letters. It can also be used in combinations with other keys to perform certain actions.

EXAMPLE: You can hold down the shift key while typing the first letter of your name; that will capitalize the first letter of your name. Also, on some computers, you can hold the shift key, tab key and ctrl key to open the task manager.

shippable: Refers to an item or product that is ready to be sent out by the creator of the product to the user of the product (shipped). Similarly, with computers this means a product is fully completed and ready to be turned over to the customer.

EXAMPLE: A computer program that was intended to keep track of household expenses, but which had errors in how it added and subtracted expenses, would not be shippable.

shortcut: 1. Also called an "alias." Something you click on (other than the original item itself) that opens up the content within. In the case of a file, you are not clicking on the original file; you are clicking on something that points to the original file. You would have saved the shortcut, or alias, somewhere besides the location of the actual file – probably for ease of access.

EXAMPLE: If you saved a copy of a file in folder G, you could create a shortcut for the file in folder A and be able to access the file from both locations. This might be done if it were easier or faster for you to access folder A than folder G; the shortcut would help often in this case.

New Folder -
Shortcut

2. Pressing combinations of keys on your keyboard (such as "s" and "ctrl" at the same time to save a file) are shortcuts. Keyboard shortcuts are also called "quick keys" and "hot keys."

EXAMPLE: On many computers, pressing CTRL + P will bring up a printer menu.

sigmoid function: *Sigmoid* literally means "s-shaped." It comes from the Greek word *sigmoeidēs*, which means sigma (18th letter of the Greek alphabet: Σ, σ). A sigmoid function is a math function whose graph has an s-shaped curve, like this:

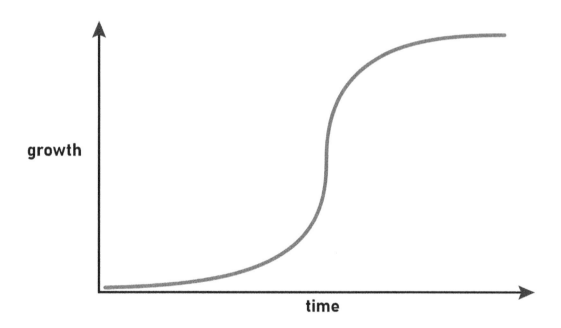

The sigmoid function limits the output of data to be between 0 and 1. This kind of function is useful for predictions of probability. This function is an "activation" function, which means that it takes in an input and activates the corresponding output.

EXAMPLE: A sigmoid function could be by an email provider to determine which incoming emails should be labeled as spam (junk mail).

signal: See "electric signal."

silicon: A very common material found on Earth. Most sand is made up of small pieces of silicon, and sand can be heated up to form larger chunks of silicon. Silicon has many uses; for example, you can use silicon when making glass. If silicon is processed in a certain way, it gains a valuable property: its physical structure can be changed back and forth between two states, just by applying a small amount of electricity to it. This property makes it very useful in making the tiny parts of a computer. This is because the two states that it can have are "able to allow electricity to flow through it" and "unable to allow electricity to flow through it."

EXAMPLE: Many parts of the computer are made using silicon.

(silicon)

silo: A system, process, department, etc. that operates in isolation from others. A siloed mentality means that you are focused on one thing. Sometimes it is used negatively to refer to the fact that someone cares only about what they're doing, with no regard for the group's needs. Siloed is being an individual, not a team. The word comes from actual silos – the tall, cylindrical containers used in farming to store grain after it's been harvested.

EXAMPLE: Someone working on a computer project who was being siloed would focus on their part of it, working on their own computer and not be very involved with the overall project.

SIM card: Stands for "Subscriber Identity Module" card. Subscriber refers to the person using a cell phone service. Module means a single entity that can be linked with other things to form a larger whole. A card is a physical component that you can put inside your computer or other electronic equipment to have it perform better or perform additional functions. A SIM card is an electronic device that can be stored inside a cell phone. The SIM card houses a unique identification number for the cell phone user. SIM cards save personal data, such as all of one's contacts.

EXAMPLE: Some cell phones cannot fully function without a SIM Card.

Simple Mail Transfer Protocol: Stands for "SMTP."

Simple Object Access Protocol: See "SOAP."

simply best fit: See "linear regression."

simulation: An artificially-created version of something that represents the actual thing. In computers, a simulation is a representation of the real world on a computer.

EXAMPLE: You might have a computer program that was used to create a simulation of a roller coaster. You could change various aspects of the construction of the roller coaster, and the program would demonstrate how the roller coaster would operate based on the changes you made.

single-page website: A website that houses all data on one webpage.

EXAMPLE: On single-page websites, typically when you click on the navbar (menu), you are taken to a lower point on the page with the relevant information.

sink: See "heat sink."

sitemap: An outline of a website that helps search engines understand and navigate your site. It typically includes a list of all pages on a website (including links), organized by subject.

EXAMPLE: You can upload a sitemap of your website to Google, which assists Google in finding your site.

sixth generation: See "generation."

6502 (Sixty-five O 2): The name of a type of microprocessor introduced in 1975. A microprocessor is a device containing a CPU and all the parts it needs to work – registers, etc. The 6502 microprocessor became very famous because it could be purchased for about 20% of the usual price of microprocessors of that era. Computers that used the 6502 microprocessor were the basic design used in many original video game systems.

EXAMPLE: Atari and the Nintendo Entertainment System (NES) used the 6502 or variations of it.

skew: See "right skew."

Skype: A service provided by Microsoft. Skype is a telephone company that uses the Internet (the largest and most-used computer network [connection that allows data transfer between machines] in the world, which is mainly utilized to access the World Wide Web) to permit people to talk as if they are on the phone, but through their computer. You can choose to hear their voice, or even talk while seeing each other's faces on the computer screen.

EXAMPLE: If you wanted to talk to someone in Germany for free, you could use Skype.

(Skype)

slash (/): A slash is a symbol that is most commonly used in the following ways:
1. To show choices – meaning literally "and or"; and example "small/medium/large" on a menu;
2. To show a ratio of things (miles/day in traveling would be how many miles you travel per day; it could be spoken as "miles per day");
3. To separate the different parts of a collection of electronic documents.

This third use is the most common use of the "/" symbol in computers, and it has been used for a long time. It was created as an aid to organizing and finding the various files (electronic documents) you might store on a computer. Files are often organized in folders – also called "Directories." Folders can contain files. Folders can also contain folders – each of which could contain further files and/or folders. The resulting structure of files and folders is called a hierarchy. A hierarchy is an arrangement of items (objects, names, values, categories, etc.) in which the items are represented as being "above," "below," or "at the same level as" one another. The "/" symbol is used to show that one item is below another. The item on the left is above the one on the right. "/" symbols are called forward slashes (because they have the appearance of leaning forward), while "\" are called backslashes (as they appear to lean backwards).

EXAMPLE: Recipes/BakedChickenRecipe.doc. This could be a folder called "Recipes," which contains a document called "BakedChickenRecipe." There is another common use of slashes in the computer industry. When using a web browser (the program people use to view web pages), the slash is used to denote a separate section of the website, or a specific web page on the site.

EXAMPLE: youtube.com/thebeatles. Here, "thebeatles" is a web page on the website YouTube that is dedicated to the band The Beatles. The "/" separates the website and the web page.

smartphone: A cell phone that you can use for other things besides simply calling someone. You can do more advanced things with a smartphone because it is essentially a small computer that is also a phone. The term "smart" refers to the ability to interact with other devices and networks wirelessly. See also "cell phone."

EXAMPLE: Using a smartphone, you can scan written documents and save them to your phone.

SMTP: Stands for Simple Mail Transfer Protocol. SMTP is a protocol (a formal agreement about how to format and send and receive a particular type of data) for formatting and exchanging email messages between computers.

EXAMPLE: One element of SMTP is that an email must have an email address it is being sent to.

snapshot: This term comes from photography, meaning a quick shot (picture) taken with a camera, but also refers to any brief look at something or summary of it. In technology, it has an additional aspect: it used to describe a recording of the state of a thing at a specific moment in time, where the thing being observed is dynamic (changing over time). For example, you might have a database that stores records of the sales for a company; you might get a report at 8:00 in the morning of all the sales ever recorded for the company. That is a snapshot of the state of the sales activity for the company at that exact moment; it is likely that sales will continue, and the actual state of the sales activity an hour later will not be the same as what you recorded at 8:00.

EXAMPLE: If you said, "I only saw a snapshot of what it will look like," you are saying that you briefly saw a summary of the thing.

SOAP: Stands for Simple Object Access Protocol. SOAP is a messaging protocol that allows for information exchange between programs built on different platforms and other programming languages.

EXAMPLE: SOAP is often used in APIs in order to transfer information between different programs.

SoC: See "separation of concerns."

social media: See "social networking."

social network: See "social networking."

social bookmarking: The action of publishing links to websites that you like so that other people on the web can see them and check them out. There are social bookmarking websites that allow people to do this broadly.

EXAMPLE: Technically, even by emailing a friend a link, you are involved in social bookmarking.

social networking: Interaction over the Web between people – using websites, email (electronic messages) and other communication methods – so they can get to know each other better. It allows people to communicate to one another socially through messages, commenting on information they have put on a website, posting pictures, etc. A social network is a website that facilitates social networking through posting information, messaging, commenting, sharing images, etc. Social media (posts, pictures, videos, etc.) is the content you put on social networks. The terms "social media" and "social network" are sometimes used interchangeably but they're technically different. The social network refers to the website, and social media is what's on the website.

EXAMPLE: Facebook is the most popular social media website and social network.

socket: In the computer industry, the term socket has a few different meanings:
1. A point where two internal parts of a computer connect.

EXAMPLE: Chips can be plugged into a socket within your computer.

2. A connector used to connect your computer to other computers and devices.

EXAMPLE: You can plug a USB thumb drive into the USB socket.

3. An important part of a computer network. Each computer in a network has a computer program running that sends and receives information with the other computers in the network. This program creates non-physical elements called "sockets" – the uniquely-named sending/receiving points for information. So a socket, here, is a "virtual" connector on a computer.

EXAMPLE: Socket addresses can be written as 146.86.19.8:80.

soft copy: See "hard copy."

software: See "program."

software developer: See "computer programmer."

software development: See "computer programming."

software engine: Refers to a central part of a computer program (a set of written instructions, entered into a computer by people, that make it execute [perform] specific tasks). The parts of a program that drive its functionality, as opposed to the look or feel, are the software engine.

EXAMPLE: "Unity" is a video game software development engine that consists of a central unit of code that all other code is built upon.

software engineer: See "computer programmer."

software engineering: See "computer programming."

software package: A group of files with information about those files. A package manager (or package-management system) is a set of software tools that automates the process of installing, configuring, upgrading, and removing computer programs for a computer's operating system in a consistent manner. Package managers deal with packages. Package managers usually maintain a database of software dependencies and version information to prevent software mismatches and missing prerequisites. One of their main uses is to eliminate the need for manual installs and updates. A package contains all the files you need for a module.

EXAMPLE: A common example of a software package is the Microsoft Office package, which includes several individual applications, including Word, PowerPoint and Excel.

software suite: A collection of computer programs that typically perform similar functions. These computer programs usually share a similar user interface (the elements on a computer that the user [person operating a computer] interacts with [such as a keyboard, screen, or login form]).

EXAMPLE: One of the most popular software suites is Microsoft Office 365. It includes several programs, including Word and Excel.

software testing: A system or process for investigating computer programs to assess their quality. This is done in order to provide those people concerned with the software (business owners, computer programmers, project managers, etc.) with vital information about such things as:

- How well the software meets the guidelines that were used in its creation.
- Whether there are bugs in the program (errors in a computer program that cause it to produce an incorrect or unexpected result).
- Whether the software responds correctly to various inputs.
- Whether the software operates within acceptable time frames (response time, etc.).
- Whether the software can be installed properly on the types of computer systems it is intended for.

There are many different types of software testing approaches, systems and processes.

EXAMPLE: You might ask a team of people who will eventually use the finished program to test various features of the program as it is developed.

solid state drive: See "SSD."

sorting algorithm: An algorithm (a list of steps to complete a task or solve a problem) that arranges a list of items in a certain order. There are different methods one can use to sort things and sorting algorithms exist for each method. Sorting algorithms allow you to sort through and organize data.

EXAMPLE: There are sorting algorithms that will have the computer look at a list of numbers, and put them in sequence, starting at the top (highest value) number and working down.

source code: The set of programming language (a system of specialized words and symbols used to communicate with a computer and to create programs) instructions that make up a computer program (a set of written instructions, entered into a computer by people, that make it execute [perform] specific tasks). Source code is the instructions a computer programmer writes (in a computer programming language) before they have been converted to machine language (commands given in a way the computer "understands" and that reflects the construction of its components – 1s and 0s). These instructions might look something like this:

```
if (age > 21)
{
        print("You may purchase this item");
}
```

(> in this case means "greater than")

A computer programmer writes instructions like this using a program called a text editor – it is basically like the word processing programs used by many people, but it is made to be useful to programmers. The end result is pretty simple, though – it is just a text document. The file is not very useful in that form; it can't make the computer do anything. When the computer programmer wants to turn these instructions into a program that the computer can execute, they use another specialized program that reads through the contents of the text file and turns them into machine language. Only then can the computer actually perform the instructions the programmer created. Those instructions in the text document are the source code. It is called "source code" because it is the source of information used to create an actual computer program. The source code for a program can be easily changed – any text editor program can open the files containing the source code instructions. The computer program that gets created from that source code, however, can't easily be changed. It can only be executed by the computer and then used by people. If you are given the source code for a program, you can make changes to it and then turn it into a program. That version of the program would then be different from any prior version of the program.

EXAMPLE: If you can access and modify the source code of a program, you could end up ruining the program entirely if you do not know exactly what you're doing. If you got a hold of the source code for a computer game, you might be able to modify it so that you could cheat while playing.

source control: Another word for "version control."

spectrum: A way to classify items in terms of positions on a scale. Spectrums have two extreme or opposite points.

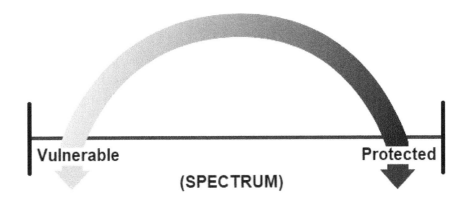

Vulnerable | Protected
(SPECTRUM)

When speaking of colors, a spectrum is the range of colors (like seen in a rainbow) as determined by refraction and according to the wavelength of the light.

EXAMPLE: You can see the color spectrum in this cartoon rainbow:

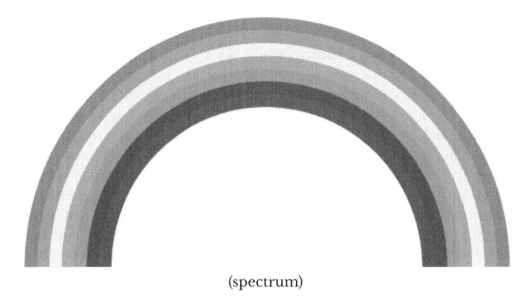

(spectrum)

spooling: Stands for <u>s</u>imultaneous <u>p</u>eripheral <u>o</u>perations <u>o</u>n-<u>l</u>ine. Peripheral refers to equipment outside of a computer that interacts with the computer (such as a printer). Spooling is when several tasks are to be done by a peripheral, and the computer is sending tasks to the peripheral faster than the peripheral can perform the tasks. The computer gives a task to the peripheral, and while it waits for the other machine to perform the task, the remaining tasks "spool" (which means the computer stacks up the tasks in a queue, gives another task to the peripheral when it's ready for one, then monitors the remaining tasks until they are done). This lets the computer get on to other tasks without having to wait until the operation on the slower-moving peripheral is done.

EXAMPLE: Sometimes when you attempt to print several documents at once, the documents spool and only the first one or two documents get sent to the printer. Then, when the printer can handle more printing tasks, more of the documents will be sent to the printer.

spreadsheet: A type of computer program (a set of written instructions, entered into a computer by people, that make it execute [perform] specific tasks) that allows you to organize, modify and analyze data. The data is stored in individual containers called cells; these cells are organized into rows and columns.

A set of rows and columns is called a table. This type of computer program was developed based on accounting worksheets where businesses could record important data on paper in a similar fashion. Spreadsheet programs that came out in the early 1980s helped the computer industry transition from a situation where only large companies used computers (and those computers were large themselves) to a situation where smaller companies were able to buy small desktop computers, get a spreadsheet program, and perform needed financial calculations much faster than they could do with a paper-based system. The popularity of spreadsheet programs helped drive up sales of these smaller "personal computers."

EXAMPLE: If you wanted to keep track of how many business sales you made each year, you could type this in a spreadsheet.

	A	B	C	D	
1	Country	Sales			
2	United States	7583			
3	United Kingdom	4359			
4	France	45995			
5	Germany	3933			
6	Spain	8738			
7	Italy	5239			
8	Greece	38282			
9					
10					

(spreadsheet)

Spring: A popular application framework for the programming language Java. It can be used to build web applications.

EXAMPLE: Spring is heavily used in the enterprise (related to a company or business) sector to build major programs and web applications.

(Spring)

spider: See "web spider."

sprint: A set period of time (usually 1 week, 2 weeks or 30 days) where a specified amount of work is assigned to get done. Sprints begin and end with meetings where tasks are assigned and reviews of past performance are done.

EXAMPLE: One development project can consist of dozens of sprints – these sprints continue until the project is complete.

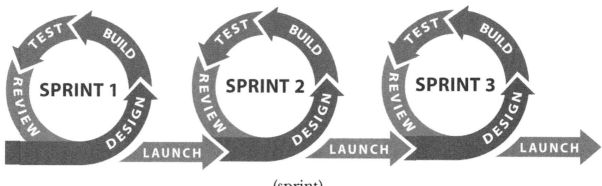

(sprint)

sprint backlog: The tasks that a team hopes to complete during a particular sprint. See "PBI."

EXAMPLE: A sprint backlog could be: "Launch a new contact form in accordance with the updated design."

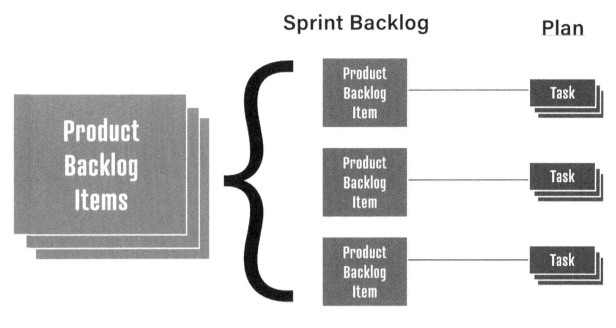

(sprint backlog)

sprint goal: In project management, this is the key focus and overall product of a particular sprint. A sprint goal is also referred to as the theme.

EXAMPLE: A sprint goal might be to complete design and development of a single web page of a website.

sprint planning: In project management, at the start of each sprint, this is a planning session which occurs with the team. During sprint planning, developers are assigned tasks and the sprint backlog is planned out – i.e. the team decides which product backlog items (PBIs) will be completed within the next sprint.

EXAMPLE: During a planning session, you might add 15 new tasks to your project.

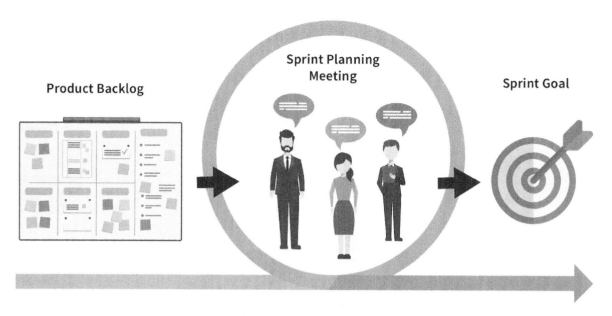

(sprint planning)

sprint retrospective: Retrospect means to review or survey past events or a period of time. A sprint retrospective is the meeting at the end of a sprint where the team determines what could be changed that might make the next sprint more productive.

EXAMPLE: Sprint retrospectives gather feedback and provide info on how a project is progressing. The meeting can be overseen by the product owner (the person responsible for defining user stories and prioritizing the backlog), but it need not be – often, this meeting involves only the members of the development team.

Sprint Retrospective

Meeting after Sprint Review to review processes

- What went well?
- What could be improved?
- How can we improve it?

30 Min - 3 hr

Self-analysis on how to work

Problem analysis and improved aspects

Framework improvements

Product owner + Scrum team

(sprint retrospective)

SPSS: *SPSS* originally stood for *Statistical Package for Social Sciences*, but was later changed to *Statistical Product and Service Solutions*. SPSS is a widely used program for statistical analysis.

EXAMPLE: The data analytics department of a company might use SPSS.

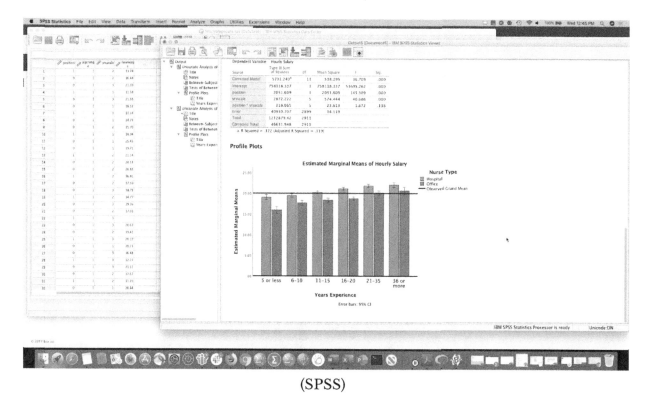

(SPSS)

SQL: Stands for "Structured Query Language." A computer language used to monitor and work with databases. SQL can edit, change, modify, delete, etc. data in a database.

> EXAMPLE: An example of a command in SQL might be this:
> `SELECT Price, ItemName FROM Products WHERE Price < 10.00`
> This would look in a database and find all the products in the table "Products" that cost less than $10.00. It would then make a list that had the price and name of each of those products.

SQL injection: SQL injection (also called "SQL Injection attack") is a code injection (see "code injection") technique. SQL injections are used to attack applications, in which malicious SQL statements are inserted into an entry field for execution (for example: to dump the database contents to the attacker). A SQL injection exploits a security vulnerability in the application's software.

> EXAMPLE: SQL injection could forward all users email addresses and passwords to a hacker from a database.

SQL join: See "join."

SQL Server: Stands for "Structured Query Language Server." SQL Server is a Relational Database Management System computer program produced by the technology company Microsoft. Whereas SQL is a language, SQL server is software.

EXAMPLE: SQL Server is one of the most popular computer programs in the world. It is used by many companies to manage their databases.

SQLite: SQLite is the most-used database engine in the world. It is a small program, which means it operates very quickly.

EXAMPLE: For small software development projects, SQLite could be a great choice to work with.

(SQLite)

squiggly: A squiggly is a short or long underline in the shape of a wavy or curvy twist that indicates an error of some sort. In most text document software, a red squiggly indicates a misspelled word, while a blue squiggly indicates a grammatical error. Colloquially, curly brackets {} are sometimes referred to as squigglies.

EXAMPLE: In coding editors, a squiggly can indicate a few different things:
- Red indicates a syntax error.
- Green and Yellow indicate a warning.
- Blue indicates a compiler error.

These colors can change based on the code editor you use.

SSD: It is now very common for drives to have no moving parts – the data is stored in a solid piece of material that can hold millions of individual pieces of data. These are called "solid state drives," (SSD) but the older term "disk drive" is often used when talking about these newer drives. Whereas HDDs (hard disc drives – see "HDD") have arms with a needle that reads the data (kind of like a record player), SSDs pass the data along various paths without any components that move. SSDs are able to store, delete and transfer data faster than HDDs. Due to their top-of-the-line performance, SSDs are more expensive than most other types of drives.

EXAMPLE: Here is an HDD (left) next to an SSD (right):

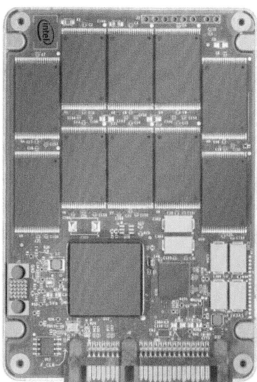

(SSD)

SSL: Stands for Secure Sockets Layer. Secure Sockets Layer (SSL) is a protocol (a formal agreement about how to format and send a particular type of data) for encrypting information on computer networks. Using SSL means that the information being sent over the Internet (the largest and most-used computer network [connection that allows data transfer between machines] in the world, which is mainly utilized to access the World Wide Web) is safe from use by someone other than the intended receiver who might intercept the information. SSL is a layer of security put over the information as it is transported on the network. An SSL certificate means that whoever you are dealing with has been inspected by an authorized security organization (a "certificate authority") and has been verified as a trustworthy organization. Over time, this protocol was improved, and eventually, renamed. The modern term for the protocol is TLS, which stands for Transport Layer Security. There are very few differences between the two protocols as far as basic operation; the differences are mainly important to those who specialize in the encryption field. You will often find references to use of SSL when, in fact, it is actually TLS that is being used. In practice, this is not a very important distinction.

EXAMPLE: It is highly recommended that if you are paying for something with a credit card on the Internet, that you ensure that whoever you are dealing with (paying) has an TLS/SSL certificate. You can often find information about this on their website.

(SSL)

stack: There are two uses for the word stack in technology:

1. The regular definition of stack is a pile of objects. In computer science, a stack is one of the basic ways of organizing and using data in a computer. It is often visualized as a vertical pile of data, with each piece of data on top of another. In computers, a stack is a set of data or tasks that are waiting to be handled. The computer (or other device) takes item 1 in the stack and handles that, then item 2, and so on. Stacks operate in this exact manner:

1) The order in which items are added to the stack is known.

2) When the computer is ready to work on another item from the stack, it takes the youngest item on the stack – that is, the one most recently added to the stack. This is called the "Last In, First Out" (LIFO) operation.

3) Taking an item off the stack to be worked on is called "popping" the item off the stack. You would say "perform a pop operation."

4) When a new item is added to the stack, it goes to the "top" of the stack – that is, it's now the youngest item in the stack, and therefore will be the very next one worked on, unless another item is added before the computer is ready to work on another item.

5) Adding an item to the stack is called "pushing" the item onto the stack. You would say "perform a push operation."

EXAMPLE: We have a stack of books in a cart at a library. The librarian is traveling throughout the library, putting books back on the shelves. She grabs the book at the top of the stack, finds out where it goes, places it on the shelf, and then grabs the next book at the top of the stack. This would be a "pop" operation. As she travels throughout the library, another librarian may walk up and put another book on the top of the stack. This would be a "push" operation. That book is now the youngest, and will be the next one handled – unless yet another book is placed on the top of the stack before she can finish re-shelving the book she is working on.

2. A stack is a set of software systems that creates a complete platform, such that no other software is needed to support a specific application. The other terms for this are

software stack or solution stack. In the case of a stack to support a web application, for example, it is a specific combination of the following items:

1) An operating system (a special-purpose computer program that supports the computer's basic functions, such as scheduling tasks, running other computer programs, and controlling peripherals, like keyboards, mice and displays);

2) A web server program (a specialized computer used to store and transmit data, such as "serving up" websites through the World Wide Web);

3) A database management system (software for managing databases);

4) A programming language (a system of specialized words and symbols used to communicate with a computer and to create programs).

With a set of those four items that can work together, a complete system exists for a web application to operate: there is a machine that has an operating system installed, the computer is running a web server program that is ready to respond to requests for web pages; there is a programming language that can be used to write programs that will run on the server to implement the logic of the web application; and there is a program to facilitate the creation and use of databases so the web application can make use of stored data as it operates.

EXAMPLE: Professionals that can use all four elements of the stack are referred to as "full-stack" developers."

stacked neural network: See "deep learning."

staging: In version control, this is the step prior to the commit process in Git. A staged file means that you have marked the file to be included in your next commit. Staging is basically a loading dock where you can determine which changes you will commit. You can perform actions in the staging area, such as temporarily storing your changes.

EXAMPLE: The following diagram shows the staging area:

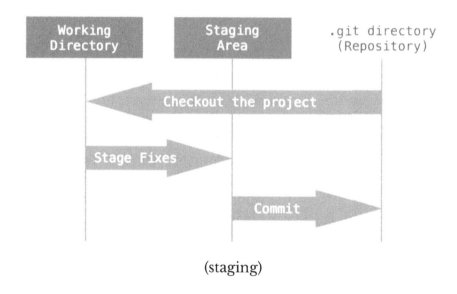

(staging)

staging environment: See "environment."

stakeholder: Someone involved in a project that is concerned with its overall success. The origin of the word is "a person involved in a bet." In project management, a stakeholder is simply anyone interested in a project's outcome. This can include members of the team, executives, users and clients. They are people affected by the outcome of a project and those who can influence it.

EXAMPLE: The financial investor behind a project would be a stakeholder.

standard definition: See "resolution, levels of."

standard deviation: A quantity that is calculated to indicate the level of deviation for a group as a whole. It is the measure of how spread out numbers are. Deviation allows you to see what is considered large or small by indicating what the "standard" is and showing the amounts that deviate from that standard.

EXAMPLE: If you were tracking the completion times of a race, you could use standard deviation to measure the variation between completion times.

standard error: A data science term that means "a measure of spread in statistics." The higher the number, the more spread out the data is. The standard error is used when working with sample data and it tells you how far your sample average deviates from the actual population of data. Standard error is an estimate of the standard deviation of a population.

EXAMPLE: You could calculate the standard error for how much you eat during the holidays vs how much you eat on average year-round.

standard HD: See "resolution, levels of."

standard resolution: See "resolution, levels of."

stand-up: See "daily stand-up."

star network: A very common type of computer network. A star network is where many computers are connected to each other via a central computer or machine. This central computer or machine is called a "hub." The hub passes information to and from computers on a star network.

EXAMPLE: There is a company using a star network. Employee A writes a supply list and saves it on the network as a document. Employee B opens the supply list document in the network. What happens here is that when Employee A saved the supply list document, it saved on the hub. When Employee B clicked on the supply list document, he got it from the hub (the hub passed the information to Employee B's computer).

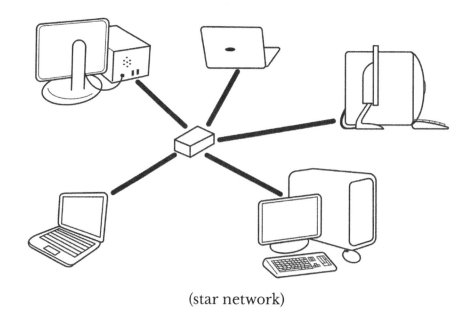

(star network)

start tag: See "tag."

state: See "class."

stateful: State is the condition of a person or thing. The terms stateful and stateless are used to describe whether or not a computer program is designed to remember prior events. A stateful program will have a mechanism for keeping track of events as the program is used; a stateless program will not. Stateful means that the interactions between the user and the computer are remembered. Stateful means that there is a record of previous interactions and each interaction that occurs can take into account the current or past events related to the desired operation.

EXAMPLE: A login page that remembers your username or password after logging in once would be stateful.

stateless: State is the condition of a person or thing. The terms stateful and stateless are used to describe whether or not a computer program is designed to remember prior events. A stateful program will have a mechanism for keeping track of events as the program is used; a stateless program will not. Stateless means that the interactions between the user and the computer are not remembered. Stateless means that there is no record of previous interactions and each interaction that occurs has to be handled based entirely on information that comes with it.

EXAMPLE: A login page that does not remember your username or password, even if you've logged in before, would be stateless.

statement: Computer instructions. These are the instructions that are used by people as they create computer programs (a set of written instructions, entered into a computer by people, that make it execute [perform] specific tasks). The simplest of these might be things like "print," "delete," "add," "multiply," etc.

EXAMPLE: The "print" statement tells your computer to display (print) whatever text you typed as part of the command.

static: See "static website."

static website: "Static" in this sense means "rigid; unchanging." Static websites are delivered to the browser exactly how they were stored originally on the web server (a specialized computer used to store and transmit data, such as "serving up" websites through the World Wide Web). Static web pages do not change. No matter who is accessing the website, it looks the same. Most websites nowadays are dynamic, meaning that the appearance and content of the web pages can be changed on the web server before the web page is sent back to the browser, or it can be changed by the browser on the user's computer before being displayed on the screen.

EXAMPLE: In the 1990s, most websites were static.

statistic: A representation of some sort of data. Typically, statistics are numerical values that show a comparison of past data amounts. Virtually anything can be represented as a statistic, and the information gained can be very useful. Statistics are a valuable decision-making tool.

EXAMPLE: You usually see statistics displayed on a graph (a picture showing the relation between various quantities), like this:

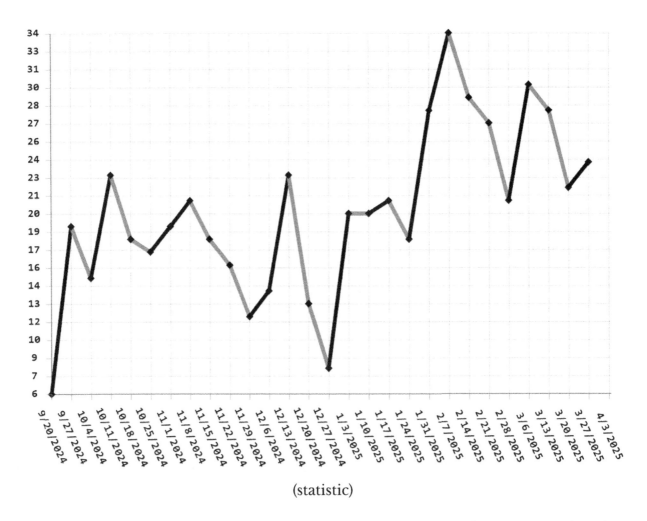

(statistic)

statistical dispersion: A way of describing the distance between data points – in other words, how spread out the data is. The question asked by statistical dispersion is, "Are the data points close together or farther apart from one data point to the next?"

EXAMPLE: Consider the following datasets:
A. 95, 97, 98, 100, 102, 103, 105
B. 75, 82, 99, 100, 101, 118, 125
Both datasets have seven data points, both also have a mean (average) of 100. The range (distance between highest and lowest value), on the other hand, in each dataset is very different. Dataset B's data points range from 75 to 125 while dataset A's range is 95 to 105. Here is what the statistical dispersion of data would look like visually:

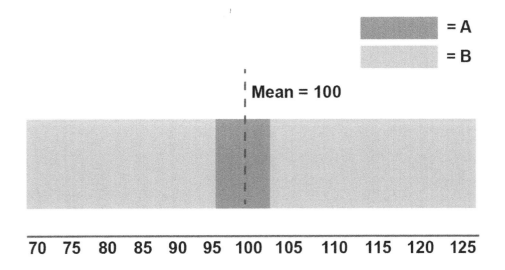

= A

= B

Mean = 100

70 75 80 85 90 95 100 105 110 115 120 125

As you can see, even though both data sets have a mean of 100, the data tells a much different story altogether when both are compared and their statistical dispersion is measured.

statistical distribution: The distribution (see "distribution") of a statistical data set shows us all the possible values or intervals of data, as well as how often each piece of data occurs and is observed. There are various methods of statistical distribution.

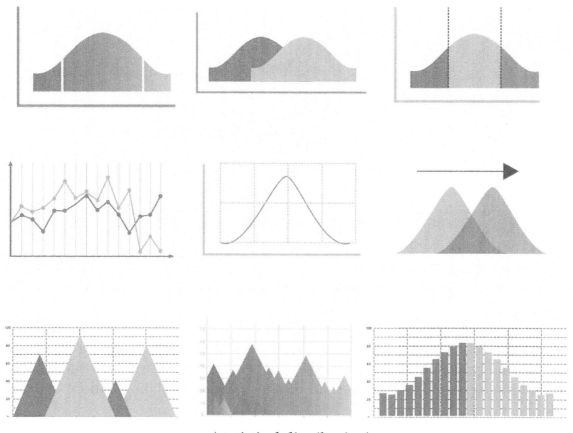

(statistical distribution)

statistical modeling: A data science term which refers to the organizing of data and creating a standard of how the data is related.

EXAMPLE: Consider this image:

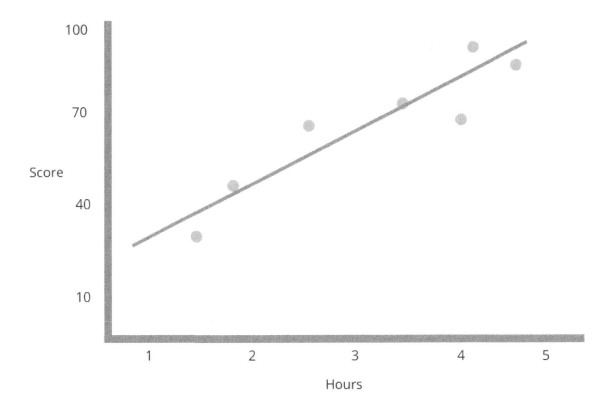

Hours

This picture is a data model of test scores that relate to how many hours a student studies before a test. The line tells you the trend of the data. Statistical modeling can help us understand the relationship between the number of study-hours and the resulting test score. The number of study-hours would be considered an independent variable (data that has a name and a value [type/amount], and can be changed), while the score would be a dependent variable. The independent variable explains, describes or predicts the dependent variable. The independent variable is often represented on the x-axis, while the dependent variable is on the y-axis. The picture above is called a *scatter plot*, *scatter chart* or *scatter graph*. A scatter plot uses dots to represent the values of two different numerical variables. The purpose of scatter plots is to show the relationships between variables. In our scatter plot, you can see that if a student studied for four hours or more before an exam, it is likely that they would get a grade above 70%. *Bivariate* means "depending on or involving two variables." Our example above is *bivariate* data. Something which involves only one variable quantity is called a *univariate*.

statistical significance: Significance means "being likely to have influence or an effect on something." Statistical significance is a data science term which indicates whether a result is due to chance or by another means.

EXAMPLE: You can do many different kinds of statistical tests for the amount of people who walk into a store. Let's say that on a Monday it was observed that 100 people walked into the store in a timespan of 4 hours, and on Tuesday only 120 came in for the same amount of time. Now let's say you surveyed each person that came in and asked what brought them in that day. On Monday there were 20% sale signs seen from outside the store, while on Tuesday they were taken down. You could perform a statistical test based on your surveys to see if the sales signs had influenced the amount of customers on Monday, or if it was by pure chance and the sale signs had little to no effect.

store: The action of storing information in a computer, or the information that is stored in a computer. To store something on a computer is to take information and put it inside the computer so it can be looked at later. This can also be used as a noun: A collection of data. It is often used in the term "data store," to describe an organized set of related data, often of various types.

EXAMPLE: A bicycle manufacturer might use computers to set up a data store containing all information related to sales, marketing and manufacturing, and then build computer programs for the various parts of the company that would let people access the data store to view and analyze data.

stored procedure: A stored procedure is a carefully designed set of SQL instructions that can be used to automate a task. Stored procedures can consist of a single line or several pages of code. They can embrace one task or a large series of tasks.

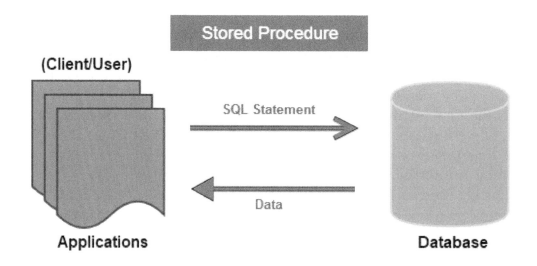

EXAMPLE: Here is an example stored procedure:

```
                                              { connects to the target database

USE AdventureWorks2014
GO                                            { creates the stored procedure

CREATE PROCEDURE dbo.HR_GetAddress
AS                                            { SQL statement

SELECT * FROM Person.Address
GO                                            { executes the stored procedure

EXEC dbo.HR_GetAddress
```

(stored procedure)

storyboard: The result of drawing out the basic ideas and sequence of a project. Storyboards are used to plan out coding projects and are based on the film industry (where storyboards refer to sequences of drawings, typically with some dialogue and directions, that represents the shots planned for a TV show or movie).

EXAMPLE: Here are a couple of examples of storyboards:

Input	Process	Output
User enters a movie name or select a genre then searches a genre then searches for a movie.	Website looks up the movie the user has searched in database, if the movie the user has searched for exist, then it will show, if not it will show similiar or related movies.	The movie or similiar related movies with reference links.

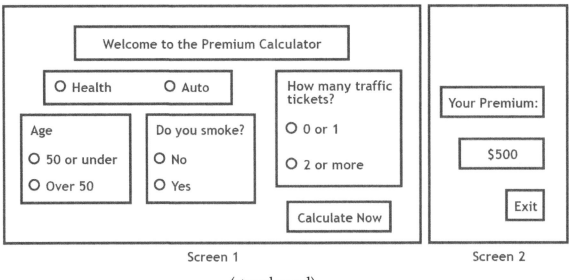

| Screen 1 | Screen 2 |

(storyboard)

story time: In project management, this is a meeting during a sprint when tasks on the backlog are discussed and clarified. Attempts are made to estimate how long each task will take to complete. Tasks are also prioritized during this time. Story time is also referred to as "backlog grooming" or "backlog refinement."

EXAMPLE: During story time, it may be decided that one task should take priority over all others.

streaming: A method of sending information from one computer to another in which the information is broken up into parts, and these parts are sent one after the other. The information is used on the destination computer as the individual pieces arrive, instead of after all of the information has arrived. This is used most often to describe a method of consuming (watching, listening, etc.) to video and audio media. In this situation, it means that a company that provides the media content has the media files (the digital information that makes up the media) on its own computers. When a remote (separate) computer connects and wants to consume that media, the company's computer starts sending the media one part at a time. As the parts arrive at the destination computer, they are processed and presented to the user. The media information is not usually preserved on the destination computer. In this situation, the source computer is said to be "streaming" the media to the destination computer. Usually, many destination computers can connect to the source computer at once. Each one will be receiving its own "stream" of information.

EXAMPLE: You could use your computer to connect to a service that lets you watch movies. You would select a movie to watch. The service would then start sending the electronic data for the movie to your computer. You could start watching the movie right away, without waiting for all the movie's data to arrive to your computer.

string: This is a data type (a specific category of information handled by a computer –

such as numbers or comparisons) used in computers that is made out of multiple characters. A string is basically a type of data that connects a bunch of characters. Often these characters signify something to the user.

EXAMPLE: In the computer instruction:
```
Print "John is smart"
```
The series of characters "John is smart" is the string.

strongly-typed: A programming language that enforces strict restrictions on mixing values with different data types. With a strongly-typed programming language, an error occurs if you attempt to intermix values with differing data types. The opposite of strongly-typed is weakly-typed. In weakly-typed programming languages, the variables are not bound to a specific data type. Technically, the fundamental difference between the two are:
1. Weakly-typed languages convert unrelated data types implicitly.
2. Strongly-typed languages typically do not allow implicit conversions of data types.

EXAMPLE: Python and Perl are strongly-typed programming languages.

structure: See "class."

structured data: Structured data refers to data that is organized into a predefined data model (a description of the structure of various sets of data, as well as the relationship between those different sets of data and how they can interact). One of the most common models is the table – an arrangement of columns (which specify the data identifier and its type) and rows (which are specific collections of the data types specified in those columns). Structured data is most commonly used in relational databases (a type of database where the data in it is organized into tables [columns and rows], and the data in each table can relate to [have a connection to] data in another table[s]). This type of data is clearly defined and can be searched for. Data contained within a field, record, table or spreadsheet is considered structured data.

EXAMPLE: Here are some data types that are considered structured data:
*   Name
*   Phone
*   Address
*   Date of Birth
*   Retail Cost

Unstructured data refers to data that is not easily searchable.

EXAMPLE: You could have hundreds of files of videos that have not been labeled properly and you're trying to find the one that shows a dolphin doing a flip in the water but all your videos are named "dolphin 1", "dolphin 2", etc. To find the required file, you'd have to manually watch each video. Therefore, this would be unstructured data.

Semi-structured data is technically a type of structured data (organized in tables), but it does not require or obey the data model structures associated with relational databases. Semi-structured data uses markers (identifiers) to locate specific elements within the data.

EXAMPLE: Word processors usually include metadata (data about data) showing the date the file was created and other information, with the rest of the document being unstructured text. This is an example of semi-structured data.

| Unstructured data | Semi-structured data | Structured data |

Unstructured data

The university has 5600 students.
John's ID is number 1, he is 18 years old and already holds a B.S. degree.
David's ID is number 2, he is 31 years old and holds a Ph.D. degree. Robert's ID is number 3, he is 51 years old and also holds the same degree as David, a Ph.D. degree.

Semi-structured data

```
<University>
  <Student ID="1">
    <Name>John</Name>
    <Age>18</Age>
    <Degree>B.S.</Degree>
  </Student>
  <Student ID="2">
    <Name>David</Name>
    <Age>31</Age>
    <Degree>Ph.D. </Degree>
  </Student>
  ....
</University>
```

Structured data

ID	Name	Age	Degree
1	John	18	B.S.
2	David	31	Ph.D.
3	Robert	51	Ph.D.
4	Rick	26	B.S.
5	Michael	19	B.S.

(structured data)

Structured Query Language: See "SQL."

style guide: A document containing a set of design standards that tell designers exactly what fonts and colors a design should have among many other aspects that should be included in the design. Its main purpose is to help designers and developers keep a product consistent. For example, a style guide would tell you exactly what size and font all main text headings should be rather than one page having one font and another page having a completely separate font. It just wouldn't look right to the end user (the person or persons for whom a computer program is being developed). Some other examples that would be included in a style guide would be:
1. Fonts.
2. Heading sizes and colors.
3. Naming conventions.
4. The exact colors that will be used on the site.
5. Exactly what the buttons should look like when inactive or clicked.
It can be used for almost any kind of design from graphic design to interior design. The guide however can change throughout the design process, as most of the time, it would simply start with some of the very basic needs for designers to get started.

EXAMPLE: Here's what a style guide could look like for a website:

(style guide)

subatomic: Literally this means "smaller than an atom" or "contained within an atom." An atom is one of the smallest units in the physical universe. It is the particle of matter that uniquely defines a chemical element. There are about 1,000,000,000,000,000,000 atoms in one grain of salt.

EXAMPLE: Electrons (particles that carry electricity) are subatomic.

subprogram: A subprogram is a set of computer instructions to be used by a main computer program that performs some task that you may want to do over and over again at various times. The main computer program could do some of its own actions in a specific sequence, then ask the subprogram to do its tasks, and then continue on where it was before it asked the subprogram to do its tasks. Another term for this is "subroutine," since a routine is just a set of computer instructions – a computer program. Subprograms are also referred to as "methods," "callbacks" or "procedures." See usage note under "function."

EXAMPLE: Within a computer program used to operate a college, there could be a subprogram that checked to see if any new students had been enrolled since you last used the program. The main program could use that subprogram as it was starting up, get the data on any new students, and then continue on with its primary functions.

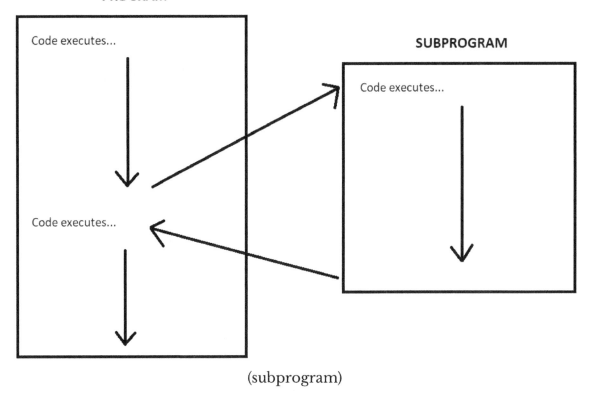

PROGRAM

Code executes...

Code executes...

SUBPROGRAM

Code executes...

(subprogram)

subroutine: See "subprogram." Also, see the usage note under "function."

subscript: A subscript is text written below a line, such as: $_1$a$_2$B$_3$c$_4$D$_5$. Subscripts can be used to indicate the base number system. The base of any number system is determined by the number of digits in that system.

EXAMPLE: Binary is a base-2 number system. The way to display that we are talking about a binary number would be 10011_2 (this would be 19). The way to display that we are talking about a decimal number would be 19_{10} (which is 19).

Subversion: Apache Subversion is an open-source (software that can be modified and used for free) version control system (a system for managing multiple versions [editions; releases] of computer files and programs).

EXAMPLE: Subversion can be used to maintain current and historical versions of code files – including source code (the original code of a program as written by the program's creator[s]), documentation and web pages.

(Subversion)

subwoofer: A speaker that is designed to reproduce very low bass frequencies.

EXAMPLE: Subwoofers can produce much lower sounds than normal speakers.

suite: See "software suite."

super key: A set of one or more keys that can be used to identify a record in a database table. A table can have many superkeys. A candidate key (column, or a set of columns, in a table that uniquely identifies any database record without referring to any other data) is a subset (subcategory; type) of super key that does not have any unnecessary information in it. Meaning, super keys can have additional information outside of the scope of a candidate key.

EXAMPLE: Consider this table of data:

Student_ID	Student_Subject	Student_Name	Student_Email
02	History	David	david@gmail.com
09	Science	Jeff	jeff@gmail.com
14	Art	Susan	susan@gmail.com
19	Art	Jeff	Jeff2@gmail.com
22	History	Jessica	jess@gmail.com

In this table, the following would be super keys:
A. Student_ID
B. Student_Subject
C. Student_Email
D. Student_ID and Student_Subject (combined)
E. Student_ID and Student_Name (combined)
F. Student_ID and Student_Email (combined)
G. Student_Name and Student_Subject (combined)

H. Student_ID, Student_Subject and Student_Name (combined)
I. Student_ID, Student_Subject and Student_Email (combined)
J. Student_ID, Student_Subject, Student_Name and Student_Email (combined)

Here are the candidate keys from the above table:
A. Student_ID
B. Student_Subject
C. Student_Email

superscript: Superscripts are smaller characters typically displayed toward the upper right of another number – like this: 4^{12}. Whereas subscripts indicate the number system we are talking about, superscripts usually indicate "power." Power simply refers to how many times a number is multiplied by itself.

EXAMPLE: 4^3 would mean 4 X 4 X 4 (which equals 64).

surround sound: A type of sound that includes three or more speakers that surround listeners. The purpose of surround sound is to provide a more realistic listening experience by emulating life (where sound comes from all directions).

EXAMPLE: A surround sound system at your home could consist of multiple speakers placed in a variety of locations in your living room.

SVG: SVG stands for Scalable Vector Graphics. It is a vector graphic (images made up of straight lines) file format. SVGs have lossless (no data is removed from the file) resizing capabilities. Meaning, instead of an item becoming more pixelated when it is enlarged, a vector graphic maintains its smooth edges. Unlike Bitmap images that have fixed pixels, vector graphics have a fixed shape. SVG images and their behaviors are defined in XML (short for "extensible markup language"; XML is a customizable markup language, used primarily in the displaying documents on the internet [i.e., websites]) text files which can be searched, indexed, scripted and compressed.

EXAMPLE: SVG is a popular file format in the field of web design because the designs can scale to any size without sacrificing image quality.

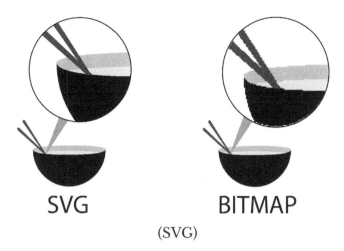

SVG   BITMAP

(SVG)

switch: 1. Something that can be placed in one of two or more physical states, and which modifies the operation of a machine based on the state it is placed in. The physical position the switch is placed in is called its "position." The most common switch you may be familiar with is a light switch. It does only two things, based on its position: 1. Stops electricity from flowing through, or 2. Allows electricity to flow through. This results in the light being "off" or "on." Some switches may have several different positions. For example, you might have three display screens set up for a computer, and a switch whose position determined which of the displays would show the information from the computer at any point in time.

EXAMPLE: There is a form of power switch on every computer, used to turn the computer on and off.

2. See "command-line option."

switch (command line): When referring to the command line, a switch behaves as a modifier to a command. It is usually a single letter preceded by either a forward slash (/) or a dash (-).

EXAMPLE: If you were to type DIR in the command line with /ON /P following, like so:
DIR /ON /P
it would list out in order all files in your computer's directory. /ON will Order the files by Name and /P will Pause after each directory page is loaded.

switch statement: Another form of branching statements, wherein the conditional element is compared to a case.

EXAMPLE: Let's say you had an input form that had different outputs based on the number a user inputs. The number choices in this example are: 1, 4, and 8. In the case the user chose 1, a prompt on the screen would appear congratulating them and the next screen would appear. The switch statement would now be broken because it is no longer needed and the code block would end. In the case that they chose 8, the switch statement would switch through the cases until it came to 8. In the case that the user chose no numbers, the switch statement would have a default at the end that would prompt the user to go back and choose one of the following numbers: 1, 4, 8. The diagram below shows the flow of how a switch statement runs:

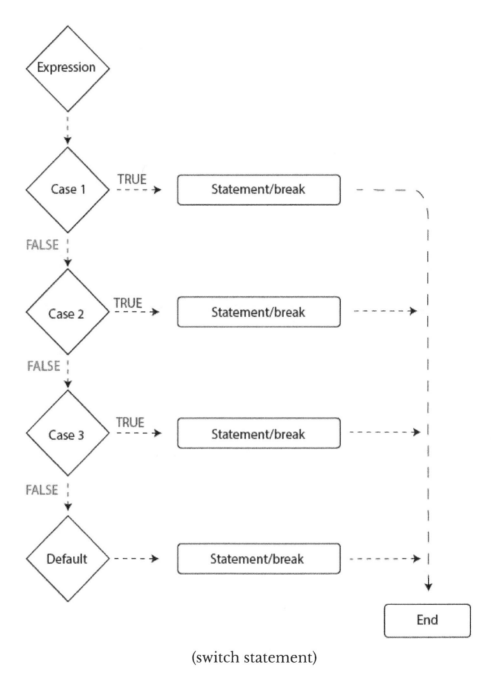

(switch statement)

symmetrical distribution: In statistics, this is a type of distribution of data where the values of variables (a placeholder for a value that can change) occur at regular frequencies, and the mean, median and mode (these are each used to calculate an average) occur at the same point. The data has one peak in the middle, and either side basically mirrors the other. This shape is called a bell curve – it curves on its way up the left side, and curves again as it goes down on the right. Symmetrical distribution is also referred to as *normal distribution* or *Gaussian distribution*. Gaussian distribution is named after the German mathematician Carl Friedrich Gauss.

EXAMPLE: This histogram illustrates the number of students and their recent test scores:

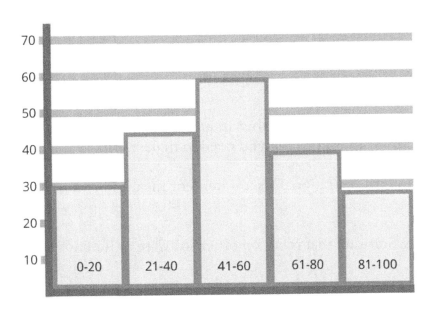

The y-axis is "students," and the x-axis is "percentage." Over 50 students scored between 41-60%, while every other student scored either lower or higher. Since this peak is in the middle, you can draw the conclusion that the average score of this class is between 41-60%.

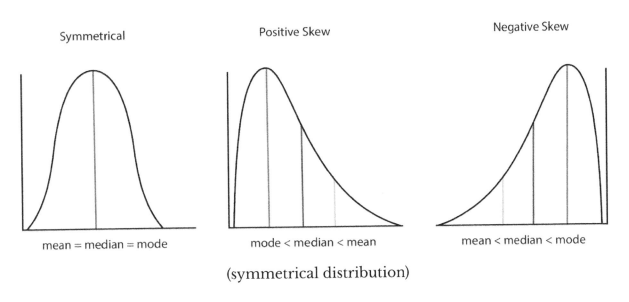

(symmetrical distribution)

synchronous: See "asynchronous."

syntax: The rules you must follow when writing computer programs (a set of written instructions, entered into a computer by people, that make it execute [perform] specific tasks). Each programming language (a system of specialized words and symbols used to communicate with a computer and to create programs) has its own syntax. Failing to use the syntax of a particular language correctly can mean that whatever program you are designing will not work at all.

EXAMPLE: If a computer language required you to write "cmd:" (meaning "command") at the beginning of each instruction, that would be part of the syntax of that language. And if you did not write "cmd:" at the beginning of an instruction, the computer would not be able to process and execute the instruction because you violated syntax.

system: A group of things that work together in an orderly fashion. A computer system is a full computer setup with everything you need to make it run.

EXAMPLE: "All systems operational" is a statement meant to mean that a computer is fully working.

system dependencies: Software that relies on other software to function.

EXAMPLE: Every computer has built-in audio software that enables speakers to play sound. Media players also have software that communicates the audio data to the speaker software. These two software depend on each other – if one does not work, sound won't play.

syntactic sugar: Refers to syntax (the rules that govern how code must be formed and ordered) of a programming language (a system of specialized words and symbols used to communicate with a computer and to create programs) that is easier to read or write. It is called this because it makes the coding language "sweeter" in terms of clarity, styling and conciseness.

EXAMPLE: In one programming language, the following lines of code both produce the same outcome (moving an item):
```
MOVE X Y
MOVE X TO Y
```
Because the second example is clearer to understand (X is moved to Y), it is considered syntactic sugar.

T

t, T: Stands for "tera." Tera means trillion. See also "byte."

EXAMPLE: $1T is $1,000,000,000,000.00.

tab: A visual representation on a computer display that identifies an element on the screen. It is similar to the tabs that are placed on file folders in a physical organizing system. It can be used in the case where a computer program allows multiple versions of a similar display element, so that each element can be identified and controlled.

EXAMPLE: Using a computer program to work on two different web pages at once. On the screen, a browser (the program people use to view web pages – e.g., Google Chrome) could present two small tabs near the top of the screen, with the name of each page on the tab. You could use these tabs to switch between the pages.

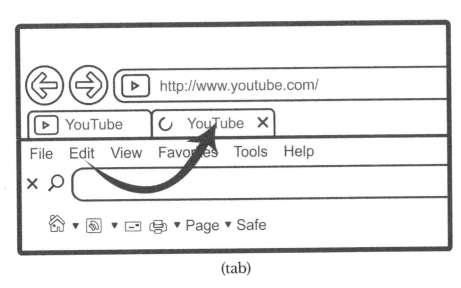

(tab)

tab key: In order to describe the tab key, you must first understand what a "spreadsheet" and a "table" are. A spreadsheet is a visual grid structure that allows you to organize, modify and analyze data. The data is stored in individual containers called cells. These cells are organized into rows and columns (each rectangle in this picture is a cell):

Here is a spreadsheet:

	A	B	C	D
1	Country	Sales		
2	United States	7583		
3	United Kingdom	4359		
4	France	45995		
5	Germany	3933		
6	Spain	8738		
7	Italy	5239		
8	Greece	38282		
9				
10				

Sheet1 / Sheet2 / Sheet3

A set of rows and columns is called a table. In a more general sense, a table is information stored in a grid (lines that cross each other to form a series of squares and/or rectangles). The "tab" in tab key is short for "tabular" or "tabulator." "Tabular" means "of or related to a table," and it refers to data presented in columns or a table. A "tabulator" is a person or thing that arranges data in columns or tables, and then works with that data. Even before the development of computers, spreadsheets were used to organize and work with data in table form; people used printed grids on paper. Spreadsheets are used in some of the most popular programs on computers; instead of the grids being drawn on paper, they are displayed on a screen. The TAB key moves the cursor (flashing bar on screen that indicates where to type) forward on the screen a set number of spaces – usually this is set to eight spaces. You may be familiar with this behavior from using computers. However, the TAB key can also move the cursor over one cell to the right in a spreadsheet.

EXAMPLE: When pressed in combination with other keys, the TAB key performs other functions as well – such alt + tab, which switches between windows.

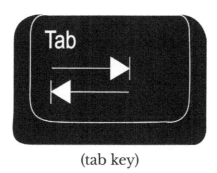

(tab key)

table: A set of rows and columns.

		— Rows —		
Columns				

In a more general sense, a table is information stored in a grid (lines that cross each other to form a series of squares and/or rectangles).

EXAMPLE: Information stored in a database (an organized collection of related data) is often saved in the form of tables.

tablet: A computer that you can operate with your fingers or a stylus (plastic rod, shaped like a pen or pencil, that you use to touch something). You click on things by just tapping on them. Tablets commonly measure between 7 and 10 inches diagonally. In terms of size, a tablet is typically between the size of a computer and a mobile phone.

EXAMPLE: Kids sometimes watch movies on tablets while riding in a car.

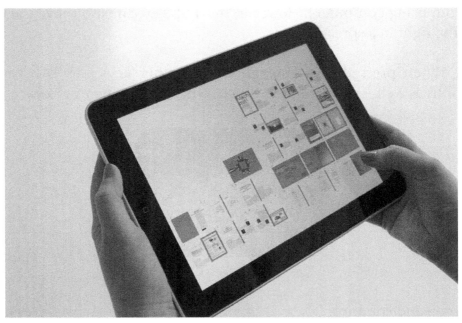

(tablet)

tag: In a markup (the action of adding instructions to a document to control the style, format and appearance of the content [text, pictures, videos, etc.] of the document) language, you surround the text that you want to modify with special words called "tags." A tag usually has two parts, a start tag (also called open tag or opening tag) and an end tag (also called close tag or closing tag). They tell the computer what to do with the text in between the start tag and the end tag. Tags are words with a special format – they have these symbols before and after them: "<" and ">." A start tag might look like this: <bold>. An end tag might look like this: </bold>. The "/" symbol is used to tell the computer that the tag is an end tag. An important thing to understand about this is the tags are not instructions – rather, they are codes that are used by other programs that will work with the document containing the tags. It is that program that would have instructions to find the sets of tags in the document and to modify the text in between those tags in a certain way, depending on what tag was found.

EXAMPLE:

```
<bold>Recipe for Peanut Butter</bold>
Peanuts
Salt
<italic>Instructions</italic>
Grind the peanuts until smooth, add salt.
```

The computer would go through the whole set of words you'd written and use the markup commands to modify the appearance of the text, like this:

Recipe for Peanut Butter

Peanuts

Salt

Instructions

Grind the peanuts until smooth, add salt.

You may notice that nothing special has been done to the words "Peanuts" and "Salt," and the sentence "Grind the peanuts until smooth, add salt." – they are not bold, or italic. This is because there is no markup language instruction applied to them – they are just plain old text to be displayed in the usual way.

tail: Looking at data distribution visually graphed, you may notice the "trails" of data move downward on either side of the mean. These *trails* are called *tails*.

EXAMPLE: Consider the following graph:

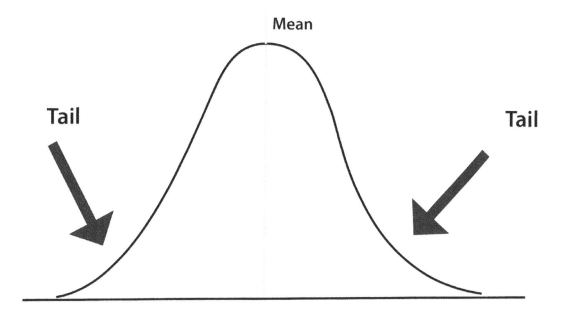

On either side of the above distribution, the tails are referred to as either *right tail* or *left tail*, when looking at the data visually. If the data were not graphed out, the tails would be referred to as upper or lower tails. An upper tail is the right tail, as that would hold the highest values in a data set – while the lower tail would be the left tail holding the lowest values in the data set.

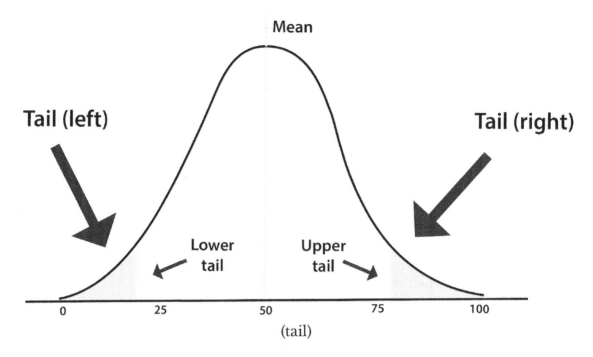

tar: A type of file format, as well as the name of a program used to handle such files. The name comes from the two words "tape archive." Tar is now commonly used to collect many files into one larger file for distribution or archiving while preserving file system information such as user and group permissions, dates, and directory (another word for "folder"; a location where a file or files are stored within a computer) structures. In order to reduce storage requirements, tar files can be compressed. The most common program used to compress tar files is a compression program called gzip. Tar files that have been compressed by the gzip program have the file extension "tar.gz." In order to access the tar file, the gzip program must be used to decompress the tar file. There are other decompression programs available that are capable of decompressing .gz files.

EXAMPLE: Tar is often used for sending software over the Internet.

task manager: A component of the Windows operating system that allows users to view various tasks being performed by the computer and the overall performance of the computer.

EXAMPLE: The task manager shows you how much computer memory is being utilized at a given moment. You can also shut down programs with the task manager, which comes in handy if something becomes frozen.

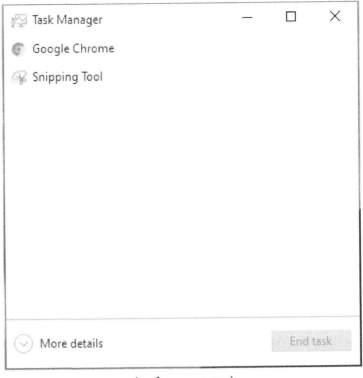

(task manager)

Tb: See "byte."

TB: See "byte."

Tbps: See "byte."

TBps: See "byte."

TCC: See "Transaction Control Language."

TCL: See "Transaction Control Language."

technology: The application of scientific knowledge for practical purposes to solve a problem. It is anything that makes activities easier. In today's world, "technology" is generally used when talking about something like a computer or any other tool or way of doing something that is considered advanced.

EXAMPLE: A printer is an example of technology – it is an electronic and mechanical device that makes it easier and faster to create printed pages.

Team Foundation Server: TFS stands for Team Foundation Server. This was a Version Control System (a system for managing multiple versions [editions; releases] of computer files and programs) developed by Microsoft. It was used in combination with Visual Studio (software used to assist in coding) to help developers manage all versions of their code, especially in a group (team) setting. It has been replaced by Azure DevOps Server, which performs all the same functions and more.

EXAMPLE: A software development team could have used TFS to manage and keep track of code.

template: In manufacturing, a template is a shaped piece of wood, metal or plastic used as a model (pattern) for various processes – such as cutting, shaping, drilling or painting. You can see templates here (these guide the lasers, jets or blades as to where to cut):

In design, a template is a reusable model.

EXAMPLE: A website template is a predefined design and layout that you can use, such as this:

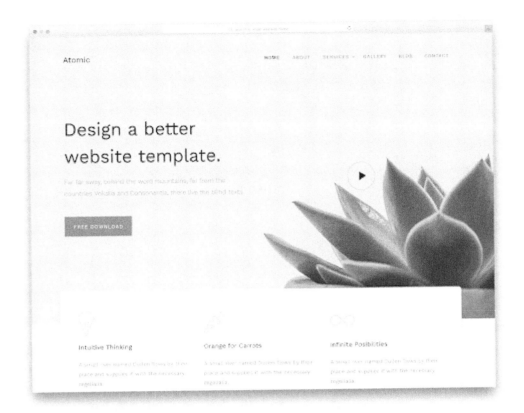

(template)

temporal: Having to do with time; limited by time. It comes from the Latin word *temporalis* which means "of time." Behavior is the way a person or thing acts or reacts. In design, temporal behavior is the way elements behave in a temporary time frame. For example, on a web page there could be a circle that looks like it bounces as the page loads. Its behavior is how it bounces and temporal would be for how long after the page finishes loading. Hierarchy refers to the order of important things. In design, hierarchy is the order in which elements should be arranged. Temporal hierarchy is the order in which motion happens and how long before the next motion or animation should start.

EXAMPLE: An example of this would be a loading ring when something is downloading or loading up. The ring would spin and spin, once done the ring would turn into a check mark indicating that the process is complete. The temporal hierarchy here is the motion for the ring to keep spinning until it is successful and then turn into a check mark once complete, not before or during.

temporary cookie: See "session cookie."

tensor: A multidimensional array of numbers or functions. Tensors can be what's called a scalar, a vector, or a matrix. However, a tensor is more commonly spoken of as a 4-dimensional array or above.

EXAMPLE: Compare tensor with less complex arrays:

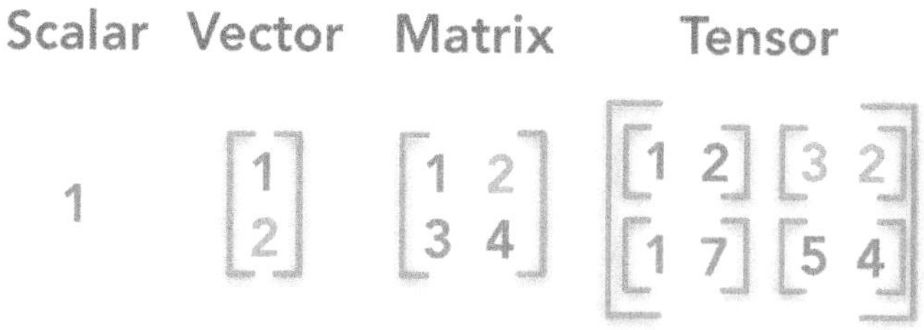

Scalar Vector Matrix Tensor

$$1 \quad \begin{bmatrix} 1 \\ 2 \end{bmatrix} \quad \begin{bmatrix} 1 & 2 \\ 3 & 4 \end{bmatrix} \quad \begin{bmatrix} \begin{bmatrix} 1 & 2 \end{bmatrix} & \begin{bmatrix} 3 & 2 \end{bmatrix} \\ \begin{bmatrix} 1 & 7 \end{bmatrix} & \begin{bmatrix} 5 & 4 \end{bmatrix} \end{bmatrix}$$

(tensor)

terabit: See "byte."

terabyte: See "byte."

terahertz: See "hertz."

terminal: Something that can give, receive or relay communication. A computer has terminals. These are sets of equipment that a user can use to do input and output tasks with the computer. Usually these are a display and a keyboard together (for input and output), and they are connected by wires to the computer itself. It is a common misconception some people have that a terminal is the computer itself; they'll see a display and a keyboard together and call it a computer. The computer is most often in a separate container, and the screen and keyboard are connected to the computer by wires. This gets complicated by the fact that sometimes, computer manufacturers will build the computer itself in the same physical case as the display – these are often called "all-in-ones," and often look no different than just a simple monitor.

EXAMPLE: If you see an older movie and a computer operator is sitting at a device with just a keyboard and a display, but there is no computer in sight, you are likely looking at someone using a computer terminal.

(terminal)

terminal area: Terminal means occurring or forming the end of something; concluding. The terminal area is the lower right portion of a page. It is the portion of the page where the user will tend to make a decision to either continue scrolling down and get more information or leave the page entirely. It is normally used to place a link or button to have the user continue interacting with a design or website.

EXAMPLE: See the terminal area below:

(terminal area)

ternary operator: Ternary means "made up of three parts." A ternary operator operates on three values. It can be used to assign a value to a variable (data that has a name and a value [type/amount], and can be changed) based on a condition. This is also referred to as a conditional operator in that it assigns a value to a variable based on a condition. The typical syntax for this is:

```
Name_of_variable = (condition) ? Value_1:Value_2
```

The ternary operator is "?".

EXAMPLE: Here's an example in the JavaScript programming language:

```
document.write(Bigger = (5 > 1) ? "Left number is bigger":"Right number is bigger");
```

In this code, we said that if it is true that 5 is bigger than 1, display "Left number is bigger." If you change the numbers or flip the symbol to <, we can change the outcome of our code to false. The document.write method is not a part of the syntax of the ternary operator, it is used to write information to the document.

test: Analyze software to locate any difference between the existing condition and the required condition. The purpose of testing is to locate defects or errors, and to evaluate features. Testing is also referred to as "QA" (quality assurance) or "QA testing." Quality assurance embraces any actions taken to maintain a desired level of product/service quality.

EXAMPLE: User acceptance testing is a form of QA that allows users to test out software – feedback can then be gathered and addressed.

test environment: See "environment."

text terminal: A terminal is a device that can be used to enter commands and data into a computer. Terminals display the output received. A text terminal is a terminal that is fully text based.

EXAMPLE: Here's what an old-fashioned text terminal looks like:

(text terminal)

TFS: See "Team Foundation Server."

the cloud: See "cloud computing."

theme: A preset package of visual elements to be used in the design of the visual display for a computer program. It usually has a set of shapes and colors that are used throughout the various visual elements created as the computer program is operating. Themes are used to customize the "look and feel" of a computer program.

EXAMPLE: You might purchase a computer program that can help a business manage sales records for its clients. It could have three themes – "industrial," "services," "retail." Each of these would have a different combination of shapes and colors for the various things presented on the screen as you used the program.

theme (project management): See "sprint goal."

third generation: See "generation."

thread: The word thread has two meanings in computers:

1. A conversation between multiple computer users that has a common subject or theme.

EXAMPLE: If you were using your computer to have typed conversations with people in other parts of the world about their pets, there might be a "Labrador Retriever" thread. The primary subject of the communication in each thread would be the dog breed Labrador Retriever.

2. A task that a computer is doing, while the computer is also doing other different tasks. This comes up where computers are set up to do more than one thing in a given period of time. Each "thing" they are doing is called a "thread." This is because each task can be seen as a length of thread, with each step of the task coming one after the next along the thread. A note here on how computers deal with threads: a computer can only do one thing at a time. When more than one thread is being worked on at once by the computer, the CPU (central processing unit – a tiny internal device that is the "brain" of the computer) will switch between the threads – it will do some work on the tasks in one thread for a time, then switch to another thread and do some work on that thread, and so on.

EXAMPLE: A computer could have one thread that was related to printing a document, while another thread was related to displaying a graph on the screen. The computer would not be working on each thread at once – rather, it would keep track of all the tasks it is doing (the "tasks") and it would switch back and forth between them.

3D plotting: See "plot."

3G: See "G (cell phone)."

throbber: See "process (processing)."

throw: In normal English, "throw" means to "cause something to enter a particular state or condition." It can also be used to mean "pass something from one place to another." In coding, throw means to raise an exception (error). It is literally used to pass (transfer) the control of a program from one block (chunk; section) of code to another. Throwing an exception means the same thing as raising an exception.

EXAMPLE: If you were writing a program and wanted to make sure that the program user does not accidentally make the program crash, you might write some code that will throw an exception where the user would have otherwise made the program crash.

thumb drive: Another word for "USB drive."

THz: See "hertz."

tilde: The ~ symbol. Pronounced "tilda."
EXAMPLE: The tilde is placed over certain letters in some Spanish words as an accent, such as the word: señor.

tint: A variety or shade of a color. The word originated from the Latin word *tingere*, meaning "to dye" or "to color." Tint is created by adding white to any color. The more white that is added, the lighter the color gets.

EXAMPLE: Here is what happens when you tint (add white to) the color pink:

(tint)

TLS: See "SSL."

token: A token is a single component in a programming language. The five categories of tokens are:
1. Constants,
2. Identifiers (names that uniquely identify a program element in the code, such as variables – data that has a name and a value [type/amount], and can be changed),
3. Operators (such as +, * or -),
4. Separators (also called "delimiters – a sequence of one or more characters that specifies the boundaries of sections of code),
5. Reserved words (words that have set meanings and uses, and cannot be redefined by a developer).

In the programming language JavaScript, keywords are tokens that have special meanings. Keywords are reserved words in JavaScript which means you cannot use them to name variables or functions.

EXAMPLE: Sometimes, if there's an error in your code, it may state: Unexpected token – which means there's a component in your code that the browser can't execute.

tone: A quality or level of something. When speaking of colors, there are two basic definitions of tone: 1. The exact quality of brightness, hue, tint, shade or deepness of a color. For example, "The sky presented a vivid tone of blue that day." 2. Refers to mixing an original color with gray. Through adding tone (mixing in gray), the original color is softened and can look less intense then the initial hue.

EXAMPLE: Here is an example of incrementally adding tone to a color:

(tone)

toner: A colored powder used to create the actual words, images etc. on the paper in computer printers. It can be used dry or suspended in liquid. The other material commonly used in printers is ink. The difference between ink and toner is that toner is a powdered substance, while ink is liquid.

EXAMPLE: Laser printers (a printer that uses lasers to fix toner on the page with a high degree of accuracy through a heating process) utilize toner.

(toner)

Torrent file: A Torrent file is made up of data that directs information to be transferred over the internet (the largest and most-used computer network [connection that allows data transfer between machines] in the world, which is mainly utilized to access the World Wide Web). These types of files use something called the BitTorrent protocol. BitTorrent is a protocol (a formal agreement about how to format and send a particular type of data) for sharing large electronic files over the Internet. This gives computer users a way to share information across computers that sometimes works faster than the traditional methods of downloading. It is a "peer-to-peer" protocol for transferring data, meaning all computers involved in the file transfer can act as both providers and consumers of data (in computers, a peer is another computer you can hook up to directly to give and share information with. This differs from earlier systems, in which your computer is required to go through a specialized third-party computer called a server in order to access information from another computer). Traditional downloading usually means one central computer has the electronic file that you want, so you send a request to that machine to send your computer the file. For example, if you download a video, you are having your computer pull the electronic files for the movie from another machine somewhere so that you can watch the video on your computer. If 100 computers are downloading a specific video from the same machine at once, the video would download slower than if only 5 computers were downloading it at once. Peer-to-peer file transfer protocols like BitTorrent provide a way to download the file you want from several computers at once; each computer would only be providing you with a smaller portion of the overall file. In BitTorrent, you are also offering your computer (in a safe way) to be a machine that others can download from. So the more people who are downloading using BitTorrent, the faster it will download because more people are sharing information and less people are using the same physical "roads" for data transfer. This is done by installing a software program called a

"BitTorrent client." This is a file transfer program that uses the BitTorrent protocol to transfer files. Torrent files are specially formatted for this system. Note: BitTorrent systems are often used for illegal activities, such as downloading copyrighted works like music and videos.

EXAMPLE: If you used a BitTorrent client to download a particular video about waterfalls, your computer would communicate with other computers that have that video and will download small pieces of the video from several sources at once – this process would involve some torrent files. The more people that have this video, the faster your computer will download. And later, when others want to download the video, your BitTorrent client could receive requests for that video, and it could send out small pieces of that video as part of the process for another BitTorrent user.

Touch: A command-line interface program for Unix that is used to update date information – such as: changing the date that a file or directory was modified or accessed. Touch can also be used to create or open a file.

EXAMPLE: You could type "touch dogstory.docx" in the command-line to create a blank Microsoft Word document entitled "dogstory."

tower: See "PC."

tracked file: The files that were last saved in Git (a system used to manage multiple versions of computer files and programs); they are files that Git is aware of. Untracked files are everything else — any files in your working directory (another word for "folder"; a location where a file or files are stored within a computer) that were not saved and are not in your staging area.

EXAMPLE: See the following diagram:

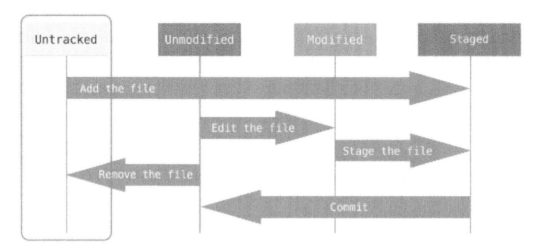

-Tracked files have been saved in the repository
-Untracked files have not been committed

(tracked file)

tracker: A large machine that keeps track of all the computers that are involved in BitTorrent (a system used for sharing files online) operations is called a tracker. The tracker lets computers know who they can connect up to and share information with so that BitTorrent can operate faster.

EXAMPLE: If you used BitTorrent to look at videos about kittens, the tracker would find other people on BitTorrent who also do so and hook each of you up so that you can all download the videos faster (resulting in less wait time). The center computer below is the tracker:

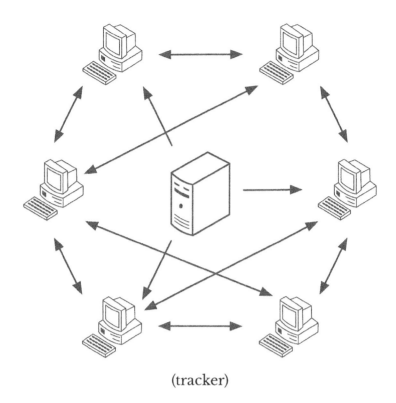

(tracker)

traffic: 1. Anything that is communicated or sent through a computer or from computer to computer.

EXAMPLE: A high load of traffic being rapidly sent to a computer would probably cause the computer to operate more slowly because it means the computer has to handle more information at one time.

2. Traffic is a measure of how many requests a web server (a specialized computer used to store and transmit data, such as "serving up" websites through the World Wide Web) is getting for a particular web page or website in a given length of time.

EXAMPLE: If 1,000,000 users visit a website in a day, that is considered good traffic.

transaction: A sequence of information exchange. It is something that needs to be completed in its entirety.

EXAMPLE: A real-life example of a transaction would be when a customer purchases something in a store. Besides a payment transaction, the transaction is not when the customer pays for the item(s) they need, rather the transaction starts the moment they arrive in the store – along with a sequence of events, then completed once they pay. Here is how it could look:
1. Customer arrives in the store.
2. Customer browses the store.
3. Customer is approached by a sales associate.
4. Customer's questions answered.

5. Customer pays for items.
6. Customer leaves the store.
7. End of transaction.

In a database, a transaction is a sequence of tasks being carried out with the use of Structured Query Language (SQL – the most common language used to create, manage, interact with, delete and edit databases). The data (when either being inputted, updated, or deleted) must be committed. Or, if the transaction can not be completed (for various reasons, such as missing data, no data, etc.), the transaction is undone (rolled back) to its previous state.

Transaction Control Language: Transaction Control Language (TCL) is used to manage transactions in a database. A database transaction is a unit of work performed within a DBMS (database management system) against a database – it represents any change in a database. TCL commands (also called Transaction Control Commands – TCC) are used to manage the changes made to data in a table.

EXAMPLE: The COMMIT command is a TCC used in TCL and SQL – it permanently stores a transaction within a database.

transistor: A device that can alter the flow of electricity in a machine. It can let electricity flow through it, it can stop the flow of electricity, or it can increase the flow of electricity. In other words, it is basically a switch (device that regulates the flow of electricity). Here is what the first one looked like:

The transistor is a solid-state (having no moving parts) switch and it lasts a long time without needing replacement. Nowadays, there are billions of transistors inside a computer that are so small you can't see them.

EXAMPLE: You can liken the flow of electricity in a computer like water through a hose. Imagine folding the hose to stop the flow of water, partially unfolding it to allow some through and unfolding it all the way to allow the water to flow freely – the "folding action" is like what the transistor does to an electrical flow.

(transistor)

transmission: The action of sending information from one place to another. Computers are often used to transmit and receive information to and from other computers or electronic devices. Transmission also refers to the sent or received communication itself.

EXAMPLE: If you print something, there is a transmission from the computer to the printer instructing what to have the printer put on the paper.

Transport Layer Security: See "SSL."

tree: A common nonlinear data structure (arrangement of data where the elements of the data do not necessarily follow one after the other) is the tree.

EXAMPLE: Let's take a look at this diagram with some of the important features of trees highlighted.

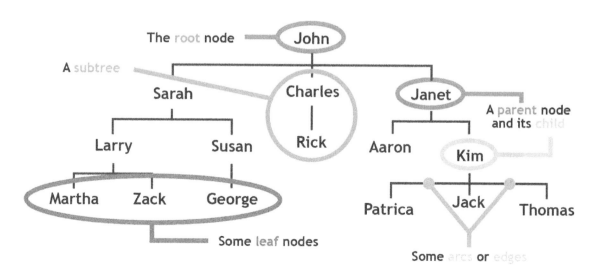

In this diagram, we can see that the starting point, or the root node, is circled in blue. A node is a simple structure that holds data and links to other nodes. In this case, our root node contains the data string "John" and three links to other nodes. Notice that the group of nodes circled in red do not have any links. These nodes are at the ends of the branches and they are appropriately called leaves or leaf nodes. In our diagram, the nodes are connected with solid black lines called arcs or edges. These edges show the relationships between nodes in the tree. One important relationship is the parent/child relationship. Parent nodes have at least one edge to a node lower in the tree. This node is called the child node. Nodes can have more than one child, but children can only have a single parent. Notice that the root node has no parent, and the leaf nodes have no children. The final feature to note in our diagram is the subtree. At each level of the tree, we can see that the tree structure is repeated. For example, the two nodes representing "Charles" and "Rick" compose a very simple tree with "Charles" as the root node and "Rick" as a single leaf node.

trend line: See "linear regression."

trigger: Something that initiates an action – it sets something off. An "event trigger" is something that indicates that an event (an action external to the program) has taken place. When an event is triggered (i.e., the event has occurred and been noted), this typically sets off (triggers) a particular action.

EXAMPLE: Let's say a user clicks the save button – this click is an event that triggers information being sent to the database. Therefore, it is an "event trigger." Or if a user inputs text in a form and presses enter, they have "triggered an event."

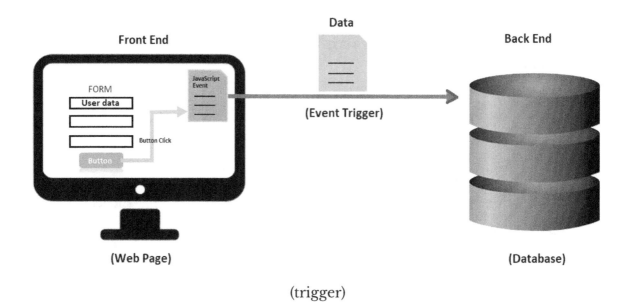

(trigger)

triple equal sign: The === (triple equal sign) symbol is used to show that a comparison should be made. Specifically, this "===" symbol is an instruction to check whether the data on the left side of the symbol is equal to the data on the right side and that it is the same type of data as that on the right. The answer to this comparison is an answer of "true" or "false."

EXAMPLE: You want to check whether two birth dates are equal. You have two pieces of data in the computer that represent these two birth dates:
"DateOfBirth1" is data of type "Date," and the value of the data is "1/1/1970."
"DateOfBirth2" is data of type "Date," and the value of the data is "1/1/1970."
You would use the "===" symbol like this:
```
DateOfBirth1 === DateOfBirth2
```
This tells the computer to check whether the two pieces of data are equal in both VALUE and TYPE. Since they are, the computer responds with "true."

trojan: A type of malware (a computer program created to perform certain harmful actions to computers). A Trojan is a program that is installed on a computer with the intention of damaging the computer, stealing information, etc. The Trojan is created in such a way that the person who receives it is led to believe that it is harmless. Trojan viruses get their name from the ancient story of the Trojan horse. According to myth, there was a war about 3000 years ago between the Greeks and the residents of the huge city of Troy. The Greeks had been trying to conquer the city of Troy for 10 years. In an effort to trick the Trojans (the name for people who lived in Troy), the Greek army constructed a large wooden horse and hid a group of soldiers inside. They then pretended to sail away, as if they were retreating. The Trojans, believing they were now victorious in defending their city, went out and brought the wooden horse into the city as a victory trophy. That night, the soldiers inside the horse crept out and opened the city gates for the rest of the Greek army, which had returned in the darkness of the night. The Greek army was then able to enter the city and defeat the Trojans. In similar fashion, a Trojan virus may be attached to a seemingly harmless message you receive on your computer. By opening the message, you might allow the Trojan to be installed on your computer, thereby allowing another person to connect to your computer and operate it without your knowledge.

EXAMPLE: Someone wants to steal your credit card information, so they create a small computer program that can search your computer for that information. They disguise the computer program as a document called "surprise birthday party – driving directions." Not suspecting the document is dangerous, you open it. When it opens, it is not a document after all – it is that small computer program.

(trojan)

troll: See "trolling."

trolling: When people try to intentionally upset others. It is most commonly used when someone puts content on a website, and then a troll (person engaged in trolling) writes something mean in an attempt to get a response or start an argument. A troll is considered someone who has a lot of time on their hands and intentionally seeks out places they can write responses to deceive, confuse, and upset other people.

EXAMPLE: Singer: "Here's my latest song. I hope you like it." Troll: "It sounds like a cat is dying. You should never sing again."

troubleshooting: To locate the sources of errors and fix them. The term originated from the 1800's term "troubleshoot" – a person who works on telegraph (system for sending written messages over long distances by wire) or telephone lines. The original trouble-shooters would find issues behind transmission problems and fix them in the physical telegraph/telephone lines, or work around them.

EXAMPLE: Software development often requires a large amount of troubleshooting.

true: Not false. This is an important element of how computers work because they are often used to make decisions based on information. They need to be able to evaluate whether a certain condition is true or false, and then perform certain other actions depending on the answer. True (also referred to as "on" or "yes") is represented as a "1" inside a computer.

EXAMPLE: The computer is asked to evaluate a list of students and determine whether or not each student has a grade point average above 3.2. The computer would look at each student in turn, and determine whether it was TRUE or FALSE that their GPA was above 3.2.

ruth table: In Boolean logic (the "logic" a computer uses to make comparisons, where only one of two possible outcomes is possible: true/false, yes/no, on/off, etc. – which is based on a system of logic developed by English mathematician George Boole), there are not any vague or 'almost' answers to a calculation or decision. A logic gate is a switch (a physical device that can be used to control whether or not electricity is passed through) that implements one of several different types of Boolean logic operations. It takes one or more "true/false" inputs and produces a single "true/false" output. Truth tables are mathematical tables laying out the possible inputs for a logic gate, along with their corresponding output.

EXAMPLE: There is a type of logic gate called an "AND gate." It takes two "true/false" inputs and produces a "true" output ONLY if BOTH of the inputs are "true." This is the symbol used for an AND gate (the two lines on the left are the inputs and the line on the right is the output):

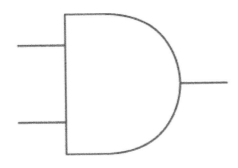

Here is a truth table for an AND gate:

INPUT A	INPUT B	OUTPUT
FALSE	FALSE	FALSE
FALSE	TRUE	FALSE
TRUE	FALSE	FALSE
TRUE	TRUE	TRUE

try/catch block: A set of two code blocks (chunks; sections), operating together, that are found in many programming languages (a system of specialized words and symbols used to communicate with a computer and to create programs). They are keywords (words built into a programming language) that are used to detect and handle exceptions (errors). The try block looks for an exception and the catch block says what to do if one is found.

EXAMPLE: Here it is diagrammed out:

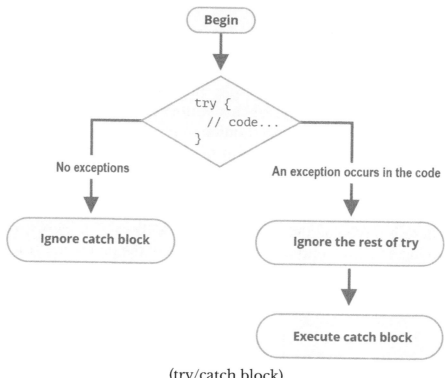

(try/catch block)

T-SQL: Stands for "transact-structured query language." This is a widely-used language Microsoft made to add additional functionality to the basic language of SQL.

EXAMPLE: You could use T-SQL to get data into and out of databases that are managed using Microsoft database management software.

2G: See "G (cell phone)."

2.4G: See "G (wifi)."

tuple: 1. An ordered list of items. In coding, a tuple is a sequence of immutable (not able to be changed) objects.

EXAMPLE: (2, 29, 13, 84)

2. See "record."

Turing, Alan (1912-1954): An English mathematician and computer scientist. He is credited with many technical achievements, including the Turing test (see "Turing test") and is considered by some to be the father of artificial intelligence (see "artificial intelligence").

EXAMPLE: During World War 2, Alan Turing helped develop technology to decrypt Nazi Germany's secret communications.

(Turing, Alan)

Turing test: A test to determine the ability of a computer to display intelligent behavior. Specifically, the test is meant to determine whether the behavior of the computer is indistinguishable from that of a human being. It is called the Turing test because it was developed by the British mathematician Alan Turing. In the test, a computer is programmed so that it will generate human-like responses when questions are typed into it. During the test, similar questions are given to the computer and to a human being. The tester cannot see either the computer or the person, and their answers are displayed on a computer screen. If the tester cannot distinguish between the computer and the human more than 70% of the time, then the computer program passed the test.

EXAMPLE: "How did you feel during your first kiss?" could be a question used in a Turing test.

2D plotting: See "plot."

type: Before digital printing, type consisted of printed letters, symbols or other characters. Each letter was individually cast (made by pouring melted metal into a mold) into metal, dipped in ink and pressed on paper. This is where we get terms like typewriter or typing. The keystrokes (the pressing of keys on a keyboard) literally pressed the type against a surface. In modern times, type is any printed letter or character.

EXAMPLE: Here is a collage of traditional types:

(type)

typed: See "untyped."

typeface: See "font family."

type safety: Refers to the degree to which a programming language (a system of specialized words and symbols used to communicate with a computer and to create programs) prevents type errors (errors caused by a discrepancy between types of data). A type-safe language is one where the only operations you can execute on data are those operations allowed by the data's type. Additionally, type-safe code only accesses the memory locations it is authorized to access (usually referred to as memory type safety). For example, type-safe code cannot read values from another object's (an item with state and behavior in a computer program) private (not able to be accessed by a different area) data.

EXAMPLE: C# is a type-safe language.

typesetting: The arrangement of type (printed characters) cast on metal in order to create lines of text to print. Typesetting as a process is similar to a stamp – the ink is pressed onto paper.

In modern times, typesetting is the preparation of the arrangement of type for display. Typesetting includes subjects like fonts, spacing (distance between characters), padding (space between characters and margin) and consistency (ensuring the display is the same – such as all body text being the same).

EXAMPLE: Text editors (like Microsoft Word) have predefined typesetting encoded within them. They also allow you to customize the typesetting (e.g., change alignment, spacing, padding, etc.).

typography: The art of arranging characters and words in a way they can be easily read and are appealing to the eye. It embraces such things as fonts, sizes, styles and spacing.

EXAMPLE: Here's one example of typography:

This is my Logo

The quick brown fox jumps over the lazy dog. The quick brown fox jumps over the lazy dog. The quick brown fox jumps over the lazy dog. The quick brown fox jumps over the lazy dog. The quick brown fox jumps over the lazy dog. The quick brown fox jumps over the lazy dog. The quick brown fox jumps over the lazy dog. The quick brown fox jumps over the lazy dog. The quick brown fox jumps over the lazy dog. The quick brown fox jumps over the lazy dog. The quick brown fox jumps over the lazy dog. The quick brown fox jumps over the lazy dog. The quick brown fox jumps over the lazy dog.

(typography)

U

UAT: Software testing is a system or process for investigating computer programs to assess their quality. This is done in order to provide those people concerned with the software (business owners, computer programmers, project managers, etc.) with vital information about such things as:

- How well the software meets the guidelines that were used in its creation.
- Whether there are bugs in the program (errors in a computer program that cause it to produce an incorrect or unexpected result).
- Whether the software responds correctly to various inputs.
- Whether the software operates within acceptable time frames (response time, etc.).
- Whether the software can be installed properly on the types of computer systems it is intended for.

There are many different types of software testing approaches, systems and processes. User Acceptance Testing is a type of software testing and is a common step in creating computer programs. UAT is typically the final phase in the software development process before the software is made available for full use. In the User Acceptance Testing phase, the software is given to the intended audience to be tested for functionality.

EXAMPLE: Before releasing an app to the general public, one should perform UAT.

UCS: See "Universal Coded Character Set."

UI: User Interface: The User Interface consists of the elements on a computer display that a user utilizes to interact with a computer program. It is where they type things in and click with the mouse, for example. This is where interaction between a machine and a user occurs. A user interface is important because a computer program usually needs some sort of user interaction in order to perform its function.

EXAMPLE: If you had a computer program that was used to enter in orders for a bicycle program, the UI would likely have an order form on the screen.

UI kit: A User Interface (UI) kit is a collection of graphic files and resources for designers. These kits usually contain small components of design such as various icons, buttons, and pre-sized elements, such as navigation for websites on desktops, mobile devices and tablets. The purpose of these kits is so designers can spend more time putting a whole design together and not waste time designing commonly used elements. Most of the time these files will contain Photoshop files so the designer can edit and customize as needed. There are many different kinds of UI kits that are all created for various purposes

EXAMPLE: Here is an example of what a UI kit could look like.

(UI kit)

Unicode: A standard for representing letters and symbols in computers. Unicode is intended to represent all languages across the world. Each letter and symbol of the various languages of the world has a specific number in the Unicode system. This is important because computers are much more useful if they can display data in the language of the user. Computer programmers needed a way to clarify what letters or symbols to use in their programs (a set of written instructions, entered into a computer by people, that make it execute [perform] specific tasks) if the user wanted the data displayed in another language. It was necessary that all computer manufacturers agree on this system so that computers could be used everywhere.

EXAMPLE: In Unicode the letter "A" could be represented as 0041.

If you look closely at some URLs (web addresses), you may see the characters "UTF." "UTF" stands for "Unicode Transformation Format." UTF is a character encoding (representing numbers, letters, etc. are represented by codes) format that is able to utilize all of the code points (numerical values assigned to specific characters) in Unicode (a system that assigns language characters to bits of code). This is needed to allow for the encoding of languages other than English. The most popular type of Unicode encoding is UTF-8. Here, the 8 means that each Unicode character is represented by one or more 8-bit (see "bit") binary (see "binary") numbers (a set of 8 binary digits is called a byte). Other UTF encodings exist, such as UTF-16, where each Unicode character is represented by one or more 16-bit binary numbers. In UTF-8, only one byte is used to represent common English characters. Hebrew, European, and Arabic characters are represented with two bytes. Three bytes are used to represent Chinese, Korean, Japanese, and other Asian characters. There are other Unicode characters that can be represented with four bytes. UTF-8 is used in the operating system (OS – the main program within a computer that manages all other programs and external devices [e.g., keyboards, mice, displays, etc.]) Linux (a free and very popular OS) by default, and is commonly used for the exchange of data on the internet (the largest and most-used computer network [connection that allows data transfer between machines] in the world, which is mainly utilized to access the World Wide Web). Around 90% of websites in existence utilize UTF-8. UTF-16 is another popular type of Unicode. UTF-8 is used far more on the web – UTF-16 is used by less than 0.01% of web pages. The main reason UTF-16 is used less in websites is due to the fact that the official documentation on HTML 5 (HyperText Markup Language version 5 – used for creating websites) strongly discourages the use of UTF-16 for websites, mainly because it wasn't originally created with web use in mind (that was left for UTF-8) and it is considered less secure for online use. UTF-16 is capable of utilizing all 1,112,064 code points of Unicode.

EXAMPLE: UTF-16 is used by Microsoft Windows and Mac OS X's file systems. It is also used in the programming language Java.

uniform distribution: Has to do with the probability that all outcomes are likely to occur, which means the possible variable (data that has a name and a value [type/amount], and can be changed) values of x will fall in a constant range or interval. There are two types of uniform distribution: 1. Continuous, and 2. Discrete.

EXAMPLE: *Uniform distribution (discrete):* An example of this would be tossing a coin and getting either heads or tails:

Discrete uniform distribution

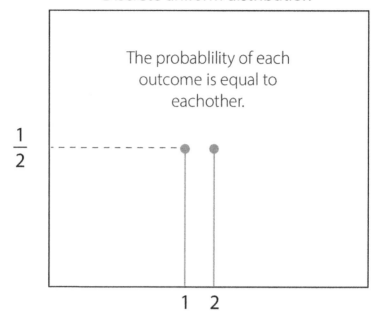

The probablility of each outcome is equal to eachother.

$\frac{1}{2}$

1   2

Uniform distribution (continuous): As an example, a child aged four could be between the range of 3'3" and 3'8". We can't ever get the exact height, but we can get an estimate of height because of the child's age. This is what a continuous uniform distribution would look like:

Continuous uniform distribution

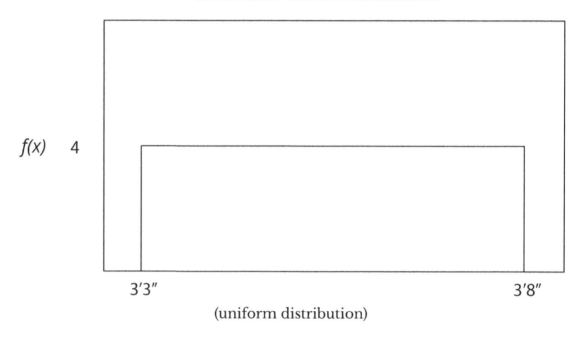

f(x)   4

3'3"   3'8"

(uniform distribution)

unique key: A key is a unique identifier for a piece or collection of information. In regards to databases, a unique key is very similar to a primary key (an attribute [column] or combination of attributes, within a database table, that uniquely identifies each record

[row] in the database table). The main difference between a primary key and a unique key is: a unique key can accept a null value (data that does not exist; nothing present; information missing), whereas a primary key can't. Unique keys cannot have duplicate values.

EXAMPLE: A unique key might be assigned to a column of phone numbers.

unit: A single item. It means literally: how many individual things are there in a collection of those things? 1 unit = one, 2 units = two, etc.

EXAMPLE: 25 is composed of twenty-five units.

unit test: A way to test software where individual units of production code (the "live" version of the code; the code users and developers interact with) are tested as opposed to the entire software all at once. These units of code are categorized by setting related sections of the computer program together and running them through various tests. A unit test is a short program that checks the results of and tests various units of code. They are valuable because they can detect when refactoring code (rewrite code with the purpose of improving its structure and readability, without changing its behavior) has resulted in the code not working as originally designed.

EXAMPLE: If you were developing an app that handled recording the steps of manufacturing a car, you could have each step of the procedure tested and this would be unit testing.

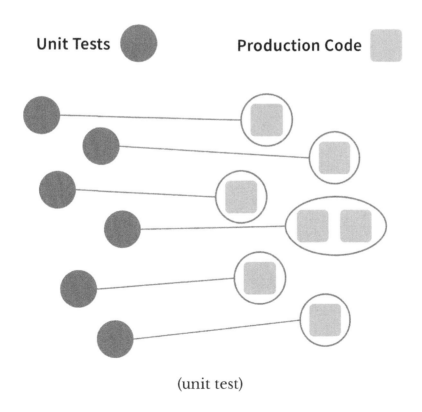

(unit test)

univariate: See "statistical modeling."

Universal Coded Character Set (UCS): UCS is a standard set of characters defined by the International Organization for Standardization (ISO) – an organization composed of representatives from various standards organizations across the world. The ISO exists to monitor and promote international industrial and commercial standards. Under the umbrella of the UCS, the ISO created the UTF (Unicode Transformation Format) character encoding systems – including UTF-8 and UTF-16. UCS-2 is a character encoding standard where characters are represented by a fixed length of 16 bits (2 bytes). UCS-2 allows for a maximum of 65,536 characters. It should be noted that in 2017, the ISO stated "UCS-2 should now be considered obsolete. It no longer refers to an encoding form in the Unicode Standard." UTF-16 is an extension of (improvement upon) UCS-2.

EXAMPLE: In UCS-2, an uppercase A is represented by 0041.

Universal Windows Platform: Universal Windows Platform (UWP) is a computing platform (a platform for running and programming specific types of programs) created by Microsoft. It was first released with Windows 10 and it supports Windows app development using C#, C++, VB.NET and XAML. UWP allows developers to create apps that can run on multiple types of devices. It is a component of .NET Core and the .NET Framework.

EXAMPLE: With UWP, you can develop software that works seamlessly on multiple Windows devices.

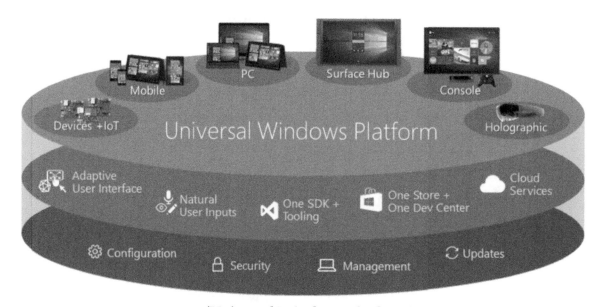

(Universal Windows Platform)

Unix: An operating system (OS – the main program within a computer that manages all other programs and external devices [e.g., keyboards, mice, displays, etc.]) created in the early 1970s. Unix was one of the first operating systems to be written using a high level (relatively easy-to-understand and similar to English) programming language (a system of specialized words and symbols used to communicate with a computer and to create programs). The original creators of Unix developed it so that anyone could alter the code to personalize it and make tweaks.

EXAMPLE: Unix is a very popular operating system; it is installed on many computers around the world.

unordered list: See "HTML lists."

unstructured data: See "structured data."

Unsupervised learning: A machine learning technique that looks for patterns in data while trying to establish meaning from them.

EXAMPLE: If a marketing company is trying to best understand a target market with a product they've never sold before, unsupervised learning could find patterns in the purchasing data. These patterns could help the company restructure their marketing of the product.

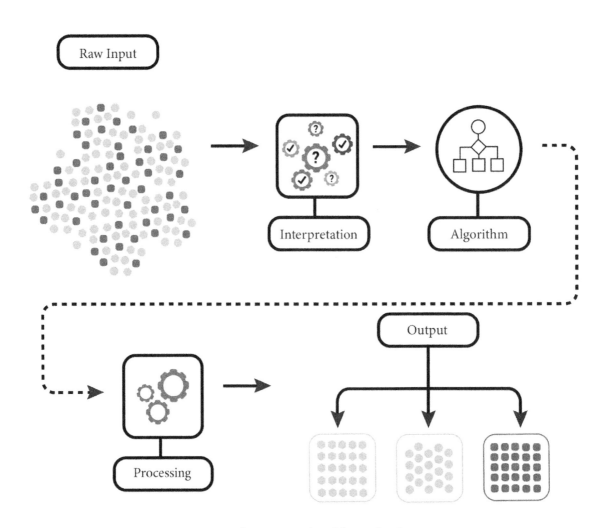

(unsupervised learning)

untyped: Many computer programming languages (a system of specialized words and symbols used to communicate with a computer and to create programs) require the programmer to specify the type of data for a variable (data that has a name and a value [type/amount], and can be changed). These are called "typed languages." When you first create a variable in a typed language, you need to specify what data type (a specific category of information handled by a computer – such as numbers or comparisons) the variable is. In a typed language, there are certain restrictions about how the various data types can interact.

EXAMPLE: You might need to make the computer instructions that calculate a person's pay for the day. Here, you could have three variables that had a data type of "integer," meaning they represented numeric data (i.e., numbers). An integer is a whole number – like 6, 99 and 182. 3.11 and 9½ are not integers. You would create the variables that calculate a person's pay for the day like this:

```
integer PayRate = 35.00
integer HoursWorked = 10
integer Paycheck
```

The third variable, the integer called Paycheck, does not have a value yet. This variable is meant to store the result of a math operation that determines how much a worker has earned. The computer instruction for this might look something like this:

```
Paycheck = HoursWorked x PayRate
```

Because all three variables are the same data type, the computer can process this math operation and store the result in the value for variable "Paycheck": 350.00. Untyped languages are programming languages that do not make you define what data type a variable is. Instead, the computer uses a predefined system to work out what data type a variable is based on its value and how it is being used. For example, let's use the earlier math example but examine how it could work when performed using an untyped language. Here, we might have three variables similar to the ones from our earlier example:

```
PayRate = 35.00
HoursWorked = "ten"
Paycheck
```

Notice that there are no data types specified. Notice, as well, that the variable "HoursWork" has a value of "ten" – a word, not a number. If we wanted to perform the same math as the above example, we might create the same computer instruction:

```
Paycheck = HoursWorked x PayRate
```

This makes math operations a bit different. The computer takes the value of the variable PayRate, 35.00, and tries to multiply it by the value of the variable HoursWorked, "ten." This does not work at first glance, of course – you can't multiply a number by a word! But untyped languages have a predetermined system that is used to infer (determine something based on the available information) the type of data that the variable represents. Here, the language can work out that the word "ten" can mean the number 10 – and since the instruction is a math operation, the language interprets the variable in that manner and multiplies 35.00 by 10 to get 350.

EXAMPLE: JavaScript is an untyped programming language in that you are not required to define the type of a variable. On the other hand, Python is a typed programming language.

update: An update is bringing something up to the newest version. Sometimes an update is done to fix any problems that might be happening with the computer or an update can be done to add something new to it. Updating software changes it in some way and can include additional features (such as enhanced security measures).

EXAMPLE: Updates can include improved security to keep your computer or device safe from the latest cyber (digital; related to computers) attacks.

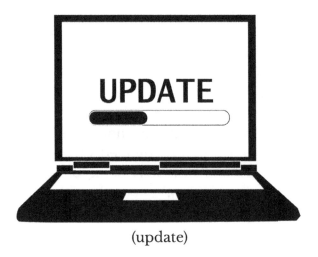

(update)

upload: At times it may be necessary to get certain electronic files from your computer onto a web server (a specialized computer used to store and transmit data, such as "serving up" websites through the World Wide Web). This process of sending a file from your computer to a web server is called uploading. Note that there are many times you may want to send a file from one computer to another. Normally, this is just referred to as a "file transfer." Uploading a file is such an action – you're sending a file from your computer to the computer that is a web server. A special word is used here because of the client/server system in effect – the web server is considered "above" or "senior" to the client computer, so the term "upload" came into use. When sending a file from one computer to another computer that is not considered to be at a different level, you would just use the term file transfer.

EXAMPLE: You could create a video and upload it to YouTube. It would then be on one of YouTube's web servers, and other people could go to YouTube and watch that video.

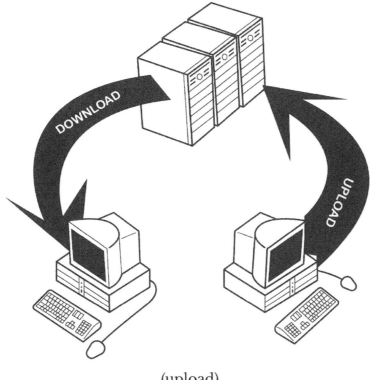

(upload)

URL: URL stands for Uniform Resource Locator. Uniform means that something is the same every time. A resource is something that helps or assists you with something. URLs are the addresses (locations) for web pages on the internet (the largest and most-used computer network [connection that allows data transfer between machines] in the world, which is mainly utilized to access the World Wide Web) you want to go to. Just like you need the address to go find someone's house, you also need the address of where you want the computer to go on the internet. The URL is that address. Everything on the web has its own URL. The URL contains the name of the website that you are going to.

EXAMPLE: When you type in "http://www.google.com" on the web, that is a URL. You are telling the computer, "take me to the website 'Google.'" Here, the method of accessing the data is also given: HTTP. HTTP stands for HyperText Transfer Protocol, and is one standard method, among others, of transferring information to and from computers over the Internet.

usability testing: Usability testing tests how easily software can be utilized by users. Some of the points evaluated in usability testing are: A. What is the level of skill required to learn and use the software? B. How long does it take to begin using the software? C. What is the user's attitude toward the software? and D. How does the user respond to the software under realistic conditions? Usability testing is the process of testing software (or other products) by having actual users use it, and then learning from the experience in order to improve.

EXAMPLE: If you want to create user-friendly software, you should implement usability testing.

Why Usability Test?

Uncover Problems
in the design

Discover Opportunities
to improve the design

Learn About Users
behavior and preferences

(usability testing)

USB card: Stands for Universal Serial Bus card. USB is a technology for storing and transmitting data. A card is a physical component that you can put inside your computer or other electronic equipment to have it perform better or perform additional functions. A USB card is a piece of hardware with a standard physical port (place to plug things into) on the computer that can be used to send and receive information. See "USB" for more information.

EXAMPLE: Computers that do not include a USB card cannot utilize USB thumb drives.

(USB card)

USB: Stands for Universal Serial Bus. Universal means "consistently done or arranged in the same way." A bus is a physical part of a computer that allows for the transfer of electronic information from one point to another. It is usually a set of wires connecting two or more parts. Electronic signals travel back and forth on these wires as the computer does its job. In a system like this, you can set it up so that when you're sending a set of data there is only one wire available for use. In that case, the data is broken up into small pieces, and each piece is sent one after the other. In other words, there is a series of pieces of data. This is serial data transfer. You can also set it up so that you use multiple wires to transfer the data. In this case, the data is broken up such that each wire is only used to transfer part of the whole data and all the wires are used at once. This way the whole set of data is moved much faster. This is called parallel data transfer. The Universal Serial Bus is a concept that all computer manufacturers agreed to use. It is a standard physical port on the computer that can be used to send and receive information.

EXAMPLE: Most chargers for cell phones can plug into the USB port on a computer and use the electronics signal from the computer to charge the phone.

USB drive: A portable data storage device. It can be used to store electronic documents, images, songs, videos, etc. This is often useful for transferring information from one computer to another using the USB port (the place where you can plug in USB drives and other USB devices) on the computer. USB drives are also called: thumb drive (due to being about the size of a person's thumb), USB flash drive, USB stick, flash drive, disk-on-key, jump drive, pen drive and memory stick.

EXAMPLE: USB drives are now inexpensive enough that they can come embedded in a rubber model of a character from popular entertainment.

(USB drive)

USB flash drive: Another word for "USB drive."

USB stick: Another word for "USB drive."

USB thumb drive: Another word for "USB drive."

user: A user is simply a person who uses something, whether that thing is a computer or a telephone or anything else. It is most commonly used when talking about using a computer in that the user is the person who, in the end, will be using that computer to do things. Also called "end user," as this is the person who will use the software "in the end" (when it is released).

EXAMPLE: When you operate a computer program that lets you create written documents, you are that program's user.

User Acceptance Testing: See "UAT."

user experience: See "UX."

user-friendly: A user is simply a person who uses something, whether that thing is a computer or a telephone or anything else. It is most commonly used when talking about using a computer in that the user is the person who, in the end, will be using that computer to do things. The term "user-friendly" is used to refer to a computer program (a set of written instructions, entered into a computer by people, that make it execute [perform] specific tasks) that is easy to operate. It usually refers to the visual appearance of a program and the sequence of actions needed to operate the program. User-friendly means it was designed from the user's perspective to give them a smooth and comfortable experience.

EXAMPLE: Facebook is very user-friendly.

user function: A user is just a person who uses something, whether that is a computer or a telephone or anything. It is most commonly used when talking about using a computer in that the user is the person who, in the end, will be using that computer to do things. The user function is a thing that the user tells the computer to do. The user is directing the computer to perform a task.

EXAMPLE: Clicking "Play" on a video on your computer is a user function.

user interface: See "UI."

user story: In project management, a user story is a tool that attempts to describe software from the user's perspective. They are written from the user's viewpoint and are used to document tasks for developers to complete by describing particular features. User stories include the type of user, what they want and why. A user story is written like this: "As a < type of user >, I want < some goal > so that < some reason >."

EXAMPLE: "As a user, I want to log into my account using a username and password, so I can access my account information."

UTF: See "Unicode."

UTF-8: See "Unicode."

UTF-16: See "Unicode."

UWP: See "Universal Windows Platform."

UX: Stands for user experience. A user is simply a person who uses something, whether that thing is a computer or a telephone or anything else. It is most commonly used when talking about using a computer in that the user is the person who, in the end, will be using that computer to do things. The term user experience is used to describe the overall experience one has in using a computer program (a set of written instructions, entered into a computer by people, that make it execute [perform] specific tasks). Things such as ease of use, aesthetics (visual appeal), how easy it is to work out on your own how to use it, etc. are all considered part of the user experience.

EXAMPLE: It is usually considered good practice, as far as UX is concerned, to provide images in a program that are indicative of the various functions of the program. For example, if there were an available function in a program to print off a document, the button you would click to start that action could have an image of a computer printer on it.

V

vacuum tube: A device that controls the flow of electricity. It is a glass tube where most of the air has been removed, and which has several electronic components inside it. In the early days of computers, vacuum tubes were used to represent the "on/off" or "true/false" or "1/0" data that a computer operates with. Vacuum tubes use a lot of electricity and give off a lot of heat – they also have a relatively short lifespan – therefore they have been replaced by improved technology.

EXAMPLE: Old televisions used to operate on vacuum tubes.

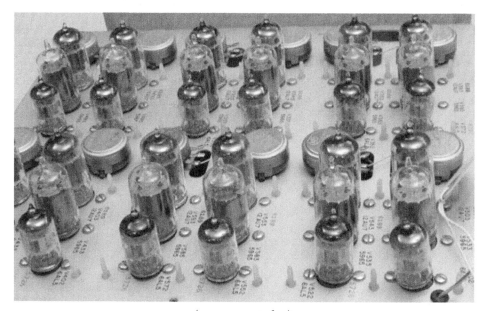

(vacuum tube)

value: A piece of information stored in a computer. A value is an actual piece of data being used by a computer. It is not the name of the data; it is the data itself. There are various types of data, just like in regular life: numbers, words, etc.

EXAMPLE: In a computer program used to track students at a school, a value for a particular student's Grade Point Average might be 3.25. The number 3.25 would be the value. The name of the data would be "Grade Point Average."

van Rossum, Guido (1956-): See "Python."

(van Rossum, Guido)

variable: In math, a variable is a symbol used to represent an unknown quantity or a quantity that may change. In computers, a variable is a piece of data that a computer program uses to keep track of values (amounts; characteristics; types) that can change as the program is executed. This might be something like "the grade of the student paper that was just graded" or "the color of paint to use for the next car on the assembly line." Variables are a vital part of any computer program because they make it so a computer program can be used for more than a single, predetermined set of values. You can imagine that if "the color of paint to use for the next car on the assembly line" was only ever able to be "blue," the computer program using that data wouldn't be very useful. It would make a lot more sense to make it so the computer program could change that value for each car that was going to be painted. When you are writing variables in a computer program, they usually are written in a manner like this:

```
[name of the variable] = [value of the variable]
```

EXAMPLE: You might have something like this:
```
color = "red"
```
Here, the variable is named "color," and the value of that variable has been set to "red." In other words, the variable named "color" is now "equal" to the word "red."

variable distribution: See "distribution."

variance: The measure of dispersion in a data set. It measures how spread out a data set is. Literally, variance is the average squared deviation of values from the mean. Meaning, we locate the variance by discovering the average squared deviation of values from the mean.

EXAMPLE: Let's find the variance in the following: 28, 30, 31, 25, 26, 35. First, we need to find the mean. To do this, we add all the numbers together and arrive at 175. Then we divide the sum (175) by 6 (the total amount of numbers in our data set), which equals 29. Now that we have the mean, we subtract the mean from each data point:

- 28 - 29 = -1
- 30 - 29 = 1
- 31 - 29 = 2
- 25 - 29 = -4
- 26 - 29 = -3
- 35 - 29 = 6

Then we square each of the differences. We do this in order to turn the negative numbers into positive numbers.

- $1^2 = 1$
- $1^2 = 1$
- $2^2 = 4$
- $-4^2 = 16$
- $-3^2 = 9$
- $6^2 = 36$

And finally, we take the sum of these numbers and divide it by the total number of data points:

- 1 + 1 + 4 + 16 + 9 + 36 = 67
- 67 / 6 = 11.17

11.17 is your variance.

VB: See "Visual Basic."

vector: An object that has both direction and magnitude. Vectors are used to determine the position of one point in space compared with another.

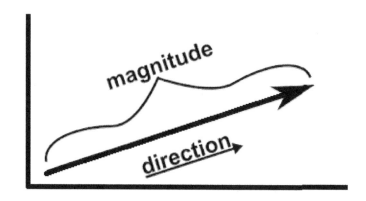

The word vector comes from the Latin would *vehere*, which means "convey."

EXAMPLE: A vector could be represented by a car that travels 20 miles at 45 mph.

Difference between Vector & Scalar Quantities

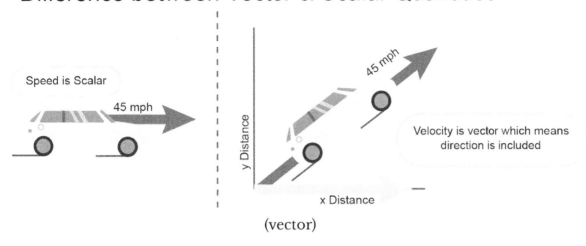

(vector)

vector graphics: Graphical representation using straight lines to construct the outlines of various objects – like so:

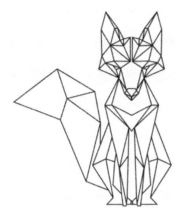

Vector graphics are computer graphic images that are defined by two dimensional points and are connected by lines.

EXAMPLE: Vector images are now so high definition that you cannot see the individual lines. Here is an example:

(vector graphics)

velocity: In project management, this is how much work people are assigned to handle in one set period of time. This can be determined by looking over how fast they took on their last assignment or by simply asking them how much they think they can get done in a set period of time. Velocity is how fast a project will be completed and its completion date can be determined thereby.

EXAMPLE: You meet up with 5 people who are creating a new computer game. You meet every two weeks, so they tell you they can finish one level in a week. You meet every two weeks, so the determined velocity is that they will complete two levels.

version control: Also called source control. Version control is the tools and processes that are used to manage multiple versions of computer files and programs as the files and programs change over time. A version control system, or VCS, provides two primary data management capabilities. It allows users to 1) prevent conflicts in a file when two people edit the exact same content at the same time, and 2) track changes to files. When you create things using your computer, you often revise them over time. This can mean the creation of documents, graphic images (pictures), computer programs, and other items. Keeping track of the changes to these items over time is called "version control." It also includes the control of changes to items like this when more than one person can make changes to the items. A version is an exact snapshot of something at a specific point in time. If you wrote a song, that would be Version 1. If you later added bagpipes over the top of the song, that would be Version 2. Version control is managing different versions of things on a computer. This is used a lot when you are creating computer programs.

EXAMPLE: If a team of writers were preparing a large textbook and each writer could add, edit, and remove content to the textbook at any time, they would find a version control system valuable in keeping track of all changes as the textbook was written.

VGA: Stands for "Video Graphics Array." A VGA connector is used to connect a video source (such as a computer) to a display device (such as a computer screen). VGA came out in the 1980s and most laptops and computers have VGA ports used to connect to a monitor. See also "DVI."

EXAMPLE: You can plug an additional screen into your laptop using the VGA port (a place on a computer where VGA cables can be plugged into).

(VGA)

video card: A card is a physical component that you can put inside your computer or other electronic equipment to have it perform better or perform additional functions. The video card is the part of a computer that handles what is displayed on the computer screen. It is essentially a small computer that handles all duties related to displaying images, thus freeing the CPU (central processing unit – a tiny internal device that is the "brain" of the computer; it is responsible for processing data and directing the operation of all other parts of the device) up for other tasks.

EXAMPLE: The better your video card is, the better the potential image quality will be on your computer screen.

(video card)

video editing: After shooting a video, you edit the footage to make it a complete, viewable video. This consists of, but is not limited to, cutting out parts, adding special effects, and adding sound. Video editing is the act of refining a filmed video so that it can be shown to others as a completed product.

EXAMPLE: In modern times, video editing is mainly done on a computer.

View: In an MVC (see "MVC") application, the part of the program that the end user actually sees. It could be just HTML, but it is commonly a mixture of the c# language and HTML, combined in one file that ends in .cshtml.

EXAMPLE: If you created an app for a bike shop, you may have an order screen where a customer could place an order. This screen would be a View, and it would be represented by a file called OrderPage.cshtml or something similar.

Vim: Stands for <u>Vi</u> <u>Im</u>proved. *Vi* is short for *Visual* and was created for the Unix operating system (OS – the main program within a computer that manages all other programs and external devices [e.g., keyboards, mice, displays, etc.] – Unix is a popular free OS) as a text editor. Vim is a version of Vi. Vim is a text editor, but unlike traditional text editors such as Notepad or Word (where inputs from the keyboard would insert the symbol or letter pressed), the inputs can be used to move the cursor around a document without the use of a mouse. Vim has three modes for editing text files:
1. Command Mode: Allows you to use the keys on the keyboard as commands.
2. Insert Mode: Allows you to input text.
3. Last-Line Mode: Inserts a colon designating the end of the file and what you want to do, such as save or quit, by typing a key command or a series of keys. For example, **:w** saves the file.

EXAMPLE: Instead of using your mouse to move the cursor one line up, you would press the letter 'j' or to move it left you would press the letter 'h.' You've probably performed a similar action while playing computer games.

(Vim)

virtual: The main English definition of the word "virtual" is hundreds of years old, and means "nearly as described, but not according to strict definition." For instance, let's say you got a secret spy message on paper and you were told to read it, then remove it from existence. So, you burned the piece of paper, put the ashes in a muffin mix, cooked the muffins and fed the muffins to your dog. You have virtually removed the original piece of paper from existence. A scientist would say the original paper still exists in altered form so it is not "removed from existence according to strict definition," but it is pretty clear that no one could read it at this point. Nowadays, "virtual" is used to describe something that seems to exist in the physical world, but instead is generated by a computer.

EXAMPLE: In "virtual reality" you wear a helmet that shows an image to each eye and blocks all other vision. It changes what you see as you move your head. If you look down and it shows your feet on the ledge of a skyscraper, and the image quality is good, you might experience a real fear of heights! It feels like reality, but of course you are not really on the ledge of a skyscraper, nor in any danger.

virtual machine: The main English definition of the word "virtual" is hundreds of years old, and means "nearly as described, but not according to strict definition." In technology, virtual is used to describe something that seems to exist in the physical world, but instead is generated by a computer. A virtual machine is software that, like a physical computer, runs on its own operating system (OS – the main program within a computer that manages all other programs and external devices [e.g., keyboards, mice, displays, etc.]) and has its own programs. Virtual machines not only exhibit the behavior of a separate computer, but are also capable of performing tasks such as running applications and programs like a separate computer. You can set up a virtual machine on your computer that allows you to access two different operating systems and sets of programs (the ones already on your computer and the separate virtual machine). When doing so, your computer dynamically allocates computing resources to the virtual machine and your actual machine as needed (i.e., whichever you're using at a given time will receive the processing power of your hardware).

EXAMPLE: Let's say you wanted to set up a Mac OS (the operating system used by Apple computers) on a Windows machine – you could access the Mac operating system through a virtual machine.

virtual private network: See "VPN."

virtual reality: The main English definition of the word "virtual" is hundreds of years old, and means "nearly as described, but not according to strict definition." For instance, let's say you got a secret spy message on paper and you were told to read it, then remove it from existence. So, you burned the piece of paper, put the ashes in a muffin mix, cooked the muffins and fed the muffins to your dog. You have virtually removed the original piece of paper from existence. A scientist would say the original paper still exists in altered form so it is not "removed from existence according to strict definition," but it is pretty clear that no one could read it at this point. Nowadays, "virtual" is used to describe something that seems to exist in the physical world, but instead is generated by a computer. In virtual reality you wear a helmet that shows an image to each eye and blocks all other vision. It changes what you see as you move your head. If you look down and it shows your feet on the ledge of a skyscraper (and if the image quality is good), you might experience a real fear of heights! It feels like reality, but of course you are not really on the ledge of a skyscraper, nor in any danger.

EXAMPLE: Here is an example of someone wearing a VR headset:

(virtual reality)

virus: A computer program (a set of written instructions, entered into a computer by people, that make it execute [perform] specific tasks) designed to do something harmful to a computer, and that can copy itself onto other computers. A virus is something that travels from computer to computer and does bad things. It is intentionally created to cause damage. There is another word here that's important: malware. Mal- means "bad" or "wrong." Malware is software (computer programs) that perform actions designed to harm a computer or other programs. A virus is one type of malware; there are others and you will learn about them here.

EXAMPLE: A virus could be something that steals confidential information off of your computer and gives it to the creator of the virus. It may also make your computer send out emails to all of your contacts without you knowing it, carrying the virus along with the email message. If any of your contacts open up the email, it might allow the virus to be copied onto their computer.

(virus)

Visual BASIC: A popular programming language (a system of specialized words and symbols used to communicate with a computer and to create programs) developed by Microsoft. It was derived from the BASIC programming language and so shares some similarities. It can perform a wide array of actions, from developing GUIs (Graphical User Interfaces – pictures on a computer display that users interact with) to accessing databases (organized collections of related data).

EXAMPLE: The popular file manager program for Windows called "XYPlorer" was written in Visual Basic.

(Visual Basic)

Visual J++: Visual J++ was a programming language developed by Microsoft with similarities to Java. The purpose of J++ was basically to make their own version of Java that would be compatible with other Microsoft technologies (i.e., Microsoft frameworks). J++ was released in 1996 and discontinued in 2004.

EXAMPLE: Visual J++ could be used to create a variety of computer programs, including games.

Visual J#: Visual J# (also simply called J#) was a programming language (a system of specialized words and symbols used to communicate with a computer and to create programs) that was basically a combination of Java and J++. Visual J# was released in 2002 and discontinued in 2007, though Microsoft support for J# continued until 2017.

EXAMPLE: As a programming language, Visual J# could be used to create a wide variety of software, including games.

Visual Studio: An integrated development environment (IDE) developed by Microsoft. An IDE is a set of programming tools for writing software programs. IDEs are a great aid to computer program creation. They combine many available tools into one place.

EXAMPLE: You can write software in a wide range of programming languages within Visual Studio.

(Visual Studio)

Visual Studio Code: A code editor (a program that can be used to write code in) from Microsoft that includes many built-in tools that assist greatly in software development. Whereas Visual Studio is an IDE (integrated development environment – software used to create, debug and manage coding projects), Visual Studio Code is an editor –

which means it focuses mainly on software development and does not include the full set of tools built into Visual Studio (IDEs have more available tools than code editors).

EXAMPLE: Visual Studio Code is the most-used code editor in the world.

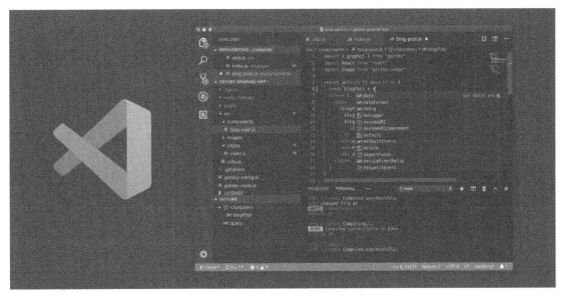

(Visual Studio Code)

VoIP: Stands for Voice over Internet Protocol. VoIP is a protocol (a formal agreement about how to format and send a particular type of data) governing the transmission of voice data over the Internet (the largest and most-used computer network [connection that allows data transfer between machines] in the world, which is mainly utilized to access the World Wide Web).

EXAMPLE: Websites exist that allow users to have voice conversations over the internet on their computers, using VoIP.

volatile: Volatile is used to describe something that can change. In computers, we use volatile when talking about a certain type of information stored in a computer. It simply means that when the power is turned off, the information is no longer there. Information that is stored in a computer that does not erase when you turn the computer off is not volatile. See also "memory" and "RAM."

EXAMPLE: You have an alarm clock plugged into the wall. That alarm clock has the time set into it by you. Someone unplugs the alarm clock. You plug it back in and now the time displays: 12:00:00. The time on an alarm clock is volatile.

volt: A unit of measurement showing the force, or potential to perform work, for an electrical current. Voltage is the electronic force expressed in volts. An electrical current with low voltage may only be able to do a small amount of work – say, light up a small flashlight bulb. On the other hand, an electrical current with high voltage may be able to do a large amount of work – say, power a car-crushing machine.

EXAMPLE: A car battery has a voltage of 12 to 15 volts or so. Cell phone batteries have a voltage of around 5 volts. The outlets in a home typically deliver electricity that is at around 100-120 volts. Outlets that power large home appliances such as clothes dryers deliver electricity that is at around 220-240 volts.

voltage: See "volt."

VPN: Stands for "Virtual Private Network." It is a special kind of computer network. It is best understood in the context of a public network. A public network is a system of connected computers that can be accessed by any computer with the necessary computer programs (a set of written instructions, entered into a computer by people, that make it execute [perform] specific tasks) installed. An example is the Internet, a worldwide network of computers; it allows access by any computer with the correct software that can connect to it. A private network is one that can only be accessed by specific computers. An example might be a network of computers in a company office building. Special software is used that controls access to all the computers that have been set up as being inside that network. A VPN is a way to safely share a private network over a public network. Basically, it is stringing a secure line from a private network (like a company's networked computers), through the Internet, to your destination point – without revealing anything to anyone beyond your intended destination point.

EXAMPLE: You have a company that handles legal documents. These legal documents are shared in your company's network. You have a lawyer working in another state that you want to be able to access your company's network. You can set up a VPN at your company and allow him to connect to that VPN, via the Internet, without exposing the information publicly. The VPN keeps the information secure and away from unauthorized viewing.

VR: See "virtual reality."

Vue: "Vue" is short for "Vue.js." It is an open-source (software that can be modified and used for free) JavaScript (popular programming language) framework (code written by others [and documentation on how to use it] that can be used by developers to enhance their programs) that is mainly used for building user interfaces (the elements on a computer that the user [person operating a computer] interacts with [such as a keyboard, screen, or login form]), websites and web applications. Vue was created by Evan You after working for Google.

EXAMPLE: Vue was one of the technologies used by Grammarly (a company that helps people write better in English) to create their software.

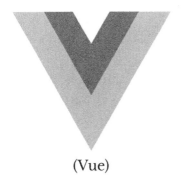

(Vue)

W

wave: A wave is a flow of energy which changes over time; it has low points and high points. Waves come in all sorts of types, patterns, and sizes. Waves are how energy moves through space. They look like this:

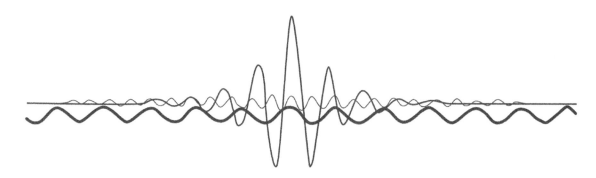

The physical distance between one point in a wave and the next identical same point in the wave is called a wavelength. Here, identical means "the same quantity and direction (rising or falling) as another point."

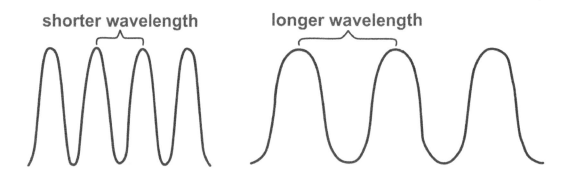

EXAMPLE: Light and sound are composed of waves.

wavelength: See "wave."

weakly-typed: See "strongly-typed."

web: See "World Wide Web."

web application: A computer program (a set of written instructions, entered into a computer by people, that make it execute [perform] specific tasks) that uses both the browser (the program people use to view web pages – e.g., Google Chrome) and the web server (a specialized computer used to store and transmit data, such as "serving up" websites through the World Wide Web) to accomplish its functions. Note that this differs from the way many computer programs work, where the entire program resides on your computer. With web applications, the browser handles the display of information to the user and gives the user a place to enter instructions for the program – while the web server handles various data processing actions based on the user instructions. Web applications are applications that run on the World Wide Web.

EXAMPLE: Dropbox is a popular web application.

web application framework: A web application framework is a pre-made set of computer code that enables the basic functions of a web application (any website that requires user-input and interaction), along with a set of documentation on how to make use of that code in creating your exact web application.

EXAMPLE: Most web applications today were created using a web application framework.

web bot: See "bot."

web browser: Called browser for short. This is a program (a set of written instructions, entered into a computer by people, that make it execute [perform] specific tasks) you use to view items on the Internet (the largest and most-used computer network [connection that allows data transfer between machines] in the world, which is mainly utilized to access the World Wide Web). The most common thing people use browsers for is to find and view websites – more particularly, the web pages on websites. There are other types of information available through the Internet that you can find and view in a browser.

EXAMPLE: Google Chrome is a popular web browser and you have probably seen its logo:

(web browser)

web indexing: An index is a tool you use to find information rapidly. There are a number of different applications of indices. ("Indices" is the plural for "index.") One type of index is a named category of information of a certain type. Specifically, this type of index tells you about what kinds of information are in a collection of data, and where to find each type of information in that collection. For example, a manual for a tractor might have an index that lists out all the key subjects in the manual, and the various places in the manual where that subject is discussed, like:

```
engine: pages 3, 10-12, 14
steering system: pages 43-50
water pump: page 22
```

In computers, an index is information about a collection of data. This information in the index tells where pieces of information with similar characteristics are located in the main data, so you do not have to search through each piece of data in the big collection, one by one, in order to get all the information that is related in some way. Indexing is sorting the contents of a website alphabetically, by subject, by date, etc. to assist with searching for things on the Internet. Web indexing refers to the various methods for indexing the contents of a website or the Internet as a whole. Indexing also includes assigning key-words or phrases to web pages so that the website can be found by a search engine (program used to search the internet – e.g., Google).

EXAMPLE: Google gathers up web pages and has a major web index it uses to list and categorize websites.

weblog: See "blog."

web crawler: See "web spider."

WebKit: WebKit is a browser (the program people use to view web pages – e.g., Google Chrome) engine (core software component utilized by web browsers) utilized by many companies, including Apple. The primary function of a browser engine is to transform HTML (HyperText Markup Language – the primary language used to create websites) documents and other resources of a web page into an interactive visual representation on a user's device.

EXAMPLE: Apple's App Store utilizes WebKit.

(WebKit)

weblog: See "blog."

webmail: A service where the email client (the computer that is requesting service from another computer) program is on a web server (a specialized computer used to store and transmit data, such as "serving up" websites through the World Wide Web). To use email services in this setup, you would access the web server using your browser (the program people use to view web pages – e.g., Google Chrome). The web pages that get sent to your browser would provide the same functions as an email client – typically to create, send, receive, and store email messages. The advantage of webmail is that you can have access to your email messages from any computer that has a browser and can connect to the Internet (the largest and most-used computer network [connection that allows data transfer between machines] in the world, which is mainly utilized to access the World Wide Web). When the email client is on your computer, you can only access your email messages from your computer. The disadvantage of webmail is that if you do not have access to the Internet, you cannot access your email messages.

EXAMPLE: Gmail and Yahoo email are popular webmail clients.

webmaster: A technology professional who creates and maintains websites.

EXAMPLE: If you see "contact webmaster" on a website, this means you can send a message to the person who oversees the website.

web robot: See "bot."

web server: The electronic files (e.g., web pages, images, etc.) that make up a website are stored on specialized computers called web servers. These computers accept requests from other, remote (located elsewhere) computers for specific web pages, and deliver those files needed to make the web page display on the remote computer. The type of program (a set of written instructions, entered into a computer by people, that make it execute [perform] specific tasks) you would use to view web pages is called a web browser. It is this program that would make the requests to the web server for the website files.

EXAMPLE: Everytime you search for data on the World Wide Web, you interact with a web server.

(web server)

website: The World Wide Web is a collection of linked electronic documents, organized into groups called websites. A website is composed of one or more individual web pages, where a "page" is an organized, specific document containing text, images, video, and other elements. The electronic files that make up a website are stored on specialized computers called web servers (a specialized computer used to store and transmit data, such as "serving up" websites through the World Wide Web). These computers accept requests from other, remote (located elsewhere) computers for specific web pages and deliver the files needed to make the web page display on the remote computer. The type of program (a set of written instructions, entered into a computer by people, that make it execute [perform] specific tasks) you use to view web pages is called a web browser. It is this program that would make the requests to the web server for the website files. Websites are locations one can visit on the World Wide Web using a web browser. They typically cover a particular topic or group of subjects, and are organized into web pages. Each web page has its own address that can be used to locate and visit it.

EXAMPLE: Facebook is a website.

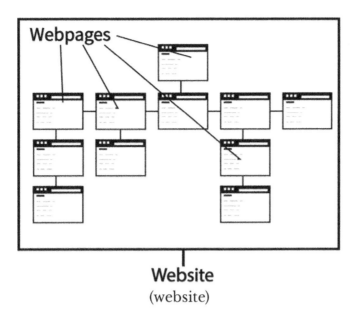

Website
(website)

website card: Like the physical object, a card is a square or rectangle design element that content is placed within. You can see some website cards here:

Cards allow for websites to present large amounts of information in a digestible fashion.

EXAMPLE: Cards on websites commonly hold preview information that, when clicked, will display the full picture/story/video to the user.

website container: In web design, a container is the concept of keeping grouped elements of the design separate from one another. The container size can vary depending on the use of the site or they can all be the same size.

EXAMPLE: Amazon uses the container concept on their site.

web spider: A "web spider" is also called a web crawler. It is a computer program that systematically searches the World Wide Web (the largest and most-used collection of linked [connected] electronic documents, organized into groups called websites, that is accessed using the internet), typically with the purpose of creating and updating an index (searchable information about a collection of data) of the Web. Web search engines (programs used to search the internet – e.g., Google) use web crawling (or spidering) software to update their web content or indexes. Web spiders can copy all the pages they visit for later processing by a search engine that indexes the downloaded pages so that users can search them much more quickly.

EXAMPLE: Google has web spider tools you can use to crawl and index websites.

wetware: See "liveware."

while loop: A type of loop (a sequence of instructions that are continually repeated until an exact condition [an item that must be true before something else occurs] is met) which means "while (blank) is occurring, do (blank)." A while loop is basically a repeating if statement (a conditional statement [computer command for handling decisions based on the outcome of "true" or "false" comparisons] that means "if ___ is true, do ___"). Meaning, with a while loop, you are telling the computer to execute certain code repeatedly while a particular condition is present. A while loop loops through a block (chunk; section) of code for as long as a specified condition is true.

EXAMPLE: While hungry, eat.

white noise: See "noise, colors of."

whitespace: Whitespace is the margin (padding; space) between elements of your design that does not include copy. Whitespace is meant to ensure aesthetic spacing and to prevent clutter. It is not always the color white – it is just the blank space between elements.

EXAMPLE: In the image below, the space around the header, body text and cakepops is whitespace:

Lorem ipsum dolor sit amet, consectetur adipiscing elit, sed do eiusmod tempor incididunt ut labore et dolore magna aliqua. Ut enim ad minim veniam, quis nostrud exercitation ullamco laboris nisi ut aliquip ex ea commodo consequat. Lorem ipsum dolor sit amet, consectetur adipiscing elit, sed do eiusmod tempor incididunt ut labore et dolore magna aliqua. Ut enim ad minim veniam, quis nostrud exercitation ullamco laboris nisi ut aliquip ex ea commodo consequat.

(whitespace)

whole number: A number that has not been broken into pieces. It is a number that has not been divided into parts (here, parts means fractions, or "parts of a whole").

EXAMPLE: 5 is a whole number. 3.2 is not a whole number. 168 is a whole number. 13 ½ is not a whole number.

widget: A widget is a simple, easy-to-use computer program, designed to be able to operate on several different types of computers. Widgets generally have only one or two primary functions.

EXAMPLE: On a computer, a widget could be a small window that stays on the bottom of your screen, always displaying the current temperature in your town.

wifi: (Also written WiFi or Wi-Fi) A technology for linking up computers or other devices in a network (connection that allows data transfer between machines) without the use of physical connectors like wires. Computers can be connected over a network by a cable (wired) or connected wirelessly. Wifi is used to connect computers and devices to the internet (the largest and most-used computer network in the world, which is mainly utilized to access the World Wide Web) wirelessly. To understand how wifi works, you must understand radio waves. Radio waves are a form of energy that moves at the speed of light. It can be sent through objects and can be used to transmit information (like data and sound). Here is a radio tower sending out radio waves:

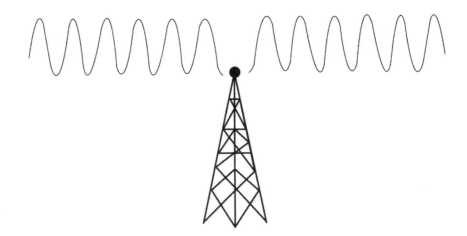

The word "radio" comes from "ray" or "beam." How it works is that a transmitter (a device that can produce radio waves) sends out the data. The data travels through the air and arrives at a receiver.

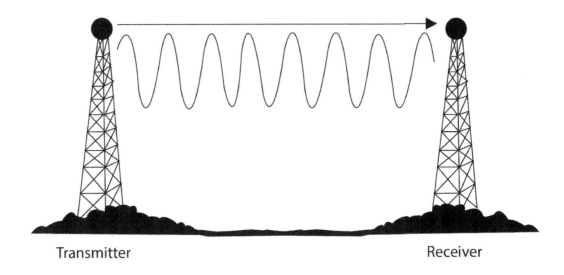

Transmitter   Receiver

Your cellphone has a transmitter and receiver built in. Wifi uses radio waves to send data through the air. Wifi-compatible (meaning, able to connect to the internet via wifi) computers are able to translate data to radio waves prior to sending it out via wifi, and can translate received radio waves into digital data that it can process. The name wifi was chosen as a pun on the word "hi-fi" (high fidelity). Fidelity refers to how exact a copy is made, compared to the original item. High fidelity sound is sound, played from a recording, that has very little distortion and sounds very similar to the original sound. Some say that wifi means "wireless fidelity" but that is not technically true. Wifi was created in 1997 by an Australian named John O'Sullivan and a team of workers.

EXAMPLE: Most homes have a wifi device that lets them access the internet using the devices they own (laptops, cell phones, etc.) while they are in the home.

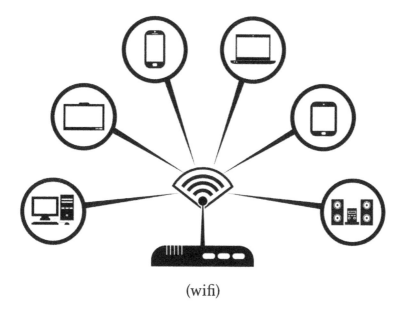

(wifi)

wiki: A wiki is a website that allows the people viewing it to add things and change the website using their browser. Wikis are a team effort where anyone can alter the website, as long as they follow the basic rules established by the operators of the wiki. "Wiki" means "quick" in Hawaiian. The creator of the first wiki was Howard G. Cunningham; he chose to use that word. Many companies set up wikis for the use of their employees or customers; these often contain knowledge about the company, its operations, its culture, etc.

EXAMPLE: Wikipedia is the largest wiki in the world.

Wikipedia: The largest wiki (see "wiki") in the world. Wikipedia is a free encyclopedia on the web created through the collaborative effort of a community of people known as Wikipedians. Anyone who signs up for the site can create and edit articles in the encyclopedia. Wikipedia is the largest encyclopedia ever created. Though there are strict guidelines for posting information on Wikipedia, not all information on Wikipedia is completely accurate or true because virtually anyone can post on it. Therefore, it is important to never take information on Wikipedia as pure fact – especially data that harms the reputation of the subject – because it can be biased and false.

EXAMPLE: If you were studying elephants, you could search Wikipedia and find articles about elephants, written and edited by various users who had specialized knowledge about elephants.

(Wikipedia)

wildcard: In SQL (Structured Query Language – the most common language used to create, manage, interact with, delete and edit databases), a wildcard is a character (a symbol used in communication; such as a letter or number) that can be used to substitute one or more characters in a string (a set of characters).

EXAMPLE: Using an underscore (_) as a wildcard in a query (searching a database) can represent a single character. Therefore, if we searched for h_m, the search results may include: ham, hem, him and hum.

Windows: An operating system (OS – the main program within a computer that manages all other programs and external devices [e.g., keyboards, mice, displays, etc.]) created by the technology company Microsoft. It is one of the most-used OSes in the world. See also "OS."

EXAMPLE: Windows comes in various versions, typically described in this way: Windows 7, Windows 10, etc.

(Windows)

Windows Azure: Azure is a bright blue color. It also refers to a small butterfly that is typically purple or blue. Windows Azure (simply referred to as "Azure" for short) is a set of tools from Microsoft used for cloud computing (using the internet's resources for work instead of using your computer's). Azure has tools for storing and managing databases, storing and running software programs, etc. – all on computers that are not located where the user is. The advantage is that the user (and their company) does not have to pay for the personnel and equipment needed to have all those computers operating. Since the computers that are being used are owned and managed by another company (Microsoft in this case), the owners can use them more efficiently and charge the users less money than the users would have to spend if they had to handle the personnel and equipment themselves.

EXAMPLE: Many companies host their websites and web applications on Azure.

(Microsoft Azure)

Windows Presentation Foundation: Windows Presentation Foundation (WPF) is a graphical user interface (GUI – any program display that can do more than take in text-input) framework (code written by others [and documentation on how to use it] that can be used by developers to enhance their programs) that is a part of the .NET Framework (software for building Microsoft-based programs). It provides developers with the tools to make Windows desktop applications with interactive user interfaces, while tying the code together that performs actions based on user input.

EXAMPLE: You could create patient monitoring GUIs for a hospital with WPF:

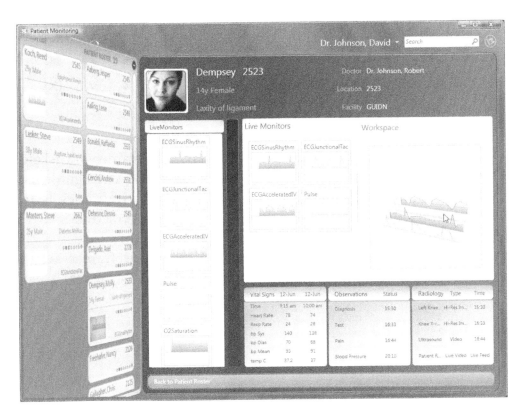

Wingding: Wingding is a combination of the words "Windows" and "dingbat." Wingdings are dingbat (a special symbol that is not a letter or number) fonts that render keys on the keyboard as a variety of symbols. For example, a capital A in wingding font is:

✌

There are various wingding typefaces (fonts), such as: Wingdings 1, Wingdings 2, Wingdings 3, etc.

EXAMPLE: Here are some wingdings:

(Wingdings)

wireframe: A wireframe is a visual guide that represents the framework (skeleton) of a website. Designers create wireframes that are used by developers as a guide for how the website, app, software, etc. should look. The purpose of wireframes is to arrange elements in a manner that best relays a designer's message, look and feel. The frame part of wireframe refers to the fact that it is a basic framework (structure). The wire part of wireframe comes from car design. In car design, wireframes are the design blueprints for a car and they look as though they're composed of "wires," as you can see here:

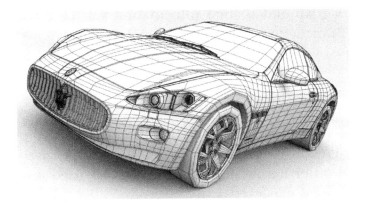

Wireframes are also referred to as page schematics or screen blueprints. Though wireframes focus on layout, they can include other design choices, such as color palette.

EXAMPLE: Here are three example of web page wireframes:

(wireframe)

wireless: This means that you are connecting to something without using wires. There are many different things that can be wireless. Wireless usually means that the information, data, etc., is being passed through the air.

EXAMPLE: Before cell phones were invented, you had to use a phone that had a wire connected to it. Now with cell phones, you do not need to have a wire. It connects "wirelessly." It is important to note here that the word "wireless" relates to how the device receives and transmits data. The way that the device receives electrical power is another matter – most devices will need to be plugged into a power source at various points in time, if only to charge the batteries (for battery-powered devices, that is). It was decided to call mobile phones "cell phones" because of how the towers that send and receive information for the phones work. These towers send and receive data. Each tower has a range surrounding it, in which it can send and receive data. Once you go beyond that range, the data can no longer be detected by that tower. The area around a tower, in which the signal is effective, is called a "cell," from its resemblance to a physical cell in the human body. Towers are physically placed close enough to each other so that cells overlap and so that information can be passed from one cell to another. That way, information can go from your cell phone, across the network of cells, to the cell phone of the person you're talking to.

whiskers plot: See "quartile."

Word: Microsoft Word (commonly referred to as "Word") is a program created by Microsoft for use in creating written documents. It is mainly used for typing content, but you can also add other items, such as pictures. It is used in almost all businesses and is also commonly used in everyday life.

EXAMPLE: Letters, invitations, and promotional materials are all things one can create in Word.

(Microsoft ® Word)

word processing: The actions a word processor performs. A word processor is a program on a computer that allows you to create, format, modify, and print documents.

EXAMPLE: Microsoft Word is a famous word processor and, as is implied, it processes words and images by creating them, editing them, deleting them, etc.

WordPress: A popular content management system (a user-friendly system for building and managing websites). It is a free program.

EXAMPLE: A company that sells framed art might use WordPress to create their website. They would take pictures of the art they want to sell, load those pictures into WordPress, write any needed descriptions for the artwork, and use WordPress to lay out the pictures and text of the website. When they were done designing the website, WordPress would convert those layouts into actual website files, which would be stored on a web server (a specialized computer used to store and transmit data, such as "serving up" websites through the World Wide Web). People could then view that website.

(WordPress)

working directory: Also called "current working directory (CWD)," "current directory" and "working tree." It is the directory (another word for "folder"; a location where a file or files are stored within a computer) you are currently working in as a developer. See also "workspace."

EXAMPLE: In the following file path, the working directory would be "Docs":
`C:\Windows\Docs\Letter.docx`

working tree: See "working directory."

workspace: A directory (another word for "folder"; a location where a file or files are stored within a computer) that holds all the source code (the original code of a program as written by the program's creator[s]) files that make up a project or program. Workspaces are also referred to as a working directory.

EXAMPLE: You might have a folder labeled "myWebsite" which holds all the files needed for your website. That would be your workspace. Only the files needed for that project should be located there.

workstation: Any computer used for any purpose. A workstation is also a computer that is typically used for some type of technical or scientific work. It is usually more powerful than a regular computer and is used for more specific tasks than your typical computer. While a personal computer could be used to watch videos or play games, a workstation would be a computer that is more high powered and would be used for more advanced, large, complex and important tasks.

EXAMPLE: If you worked at Ford and had a special computer to help you design cars, that computer would be called a workstation.

(workstation)

World Wide Web: The World Wide Web (the "Web") is a collection of linked electronic documents, organized into groups called websites. For more information, see "internet" and "website."

EXAMPLE: There are websites on the World Wide Web dedicated to the films of famous actors.

worm: A type of malware (harmful software) that replicates itself so that it can be installed on more computers. Once a worm program has been installed on a computer, it copies itself and leaves a worm in the original computer and puts the copy in the next computer it travels to, and so on. Worms can be used to cause harm to computers. They can include other programs that can allow damage to the already-installed programs on a computer.

EXAMPLE: A worm is created by someone and saved on computer A. The worm is sent from computer A to computer B. Now there are two worms (one on computer A and one on computer B). Then it goes from computer B to computer C, and we have three worms (computer A, computer B, and computer C now all have trojans) – and so on.

(worm)

www: Short for World Wide Web (see "World Wide Web").

X

x86: x86 is a term that is used to describe a CPU (Central Processing Unit – the "brain" of the computer; a physical piece within the computer that processes [handles; performs actions with and on] data) instruction set (machine language [1s and 0s] handled by the processor) that is compatible with various Intel [a popular computer parts manufacturer] processors. x86 is compatible with 16-bit and 32-bit processors. It is also backwards compatible (can work with older versions) – for example, if you have a 32-bit processor, x86 allows for 32-bit processing and less. x86 is not the CPU itself, it is the word for the instruction set handled by the CPU.

EXAMPLE: Modern computers typically do not use x86. Instead, they use x64, which is compatible with 64-bit processors.

Xamarin: Software from Microsoft that allows for cross-platform (works on multiple platforms, such as Apple, Android, etc.) mobile app development.

EXAMPLE: The Alaska Airlines app was built with Xamarin.

(Xamarin)

XAML: XAML stands for "Extensible Application Markup Language." It is pronounced "zam-ull." XAML is a markup language (a system of specialized words and symbols used to add instructions to a document in order to control the style, format and appearance of the content [text, pictures, videos, etc.] of the document – markup languages are primarily used to make websites) developed by Microsoft. Its primary use is creating interfaces for applications. The syntax (rules that govern how code must be structured) is very similar to HTML (HyperText Markup Language – the primary language used to create websites). Just like other markup languages, XAML uses tags to define objects. The attributes of an object (such as the size, color, name or shape) are specified within the tag.

EXAMPLE: XAML has been used to help create apps for multiple platforms (a specific combination of hardware and an operating system).

XAMPP: A free and open-source cross-platform (works on multiple platforms, such as Windows, Mac, etc.) web server (a specialized computer used to store and transmit data, such as "serving up" websites through the World Wide Web) solution by Apache that consists of a server software, databases and code. It unofficially stands for:
- X – cross-platform (x being the abbreviation for "cross")

- A – Apache (web server software)
- M – MariaDB (relational database management system)
- P – PHP (popular programming language for creating dynamic and interactive websites)
- P – Perl (popular programming language that can be used for a wide range of tasks, ranging from computer graphics to general scripting)

EXAMPLE: You can host your own website using XAMPP.

x-axis: See "axis."

XHTML: Stands for "Extensible HyperText Markup Language." It is an advancement of HTML (HyperText Markup Language – used for creating websites) created to help give web pages more functionality. XHTML is no longer commonly used, and HTML has been advanced in other ways.

EXAMPLE: When you look at a website, you see words, pictures, sounds and videos. One language that could be used behind the scenes to tell the computer to show you those words, pictures, sounds, and videos is XHTML. The thing to remember is that there are many different languages you can use to write websites.

XML: Stands for "Extensible Markup Language." This means that computer programmers can create their own document structure, and then use XML to specify markup instructions for the data in those documents. These markup instructions give the computer data about the elements of the document – text, images, video, etc. When the document is processed by a computer program, those markup instructions are not used as the data in the document – rather, they are used to control how the actual content of the document is used or displayed.

EXAMPLE: An XML document that represents an order from a manufacturing company might look like this (NOTE: that there is no data in this document yet; as the document stands here, it is just a definition of the structure of the data that we want to represent):

```
<shippingorder>
        <ordertaker></ordertaker>
        <customer></customer>
        <customerId></customerId>
        <shiptoaddress>
                <name></name>
                <address></address>
                <city></city>
                <state></state>
        </shiptoaddress>
        <orderitems>
        <itemdata>
```

```
            <title></title>
            <note></note>
            <quantity></quantity>
            <price></price>
        </itemdata>
    </orderitems>
</shippingorder>
```

An XML document that includes actual data might look like this:

```
<shippingorder>
        <ordertaker>John Smith</ordertaker>
        <customer>Bob Smith</customer>
        <customerId>THX-1138</customerId>
        <shiptoaddress>
            <name>Bob Smith</name>
            <address>123 Main Street</address>
            <city>New York</city>
            <state>New York</state>
        </shiptoaddress>
        <orderitems>
        <itemdata>
            <title>Red balloon</title>
            <note>Birthday message</note>
            <quantity>1</quantity>
            <price>9.99</price>
        </itemdata>
        <itemdata>
            <title>White tablecloth</title>
            <note>cotton</note>
            <quantity>1</quantity>
            <price>20.00</price>
        </itemdata>
    </orderitems>
</shippingorder>
```

Because the XML instructions here define an exact structure for the data in the file, a computer program could be created that could read through the document and locate exact data that was needed – for example, it could determine how many items were in the order by seeing how many pieces of data there were that were marked by the instruction "<orderitems>" – in the example above, this would be two.

XHR: Stands for XML HTTP Request. XHR is a set of APIs (Application Programming Interface – a program used for transferring and editing specific information) that can be used by some scripting languages (such as JavaScript). It is used to transfer XML (short for "extensible markup language"; XML is a customizable markup language, used primarily in the displaying documents on the internet [i.e., websites]) to and from a web server (a specialized computer used to store and transmit data, such as "serving up" websites through the World Wide Web) using HTTP (HyperText Transfer Protocol

– a system for transmitting information). XHR works by establishing a communication path between a web page's client-side and server-side and can be used to transmit many different types of data accurately.

EXAMPLE: Google Maps uses XHR in transmitting data (maps, directions, etc.) to and from your computer.

XNOR gate: A logic gate (gate for short) is a switch (a physical device that can be used to control whether or not electricity is passed through) that implements one of several different types of Boolean logic (the "logic" a computer uses to make comparisons, where only one of two possible outcomes is possible: true/false, yes/no, on/off, etc. – which is based on a system of logic developed by English mathematician George Boole) operations. It takes one or more "true/false" inputs and produces a single "true/false" output. In computers, if electricity is allowed to flow, that is considered "true"; if it is not allowed to flow, that is considered "false." Gates are part of how we can use computers to make decisions based on the results of analyzing data. An XNOR gate takes two "true/false" inputs and produces a "false" output if EITHER of the inputs are "true," but not if BOTH of them are true. Here is the symbol used for an XNOR gate:

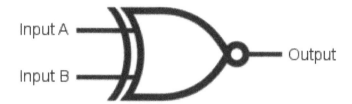

Here, the inputs are the two lines on the left, and the output is the line on the right. The inputs on the left are commonly labeled "Input A" and "Input B." To show how the XNOR gate works, we will use a truth table. Truth tables are mathematical tables laying out the possible inputs for a logic gate, along with their corresponding output. Here is a truth table for an XNOR gate:

INPUT A	INPUT B	OUTPUT
FALSE	FALSE	TRUE
FALSE	TRUE	FALSE
TRUE	FALSE	FALSE
TRUE	TRUE	TRUE

EXAMPLE: You are in charge of controlling who can access a final exam summary page in a computer program for college students. Access is based on two factors: age and Grade Point Average (GPA). The page is intended for use by students who are adults

OR who have good performance in their studies, but not both. In this instance, you might want to deny access EITHER if the student is 18 years of age or below OR has a GPA of 3.20 or below, but not both. When you put instructions in a computer program to this effect, the computer could use an XNOR gate to decide whether or not to allow the student to access the summary page. The truth table for that XNOR gate would look like this:

Input 1: Age <= 18?	Input 2: GPA <= 3.20?	Output: Allow access?
FALSE	FALSE	TRUE
FALSE	TRUE	FALSE
TRUE	FALSE	FALSE
TRUE	TRUE	TRUE

XOR gate: A logic gate (gate for short) is a switch (a physical device that can be used to control whether or not electricity is passed through) that implements one of several different types of Boolean logic (the "logic" a computer uses to make comparisons, where only one of two possible outcomes is possible: true/false, yes/no, on/off, etc. – which is based on a system of logic developed by English mathematician George Boole) operations. It takes one or more "true/false" inputs and produces a single "true/false" output. In computers, if electricity is allowed to flow, that is considered "true"; if it is not allowed to flow, that is considered "false." Gates are part of how we can use computers to make decisions based on the results of analyzing data. An XOR gate takes two "true/false" inputs and produces a "true" output if EITHER of the inputs are "true," but not if BOTH of them are true. Here is the symbol used for an XOR gate:

Here, the inputs are the two lines on the left, and the output is the line on the right. The inputs on the left are commonly labeled "Input A" and "Input B." To show how the XOR gate works, we will use a truth table. Truth tables are mathematical tables laying out the possible inputs for a logic gate, along with their corresponding output. Here is a truth table for an XOR gate:

INPUT A	INPUT B	OUTPUT
FALSE	FALSE	FALSE
FALSE	TRUE	TRUE
TRUE	FALSE	TRUE
TRUE	TRUE	FALSE

EXAMPLE: You are in charge of controlling who can access a final exam summary page in a computer program for college students. Access is based on two factors: age and Grade Point Average (GPA). The page is intended for use by students who are adults OR who have good performance in their studies, but not both. In this instance, you might want to allow access EITHER if the student is above 18 years of age OR has a GPA above 3.20, but not both. When you put instructions in a computer program to this effect, the computer could use an XOR gate to decide whether or not to allow the student to access the summary page. The truth table for that XOR gate would look like this:

Input 1: Age > 18?	Input 2: GPA > 3.20?	Output: Allow access?
FALSE	FALSE	FALSE
FALSE	TRUE	TRUE
TRUE	FALSE	TRUE
TRUE	TRUE	FALSE

X Window: To start, X Window has nothing to do with Windows from Microsoft. It is a program. It is called "X" Window because it adds windows-functionality to Unix (a free operating system – the main program within a computer that manages all other programs and external devices [e.g., keyboards, mice, displays, etc.]). Meaning, it lets the user operate his/her computer through use of windows (an enclosed area that shows a picture or some information for you). Prior to X Window, Unix was controlled only through a Command Line Interface (CLI – a program that only allows text-input). X Window forms the basis for most GUIs used in Unix. It allows the user to navigate on his computer graphically .

EXAMPLE: X Window allows you to open a file in Unix by clicking on an icon, rather than by using the CLI to navigate to, and then open, the file.

Y

YAML: Stands for "YAML Ain't Markup Language." This is referred to as a "recursive acronym." "Recursive" means "repeating" or "repetitive." An *acronym* is a word formed by the first letters of the words that make it up – for example: TTA is the acronym for The Tech Academy. A recursive acronym is an acronym that refers to itself – meaning, the acronym itself is inside the acronym. YAML deals with data serialization. Data serialization is the process of converting objects within complex data structures into bits for storage, transfer and distribution purposes on physical devices. YAML is a data serialization standard for all programming languages (a system of specialized words and symbols used to communicate with a computer and to create programs).

EXAMPLE: YAML is similar to English (it is a high-level language).

y-axis: See "axis."

Z

z-index: A property which specifies how elements will be stacked – i.e., which will be in the front, the back, etc. It only works on positioned elements (e.g., position: absolute, position: relative). The higher the number value, the higher the element is stacked.

EXAMPLE: An element assigned z-index: 4, would be placed on top of z-index: 3.

Z-score: This diagram is of a symmetrical data model. Each area to the left and right of the mean (0) represents one standard deviation (a quantity of deviation from the standard).

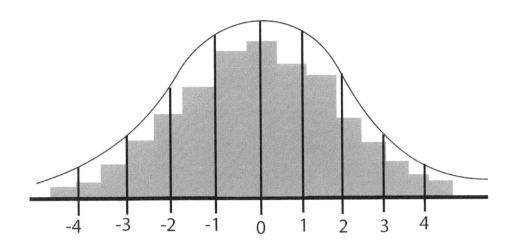

Z-score measures exactly how many standard deviations above or below the mean (average) a data point is.

EXAMPLE: To find the z-score, you subtract the mean from the data point, then you divide it by the standard deviation. Here it is written as a formula:

$z = (x - μ) / σ$

Let's say Jake was on time to work for 180 days. The average employee was on time for 160 days (mean), with a standard deviation of 10.

180 - 160 = 20

20/10 = 2

Jake's z-score is 2.

Below you'll see what's called a "z-score table." With this table, we can take Jake's z-score and find the percentile he lands in. To do this, let's take the number in the ones and tenths place of Jake's z-score (2.0) and find it in the z column. Then take the number in the hundredths place of his z-score (there is no number in the hundredths place, so it would be 0) and find that in the z row. Now find where the two intercept. .9772 is the answer. But we're not quite done yet. Let's convert this number to a percentage: 97.72%. Jack is basically in the 98% percentile, which means he arrived to work on time more often than approximately 98% of the other workers.

z	.00	.01	.02	.03	.04	.05	.06	.07	.08	.09
0.0	.5000	.5040	.5080	.5120	.5160	.5199	.5239	.5279	.5319	.5359
0.1	.5398	.5438	.5478	.5517	.5557	.5596	.5636	.5675	.5714	.5753
0.2	.5793	.5832	.5871	.5910	.5948	.5987	.6026	.6064	.6103	.6141
0.3	.6179	.6217	.6255	.6293	.6331	.6368	.6406	.6443	.6480	.6517
0.4	.6554	.6591	.6628	.6664	.6700	.6736	.6772	.6808	.6844	.6879
0.5	.6915	.6950	.6985	.7019	.7054	.7088	.7123	.7157	.7190	.7224
0.6	.7257	.7291	.7324	.7357	.7389	.7422	.7454	.7486	.7517	.7549
0.7	.7580	.7611	.7642	.7673	.7704	.7734	.7764	.7794	.7823	.7852
0.8	.7881	.7910	.7939	.7967	.7995	.8023	.8051	.8078	.8106	.8133
0.9	.8159	.8186	.8212	.8238	.8264	.8289	.8315	.8340	.8365	.8389
1.0	.8413	.8438	.8461	.8485	.8508	.8531	.8554	.8577	.8599	.8621
1.1	.8643	.8665	.8686	.8708	.8729	.8749	.8770	.8790	.8810	.8830
1.2	.8849	.8869	.8888	.8907	.8925	.8944	.8962	.8980	.8997	.9015
1.3	.9032	.9049	.9066	.9082	.9099	.9115	.9131	.9147	.9162	.9177
1.4	.9192	.9207	.9222	.9236	.9251	.9265	.9279	.9292	.9306	.9319
1.5	.9332	.9345	.9357	.9370	.9382	.9394	.9406	.9418	.9429	.9441
1.6	.9452	.9463	.9474	.9484	.9495	.9505	.9515	.9525	.9535	.9545
1.7	.9554	.9564	.9573	.9582	.9591	.9599	.9608	.9616	.9625	.9633
1.8	.9641	.9649	.9656	.9664	.9671	.9678	.9686	.9693	.9699	.9706
1.9	.9713	.9719	.9726	.9732	.9738	.9744	.9750	.9756	.9761	.9767
2.0	.9772	.9778	.9783	.9788	.9793	.9798	.9803	.9808	.9812	.9817
2.1	.9821	.9826	.9830	.9834	.9838	.9842	.9846	.9850	.9854	.9857
2.2	.9861	.9864	.9868	.9871	.9875	.9878	.9881	.9884	.9887	.9890
2.3	.9893	.9896	.9898	.9901	.9904	.9906	.9909	.9911	.9913	.9916
2.4	.9918	.9920	.9922	.9925	.9927	.9929	.9931	.9932	.9934	.9936
2.5	.9938	.9940	.9941	.9943	.9945	.9946	.9948	.9949	.9951	.9952
2.6	.9953	.9955	.9956	.9957	.9959	.9960	.9961	.9962	.9963	.9964
2.7	.9965	.9966	.9967	.9968	.9969	.9970	.9971	.9972	.9973	.9974
2.8	.9974	.9975	.9976	.9977	.9977	.9978	.9979	.9979	.9980	.9981
2.9	.9981	.9982	.9982	.9983	.9984	.9984	.9985	.9985	.9986	.9986
3.0	.9987	.9987	.9987	.9988	.9988	.9989	.9989	.9989	.9990	.9990
3.1	.9990	.9991	.9991	.9991	.9992	.9992	.9992	.9992	.9993	.9993
3.2	.9993	.9993	.9994	.9994	.9994	.9994	.9994	.9995	.9995	.9995
3.3	.9995	.9995	.9995	.9996	.9996	.9996	.9996	.9996	.9996	.9997
3.4	.9997	.9997	.9997	.9997	.9997	.9997	.9997	.9997	.9997	.9998

If the z-score were a negative number, we would use the negative z-score table instead:

z	.00	.01	.02	.03	.04	.05	.06	.07	.08	.09
−3.4	.0003	.0003	.0003	.0003	.0003	.0003	.0003	.0003	.0003	.0002
−3.3	.0005	.0005	.0005	.0004	.0004	.0004	.0004	.0004	.0004	.0003
−3.2	.0007	.0007	.0006	.0006	.0006	.0006	.0006	.0005	.0005	.0005
−3.1	.0010	.0009	.0009	.0009	.0008	.0008	.0008	.0008	.0007	.0007
−3.0	.0013	.0013	.0013	.0012	.0012	.0011	.0011	.0011	.0010	.0010
−2.9	.0019	.0018	.0018	.0017	.0016	.0016	.0015	.0015	.0014	.0014
−2.8	.0026	.0025	.0024	.0023	.0023	.0022	.0021	.0021	.0020	.0019
−2.7	.0035	.0034	.0033	.0032	.0031	.0030	.0029	.0028	.0027	.0026
−2.6	.0047	.0045	.0044	.0043	.0041	.0040	.0039	.0038	.0037	.0036
−2.5	.0062	.0060	.0059	.0057	.0055	.0054	.0052	.0051	.0049	.0048
−2.4	.0082	.0080	.0078	.0075	.0073	.0071	.0069	.0068	.0066	.0064
−2.3	.0107	.0104	.0102	.0099	.0096	.0094	.0091	.0089	.0087	.0084
−2.2	.0139	.0136	.0132	.0129	.0125	.0122	.0119	.0116	.0113	.0110
−2.1	.0179	.0174	.0170	.0166	.0162	.0158	.0154	.0150	.0146	.0143
−2.0	.0228	.0222	.0217	.0212	.0207	.0202	.0197	.0192	.0188	.0183
−1.9	.0287	.0281	.0274	.0268	.0262	.0256	.0250	.0244	.0239	.0233
−1.8	.0359	.0351	.0344	.0336	.0329	.0322	.0314	.0307	.0301	.0294
−1.7	.0446	.0436	.0427	.0418	.0409	.0401	.0392	.0384	.0375	.0367
−1.6	.0548	.0537	.0526	.0516	.0505	.0495	.0485	.0475	.0465	.0455
−1.5	.0668	.0655	.0643	.0630	.0618	.0606	.0594	.0582	.0571	.0559
−1.4	.0808	.0793	.0778	.0764	.0749	.0735	.0721	.0708	.0694	.0681
−1.3	.0968	.0951	.0934	.0918	.0901	.0885	.0869	.0853	.0838	.0823
−1.2	.1151	.1131	.1112	.1093	.1075	.1056	.1038	.1020	.1003	.0985
−1.1	.1357	.1335	.1314	.1292	.1271	.1251	.1230	.1210	.1190	.1170
−1.0	.1587	.1562	.1539	.1515	.1492	.1469	.1446	.1423	.1401	.1379
−0.9	.1841	.1814	.1788	.1762	.1736	.1711	.1685	.1660	.1635	.1611
−0.8	.2119	.2090	.2061	.2033	.2005	.1977	.1949	.1922	.1894	.1867
−0.7	.2420	.2389	.2358	.2327	.2296	.2266	.2236	.2206	.2177	.2148
−0.6	.2743	.2709	.2676	.2643	.2611	.2578	.2546	.2514	.2483	.2451
−0.5	.3085	.3050	.3015	.2981	.2946	.2912	.2877	.2843	.2810	.2776
−0.4	.3446	.3409	.3372	.3336	.3300	.3264	.3228	.3192	.3156	.3121
−0.3	.3821	.3783	.3745	.3707	.3669	.3632	.3594	.3557	.3520	.3483
−0.2	.4207	.4168	.4129	.4090	.4052	.4013	.3974	.3936	.3897	.3859
−0.1	.4602	.4562	.4522	.4483	.4443	.4404	.4364	.4325	.4286	.4247
−0.0	.5000	.4960	.4920	.4880	.4840	.4801	.4761	.4721	.4681	.4641

(z-score)

Zuse, Konrad (1910-1995): A German engineer and computer pioneer. He was an innovator in the computer industry and he designed and built one of the first working program-controlled computing machines.

EXAMPLE: Zuse Konrad created one of the first simple programming languages (a system of specialized words and symbols used to communicate with a computer and to create programs) called Plankalkül.

(Konrad Zuse)

OTHER READING

Be sure to check out other Tech Academy books, which are all available for purchase on Amazon!:

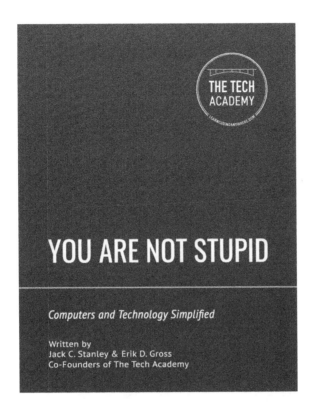

LEARN CODING BASICS

For Kids, Young Adults and
People Who Are Young at Heart

With Python

Written by:
Jack C. Stanley and Erik D. Gross,
Co-Founders of The Tech Academy

Illustrated by:
Afra Amin Orony,
based on the sketches by Jack C. Stanley

THE TECH ACADEMY

LEARN CODING BASICS IN HOURS WITH JAVASCRIPT

Programming for Absolute Beginners

Written by: Jack C. Stanley & Erik D. Gross,
Co-Founders of The Tech Academy

PROJECT MANAGEMENT

HANDBOOK

Simplified Agile, Scrum and DevOps for Beginners

Written by
Jack C. Stanley & Erik D. Gross
Co-Founders of The Tech Academy

Made in the USA
Monee, IL
27 April 2022

95509284R00319